WHAT COMES NEXT

WHAT
COMES NEXT

THE END OF BIG GOVERNMENT—
AND THE NEW PARADIGM AHEAD

James P. Pinkerton

New York

*Excerpt from "Stop All the Clocks" from W.H. Auden: Collected Poems by W.H. Auden
© 1940 and renewed 1968 by W.H. Auden. Reprinted by permission of Random House,
Inc.*

*Lyrics from "Born in the USA" by Bruce Springsteen © 1984 Bruce Springsteen ASCAP.
Used by permission.*

*Lyrics from "Wernher Von Braun" by Tom Lehrer © 1965 Tom Lehrer. All rights reserved.
Used by permission.*

Library of Congress Cataloging-in-Publication Data
Pinkerton, James P., 1958–
    What comes next : the end of big government—and the new paradigm ahead /
by James P. Pinkerton.—1st ed.
        p.   cm.
    ISBN 0-7868-6105-3
    1. Bureaucracy—United States.   2. Administrative agencies—United States—
Reorganization.   3. United States—Politics and government.   4. Waste in govern-
ment spending—United States.   5. United States—Economic policy.   6. United
States—Social policy.   I. Title.
    JK469   1995a   95-18432
    353—dc20   CIP

Designed by Paul Chevannes

FIRST EDITION

10   9   8   7   6   5   4   3   2   1

To my mother, who taught me the power of ideas.

CONTENTS

Part 4   A Third Party and the Next Big Offer

Part 5   The New Paradigm Big Offer

Acknowledgments

First, to Pat Mulcahy and Rafe Sagalyn, whose helpful encouragements—and timely threats—spurred me onward.

Second, to Mike Horowitz, who would have been more than happy to rewrite every word of this book. His extraordinary energy and generosity made a huge difference. And to Chris Hull, who will write a better book of his own someday.

Third, to all the other people and institutions who helped. Their contributions were so enormous that only an alphabetical listing will provide some rough justice: Ruth Berenson, Greg Besharov, Mary Kate Cary, Misty Church, John Gardner, Doug Greene, Lloyd Green, Jennifer Grossman, Bob Hahn, Hoyt Hudson, Randy Hudson, Ron Jensen, Kaveri Kalia, Elaine Kamarck, Joe Klein, Charlie Kolb, Hanns Kuttner, Spencer Lehv, Beth Levine, Larry Lindsey, the Manhattan Institute, Seth Masket, Yvonne Murphy, Hans Nichols, Peggy Noonan, Jack Pitney, Ramesh Ponnuru, the Pope family, Ed Rogers, Ben Rosen, Noel Rubinton, Chris Schroeder, Ruth Shalit, Jeremy Shane, Fred Siegel, Bob Simon, Elliot Vermes, and the gang at Mr. Eagan's.

WHAT COMES NEXT

Introduction

THE BIG SLEEP

Early in 1989, when I was deputy assistant to President Bush for policy planning, I participated in an extended meeting in the west wing of the White House. The subject was education—specifically, helping the self-proclaimed "Education President" live up to his billing. Bush was scheduled to address the Congress soon, on February 9. The speech wasn't written yet, but it had a title: "Building a Better America." The purpose of this evening session was to "put meat on the bones" of the administration's education agenda. In the room were staffers from the Domestic Policy Office and other White House shops, as well as the Office of Management and Budget and the Department of Education. A couple of spin doctors and politicos drifted in and out. One floor down was the Oval Office. I had the same 456 telephone prefix as the Commander in Chief himself, although my own office in the OEOB, the Old Executive Office Building, was about as far away as one could get and still be in the White House complex.

The meeting dragged nearly to midnight, but I never minded working late. Thirty-year-olds have lots of energy; besides, I knew that the bureaucratic culture of the White House measures inputs more readily than outputs. Enthusiasm, faithful attendance at meetings, and willing-

1

ness to pull all-nighters counted for more than whatever product might emerge from the executive–legislative moil months or years in the future.

Higher-ups had already set the ground rules: we had $500 million dollars to allocate for the fiscal year 1990 budget. That was puny in proportion to the $23 billion the Department of Education would spend in the coming fiscal year, but it was "new money," so with creativity we hoped to get the most PR bang for each one of those bucks. We kicked around various ideas for new programs, all of which sounded pretty good. It's been called "legislating by titling"; if we had thought we could get away with it, we would have called our opus "The Better Schools Through Motherhood and Apple Pie Act."

Not being an expert on education, I mostly listened. Yet as my mind started to wander, I imagined that the bureaucratic buzzwords, sports metaphors, and flakes of stale imagery being tossed about the room were solid objects—and that I could see them bounce off the white-plaster walls and plop down on the wall-to-wall carpeting. "Invest in our future," went one. Then whoosh! Another platitude went past my ear: "The ball's in their court." And boing! "Hit the ground running" skidded to rest near my foot.

Someone had what seemed a great idea: an "education superfund." It would be like the Environmental Protection Agency's superfund program, only better. The EPA superfund program is intended to clean up toxic waste sites, although most of the money goes to lawyers. The Education Department's superfund would target . . . well, we couldn't quite decide: should this superfund target bad schools that needed cleanup? Or should we be "proactive" and reward good schools with extra money? The point of such a program, of course, was to give the president an excuse to travel around the country ladling money-nuggets from the federal cornucopia. I looked at the heaps of clichés scattered about the floor and thought that the cleanup might start here.

The naked cynicism of the superfund idea was so obvious that eventually we dumped it. Yet most of the discussion meandered through a valley of abstraction obscured by clouds of jargon. Endless high-flown words—capability, flexibility, responsibility—ping-ponged over the polished maple conference table. If I didn't understand how these programs worked when the meeting began, I certainly didn't know the answer three hours later. Then it hit me: *neither did anyone else.* We were reaching a consensus on Bush administration policy based mostly on what sounded good without giving any thought to whether or not the programs would help—or even how they would operate in what we called "the real world."

The evening wore on, and the thinking wore thin. I mused over the legend surrounding the filming of Raymond Chandler's novel *The Big Sleep.* At one point during the 1946 shooting, director Howard Hawks realized that he didn't understand the plot of his own movie. Stars Humphrey Bogart and Lauren Bacall could only shrug with an I-just-work-here fatalism, and so Hawks called the scriptwriter, one William Faulkner. Typically, the Mississippi novelist was too soused to be of much help; the director had to track down Chandler himself, in London, and ask him to explain the plot of his story via a long-distance call. It must have been a bad connection; the film is a classic, but its story line non-sequiturs through 114 minutes of smoky murder and shadowy betrayal. In the end, Bogey and Bacall huddle in the darkened house, safe at last; that's about all *cinéastes* can be sure of.

My White House colleagues might not have had as much sultry film-noir style, but they were smart as well as sober. Everyone around the table that night, except me, could fairly claim great educational expertise. Most had advanced degrees or had spent years working in the field. All of them could have given a detailed and persuasive speech about the future of American education, about the pressing need to expand opportunity for all children, about the linkage between education and American competitiveness. As we talked and talked and talked, we considered the likely public reaction: how the Congress would respond and what the "education community" would think of our package. We figured that since we proposed spending more money, the educratic establishment would consider us to be at least a little "kinder and gentler" than Reagan and hence not complain too much. But since we were going to propose spending just a little bit more money, we figured that conservatives would bark but not bite.

However, for all our attention to detail we were acting out our own Washington version of *The Big Sleep*; we had lost the plot of the story. We'd been tasked with improving American education, but none of us were awake to what was truly happening in the schools and what needed to be done. The real issue wasn't money, it was what the schools were doing with the money. We could add or subtract zeros from dollar totals, but we had no reason to think that either a lot of money or a little money would be spent well.

Our planning process was a microsnapshot of the difficulties that twentieth-century bureaucratic planners face everywhere. All the technocratic talent in the room that night was not connected in any meaningful way to the actual process of helping some kid learn. That wasn't our problem. I was reminded of the Tom Lehrer song about the Nazi rocket scientist Wernher Von Braun: "Once they go up/Who cares where they come down?/That's not my department/Says Wernher Von Braun." But we weren't bad people; we were more like scriptwriters with no sense of story line. And we had no Raymond Chandler to explain it all to us.

Having agreed on four themes for the president's upcoming speech— "excellence," "choice," "targeting," and "accountability"—we then fleshed out the proposal. That meant writing a fact sheet or, as the White House puts it, a Fact Sheet.

We worked hard on that Fact Sheet. We muscled up the language, eliminating passive-voice constructions and adding muscle words like "commitment" and "strengthen." We plugged in positive terms like "family" and "patriotism." "Nation," for example, was better than "America," because we could give it a noticeably solemn capital "N," to better communicate the majesty of our Fact Sheet.

The physical appearance of the Fact Sheet was important. We wanted as many separate factoids, or "bullets," as possible, studding the page like the medals on the chest of a Soviet general. Not only did a bounty of bullets make it look as if we were doing more than we were, but every separate item was an opportunity to include peripheral players, such as the Labor Department. If the DOL had a bullet with its name on it, then Secretary Elizabeth Dole would feel that she had some "equity" in the endeavor. Thus she would be more likely to "be a team player" and "get with the program."

The Bush White House had various schools of bureaucratic aesthetics. In the policy shop, underlining was <u>good</u> and all-caps was EFFECTIVE, if used sparingly. Were we better off with little "o"-type bullets, or were dashes better? If "o"s, should they be filled in to look solid and imposing on the page, or should they retain their natural, open-donut look? Or if we went with numbers instead, should they be Arabic or Roman numerals? If Roman, should they be big (I) or small (i)?

With such an electron-microscope focus on fonts and format, it was easy to miss the bigger picture. Nineteen eighty-nine was the year the Wall fell. It was the year that Bush was supposed to put a human face on Reaganism, but the continuing failures of the bureaucratic welfare state meant there would be no light at the end of the Reagan tunnel. Yet nobody in Washington—at least not in the Bush White House—seemed to be absorbing the real import of all this change. I, too, felt like the fly in Wittgenstein's bottle, unable to describe the vessel because I was inside it.

Searching for some tool of understanding, I picked up Thomas Kuhn's 1962 work, *The Structure of Scientific Revolutions*. I had first read the book in high school and didn't really "grok" it, to use a voguish verb of the day derived from Robert Heinlein's *Stranger in a Strange Land*. But even in the early seventies, I had grasped that Kuhn was on to something important about the way systems of belief and practice change. In 1989, I reread it. Click.

Structure is a history of science, but its deepest insight is into human nature. Kuhn argues that all scientists work from models, sets of assumptions about how things work, which he calls "paradigms." His book describes the scientific "revolution" that overturns an old, discredited paradigm, replacing it with a new and more useful paradigm—a better mousetrap, a better model for the way things work.

In the second century A.D., the astronomer Ptolemy constructed an astrophysical model based on the assumption that the sun revolved around the earth, a "geocentric" paradigm that dominated astronomy for over a thousand years. One reason was that nobody had a better idea. Moreover, Ptolemy's geocentrism came to be embraced by the church, whereupon it ossified into creedal institutionalism. Science reached a crisis in the sixteenth century as improved devices, such as the telescope, made it increasingly apparent that celestial reality was not in conformity with Ptolemy's paradigm. Nobody could explain what Kuhn calls "anomalies" in the Ptolemaic theory, such as why the stars and the planets were not where they were supposed to be. But in the absence of a better theory, the scientific establishment, such as it was, dismissed the anomalous results.[1]

Enter Copernicus and Galileo. They looked at the same data and came up with a completely different theory that better fit the facts—the "heliocentric" paradigm. After an inquisition or two, their truth prevailed over dogma, and scientific astronomy advanced.

A paradigm is a two-dollar word for the pattern of thinking around which human beings create their view of reality. Orthodoxies build up like barnacles to defend a particular world view: in astronomy, medicine, politics. It's human nature to stick with traditional beliefs, even after they outlast any conceivable utility. Experience shows that people won't let go of the paradigm they know—even if it's no good—for a paradigm they don't know.

In the absence of a new explanatory model, the intellectual corruption of the old can go on forever. After 1,300 years of Ptolemy, his paradigm stank and shone like a mackerel in the moonlight. As Kuhn puts it, "The state of Ptolemaic astronomy was a scandal before Copernicus' announcement."[2]

It was right there—on page 67—that it hit me between the pupils. My work in government was a small part of a Big Lie, a massive attempt at alchemy, in which we tried to turn gold into lead. It was all legal, but what we were doing, in terms of direct expense and lost opportunity, was costing America far more than all the political scandals combined.

What Kuhn writes of scientists struggling with scientific "puzzles" applies equally to politics. In Kuhn's dry phraseology, "Paradigms gain their status because they are more successful than their competitors in solving a few problems that the group of practitioners has come to recognize as acute."[3] Put another way, new paradigms win if they work. Only when the proof that the earth did in fact revolve around the sun was overwhelming did the "paradigm shift" in astrological thinking occur. Suddenly science leapt to a new level, and we could chart the stars. That's the point about a theory that matches reality: it enables knowledge to progress. Things go better with truth.

Our political paradigm today is bureaucracy. To borrow a term from computers, bureaucracy is our "Operating System," how we get things done—from delivering aid to the poor to providing education to all. Large-scale redistributionist bureaucracy was a great new idea a century ago, when Bismarck first implemented it in the Kaiser's Germany. It's a bad old idea today, as useless as spiked helmets. Like Ptolemy's geocentric paradigm, bureaucracy worked reasonably well for a while, but it survives today only because no one has yet developed a coherent replacement model.

In a speech to the World Future Society in February 1990, I announced somewhat grandly that we were in the era of the "New Paradigm." I identified five appropriate policy responses: acknowledging the supremacy of the global market; decentralization; choice; empowerment; and, finally, cleaving to "a principled commitment to what works." The first four elements of the New Paradigm seemed self-evident enough, but the fifth was politically motivated: as a small-"d" democrat, I feared revolutions from above; action taken without the informed consent of the governed always generates a backlash. I argued in that speech that after decades of wrangling over the New Deal and the Great Society, Americans had arrived at something of a consensus about enduring values, such as democracy, markets, nondiscrimination, and compassion. If we could agree on such goals, then the only thing left to argue about was technique. And argue we must. As the bureaucratic system leaked out its lifeblood of legitimacy, I maintained that all Americans should have the chance to participate in the next idea-transfusion.

Late in 1990, after my little-noticed speech and the much-noticed budget agreement, OMB director Richard Darman—architect of the tax-increasing, pledge-breaking deal I had publicly questioned—attacked the idea of an empowerment-centered agenda in general and the New Paradigm in particular, jibing, "Brother, can you paradigm?" Jack Kemp, Newt Gingrich, and others came to my defense, and a mini-brouhaha erupted in the *Washington Post* and the *New York Times* and even on *The McLaughlin Group*. I survived, but my clout inside the building, never great to begin with, was at an end. I became the White House black sheep.

Early in 1992, I moved to the Bush–Quayle reelection campaign as counselor. It was an august title, but I still didn't have much to do. Throughout the year, candidate Bush was completely paralyzed, unable to do anything about urgent problems, such as the recession or the Los Angeles riot, or chronic problems, such as worsening education or collapsing public housing. I used up what remained of my influence to argue for a Bush proposal to offer work to the poor. My centerpiece idea was a revived Civilian Conservation Corps. The CCC wasn't new, but that was the point: it was a social program that had worked in the past. I was convinced it would work in the nineties, because its principles—rigor and reciprocity—were timeless. Just as Franklin D. Roosevelt confronted "stagnant pools of capital" in the thirties, so America today has stagnant pools of humanity, much in need of pump priming. If the only available catalyst is government, then why not use demobilized drill sergeants and shut-down military bases as part of the solution? I argued that "work" was one value Americans could agree on. I knew that the EPA had suggested reforesting 40 million acres in the United States to help combat the greenhouse effect—and was casting around for ways to get that task accomplished. That struck me as a perfect match: save inner-city kids by saving the environment. Nothing came of my efforts. Darman, who possessed the administration until he and it were finally exorcised by the voters, dismissed the CCC as "communist."

By the end of the summer I had no real influence left, so I spent the rest of the 1992 campaign observing the decline and fall of the Bush Empire. However, I thought less of things ending in a bang and more of things ending in a whimper. I thought of poor Prufrock. Bush reminded me of him, with his WASP niceness and indecisiveness, walking on the beach, pondering his peach—till the voters woke him, and he drowned.

People said that Bush just didn't get it, and so the voters got rid of him. Bill Clinton talked the talk of reinvention in 1992; his New Democrats thought they were ushering in a new paradigm of their own. As I walked past the White House in 1993–94, I often thought of the new people who must be sitting around that polished maple table in the second floor of the West Wing. Clinton staffers were at least as knowledgeable as we were—and surely more enthusiastic about the idea of activist government. They had even longer meetings than we did; yet they, too, accomplished little of their agenda.

The voters were even angrier in 1994 than they had been two years before, and so the incumbent party was once again clobbered. Those who dismissed Newt Gingrich's electoral earthquake as a mere blip were deluding themselves; the Georgian was dead right when he said he was "a revolutionary." For the first months of 1995 the new speaker of the House capitalized on his enormous electoral mandate to roll over his demoralized opponents. Yet later in the year the GOP's momentum was slowed by its heavy cultural baggage and the unresolved contradictions in its own thinking. And so the great work remains undone: to replace the Old Paradigm with something better.

My experience in the White House convinced me that the government–political complex, constructed over the last century, is destined inevitably for the ash heap of history. While many, if not most, Americans share this feeling, no consensus yet exists about what to build in its place. And so, as markets continue to crush old-style politics, and as the trend toward de-bureaucratization accelerates, older visions of community are mooted, and honored institutions are disequilibrated.

I believe that limited government can be combined with empowering, compassionate, collective action to make a better America. But the nation can't achieve that goal so long as the bulk of the bureaucratic system—the Old Paradigm—remains sunk in place, in spite of the best efforts of the best minds and fullest hearts our country has to offer.

All Americans, whether they deem themselves Democrats, Republicans, independents, or anything else, must sooner or later adapt to the reality of the New Paradigm. Today, the bad news is that neither party possesses a complete vision for America in the next century; the good news is that no party or coalition is precluded from seizing the high ground of the future by embracing the new thinking America needs. But before any would-be leader can develop and implement the New Paradigm, he or she will need a better understanding of what came before, as well as what comes next.

In my three years in the Bush White House, a frequent duty was "working" room 450 in the OEOB. Every day, outside-the-Beltway groups, from CEOs to college students, were brought in for propaganda briefings. Naturally, they all wanted to see the stars—Bush, Dan Quayle, Jim Baker—and were disappointed when they got mid-levelers like me instead. My usual assignment was to offer an "overview" of administration domestic policy—which gave me a lot of latitude for ad libbing. By 1990, I sensed that audiences weren't much interested in listening to me tick off the key points of the Bush agenda, especially since virtually none of those policies, including the Education President's 1989 proposals, had passed the Democratic Congress.

Because I sensed that none of my superiors much cared about what I did, I began to deviate from the Fact Sheets in my talks. The stiff sessions in room 450 became loose conversations. I tried to listen more than I talked. In the Q & A sessions, few wanted to follow up on this or that aspect of Bush domestic policy; if Bush didn't seem to care about his domestic agenda, why should they? Instead, audiences expressed concern about the way things were going and alarm that nobody in Washington seemed to be doing anything about it. There were reasons for the drift, of course. Neither Bush, nor Senate Majority Leader George Mitchell (D-Maine), nor anyone else in a position of power, had ever asked the voters for a real mandate to change the way Washington worked, so, naturally, the bureaucratic system remained in place. A body at rest tends to remain at rest.

Being a tad radioactive within an administration that put such a premium on the ability to "work and play well with others" had its advantages. Left to luxuriate in my own comfortable alienation—I still had my corner office—I resolved to do what I could to craft a mandate for better policy in the future. I knew that Bush wasn't interested, but I figured some future politician would be. If I hurled seaward enough messages-in-bottles, maybe someday one of them would wash up on a hospitable shore.

I tried an illustration from my own experience to show the way the current system worked—and the pathetic irrelevance of what passed for "reform." I reminded my audiences of the big scandal that had erupted at the Department of Housing and Urban Development in 1988, with revelations that Secretary "Silent Sam" Pierce and his aides were deeply involved in allocating millions of dollars' worth of public housing contracts to favored friends and associates. Some HUD officials were convicted of receiving bribes in return for government subsidies, but most of the billions were spent according to the then-rules of the game. It was "influence peddling,"[4] as one Republican lobbyist conceded, but it was *legal* influence peddling.

I asked my room 450 audiences to think back to where they were in 1988. As for me, I'd been working on the Bush presidential campaign. I knew a lot of the HUD people. They were my age, give or take a few years; many of us had been in Washington since the 1980 Reagan campaign. So while I didn't defend their actions as they shoveled money in the direction of their Republican cronies, I could still imagine what it must be like for them. And I thought to myself: what if I had zigged, careerwise, when I should have zagged, and wound up at HUD instead of the White House? What if someone at Presidential Personnel had called me a few years prior and said, "Hey, Jim! You'd make a terrific deputy assistant secretary for Multi-Family Housing. The job may not have the cachet of the White House or a presidential campaign job, but it's a pay raise and you'd get hands-on experience actually running something." I might have been tempted.

So I'd get over to HUD, and I'd realize the essential nature of the job. Mostly, I'd sit at the dock of my desk watching federal money slip away. The bulk of HUD's money flows according to fixed formulas, and so "Schedule C" political appointees have little to do except get into trouble while career bureaucrats rubberstamp reports and write checks. But a small percentage of HUD's $20 billion budget at that time was "discretionary." That is, the department had some leeway as to where the money went. Naturally, mayors, governors, members of Congress, and an infinite number of lobbyists and pressure groups all petitioned to get their share.

At the level of deputy assistant secretary, I'd try to balance pressure from the White House, from Secretary Pierce, and from my immediate superior in the HUD hierarchy. I'd also hear from members of Congress, especially the majority Democrats who chaired the various congressional committees with jurisdiction over my activities. They could make my life miserable, to be sure. Finally, there'd be the constellation of GOP politicos, current friends, and future employers. All of them would be calling me.

I like to think I'm honest and ethical and would never break the law. So in this hypothetical scenario, I'd immediately report anyone who offered me a bribe or a future job in return for steering a HUD contract his or her way. Yet with illegality removed from consideration, let's consider what might nevertheless occur.

I'm sitting in my office overlooking Seventh Street, and I see that three phone lines are ringing at once. My assistant answers them all and, with all three of them holding, tells me the following:

> Line 1 is a well-connected Republican political consultant, someone with access to the White House, someone who maybe did me a favor in the past—or could help me in the future. I certainly don't want him to spread the word that I've "sold out" to the bureaucrats, that I'm not "a team player."

> Line 2 is a Democratic congressional subcommittee chairman, someone who, if he decided to teach me a lesson, could call me down to a hearing, put me under oath, and then check the accuracy of every word of my testimony by subpoenaing every phone log, every memo, every piece of HUD correspondence I'd ever signed or seen. That sort of proctoscopic examination can take months, and one needs a lawyer. By the time they figured out that I once xeroxed a crossword puzzle on a government machine, I'd be more than ready to cop a plea; it would be cheaper than contesting my innocence.

> Line 3 is a woman in St. Louis whose children are being jeopardized by crack-gang crossfires, someone I'd never met. She's not connected to anyone, except to me, temporarily. And she'll never be powerful.

Whose call, my assistant would ask, would I like to take? And should the other two be kept on hold? Would I call 1, 2, or 3 right back? As a rational bureaucrat, the answer is obvious. I would talk to the Republican honcho first; the Democratic congressman second; and the woman in St. Louis, never. I would sympathize with the poor woman—but why couldn't her Public Housing Authority or the HUD regional office take care of that? Now there's nothing illegal about this decision making that has taken place. But it's rotten. As the pundit Michael Kinsley puts it, the scandal in Washington is not what's illegal; it's what's legal.

We'd all like to think we'd behave nobly, but presumption of nobility is no way to run a multibillion-dollar government agency. Over time, the best we can hope for is that people play by the rules and that those rules are fair. But at HUD, in the Education Department, in the White

House itself, the rules aren't fair. And there's no way, within the existing paradigm of bureaucratic governance, to make them fair.

And so the Big Sleep of American politics continues. Meetings held. Money spent. Millions wasted. Many have come to believe, or at least accept, that the bureaucratic system will go on forever, taxing more and more, delivering less and less. But bureaucracy is just one form of government. Something different came before it, and something different will come after it. There *are* alternatives. This book is about them.

In Charles Dickens' *A Christmas Carol*, the Ghost of Christmas Yet to Come beckons Ebenezer Scrooge to the churchyard and points down to a tombstone. Scrooge asks the specter, "Are these the shadows of the things that Will be or are they shadows of the things that May be, only?" The Ghost is silent.

Scrooge reluctantly looks and sees his own name on the grave. He now knows that the chains he has forged in life will surely drag him down to the same grinding destiny as his dead partner, Marley. But he has his epiphany: "Men's courses will foreshadow certain ends, to which, if persevered in, they must lead. But if the courses be departed from, the ends will change."

Dickens anticipated twentieth-century science fiction writers in this tale of time travel in which Scrooge visits both the past and the future. Yet, unlike many contemporary writers, Dickens offers redemption. At his lowest point, Scrooge demands: "Why show me this, if I am past all hope?" Then he learns that he can repent—and thus prevent the inexorable Will Be.

Writers of the current near-millennium, especially those of the science fiction "cyberpunk" genre, show us a tomorrow without hope, a brutal and decaying world that we scuttle toward inevitably. Can we hope, as Scrooge did, that "courses be departed from"? If so, we have little time; we must do much so that "the ends will change."

Otherwise, the Cyber Future is coming.

PART 1

PROLOGUE
THE CYBER FUTURE

CHAPTER 1

NIGHT OF THE LIVING PARADIGM

The fears Americans have about the future of their country—that the middle class is shrinking, that the rich are reaching new heights while the poor sink to new depths, that we are entering a period of chronic chaos and entropy—found an early voice in New York governor Mario Cuomo's keynote speech to the 1984 Democratic convention in San Francisco. Cuomo pointed to a widening rift in the country, arguing powerfully that President Ronald Reagan and the Republicans "divide the nation . . . into the lucky and the left-out, the royalty and the rabble."[1] Cuomo's speech was the most eloquent articulation of the Democratic faith heard in years. For at least that one evening, it seemed as if New Deal liberalism might live again.

That same year, William Gibson, in his novel *Neuromancer*, offered an even more vivid projection of the bifurcated future. The evocative power of Gibson's words came from the stark contrast he sketched in hard-bitten noirish strokes between the corrupted outer landscape and the thriving inner realm of the neuroelectronic. *Neuromancer* begins: "The sky above the port was the color of television, tuned to a dead channel."[2] In Gibson's future-shocked world, the well-off have left this dreary—as well as crime-ridden and dangerous—external world for the safety and serenity of cyberspace.

Whereas Cuomo's motif was the gap between rich and poor in 1984, Gibson carried his critique into the twenty-first century, defining older cleavages based on wealth or race anew: the plugged-in powerful versus the unplugged powerless. Gibson's startling dichotomy extrapolates from the present; as the commonweal is torqued apart, we can e-mail across the planet but are afraid to cross the street.

Neuromancer swept the three major awards for sci-fi literature[3] and spawned the bent genre of cyberpunk, which simulcasts technological progress alongside societal regress. Cyberpunk is light years away from *The Jetsons* or *Star Trek*. Its snarling prose is a naked-lunch look at a noxious and hellish future whose roots are visible today. Cyberpunk posits "canon crackup"—the end of the shared values that humanity has accumulated over the centuries. The genre is a distant early warning of dystopia, filling the gap between dry statistics and lurid anecdotes.

Both Cuomo and Gibson witnessed a polarization of incomes, opportunity, and quality of life, and both articulated it as best they knew how. But while Cuomo lamented the present and looked fondly backward to the old order, Gibson looked ahead to the entropic demise of twentieth-century hopes. Cuomo blamed everything on Reagan's politics; Gibson skipped over personalities and platforms to describe what happens when politics itself peters out.

Ten years after Gibson's and Cuomo's jeremiads, the simultaneity of suffering and surfeit is unmistakable. The good times are better, and the bad times are worse. More are rich, but more are poor. The earnings of a few have leapt; the earnings of many have dwindled.[4] We have more Emerald Cities—physical as well as virtual—and yet we have more neo-Hoovervilles as well. More Americans know how to program the genie of technology to profitable use, yet more of their fellow citizens possess no skill that guarantees them a wage higher than that of a Third World striver. The overclass of info-aristocrats never had it so good; the underclass have never had it at all. And in between, the middle class, buffeted by the gusts of the planetary economy, wonders whether it will be lifted in an exhilarating globally competing updraft or windsheared in a demoralizing dollar-falling downdraft. The economic and social tornado that Cuomo and Gibson saw a decade ago has swept the country up and is carrying it toward a new and terrifying Oz. No one can set us down safely in the innocent Kansas past again.

On a superficial level, both Cuomo and Gibson have been vindicated. We are disuniting into a society of program traders, Think Pads, and the Internet at one extreme—and crack, Uzis, and three-strikes-you're-out on the other. Gibsonian technology has widened the contradictions within the old system that Cuomo extolled. Through the resulting clefts have stepped both cyberbillionaires and Central Park wilders.

Nineteen eighty-four, the year of Cuomo's speech and Gibson's novel, was in some ways an anticlimax. That year was George Orwell's target date for totalitarianism—the time by which history would have ended, when humanity had sunk into perpetualized despotism. But in nonfiction 1984, the ebbing of top-down tyranny was already apparent. People sensed that tremors were beginning to crack the foundations of government giantism on the eastern side of the Wall; yet few noticed the hairline fractures in the masonry of the Western welfare state.

A decade after its delivery, Cuomo's polemic has survived longer than Cuomo. Images of division—two cities, two tiers, two nations—are all around us. Like waves in the wake of a long-gone ship, the swells of American society have rolled off to different shores. The question is causation. Cuomo had his answer, asserting that Reaganomics had "cut this nation in half." The solution? The first step, according to the New York governor, was to "insist on all the government we need."[5]

For all his histrionics, Cuomo misnamed the wound at the heart of the nation. It was precisely the well-funded failure of his old order to educate, empower, and protect Americans that had caused not only the divide that Cuomo bemoaned but the deeper divisions we see today and the radical cyberskew that Gibson saw ahead. It seems clear now that rote redistributing, bureaucratic burgeoning, and ministerial mandating aren't the cure for that Cyber Future. They are the cause.

While pols and pundits chew tax-funded lotus leaves inside the Washington pleasure dome, artists have stepped forward to offer the slapping tonic of fictional truth. Gibson and his fellow cyberpunkers have spurred people to imagine what happens when creaking politics crumples and technology overwhelms bureaucracy. Cyberpunk hears the call-of-the-wild cacophony that howls beyond the cold comfort of platitude.

In 1948, the same year that Orwell wrote *1984* on a bleak island in the Scottish Hebrides, MIT professor Norbert Wiener labored in Cambridge, Massachusetts, to explain how the entire world would be turned upside down by the new science of computers. Wiener coined the word "cybernetics" from *kybernan*, the Greek word for "steering." His farseeing work *Cybernetics: Or Control and Communication in the Animal and the Machine* compared electronic and neurologic control of systems; whereas the refinements of industrial technology were the equivalent of building bigger biceps, cybernetics would in effect construct a better brain. Wiener foresaw that the technology would create a revolution—mind-storming the Winter Palace of matter.[6] And it happened: the electric juggernaut has rolled over extant institutions, flattening tender mercies as well as totalitarian rigidities. The ghosts of both Hubert Humphrey and Leonid Brezhnev have been plowed under by the cyber-reaper.

The earlier antiutopian tradition of sci-fi had predicted that the state would swell forever, consuming everything in its orbit in a roiling holocaust of repression. But Gibson and others of his generation saw differently: having expanded to its maximum circumference in the age of the mainframe, the old command-and-control system burned itself out—and went supernova, leaving only charred cinders at its center.

The most evocative and emblematic of all cyberspeculation is *Blade Runner*; one critic called it "the paradigm of the new sci-fi."[7] Ridley Scott's 1982 movie derived its rainy, irregular vision from author Philip K. Dick, who scattered the smithereens of society all over his pages. It's 2019: welcome to LA. The mainspring of Western civilization has snapped, leaving drugged-out, whacked-out, left-out masses disconnected to the interplanetary economy. In the environmental meltdown, every day is a monsoon. Massive hovering blimp advertisements— starry dynamos of flaring neon—blare encouragements to the surplus populace to emigrate to off-world colonies. Meanwhile, the quest for better workers has led the Tyrell Corporation to fabricate techno-helots called "replicants." These futuristic *Untermenschen* are programed to pass into oblivion after a few years of overwork. However, a small group of them rebel and murder their corporate creator atop his 700-story halogen-lit pyramid.

Replicant Roy Batty is the film's cyborg-Spartacus, illuminating the darkness around him with his dignity in death. Sparing the life of his tormentor, Batty the android expresses in all-too-human terms his agonied and ecstasied living of life:

> I've seen things you people wouldn't believe. Attack ships on fire off the shoulder of Orion. I watched C-beams glitter in the dark near the Tannhauser gate. All those moments will be lost in time, like tears in rain. Time to die.

The enduring popular appeal of such cybernoir is its high-tech rendering of themes of alienation, identity, and class exploitation. A decade after its release, *Blade Runner* stalks our dreams because the film's vision—swank decadence amid social desolation—seems more revelatory with every passing year. In 1993, a *New York Times* reporter noted that the stump speeches of mayoral candidate Rudolph Giuliani, in which cops and kids are "slaughtered" and criminals "roam unhindered by arrest," echoed *Blade Runner*'s scenario of "grim social havoc."[8] Giuliani won the election.

What's the basic economic system of the Cyber Future? It's clearly "capitalist"—filled with the filthy rich and teeming with sharp practitioners. Cyberpunkers envision capitalism as a Capone-like kleptocracy, without even the pretense of virtue. There will be plenty of business, but no Better Business Bureau. Amid the wreckage of toppled scruples in the cyberpunk's tableaux, corporate raiders and "hood" crews blend into one. The capitalists in cyberliterature are a Marxist's dream—unreconstructed, unredeemed villains twirling data streams instead of mustaches. The cyberprinces of plutocracy owe more to Machiavelli, preferring to be feared rather than loved, or even trusted.

Cyberpunkers thus eliminate any pretense of ethics within capitalism. They backhand such thoughtful and well-meaning observers as Michael Novak, who has argued that, regardless of the specific religion, "both democracy and capitalism have a moral basis, without which they perish."[9] Indeed, the rise of Asia, Inc., suggests that not only is there nothing particularly "Protestant" about dynamic capitalism—belying Max Weber's assertion early in this century—but there's nothing inherently democratic about it, either. As cyberpunk makes clear, capitalism is an amoral system; like Darwinian evolution, it happens to be the most efficient way to allocate goods—rewarding the fittest without regard to the finer theories of civil society or moral sentiments. In the Cyber Future, the profit motive is all that's needed; we get a byte-driven bobsled to the bottom line.

Cyberpunk capitalism no longer needs ethics—because the gimlet gaze of technology makes up for it. The night of cybercommerce has a thousand eyes: scanning, scrutinizing, and decrypting. If the current technological confidence builders—cameras, credit histories, polygraphs, and fingerprints—aren't sufficient, we move then to retina-readers and DNA detectors. Cyberpunk capitalism works fine in semi-anarchy; in the Cyber Future, the human face is ripped from capitalism's hideous skull.

Neal Stephenson's 1992 cyberpunk novel *Snow Crash* puffs with prophecy about future politics: there will be none. All that's left of the American government is a few isolated high-security strongholds. In the rest of the country, privatized white-only "burbclaves" have sprung up where "non-caucasians must be processed" to help further buttress the high-and-dry rich from the brackish, tidal poor.[10] Stephenson's "franchulates"—franchise-organized quasi-national entities—deploy armored, liquid-cooled bionic guard dogs, so sophisticated they can sniff the difference between a Beretta and a Browning.

Stephenson's device of apartheid as a crime-fighting technique is an easy projection of the current trend toward walled, white-flighted communities. Compare the if-present-trends-continue forebodings of Robert Reich, writing in 1991, the year before Stephenson's novel appeared:

> Distinguished from the rest of the population by their global linkages, good schools, comfortable lifestyles, excellent health care, and abundance of security guards, symbolic analysts [the top-feeding fifth of the future work force] complete their secession from the union. The townships and urban enclaves where they reside, and the symbolic-analytic zones

where they work, will bear no resemblance to the rest of America; nor will there be any direct connections between the two. America's poorest citizens, however, will be isolated within their own enclaves of urban and rural desperation; an ever-larger proportion of young men will fill the nation's prisons. The remainder of the American population, gradually growing poorer, will feel powerless to alter any of these trends.[11]

Reich is no fantasist; he became President Clinton's Secretary of Labor. His prognostics focused on labor policy: the need to improve job skills for Americans, lest they fall into the rut that Stephenson foresees; *Snow Crash* America boasts only four competencies—music, movies, software, and high-speed pizza delivery.[12] What societal order exists in Stephenson's Cyber Future comes not from civic virtue but from profit-minded self-interest. The utterly unforgiving corporate *keiretsu* are the only institutions able to get anything done—and therefore, the only institutions that have survived. In the absence of law, either civil or common, organized crime and multinationals have become indistinguishable.

Stephenson answers Oscar Wilde's question: If the bourgeoisie doesn't provide standards for the rest of us, who will? In his bifurcated world to come, the answer is—no one. No middle-class ethic exists because no middle class exists. Once the connection of community is broken, loyalty and fidelity shrink from the larger polis to more defensible outposts on the alienated outskirts. In the past, those mores were maintained within the family, the clan, or the country. But in the technologically driven diversity of the future, the cyberpunkers predict, the new organizing units will be corporations, burbclaves, cults, and covens.

Gibson's 1993 novel, *Virtual Light*, is yet another sting of contemporary commentary masked as fiction. Set in the year 2005, decades closer to the present than *Neuromancer*, the blade of cyber-anticipation cuts closer to home. Freed from anything so pedestrian as law or patriotism, Gibson's unhindered characters live debauched lives, smoking Ice and snorting Dancer, doing virtual reality in wraparound sunglasses to shut out the daily dreck. Gibson's Raymond Chandler-meets-*Popular Mechanics* prose is in full fly as he describes "rent-a-cops" sporting air-conditioned helmets on search-and-destroy SWAT missions. Riots erupt when San Francisco privatizes the parks, but the free market—unleashed at last by the breakdown of civic and civil restraint—prevails. In Gibson's refraction of the future, mirrored ziggurats line city streets, a "jackstraw tumble of concrete tank traps"; warm whirlwinds blow fecal snow from frigid sewage flats. Those who can afford it drink quadruple-distilled water and breathe through catalytic masks. After the collapse of the public sector, entrepreneurs move in to provide everything—life, liberty, and property—for a price; cross-oceanic privatization gives us a Nissan County. Gibson's tone is sardonic: "I'm not okay, you're not okay—but, hey, that's okay."

In Gibson's and Stephenson's imagined morrow, selfishness and nihilism are the prime values rising from the shards of a system left for broke. All the familiar sentimentalities—flags, family, faith—are devalued and devolved. Urban rot devours visible community while technology opens up, for the few, the portal to a wondrous invisible commonwealth. Old standards of balance and beauty choke on the smoggy exhalations of the vertical high-rise wasteland. The Judeo-Christian tradition of alms and altruism spends itself out. Pitiless and spiritually demolished ramblers stalk the Las Vegas-goes-to-hell landscape looking for their S & M jackpot.

Gazing past millennium's turn, the cyberpunkers see that the towering immobility of authority will swoon into a free-form sorcerer's frug. The wizened hands of the old bureaucratic politics can no longer grip the heavy-metal motion of jacked-in high-tech demi-monders.

Cyberpunk, for all its prophecy, is really about the here and now. As Gibson admits, "I'm not trying to predict the future, I want people to see the present." One suspects that he gets as much inspiration from the Metro sections of city newspapers as from *Scientific American*. What seems most overdrawn in his work, the violent shipwreck of his drunken-boat prose, is what he considers most accurate: "the bleak aspect is just my attempt at realism."[13] Cyberpunk's primary source material is all around us.

More than a decade after his great keynote speech, the bureaucratic welfare state that Cuomo championed in his baroque retro-rhetoric has survived Reaganite assaults—only to fail in its basic mission of protection and uplift. Cuomo may have evocatively described what was happening, but he was not able to learn from it. From Albany, Cuomo watched with loquacious passivity as the cyberwedge cleaved his "family of New York." As Manhattan's gilded infocrats profitably exported their nano-Nietschean ideas about stocks and software to the planet, the rest of the state languished. Indeed, during Cuomo's tenure, New York was the first state in the nation in income growth, but forty-ninth in income distribution;[14] inequality in the borough of Manhattan was greatest of any county in the nation, with the rich gaining wealth at thirty-two times the rate of the poor.[15]

Cuomo called for an uprising against Reaganomics. Subtitling his speech "A Tale of Two Cities," he described a ragged realm, ready for revolution. But he ignored the fact that his own policies had been nonrevolutionary, even reactionary. For a decade more, Cuomo concealed his failings in the shadow of the larger national decline, all of which he could blame on the Republicans. Bill Clinton's election took away that exculpatory penumbra; in 1994, the cyber-tumbrel finally came for him.

The irony is this: Cuomo warned against that which he helped create. As cybertech shifted the world's paradigm, he tried to replenish the welfare state instead of replacing it. The senescent structure that has survived the eighties is not Reaganomics but bureaucracy; the Cyber Future is simply a fast-break fortelling of the breakdown of bureaucratic government. The future Cuomo predicted a decade ago is coming true—not in spite of him, but because of him.

The failure of the old system is the subtext of Gibson's cybertext. Cyberpunkers have taken the system we have now and spun it through the liquid-crystal looking glass to its utmost extremities, imagining us staggering endlessly across the imbalanced terrain of inequality, through a whipping wind of excremental sleet. Yet like Dante's guide through the circles of Inferno, Gibson has his own moral compass; he is a virtual Virgil. Gibson's prose is set on stun, but his aim is to make change: "We have a responsibility to posterity to try to influence the outcome."[16]

Cyberpunk provides us with a pulsing and painful vision of what comes next. Some will look at its predictions and wonder if the sky is falling. That's not the point—it's the *system* that's falling. The cyberpunkers look at the decrepitude of the Old Paradigm today and project its demise, leaving only amoral nihilists and avaricious profiteers swarming over the rubble. We may hope that as in *A Christmas Carol*, the telling of the tale changes the ending. But such a happy fate requires that we learn, so that we can prevent the otherwise inexorable Will Be.

If the public sector fails to educate us in basic civic virtues, let alone the vital technologies of the wired world; if it fails to provide even the most basic security, leaving most citizens to live by their wits in a war zone; if we soak for another decade in the bladerunner runoff of a rusting paradigm—then Gibson's vision will inherit the earth.

The Cyber Future has begun.

CHAPTER 2

THE CYBER-ECONOMY

In the summer of 1984, Bruce Springsteen released his biggest album, *Born in the USA*. The ringing anthemic chords of the title track confused some listeners, including President Reagan, into thinking that it was a song of optimism, in keeping with his "Morning in America" reelection theme. Reagan cited Springsteen's "message of hope" in a campaign speech in the Boss's own New Jersey.[1] Springsteen was on tour at the time and told an audience that Reagan was wrong; "there's a bad moon rising" over America, he said. Yet like much of Springsteen's songs, "Born" expresses a folkish faith in the basic decency of ordinary people—a decency sorely tested by the times in which they live:

> Come back home to the refinery
> Hiring man said "son if it was up to me"
> Went down to see my V.A. man
> He said, "son don't you understand now"[2]

By the end of the song, the protagonist, having survived Vietnam and unemployment, is resigned to his life; he's just another hometown hotrodder with nowhere to run and nowhere to go.

27

The vectors of the two Americas are veering apart, as both Cuomo and Gibson foresaw. Yet the current contrast is just a pale preview of what's to come: a worldwide "cyber-economy" in which capital and information flow so quickly that only the electronically empowered can take full advantage of the opportunities whizzing by at the speed of light. The result, in the coming century, is that one lobe of the transnational gray matter grows a rich green, while the other lobe fades away.

On the bottom of the split: a sinking poverty that includes not just low incomes but even lower, deeper social disintegration. On the top side of the split: riches and freedom of a magnitude never seen in world history. *Business Week* has already noted "the biggest spurt in family-income inequality since the Depression."[3]

The great struggle between capital and labor has been won by capital. Yet if the political Right hates to admit that capitalism bestows its blessings unequally, so the Left is loathe to concede that the separation is not the exclusive fault of Ronald Reagan. The cyber-economy has its own rules, which transcend both presidents and parties.

When Ken Auletta's *Greed and Glory on Wall Street* appeared a decade ago, readers were shocked to learn that investment bankers were taking away severances of five, six, or even ten million dollars.[4] Yet today, such sums are given away in annual bonuses to third-echelon thirty-year-old coheads of fixed-income arbitrage groups. Wall Street pooh-bahs know that if they don't pay that much to their cybercharged bratpackers, a rival firm across Vesey Street will.

In inflation-adjusted dollars, the revenues of American securities and commodities brokers have quadrupled in the past fifteen years.[5] Cybertechnology has opened up new vistas for financial instruments that few PhDs can comprehend, ranging from swaps and derivatives to ELKS, DECS, REMICS, and any number of other money-making acronyms that remain proprietary secrets. Measures of activity—shares traded, futures contracts executed—all show ten- or twentyfold increases in the past two decades. The notional value of the derivatives market has been estimated as high as $40 trillion; yet such intangibilities have become very real to investors and taxpayers from London to Singapore to Orange County, California.

In the market, capital seeks out its highest and best use; technology has accelerated the flow and flight of capital to the speed of light. The fastest player of all has been George Soros; in 1992, his Quantum Fund shorted the British pound and made a $1 billion profit just in that transaction, driving the Bank of England out of the European exchange-rate mechanism. In 1993, Soros personally took home an estimated $1.1 billion, a profit that put him ahead of all but thirty-six U.S. corporations and exceeded the gross national product of forty-three countries.[6] Hedge funds haven't done so well since, in part because so many more players now divvy the profits from the trillion-dollar-a-day currency markets.

Computers have created their own world order; Sorosians now discipline the fiscal policies of once-sovereign entities, from Russia to Mexico to the United States. The new technology will never go home again; just as sports equipment, from tennis rackets to running shoes to weight-training machinery, ratchets forward toward greater refinement, so the twenty-four-hour planetary market is never going to return to the days of ticker and telegraph. Since even the rumor of war or devaluation is bad for business, nation-states find their ability to nationalize, to tyrannize, or even to tax severely limited by some money changers half a world away who can bet against the national exchequer. Jealous governments would love to put an end to such lèse majesté, but they don't know how. In Michael M. Thomas's novel *Black Money*, one character explains the new secret protocols of hot capital:

> You must not think of "offshore" as having a defined physical geography. . . . it exists in what is called cyberspace; its cartography is digital. You can be in the bar of this very hotel, and if you have a palmtop computer and a phone jack you can make yourself every bit as "offshore" as if you were sitting on a Swiss mountaintop or a beach on Vanuatu.[7]

Soros himself operates out of New York City, but his Quantum Fund is officially domiciled offshore, on the island of Curaçao, where it pays an estimated $10,000 per year in tax on $3.8 billion in assets.[8]

In the cyber-economy, the greatest fortunes are made from products that can barely be seen. The five "C"'s of the cyber-economy are currency, computers, cinema, CDs, and cable. Richer perhaps even than Soros is Microsoft's Bill Gates, whose eleven-digit fortune is from floppy discs. Pop music groups that few have heard of turn up on the MTV Music Awards with triple platinum albums. Baubles that nobody would buy in a store sell like diamonds on discount on the Home Shopping Network.

The advantage these cyberworkers have is this: after the Fall of the Wall and the passage of NAFTA and GATT—and with still more trade agreements in the offing—they can hawk their intangible wares to 6 billion potential customers, from Albania to Zimbabwe. Mickey Kaus, author of *The End of Equality*, calls it the "Hollywood Effect": America's stars are now the world's stars, who can sell their wares to billions, not just millions, of fans. It's the twenty-first century vision of infinity. After centuries of clawing their way up the hills and mountains of earth-bound industry, tycoons have gone virtual; now they scale thunderbolts into heaven, walking on clouds of commerce from continent to continent, leaving ordinary fans and consumers down below in the dirt.

In the last dozen years, per capita disposable income has doubled. However, statistical averages conceal the high and low extremes; those with an oar in the great planetary streams of capital, information, and technology are the ones who pull ahead of those with less stroke. Since 1982, the total net worth of the folks on the Forbes 400 has quadrupled.

Such economic polarization is part of the coming inversion of the familiar. From the first, the cyberpunkers looked to Asia: much of *Neuromancer* is set in Japan; the protagonist of *Snow Crash* is named Hiro. Now other once-poor Asian countries are catching up. *The Economist* projects that by the year 2020, China will have a gross national product 40 percent larger than that of the United States. A quarter century hence, four of the world's five largest economies—China, Japan, India, and Indonesia—will be Asian; South Korea will output almost as much as Germany's; Thailand will be richer than France.[9] Put simply, the U.S. can no longer afford to impose its Jeffersonian ideals on the rest of the world. Two decades ago, the dollar accounted for 80 percent of currency reserves held around the world; today that percentage has fallen to 60 percent.[10]

As the planet's A-list players print out their invitation list for the new-millennium bash, many if not most Americans won't be invited. The next century will be no party to them. The nation is now learning what the Old World always knew: for every empire that rose, another empire fell. The postwar bubble of high wages and near-monopoly amid bombed-out competitors has burst. The first shock wave washed over the eighties; by now, millions of Americans have grown accustomed to the rackety clatter as further shards of their futures crash down. While the cyber-tsunami ebbed during the recession of the early nineties— replaced temporarily by old-fashioned pinkslips and bankruptcies— such restructuring never stopped, nor will it recede in the future. Briefcased barbarians are back, besieging every corporate gate.

As the capitalist centrifuge spins faster, income distribution patterns splatter. In 1980, the average American worker made about $18,000 a year; by the midnineties, that wage increased about 60 percent, to $30,000. In 1980, the average CEO made $625,000; yet during the same period that worker salaries rose 60 percent, CEO incomes rose more than 600 percent, to $3.8 million.[11] The president's Council of Economic Advisers reports that the share of the nation's income received by the richest 5 percent of American families rose from 18.6 percent in 1977 to 24.5 percent in 1990, while the share of the poorest 20 percent fell from 5.7 percent to 4.3 percent.[12] Reich says that 98 percent of the growth in average family income has gone to the top 20 percent of earners. The Census Bureau found that in 1993 median family income fell nearly 2 percent, the fourth consecutive annual decline. In 1994, overall U.S. household wealth fell by 0.5 percent. Meanwhile, the income share of the top fifth of American earners rose three percentage points in 1993, and the income share for the bottom fifth fell by even more. In other words, despite the best efforts of Clinton, Reich, and the Democratic 103rd Congress, the rich still get richer and the poor still get poorer. Columbia's Katherine S. Newman writes: "If our current trajectories continue, fewer than half of all Americans will be middle class by the year 2000."[13]

White-collar employment may be rising, but raises in base salaries are decreasing: 90 percent of the Fortune 500 firms no longer provide automatic across-the-board cost-of-living adjustments,[14] a growing share of compensation comes in the form of variable bonuses.[15] More ominous is the endless wave of layoffs, which undermine the proud tower of bourgeois faith. In the 1980s, 3.4 million workers were laid off; the nineties have seen another 2.5 million layoffs,[16] despite strong growth in the GNP. Most of those losses were permanent, two-thirds of them due to plant or office closings. Researchers at Cognetics, Inc., sampled 13 million U.S. companies and found that "fully 30 percent of all jobs in 1989 had disappeared by the end of 1993." The American Management Association found that half of major U.S. companies laid off an average of 10 percent of employees in the nineties, with the white-collar share of such cutbacks rising by almost a fifth. Even the best and the brightest are not immune: one study of the Harvard Business School class of 1974 concluded that 40 percent of its members had been fired or let go in the previous two decades.[17] As one expert said, "Downsizing is not an event anymore. It's become a way of business life."[18]

The Labor Research Association's "Job Opportunity Barometer"—which measures not only unemployment but other indicators, such as the duration of unemployment, average weekly earnings, and help-wanted advertising—peaked in the seventies. We can expect more of the same decline in the future. According to a recent National Academy of Sciences study, in the eighties service companies invested $862 billion in information technology to automate everything from inventory to cashiering; the productivity benefits are just now beginning to be reaped, with suddenly superfluous service workers destined to get the cut.[19] That's the bad news. The not-so-good news is that if the dollar continues to go lower, American workers will suddenly become bargains on the world market.

Remember TV sitcom dad Ozzie Nelson? He must have worked an office job somewhere, but his duties never seemed to weigh heavily on him; he always had time for his spic-and-span wife and his apple-cheeked kids. Indeed, the hulking edifice of postwar corporate America provided plenty of desk day-dreaming at the office and La-Z-Boy time at home for Ozzie Nelson and Ward Cleaver and all the other fathers-who-knew-best. Woody Allen was right many years ago when he said that 90 percent of life is just showing up. That was true when America benefited from the pleasant-but-shortlived advantage of competing with market neophytes from Asia, WWII losers, and bombed-out winners. But if the working class has been filleted by international competition, the three-martini-lunch class has been sliced by cybertechnology.

Today, it's not Mr. Dithers keeping haphazard track of white-collar output; it's an Excel spreadsheet. Such machinery can't be scammed by a Dagwood Bumstead turning back the hands of the time clock as he slinks tardily into work. And whatever happened to Della Street and the gals in the steno pool who did all the real work? Even corner-office-rated executives now do their own word processing and screen calls via voice mail. The new executive work ethic isn't driven by Calvinism; it's spurred by competitive survivalism.

A revealing headline in the *Washington Post* read as follows: "Mobil to Cut 1,250 Jobs in Fairfax/Downsizing Part of Restructuring, Stock Hits New High."[20] The trapezoidal structures of white-collar existence have been management-consulted down to slivers. The percentage of Americans working for Fortune 500 companies rose from 14.6 percent in 1954 to 19.4 percent in 1974, then fell to 10.9 percent in 1992.[21] All that's left of many palatial company headquarters is a tiny control unit hanging like a mirrored sphere at a disco, beaming instructions onto the teeming subordinates spread over six continents below.

Meanwhile, the grandchildren of FDR's "forgotten man," the off-spring of Nixon's Silent Majority—the people who, as Bill Clinton said in his 1992 nomination acceptance speech at the New York convention, pay the taxes and play by the rules—are getting middle-class-squeezed. Stanford economist Paul Krugman reports that the proportion of full-time workers whose earnings were below the poverty line increased from 12 percent in 1979 to 18 percent in 1990.[22] Unions are almost helpless; they may be able to preserve labor solidarity in one industry or one region, but they can't maintain their impermeability when national borders are fully osmotic to trade and capital. And so the nineties are turning into the auxiliary annex of the eighties; and the trend toward temps, consultants, and contractors working in "virtual organizations" continues,[23] leaving old-line workers searching in vain for their jobs.

Yet it is the young, those born during the sixties' Summer of Love, who are now in their winter of twentysomething discontent. The Economic Policy Institute reports that "the most severe wage reductions . . . have been for young, high school graduates, a group comprising two-thirds to three-fourths of all young workers." The EPI found that

1993 wages paid to male high school graduates under 25 were 30 percent lower than in 1979, while those of young male college graduates were 8 percent lower.[24]

Jeff Spiccoli, *Ridgemont High*'s ur-Slacker, endures forever on home video, typifying the downwardly mobile pathfinder for a generation to come. While every age cohort produces its share of young go-getters armed with firm handshakes and killer smiles, Spiccoli resembles growing numbers of fiscally challenged, expectationally diminished neo-deadheads who seem content to finance their couch-potato-and-fridge-raiding lifestyle by sponging up what remains of their parents' home equity.

The exaggerated ups and downs—from the greed on Wall Street to nightmares on Elm Street—inspired Doug Coupland, author of the cult book *Generation X*, to coin an apt term for these barbed and spiked bifurcations: "Brazilification."[25] Even before Clinton pledged to "create millions of high-wage jobs" on TV shows such as *Roseanne*, *The Simpsons*, and *Married With Children* were depicting the re-proletarianization of the American bourgeoisie.

Latchkey kids, raised by the media, relate to MTV's *Beavis and Butthead*; like a diminished Narcissus, they recognize the parody of their no-talent/no-future selves and fall in love with their mirror image. Likewise, they laugh knowingly when they see Mike Myers's collection of hair nets and name tags from the MacJobs held by the protagonist of the *Wayne's World* movies. The still-living-at-home "baby boomerangs" torment each other with the prospect of service-job drudgery; as one character puts it, the future consists in living at home, working at a mall or theme park, "mopping up hurl and lung butter." In *Reality Bites*, the valedictorian-turned-grunt worker is assaulted by her villainous boss with blunt truth: "I can find an intern who will do your job for free!" During the 1994 commencement season, *Doonesbury* featured college graduates with no higher aspiration than working at the Gap.

In the cybertrends of the eighties, decisions made outside of Washington—in Silicon Valley, Beijing, Moscow, and Mexico City—made it easier for decision makers to accrue serious wealth. Ordinary folks, including twentysomething Gap workers, will never know that the decision to locate or relocate elsewhere was made over coffee by an

MBA with his cyberworkman's tools: an HP-19B calculator and a copy of the *Financial Times*. They'll know only that life sucks.

The mainstream media, which generally believed their own line that the "casino economy" was a temporary byproduct of Gordon Gekko–style Reaganism, have been left to puzzle over how this economic roulette could occur in the era of President Clinton's New Covenant of "putting people first." The *Washington Post* headlined, "Wall Street's Prosperity Makes the Go-Go '80s Look Small Time," reporting that the early nineties boasted the three most profitable years in securities industries history, with the total for the half-decade nearly matching the entire sum earned in the eighties.[26] Even the sleazeball signature of the Drexel-Boesky-Levine epoch, the hostile megamerger, has resurfaced;[27] *Business Week* lamented that the "sudden resurgence of merger mania"[28] makes the nineties look remarkably like the eighties—and then some. In the words of Lehman Brothers economist Allen L. Sinai, "We are on the cusp of a major takeover boom, and it will be global in scope."[29] In particular, the jousting between QVC and Viacom for the hand of Paramount seemed like the ghost of the greed decade; the *Los Angeles Times* described the Diller–Redstone battle as "an unsettling throwback to the 1980s." The *New York Times*, at ground zero of the cyber-economy, worried: "It's only 1994, the middle of a decade that was supposed to be the low-key antithesis to the greedy and arrogant 1980s. But the 1980s may be making a comeback already." The evidence cited ranged from the return of the high heel to the rehabilitation of Reagan-era socialite Betsy Bloomingdale, her life revalidated by her appearance on the QVC home shopping channel.[30] Jewelry, fur, and caviar purveyors all had terrific 1994s, and prices for Andy Warhol silk screens, a reliable measure of surplus capital available for conspicuous consumption, are approaching the record highs of the eighties.

Welcome to the new economic world without end. The global forces that created "the eighties" are even stronger in the nineties. One can imagine Michael Milken singing the old labor agitprop song "Joe Hill": " 'I never died,' he said." Joe Hill may be dead, but Milkenism isn't. People realize now that there's no exit from the cyber-economy. Verbal hand-wringing or even legislative screw-tightening won't stave off America's rendezvous with its globalized destiny. In the Darwinian world to come, governments can't protect everyone from the consequence of maladaptive policies and practices; what happens instead is that a few learn to work the new system to maximum advantage. As one Wall Streeter said in 1994, two years into the people-first Clinton era, "It's a great time to be an arbitrageur."[31]

Market pressures and technological progress continue to bear down on what Reich calls "the anxious class." The introduction of the automated teller machine was an early warning of what could happen to clerical jobs; half of all bank branches are expected to disappear in the next decade.[32] Hyatt Hotels are installing lobby check-in kiosks, and in New Jersey, Merck is using computer terminals instead of people at desks to handle its employee benefits and services. The pharmaceutical giant realized that shifting its one-size-fits-all benefits package to flexible plans for each of its 15,000 employees would require the hiring of more paper shufflers; that was too much expense, so Merck automated the fringe-benefit scut work, scrapping 40 jobs.[33] And so the cybernetic mowing continues; clerks and typists are going the way of milk deliverers and hod carriers, automated out of existence—or into subsistence.

Ruminating on the future of work, William Bridges observed:

> We used to read predictions that by 2000 everyone would work 30-hour weeks, and the rest would be leisure. But as we approach 2000, it seems more likely that half of us will be working 60-hour weeks and the rest of us will be unemployed.[34]

On paper, it may appear that a fairly small number of infopreneurs and cyberyuppies could generate enough wealth to subsidize both nonworkers and sub-subsistence workers. Already, one in five workers is eligible for the Earned Income Tax Credit, a subsidy to the working poor that has ballooned from less than $2 billion in 1980 to more than $22 billion in 1995.[35] All that's needed is for the golden geese of the cyber-economy to continue patriotically to lay their eggs in the home nest. Yet *Time* reports that "a quiet brain drain is under way": the percentage of Stanford MBAs looking for work abroad, as well as the number of Americans working in Hong Kong, has doubled in the past five years.[36] A study for the Hudson Institute found that the percentage of Americans considering emigration has doubled since 1971.[37] Furthermore, substantial numbers of foreign-born Americans are emigrating; Asians in particular are returning home with their high-tech skills.[38] Economic theory holds that all this churning helps make markets liquid; such lubrication makes the great gears of global commerce mesh smoothly. However, it's harder to accept such dispassionate theorizing when one's country—home, hearth, kith, kin—is at stake.

In *Snow Crash*, set in c. 2010, cyberpunker Stephenson treats patriotism and national loyalty as quaint artifacts of another age, harrowed under by the combine of capital and comparative advantage. As he contends,

> once we've brain-drained all our technology into other countries, once things have evened out, they're making cars in Bolivia and microwave ovens in Tadzhikistan and selling them here—once our edge in natural resources has been made irrelevant by giant Hong Kong ships and dirigibles that can ship North Dakota all the way to New Zealand for a nickel—once the invisible hand has taken all those historical inequities and smeared them out into a broad global layer of what a Pakistani brickmaker would consider to be prosperity[39]

—then we'll see what remains of the American Dream. Chic cyberculture exults in this deracination of social rootedness. Yet, alas, the conditions that inspire vivid literature imply vicious social policy. As we move from nation-state to solid state, the old systems of political redistribution are reduced to rank and rutted turbines out of gas. But even this vision of the cyber-economic future fails to capture the full fury of things to come. We must confront a new phrase to describe this dizzying and disturbing phenomenon: hypercrime.

CHAPTER 3

HYPERCRIME

The Cyber Future is also a criminal future. As befits cyberpunk's roots in the seventies outlaw culture of protohacker "Captain Crunch" and the original Ma Bell–beating "phone phreaks," high-tech ripoff is a major motif of the genre. Case, the protagonist of *Neuromancer*, is an amoral techno-grifter. Yet he is also a victim of society, he's merely trying to stay alive in a Thomas Hobbes-in-hell world that's nasty, brutish, and shorted out.

Cybercriminals don't much resemble the marauding contemporary street hoodlums that Americans today fear most, those whose bravado is usually matched by the brevity of their not-so-brilliant careers. The cyberpunkers are writing about a world in which middle-class virtue and civil society have been so eroded that cyberwilders of all classes, races, and genders tap whatever they don't trash. Like everything else in cyberpunk fiction, Gibson's crooks are the *reductio ad absurdum* of every present pathology.

Ironically, this fear is coming to fruition at a time when indicators show that the overall crime rate is leveling off. The FBI's violent crime index more than tripled from 1960 to 1980, but upward movement has slowed in the past few years. The murder rate per 100,000 Americans actually peaked in 1980. Of course, 25,000 murders a year, especially when so many of them are media-multiplied into our consciousness, makes an impression.

Yet while crime in the aggregate may not be rising, the incidence of victimization is deeply skewed—and is walloping the poor. The Justice Department found that the rate of violent crime victimization for Americans earning over $50,000 a year was 21 per 1,000; yet the rate for those earning less than $7,500 was three times as high—64 per 1,000.[1] Those most at risk are the low-paid definers of public norms—movie ushers, bouncers, fast-food clerks. They must do their job knowing that every disgruntled customer is a potential shooter. FBI Director Louis Freeh, when asked about the seeming plateau in statistics, put his finger on the real issue: "the more reliable index . . . is fear."[2]

Hypercrime is the convulsive paradox of declining crime rates accompanied by increasing fear. Most Americans are more afraid, even as they desperately make themselves more safe. Declining victimization is simply the result of evacuation; Americans are "cocooning" with a vengeance, retreating into bunker habitats, telecommuting to work and socializing on-line to escape the spiraling dread of the streets. In Tom Wolfe's novel *The Bonfire of the Vanities*, Sherman McCoy, master of his Wall Street universe, takes this advice to his debentured heart: "If you want to live in New York . . . you've got to insulate, insulate, insulate."[3]

The response to hypercrime comes in two tiers, public and private. The first-tier response is the attempt to bolster the public sector.

According to *U.S. News & World Report*, Americans believe that crime is the number one issue facing the country, and 65 percent think that the government should play a "large role" in solving the problem; 60 percent say they'd be willing to pay more taxes. So far, so good. Yet fully 78 percent agree that "the government would end up wasting most of the money."[4] This is the Hobson's choice of the Old Paradigm: do nothing and let the problem get worse, or spend more and know that amid all the incompetence, the problem will get slightly less worse.

Upping the cash flow into the existing mechanisms of law enforcement is always popular. However, if the basic paradigm is dysfunctional, more money will not equal more justice. In Jersey City, New Jersey,

Mayor Bret Schundler discovered that two out of three officers never patrolled the streets; when he tried to make manifest these invisible men, the police unions sued him.[5] Yet Schundler notes that the average compensation for a Jersey City cop totals nearly $90,000 a year, when salary, overtime, and benefits are all totaled up—this in a city with a per capita income of $10,000. He says: "Our problem is not that we spend too little on policing, but that in return for our money we get too little." But Schundler may be one of the lucky ones: Los Angeles Mayor Richard Riordan says that only one out of seven of his police officers is actually on the beat.[6]

Moreover, with no better model to build on than that inherited from eighteenth-century England, we are putting a significant percentage of our young people in jail. Nationwide, the prison population has doubled in the past decade to more than a million—more than in any other country in the world. And as legislatures repeal "prisoner bills of rights", time spent in U.S. correctional facilities is getting longer and harder:[7] after a thirty-year hiatus, Alabama is bringing back roadside chain gangs.[8] Any pretense of rehabilitation is forgotten at formidable "maxi" fortresses found in Marion, Illinois, or Florence, Colorado, or Pelican Bay, California.[9]

Another public-sector response is the curtailment of civil liberties. It's been done before. In 1880, New York City police established a "dead line" at Liberty Street in lower Manhattan, below which any "suspicious individuals" could be stopped and, if they lacked an adequate justification for their presence in the forbidden zone, jailed for the night. It worked. Historian H. Paul Jeffers records the boast of one official: "Not even so much as a ten cent piece was lost in Wall Street through thievery by outsiders," adding slyly that "whatever stealing has been done has been accomplished by the employees of the financial institutions."[10] This Fourth Amendment–free zone was eliminated in 1895 in response to civil libertarian concerns. However, even today hundreds of neighborhoods and towns are ignoring ACLU complaints and blocking off neighborhood streets to "outsiders." The argument that reducing freedom "works" has a powerful lure in the hypercrime era.

National Guard troops are already in the public housing projects of Puerto Rico,[11] and federal agents dressed in full combat gear, including assault weapons, launch drug raids from helicopters.[12] Fresno, the crime capital of California, doesn't need the Guard and its firepower; its own SWAT teams cruise the dire streets with their assault weapons at the ready.[13] Yet even ninja-suited Darth Vader lookalikes seem inadequate to the challenge of inspecting each package that comes in the mail and every unattended Ryder truck parked in front of every office building.

The second tier of response to hypercrime is private: privatized "surrogate government." People's taking the law into their own hands is nothing new; vigilantism has been the normal mechanism of crime control for most of human history. State-sponsored, bureaucratized law enforcement was a reform mostly of the last two centuries. But when the public-sector approach was seen to falter, the older, meaner techniques of feuds and vendettas naturally recrudesced.

In the hypercrime regime, the rich lead the retreat from public-sector crime control. Here the now-familiar cyberskew is at its widest: the gap between those who can afford to provide themselves with protection and those who must hope that the first-tier responses of government will keep them safe and whole. Hypercrime mirrors the central cyberpunk aesthetic: safety and productivity on the inside, fear and destruction on the outside.

A new bumperstrip reads: "Fight Crime. Shoot Back." A gun-buying binge is a further private-sector response to hypercrime. Two decades ago, 50 million guns filled America's closets and drawers. Today 220 million guns, a third of them handguns, fill glove compartments and waistbands as well.[14] Gun sales are growing 30–50 percent a year.[15] The fastest growth market is handguns for women: 88 percent of gun dealers have reported increased sales to women.[16] Smith and Wesson thoughtfully provides the "Ladysmith" model, and New England Firearms offers the "Lady Ultra."

Another market response to hypercrime is the conversion of the home into a true castle, as homeowners invest in cybersecurity. Property crime, as opposed to violent crime, is down sharply—because people lock, shutter, guard, or relocate everything they want to keep.[17] One San Antonio entrepreneur, responding to the market need created by 1,262 drive-by shootings in a single year—ricochets galore—is selling bulletproof armored panels for houses.[18] And as those fleeing danger retreat into their fortresses, the dream of defensible public space fades.

In the Cyber Future, public parks and beaches will be remembered as a great idea from the uninsulated twentieth century.

A visit to a state-of-the-art secured office building is a near-sci-fi experience; cyber-era buildings feature cameras, key cards and *Rising Sun*–type technology to keep track of the human element. The maximum security at casinos today is a foreshadowing of tomorrow as elaborate equipment monitors employees as well as customers.[19] The Los Angeles County Museum of Art deploys robo-nightwatchers. A British firm has invented a burglar alarm that sprays trespassers with a harmless but indelible dye; the company brews a specific chemical signature for each location so that law enforcement can later prove that the stained suspect was at a particular location.[20]

Thus technology reinforces the new surrogate government order. Automakers have found that the hottest selling points for new cars are keyless entry systems and "panic buttons" that set car alarms wailing and lights flashing.[21] Cameras are at every ATM and increasingly gaze into garages and stores; the new Denver airport has 1,500 of them. Suspects in the 1994 slaying of two Japanese students in an empty San Pedro, California, parking lot were arrested because a nearby bank camera was watching. Further technological fixes are on the way— instant DNA testing, retina scanning, someday perhaps *in utero* personality divination and/or behavior modification.

The most significant private-sector response to hypercrime is Gibsonian rent-a-cops—hiring a whole new set of security personnel to serve as a private, antimatter police department. To paraphrase the old Federal Express ad, when you absolutely, positively want to be safe, hire someone to watch over you. It works for those with the wherewithal to do it right; as in the film *The Bodyguard,* every Whitney Houston will be safe with her own Kevin Costner. But everyone else is on her own.

In San Francisco, a little-used law enforcement mechanism providing for private police is being revived and expanded. In 1851, at the height of the criminal chaos of the Gold Rush, the city made allowance for private security guards to patrol the Barbary streets. Today these "specials," as they are called, often come into conflict with the regular San Francisco police, who themselves have long been offering their own deluxe security service, providing extra cops to merchants for $58 an hour. However, the SFPD is outraged because the specials charge just half the cops' hourly rate.[22] The prospect of public and private police waging a price war is Gibsonian in its truth-is-stranger-than-fiction twistedness.

In the last ten years, the number of police nationwide has stayed the same, hovering at 500,000; yet since 1980, 1 million private security guards has grown to 1.6 million,[23] and further reinforcements are on the way. Today, Americans spend twice as much on private police as they do on public police. For reasons that perhaps mayors Schundler and Riordan can explain, even governments are hiring rent-a-cops. In the wake of spectacular roadside crimes against foreign visitors that cost Florida an estimated billion dollars in lost tourism revenue in 1993 alone, the Sunshine State contracted with a private security firm to guard its highway rest stops.

So-called business improvement districts (BIDs) have already banded together companies to provide services once expected from tax-funded municipalities. In New York's Times Square, 5,000 building owners instituted their own 2 percent sales tax to hire street cleaners and private security guards to bolster slumping sales and real estate values. In 1993, the second year of the BIDs' operation, the percentage of clean sidewalks jumped from 52 percent to 90 percent—and the crime rate dropped by a fourth.[24] The Big Apple now has dozens of BIDs, and such surrogate governments are cropping up around the country.

NIDs—neighborhood improvement districts—aren't far behind. In many affluent burbclaves, homeowners are pooling resources to hire their own security guards. In Washington's tony Georgetown neighborhood, Wells Fargo security guards patrol the streets at night.[25] Americans beyond the Beltway should bear this in mind: when the Washington elite want to feel secure, they bring in muscle, even if they have to pay for it out of their own pockets. The entire Upper East Side of Manhattan is considering spending $20 million a year to hire its own private 600-person army.[26] The upscale *New York Observer* opined that the proposal "is well worth the price, considering the cost of doing nothing."[27] Of course, the city is already doing plenty; this silk-stocking district has more than its share of the Big Apple's 30,000 blues.

An estimated 3-4 million Americans live in guarded communities, 500,000 in trend-setting California alone.[28] For them, security becomes a simple cost–benefit proposition: why bother petitioning indifferent bureaucrats when a call to an 800 number will bring instant relief? It's easier, let alone safer, just to pay and get it done. More than 300 pay-to-play Discovery Zones exist today, up from zero in 1989. For a fee, parents can bring their children to a crime- and gang-free playground; some lots even use metal detectors to screen customers.[29] Meanwhile, poor children, with no one but the distant police to protect them, huddle at home, afraid to venture outside into a crack deal or a crossfire. Says one teenager, "Nowhere is safe."[30] Perhaps—but those with platinum Amex cards are likely to live longer.

Shopping malls have been an early inkling of the Cyber Future. They may have no soul, but at least their bathrooms are clean. Author Joel Garreau coined the term "Edge Cities" to describe the suburban and exurban office and shopping complexes springing up miles away from the perilous urban core. He writes of one such place, Bridgewater Commons in New Jersey; nine million people a year pass through its doors, and yet in the first two years of its existence, just two assaults violated the cyberized peace. Why? "Because Edge Cities have privatized the domains in which large numbers of strangers come together,"[31] and so "patrol and control can operate at a high level."[32] In a hundred different ways, Americans are leaving behind the used-up husks of their cities with their bottom-line-insensitive bureaucracies, and they are fabricating new, outland communities. This ongoing tale of new cities was never scripted in advance but is the collaborative effort of millions of apolitical Americans, voting with their feet on the gas pedal.

What a waste: it's a trillion-dollar two-tier cost to recreate the peripheral infrastructure of everyday life in Edge Cities and suburbs—after we've already paid for one at the core. All the subways, streets, museums, libraries, and auditoriums are currently underutilized because most downtowns become nothing more than 9-to-5 "day cities."

The idea of retreat from a dangerous world into a cyberized environment reached its logical extreme in Biosphere 2. The Biosphere project was the harmonic reconvergence of an old idea, the quest for utopia raising a polymer roof in Arizona. From medieval monasteries to nineteenth-century free-love experiments, from hippie communes in the sixties to the AR-15-armed Aryan survivalists in backwoods Idaho today, the desire to retreat into a better world is deep-rooted. Today, when people feel overwhelmed by AIDS, advertising, and additives, they feel the attraction of a gun-controlled, crime-free haven where they can lose weight, relax, and recycle. Biosphere 2 repositions "white flight." People fleeing the cities will no longer be seen as compassion-fatigued race-conscious urban refugees; they will be viewed as bold eco-pioneers for the New Age. Biosphereans are a leading indicator: if the political system fails to deal with crime and fear, more and more Americans will withdraw from civil society and tend their own personal gardens.

All these second-tier responses have worked to channel crime away from those with money and toward those who can afford it least. Criminals may have declared war on society, but the rich and powerful prevail, at least on their own turf. But for those who can't afford to bear every domestic defense burden, the situation will be ever more desperate. Must poor and working people pay a second time for protection, using their dwindling quantity of after-tax dollars?

Author Doug Coupland calls this doleful phenomenon "2-ply taxation." The second tier of surrogate government is moving society in the direction limned by the cyberpunkers—privatized everything, accountable to those who foot the bill and to no one else. Second-tier responses are pure value-free market-driven pragmatism. People pay their taxes because they have to; yet as Old Paradigm solutions falter, participation in the general society beyond the mandatory minimum becomes a bad bargain. Taxpayers make their own provisions for what they need, reckoning the additional expense as just a cost of doing the business of life. And as the economics of crime and punishment sink in, few people will volunteer or vote more tax money to the government to fight lawlessness. Why should they, when they can hire their own surrogate cops, targeting their resources precisely, with no waste and no free riders?[33]

The cyberscenario holds that the struggle between tax consumers and taxpayers will not be resolved through the political process. Instead, market forces will redistribute the rich to distant—and defensible— hills and hollows across the planet. The rich have their quicksilver capitalism, enabling them to buy their way out of bureaucracy. Using private eyes and private dicks, the affluent can Gold-Card their way out of Quentin Tarantino-esque danger; the poor are left with leaden bureaucracy.

Surrogate government is means-tested—based on ability to pay—so it's inherently unequal. Two-tier law enforcement affronts the ideal of equal protection, even as it widens the cyberdivide. Although second-tier responses may represent the optimal solution for the individual, they do nothing to improve the commonweal. And with such surrogate government in place, the real government—once the repository of citizenship and patriotism—eventually becomes irrelevant.

If the dominoes of the high–low Cyber Future continue to fall as they have, then someday soon the idea of what it means to be an American will tip over. Will we trust our coworkers if we fear that they are carrying a concealed handgun to the office—or are keeping an assault weapon in the trunk of their car? And how can we expect poor kids to risk their lives in wartime for a country that is mostly walled off to them? Cyberpunkers riposte: "Who cares? After the collapse of nation-states, only anarchy will reign; the wars of the future will be fought between corporations—who will be able to afford their own cyber-Hessians." In *Snow Crash,* one of the characters muses that the federal government "was invented to do stuff that private enterprise doesn't bother with, which means that there's probably no reason for it."[34]

This is not what the Founders had in mind. But if Thomas Jefferson were alive today, he would be less angry at Americans trying to adapt to danger than disgusted by leaders who fail their Constitutional duty to "ensure domestic tranquility."

How did all this happen? How did the century that began with President McKinley's hope of a full dinner pail end with streets filled with fear? Gibson sees the bright streaks of Western Civ, which arced so high for so long, crashing in the near horizon, at the beginning of the Cyber Future. Its dawn coincides with the sunset of the Old World. *Virtual Light* contains this terse elegy:

> We are come not only past the century's closing . . . the millennium's turning, but to the end of something else. Era? Paradigm? Everywhere, the signs of closure. Modernity was ending.[35]

Today, modernity is already ending, and the assumptions that guided America for a century are being repudiated. Yet current politics are still mired in the precepts of the Old Paradigm. It is the persistence of these old ways that brings the divided cyber-economy and the paralyzing fear of hypercrime. Together, they bring the Cyber Future.

If the Old Paradigm is so bad, why was it ever put in place? And why has it lasted so long? We must consider the origins of the Old Paradigm and the greatness of what it accomplished; we must know it in its youth to recognize it on its death bed. Before we can comprehend what comes next, we need to understand what came before.

PART 2

THE BUREAUCRATIC OPERATING SYSTEM

CHAPTER 4

BUREAUCRAT

Tony Kushner's Broadway play *Angels in America, Part Two: Perestroika* opens in the Kremlin. An ancient man, "the world's oldest living Bolshevik," hobbles onto the stage. Summoning all his passion, he lectures Gorbachev-era reformers who, having lost their communist fervor, now flounder with reform. The old Bolshevik asks them: "How are we to proceed without *Theory?*" Recalling the clarities and enthusiasms of his youth, he tells his audience, "You can't imagine, when we first read the Classic Texts, when in the dark vexed night of our ignorance and terror the seed words sprouted and shoved incomprehension aside." The old man says that he pities this new generation, which never had the chance to see "the grandeur of the prospect we gazed upon: like standing atop the highest peak in the mighty Caucasus, and viewing in one all-knowing glance the mountainous granite order of creation."[1] Three thousand years after God took Moses to the mountain of Nebo and showed him the lands of Gilead unto the utmost sea, communist revolutionaries surveyed the scientific socialist future laid out by Marx with equal exhilaration—and believed that, unlike Moses, they would reach the Promised Land.

51

The Synoptic Aspiration: The Guardian Angel of the Old Paradigm

Humankind is always drawn to ecstatic epiphanies—in religion, in philosophy, in politics. Karl Popper refers to the "Spell of Plato":[2] the dream of one ideal, one form, one final answer. Such yearning for an all-encompassing theory has also been called the Synoptic Aspiration.[3] It names the quest for the Good, for the Infinite, which has animated much of human endeavor. Every physicist who sees the end of time in an atom, every biologist who sees the fingerprint of God in a chromosome, every poet who sees all Beauty in a flower or a face—all are moved by the Synoptic Aspiration.

The urge to discover every truth in One Big Answer is a splendor of human nature, inspiring men and women to do their best inquiring, creating, and discovering. Yet in the world of politics, the Synoptic impulse must eventually find an anchor in institutions—and Synoptically inspired institutions have oppressed more than they have liberated. In this century, the Synoptic Aspiration has led to mass-scale tragedy; humanity, in its diversity and complexity, is not easy to "Synopticize"— though much blood has been spilled in the attempt.

The Russian Bolsheviks didn't have God, but they had their Marxist theology: the Synoptic longing for secular salvation, for an end to exploitation and alienation, for the delivery of humankind from the nightmare of the past.[4] Yet since the workers' paradise did not arise spontaneously, as Marx had hoped, Lenin had to resort to more practical means. Thus the irony: in the name of communism, the Soviets established a system of bureaucratically controlled state capitalism. How could the brutal Bolshevik system hold the high moral ground for so long? How could intellectuals and idealists who hated private capitalism so love public capitalism? The answer reaches back further than Lenin or even Marx—to the philosopher who most embodies the union between philosophy and state power, Georg W. F. Hegel. Hegel was the thinker of modern times who pulled the Synoptic Aspiration down to earth, taking it from the Olympian province of philosopher kings into the mortal coil of real Kaisers.

In 1806, Hegel had a vision of the progressive, propulsive future of humankind, as it marched forward to its manifest enlightened destiny.

As a professor at the University of Jena, he looked out his window and watched the victorious Napoleon and the *Grande Armée* passing by. "I saw the World Spirit riding upon a white horse!" he famously exclaimed. Although the French were the enemy, he saw them as embodying Progress: the modernizing force that would galvanize the apathetic, array the undisciplined, and spur the longed-for unification of Germany.

Few men of power have read Hegel's dense tomes *The Phenomenology of the Spirit* and *Philosophy of Right and Law.* Yet rulers can appreciate his most enduring contribution to political praxis: the fusion of ethereal, intoxicating idealism with the wrought-iron structure of government— Synoptic Statism. Any leader planning a vast enterprise, from public works to racial purification to class warfare, would appreciate Hegel's words:

> The Universal is to be found in the State . . . The State is the Divine Idea as it exists on earth . . . We must therefore worship the State as the Manifestation of the Divine on earth . . . the State is the march of God through the world.[5]

Believing in the idea of the Absolute, Hegel readily transferred his devotion to one particular absolutism: the Prussian monarchy. As a professor by royal appointment, he had what today would be called a conflict of interest; yet for whatever motives, Hegel, more than any other philosopher, injected nineteenth-century bureaucracy with the steroids of world-changing ambition, bulking up government for the heavy lifting to come.

Born half a century later, Karl Marx saw himself as an anti-Hegelian, determined, as he said, to stand Hegel on his head. If Hegel was an airy theorist who saw human development as the growing self-awareness of the Universal Spirit, Marx deemed himself the hard-nosed materialist who saw change and growth through technology and material development. Yet in spite of his substitution of the sociological for the spiritual, Marx remained always in the shadow of Hegel[6]—another German Synoptic Aspirer searching for the immutable dialectic of historical progression, swept up in the same universalist grandiosity that proved to be an enslaving opiate to idealists.

Hegel died in 1831 and Marx in 1883, so it's hardly fair to blame them for the abuses and atrocities committed by their heirs in this century. However, since both wrote with the intention of influencing the world, their legacies must include their becoming tools for tyrants and front men for totalitarianism. If Hegel was the progenitor, Marx was the popularizer. Marx's vision of workers throwing off their chains and winning the world for equality and peace gave appealing substance to Hegel's neo-Platonism.

Both thinkers contributed toward the same end: to give sanction to the sweeping expansion of state power. Suddenly, "raison d'état" became raison d'être—on the Right as well as the Left. As the government took on new majesty, sanctified by the new ideology, the leader was seen as answering only to History.

Marx thought, wrongly, that the utopian state of the future would wither away. But since Hegel had approved of the State's status quo, the thinking of this philosopher was particularly useful to *Macht* politicians like the Iron Chancellor, Otto Von Bismarck, and later to Lenin and Hitler. With Hegel's posthumous blessing, they planted a quasi-religious halo atop such concepts as "the general will," "the proletariat," and "the people." The Austrian economist Ludwig von Mises labeled this apotheosizing as "statolatry," the worship of the State. Modern bureaucrats, von Mises added, rather than intone about the divine right of Kings, were more modest—and more cunning. "You could revolt against a Bourbon king, and the French did it," he wrote in *Bureaucracy,* "but you cannot revolt against the God State and his humble handy man, the bureaucrat."[7]

For the last hundred years, even nontotalitarians—those committed to democracy—have shared in the Synoptic exuberance. Government action became the fixation of all who wanted to cut through the sludge of reactionary custom and get on with the business of winning wars and solving people's problems. The instrument, the all-purpose tool, was bureaucracy.

Yet now that so many One Big Answer bureaucracies have crashed, the millenarian zeal has ebbed from the God-State faith. Little of the Synoptic Aspiration is visible today, although its currents run deep through our psyches. Meanwhile, although the iridescent neon of Hegelian ideology has faded, the structure of twentieth-century statism still stands: gray drab solids, concreted across the landscape. Many Americans still get a warm feeling when they think about the federal government, but that glow comes from nostalgia, from thinking of the glorious accomplishments of the past. Old Paradigm believers mostly concede that the present offers no hope for paradise—and the future, even less.

Today's world makes us wonder if the clash of past Synoptic titans was just a dream. It wasn't; it was *about* a dream. But it was real. Just as we might look at a Mongolian shepherd and strain to the realization that the blood of Genghis Khan flows through his veins—that once his ancestors terrorized the world in their Golden Horde—so we look at bureaucrats today, in their short-sleeved shirts with pocket protectors and wonder how they ever could have been so powerful.

The Bureaucratic Operating System

Bureaucracy was the human institution in which Synoptic yearnings and ambitions found grounding. Since its modern foundations were laid during the Industrial Revolution, the model was of government as a machine—a neutral system that would act efficiently, competently, and dispassionately to resolve problems.

As early as 1761, a German political theoretician was moved to postulate:

> A properly constituted state must be exactly analogous to a machine, in which all the wheels and gears are precisely adjusted to one another; and the ruler must be the foreman, the mainspring, or the soul . . . which sets everything in motion.[8]

Bureaucracy, because it boomed during the industrial era, assumed the rhythm of mass production—assembly lines, interchangeable parts, standardized work rules. As the critic Robert Hughes observes, machines were once seen "as unqualifiedly good"—whereas today, only "exceptional sights, like a rocket launch, can give us anything resembling the emotion with which our ancestors contemplated heavy machinery." In an earlier era, people "did not feel the uncertainties about the machine that we do."[9] The new machines produced great gains in economic productivity, and it seemed logical that mechanistic modes of politics could enable social engineers to secure equally large outputs.

Thus the guiding metaphor for nineteenth- and twentieth-century government was the factory production system, cranking out educated citizens and pension checks like widgets. For the twenty-first century, the apt analogy can be drawn from computers—the Operating System.

An Operating System is a computer's paradigm, the software program that runs all other programs. Just as bureaucracy is designed to carry out the tasks given it, so the Operating System performs the functions of the computer, storing and retrieving files, processing input and output.

The most familiar Operating System today is Microsoft MS-DOS, which went from its inception in 1980, achieved near-universality within ten years. MS-DOS, or the Microsoft Disk Operating System, is the product of continuous evolution, progressing through versions 1.0 to 6.22 and constantly receiving new features, from mouse drivers to memory managers to disk doublers to windowing multitaskers. Because the goal of getting things done faster and better drives the technique, Operating Systems are endlessly reengineered, or upgraded.

Eventually, an Operating System reaches the edge of its envelope. In a Kuhnian sense, the "anomalies"—bugs, kluges, and incompatibilities—overwhelm the old paradigm of the Operating System. Thus the way is clear for a new paradigm, a new Operating System. Fifteen years ago, MS-DOS was a paradigm shift away from more primitive Operating Systems, such as CP/M. In the midnineties, it is scheduled to be replaced by a new Operating System, Windows 95. If the new Operating System "works," Bill Gates will make more billions. If it doesn't, then the entrepreneurial equivalent of Darwinian selection will march on without him.

An old joke runs: How many Virginians does it take to change a lightbulb? The answer: ten—one to change it and nine to talk about how great the old one was. Yet in the software business, the hunger for competitive edge leaves little time for sentimentality; an obsolete Operating System is a luxury few can afford. Even a cavalier, punch-drunk-on-Old-Dominion nostalgia, would not get weepy-eyed over an obsolete Operating System.

Most human techniques must withstand the test of a rival system.

The story of "progress" is the story of one "Operating System" being supplanted by another. As we have seen, the heliocentric paradigm displaced the geocentric paradigm because it worked better. Centuries later, Nikolai Tesla's idea of alternating current proved superior to Thomas Edison's plan for direct current and became the new electrical standard. Some of the simplest but greatest inventions, such as the spoon, the button, and the stirrup, can all be thought of as superior Operating Systems for eating, dressing, and moving. In written communication, the stylus replaced the stick, which gave way to the quill and then the fountain pen and then the ball point. These in turn were muscled out by movable type, linotype, and word processing—and on into virtual reality.

Like an Operating System, bureaucracy is made up of procedures and hierarchies. It coordinates activities, gathers and disseminates information, and organizes input and output.[10] We can call the current mechanisms of government the Bureaucratic Operating System, or BOS.

The BOS has dominated world politics in this century. With a few exceptions, it has ruled over individuals and parties, and its empire still stands. Bureaucracy can be upgraded endlessly—although with diminishing returns—but the world won't shift its paradigm until something new arrives to replace the old Operating System.

In the spirit of computers, we can say that our BOS runs its own special software: BUREAUCRAT. This software, the primary application of the BOS, has the same limitations as any software: in spite of frequent Upgrades, it is subject to both Bugs and Viruses.

BUREAUCRAT: The First Version and Early Upgrades

The word "bureaucracy," which emerged from eighteenth-century France, means "rule by offices."[11] Yet long before then, bureaucrats were running BUREAUCRAT.

One of the first bureaucrats was Joseph, son of Jacob and Rachel. According to Genesis 39–41, Joseph started his career in Egypt as overseer of the house of Potiphar, the captain of Pharaoh's guard. After being falsely accused by Potiphar's wife, he was imprisoned, but his organizational talents were such that he was soon running the prison.

Staying in touch with his Synoptic side, Joseph further distinguished himself as an interpreter of dreams. When Pharaoh dreamt that seven fat-fleshed cows were eaten by seven lean-fleshed cows, Joseph interpreted the dream as signifying that seven years of plenty would be followed by seven years of famine. Joseph urged Pharaoh to create a system for food conservation and rationing—to "appoint officers over the land, and take up the fifth part of the land of Egypt in the seven plenteous years . . . gather all the food . . . and that food shall be for store to the land against the seven years of famine." It worked, and Joseph was rewarded: "Pharaoh took off his ring from his hand, and put it upon Joseph's hand, and arrayed him in vestments of fine linen, and put a gold chain around his neck." What more could a bureaucrat want?

Max Weber, the early twentieth-century student of bureaucracy, has written that ancient Egypt was indeed where bureaucracy started. The land of the Nile, he notes, provides "the historical model of all later bureaucracies."[12] So the history of BUREAUCRAT begins there.

Why did the Egyptians need a Bureaucratic Operating System? One reason was control. Around 3100 B.C., Menes, king of Upper Egypt, gained sway over Lower Egypt; to secure allegiance, he and his successors proclaimed themselves divine kings, whose personal names became too sacred to utter. Thus they took the title of "pharaoh," or "great house," and soon out of the royal household in Memphis the first state bureaucracy emerged. Different administrative functions were executed out of different rooms—fledgling bureaucrats staking out their turf. Egyptian papyrus pushers conducted the census, collected taxes, and administered the law.

A second purpose of bureaucrats was to accomplish the great public works of the pharaohs: flood control and pyramid building. Weber writes that Egypt set up "public regulation of the water economy for the whole country"; the project was administered from the top down, thus creating an "apparatus of scribes and officials."[13] Long before the Tennessee Valley Authority came into being, government planners and hydraulic engineers—officials with titles like superintendent of the inundation and royal constructor—were supervising a vast system of canals, dikes, and levees designed to ensure the bounty of Nile Valley agriculture.[14] Meanwhile, the state consumed much of Egypt's surplus value in other pre-Keynesian public works, including pyramids and mortuary temples. These colossal projects were built by forced labor, overseen by bureaucrats.

It is important to recognize that this top–down bureaucratic system "worked." Weber speaks of "the rationalization of charisma," describing the process by which the authority of a great leader is transferred to a long-lasting system. Egyptian bureaucrats, rationalizing the charisma of the pharaoh, provided continuity and competence for three millennia, etching the deeds of the pharaohs onto the tablets of civilization. That Egyptian bureaucrats today are best known for upturned-palm *baksheesh* should not blind us to the fact that their ancestors created the first effective software of the Bureaucratic Operating System. We can call it BUREAUCRAT 1.0, the Ur-software for bureaucrats everywhere.

The longevity of the Egyptian system provides a contrast with the abbreviated career of Alexander the Great, who captured Egypt in 332 B.C. Alexander was a giant of history, conquering from Greece to India, although his vast domain splintered within a few years of his death; he established no system to rationalize his charisma. As Hellenic scholar Peter Green puts it, the Alexandrian empire was held together only by Alexander's "unique and irreplaceable personality." On his deathbed in Babylon, the Macedonian charismatician, ignoring rationalization, bequeathed his empire "to the strongest," predicting that his generals "would hold a great funeral contest" over the fate of the empire. They did just that, and Hellenic hegemony, spanning lands from the Nile to the Indus, was sundered.[15]

The Romans were less audacious on the battlefield than Alexander, but their conquests stayed conquered longer because they had a bureaucratic system for consolidating their gains. A pillar of the Roman imperium, in the words of historian Eugene Kamenka, was "a centrally controlled professional bureaucracy, holding the capital and the provinces together."[16] The Romans developed an elaborate modus operandi, with titles based on pay grade: at the bottom were the *sexagenarii* (officials earning 60,000 *sesterces* a year); above them were the *centenarii* (100,000), the *ducenarii* (200,000), and the *trecenarii* (300,000).[17]

None of this system would have survived except for one thing: it worked. As Weber put it, "The decisive reason for the advance of bureaucratic organization has always been its purely *technical* superiority over any other form of organization."[18] Roman bureaucrats kept control not because they were despots but because they kept busy: they built roads and fortifications; they coined money and collected taxes; they meted out justice that was, by the standards of the time, remarkably fair. Credit the Romans with a massive Upgrade, developing BUREAU-CRAT 2.0.

The structure of an even longer-lasting bureaucracy, the Roman Catholic church, was modeled after that of the empire. The church's origins were supremely Synoptic; yet by the end of the first century A.D., when it was clear that Christ's return was not imminent, His vicars set to work rationalizing His charisma. The organization they created provided continuity through pagan persecution, barbarian invasion, and Dark Ageification. St. Peter's successors survived and thrived because they were technically superior: they could read and write. Since BUREAUCRAT couldn't function if its functionaries couldn't communicate across time and distance, the church invested heavily in its dogma- and document-driven educational Program.[19]

The church's administrative machine built not only cathedrals, universities, libraries, and records depositories but also the rudiments of a social welfare system, with hospitals and systematized charity.[20] At the zenith of its secular power, the church divided Christendom into some 400 dioceses, each ruled by a bishop or archbishop with administrative, judicial, and military power, in addition to spiritual puissance.[21]

As the Romans' BUREAUCRAT 2.0 was Upgraded to Roman Catholic BUREAUCRAT 3.0, we should note the basically unchanging nature of the economic and social environment. From the pharaohs to the popes, labor-intensive agriculture and preindustrial artisanry were the dominant modes of production. Whether the dominant deity was Horus or Zeus or God, the Programs the system ran didn't much change—keeping the realm together as well as building pyramids, pantheons, and Notre Dame. Bugs were evident, but no terminal Viruses. The Programs could be tweaked and patched in response to the problems that arose.

Yet by the nineteenth century, the combination of Hegelian ideologizing and industrial revolutionizing led to a vast expansion of state power. BUREAUCRAT 3.0 may have been sufficient for use by tradition-bound kings, queens, and priests, but it was no longer sufficient for the great work to come. The new era of politicians and commissars had arrived, and new software was needed.

BUREAUCRAT: Later Upgrades

One new Program needed for BUREAUCRAT was crime control. During the Industrial Revolution, mechanization and industrialization pushed people off the land and into the cities, concentrating a *lumpenproletariat* whose behavior overwhelmed the old mechanisms of vigilantes and constables. The population of London nearly tripled during the Georgian era, from 600,000 in 1714 to 1.7 million in 1830. The antisocial stresses associated with that population explosion forced the creation of the first modern bureaucratized police force, London's "bobbies," in 1829.

Yet more police were only a partial answer to the larger questions of social control and societal preservation. All manner of radicalisms abounded in the nineteenth century; governing regimes knew that they had to Upgrade or perish amid riots, strikes, and revolution. BUREAUCRAT was further modified to meet these threats.

It was Hegel and Marx's own Germany that took the lead in social reform. Bismarck, a Prussian who engineered the unification of Germany while preserving the suzerainty of the Hohenzollerns, is best known for provoking three wars in the 1860s and 1870s that led to the unification of Germany. But Bismarck was the founder not only of the modern warfare state but of the modern welfare state: BUREAUCRAT 4.0. After all, what chance did the German *Reich* have to gain its rightful place in the European sun if it was shadowed by the threat of insurrection and chaos at home? The Germans took the militaristic bureaucracy inherited from Prussia[22] and combined it with industrial mass-production techniques to create the first bureaucratic welfare state. Bismarck was neither a liberal nor an intellectual; he was a pragmatist who could see that *Realpolitik* required an effective social contract at home. As he explained, "Social evils are not to be remedied by repression alone, but rather by concurrent promotion of the welfare of the working classes."[23] Because he considered it the duty of the statesman to preserve the divine-right authority of the Prussian kaiser, Bismarck preempted the socialist opposition by adopting much of its agenda.

The Programs Bismarck booted up on BUREAUCRAT for the first time established a spectrum of social insurance benefits, for accident victims (1881), for the sick (1884), for the elderly (1889). The pattern that emerged was that the Right and Left, in spite of their mutual hostility, worked together to build the Old Paradigm—although at the time it was the new paradigm. The one thing they could agree on was that bureaucracy was the tool to undertake whatever social functions they decided on.

Other nations with similar problems looked upon the Germans' model as an efficient, dynamic cure for the fashionable *Ende des Jarhunderts* pessimism, and by 1914, most European countries were well on their way toward the creation of a welfarist safety net. In the words of Princeton historian Harold James, "Germany produced her . . . model that the rest of the world might and did imitate."

Thus the irony: the true progenitors of today's social welfare bureaucracy looked nothing like Eleanor Roosevelt. They favored dueling scars, handlebar mustaches, and helmets with spikes on top.

Bugs in the BOS

No software is trouble-free; over time, it accumulates Bugs, like lint in a belly button. There are five Bugs, not only in the program called BUREAUCRAT, but at a more profound level in the Bureaucratic Operating System itself: what might be called Parkinsonism, Peterism, Oligarchism, Olsonism, and Information Infarction.

Bug #1: Parkinsonism

In his famous little book, *Parkinson's Law,* C. Northcote Parkinson puts it simply: "Work expands so as to fill the time available for its completion." There is "little or no relationship," he adds, "between the work to be done and the size of the staff to which it may be assigned."[24]

The Bureaucratic Operating System, in other words, is prone to Parkinson's disease: brain-bloat. Without getting any smarter, its cerebrum swells while its sinew shrinks. In his famous example, Parkinson found that the number of capital ships in the royal navy fell by 67 percent from 1914 to 1928, while the number of admiralty officials rose by 78 percent during the same period.[25]

Bug #2: Peterism

Another ghost in the machine is Peterism, a Bug first identified by Dr. Lawrence Peter in *The Peter Principle:* "In a hierarchy, every employee tends to rise to his level of incompetence."[26] In other words, effective employees will continue to be promoted until they arrive at a level of responsibility where their performance falters. And since nobody gets fired in BUREAUCRAT, "In time, every post tends to be occupied by an employee who is incompetent to carry out its duties."[27] Glorying in the gloomy discipline of "hierarchiology," Peter waxes Spenglerian: the accumulation of ineptitude will eventually drag civilization down.[28]

Bug #3: Oligarchism

Sociologists know the "iron law of oligarchy": someone has to be in charge. Marx was wrong about many things, but he was right about one: the state is the tool of the ruling class. The composition of the ruling class has changed, and yet a ruling class still exists in every society.

All the way from Moscow came a new word, *nomenklatura,* to describe this bureaucratic elite. Yet the most enduring moniker was given by Milovan Djilas, the Yugoslavian dissident, in his 1957 volume *The New Class,* where he spoke of this group's own distinctive consciousness— mostly a determination to stay on top.[29] Since then, neoconservative Irving Kristol has elasticized the "New Class" label to cover the postindustrial power elite in the West: "those who make their career in the expanding public sector"—the nonprofit knowledge workers, bureaucrats, planners, grant makers, and idea mongers. "They are not much interested in money," Kristol notes, "but they are keenly interested in power."[30] In other words, what has happened around the world is that the biggest single obstacle to change in the public sector is the public sector itself. BUREAUCRAT has proved more effective in its self-defense than in its putative purpose. Marx explains it: the ruling class is acting in its own class interest. What did we expect, altruism?

Bug #4: Olsonism

University of Maryland economist Mancur Olson argues that advanced economies ultimately face death by another kind of "interest": special interest. Olsonism is James Madison's nightmare: "the mischief of faction," which Madison decried in the *Federalist Papers*. Olson's two books, *The Logic of Collective Action* and *The Rise and Decline of Nations*, make a powerful argument that the accretion of special interests buries economic growth.

In a democracy, the taxing and regulating power of the government—the power to destroy or to enrich—becomes the object of intense interest-group focus. And if one asks which interest group, the answer is—all of them, eventually. Yet Olson argues that the wealthy and well connected are at the head of the favor-seeking line; they are relatively few and easy to organize. Moreover, they have the disposable money and time to invest in the effort to bend the government to their will, and they already have a chummy relationship with their neighbors atop the commanding heights of the political economy. In America's past, the rich blatantly pressed for railroad subsidies and protective tariffs; today, standards of propriety have changed, but the well-off still get what they can by means of industrial-policy-type subventions.

Next in line is the middle class, as the realization that lobbying can be lucrative trickles down to this group. The middle/working class is usually so big that it's hard to mobilize, but when it does, like an 800-pound gorilla, it gets to sit where it pleases. Two results of past middle-class politicking are legal protection for labor unions and state-administered retirement pensions. Finally, the lower class gets into the act, demanding various forms of income transfer. So at the end of the Olsonistic process, no one is left out; yet everyone is poorer, because the transaction costs of what economists call "rent seeking"—politicized wealth transfers—are enormous.

In the Olsonian scenario, BUREAUCRAT seeks to preside over all those political connections and strangles itself in the tangle. Olson offers little but ironic pessimism; countries known for their democratic, pacific stability are punished for their virtue:

> Countries that have had democratic freedom of organization without upheaval or invasion the longest will suffer the most from growth-repressing organizations and combinations. This helps to explain why Great Britain, the major nation with the longest immunity from dictatorship, invasion, and revolution, has had in this century a lower rate of growth than other large, developed democracies.[31]

In a view that is dismal even by the standards of his profession, Olson comes close to suggesting that the solution to "national declinism" is to lose a war and start with a clean slate.[32]

Bug #5: Information Infarction

The central tenet of Austrian economics, the school of thought led by von Mises and Friedrich Hayek, holds that bureaucratic decision making must fail because it cannot know all relevant information. As Hayek put it, "What cannot be known cannot be planned."[33] In other words, a permanent Information Infarction cuts off the central planner from the blood supply of knowledge, clotting judgment and swelling the body politic's most painful failures. People sitting in marble office buildings suffer from the Big Sleep of ignorance about what is happening in the real world—even when they're wide awake. The Austrians, the most resolutely anti-Synoptic of all twentieth-century economists, preached humility and a necessarily constricted vision. Since we can never know all the answers, they argued, the most that humanity can aspire to is the cumulative knowledge that comes from trial and error, spread out among the largest possible number of economic actors.

Cyberpioneer Norbert Wiener has also noted the negative synergy of top-down information occlusion, writing that "the State is stupider than most of its components."[34] Only the multivariate verities of feedback can provide the intelligence needed to operate even a small sector of the economy.

The Information Infarction has been most evident in the socialist East, but on a smaller scale it is equally apparent in the bureaucratic West. BUREAUCRAT 1.0—the software the Egyptians used to build pyramids—was effective at the simplest tasks of counting noses and granite blocks. Even an Upgrade such as BUREAUCRAT 4.0 once seemed able to cope with the information brought through pneumatic tubes and telegraph wires. But further Upgrades in the twentieth century were too little, too late; they fell further and further behind the emerging cybertechnologies of transistor, chip, and PC. BUREAUCRAT's obsolete system cannot cope with the cyberflood, the gushing gigabyte magma of cognition.

Thus the five Bugs of the BOS. They are all present in the American version of BUREAUCRAT, which we will call AMERICRAT, the subject of the next chapter.

Yet a Virus lurks, too, in the Bureaucratic Operating System: totalitarianism. Unlike Europe, America has never been swept up in the totalitarian version of the Synoptic Aspiration; playwright Kushner had to look to Moscow to find his Synoptic Bolshevik. Yet the oldest living Bolshevik seems to speak for his author when he tells his Kremlin audience: "Show me the book of the next Beautiful Theory, and I promise you these blind eyes will see again, just to read it, to devour that text. Show me the words that will reorder the world."[35] Few folks are Marxists anymore, but we will always have Synoptic politics, because the Synoptic Aspiration—to walk with the Divine—is within all of us.

The United States has had its share of neo-Hegelians, of the communist as well as anticommunist persuasion, but they could never sell their One Big Answer vision to this heterodox nation. Even in its biggest big-government excrescences, AMERICRAT has been immune to the totalitarian Virus. Yet as Americans guarded against the Virus, the Bugs proliferated. If death camps or gulags never happened here, our recent history is nevertheless the sad story of systemic decline—and of the resultant quotidian but cumulative disasters we see around us every day.

We look back at the apogee of twentieth-century BUREAUCRAT with fear and loathing, with gratitude and awe. We think of both the enobling visions that lifted the human condition and of the great leaps forward that crashed down to earthbound reality in a cascade of unintended consequences. In our historical imagination we listen to an aural pastiche of Nuremberg rallies, railway whistles, air-raid sirens, blaring propaganda, and heavy machinery. Together they compose the grinding, lamenting fugue of the twentieth century.

"The essence of dramatic tragedy," explained the philosopher Alfred North Whitehead, "is not unhappiness. It resides in the solemnity of the remorseless working of things"— that is, the workings of paradigms. In the following chapter, we will consider the working of AMERICRAT, past, present, and future.

CHAPTER 5

AMERICRAT

It's said that every civilization goes through its "republican" phase, when things are built, and its "imperial" phase, when things are consumed. In America, the Bureaucratic Operating System is in its imperial phase. The country isn't crumbling all at once, but the bureaucratic parts are in a state of decline and fall. Shattered hopes and derelict lives scatter across the distressed political landscape.

BOSS: The Old Old-Paradigm

As we have seen, the Industrial Revolution inspired European politicians to conceive of large-scale redistributive bureaucracy as a factory for producing desired social outcomes. Bismarckian bureaucrats displaced older systems of aristocratic and feudal control to create the first welfare state in Germany in the late nineteenth century; and other countries followed suit. We gave this ambitious new Program a name: BUREAU-CRAT.

Across the Atlantic, American leaders were also impressed by the power of bureaucracy. Yet the bureaucratization of American politics did not displace kings and queens but rather another kind of ruler, the political boss. American bosses had gained power in the first century of American independence as a result of the "spoils system" of patronage politics. They created what we might call boss politics, the paradigm before the Old Paradigm—the "old old-paradigm." It was this patronage system that the New World software for the Bureaucratic Operating System, AMERICRAT, replaced.

Ironically, such patronage politics was known as "machine politics," a phrase originated by Aaron Burr at the end of the eighteenth century. In the case of the old old-paradigm, the machine metaphor had little to do with industrial-era precision and everything to do with raw power.

The archetypal political machine was New York City's Tammany Hall, the common name for Gotham's Democratic Party, headed by the notorious "Boss" Tweed. We can say that in America the predecessor to BOS was BOSS. Having little regard for such trivia as legalism or honesty, Tweed types had their vision of redistribution—with themselves at the front of the queue. However, the BOSS system "worked" in its own fashion. Rough-hewn folk trusted their own kind; ethnic loyalties—not just rivalries—made the trip across the Atlantic. BOSS had a Robin Hood–like sensibility that was particularly popular among the Irish, who updated their ancient animus toward English Protestants when they confronted them once again in America. Thus a certain amount of corruption was tolerated in return for user-friendly politics. As Thomas Sowell writes,

> The Irish were by no means the originators of corrupt politics. They were simply more successful at it, and performed with a warmer human touch. The poor usually ended up preferring corrupt politicians, who understood them, to distant theorists, who did not.[1]

Long before bureaucrats got into the business of feeding, clothing, and sheltering, BOSS workers were helping their constituents. As Tammany chronicler Oliver Allen observes, BOSS "actually performed a service to society":

> Tammany's minions, its far-flung network of ward heelers, block captains, and district leaders, provided a visible, personal link between the

poor immigrant and the otherwise faceless city government, parceling out jobs . . . functioning as a kind of private welfare service.[2]

Yet as with any Operating System, eventually the Bugs in BOSS brought it down. The most notable of these was greed. As Allen puts it, "Under Tweed, Tammany changed from an organization primarily dedicated to winning elections to one brazenly employed for wholesale thievery."[3] Tweed went to jail, and BOSS went into eclipse, although it has survived in some cities virtually to this day.[4]

At the federal level, however, BOSS was unsustainable after 1881, when President James Garfield was assassinated by one Charles Guiteau, perpetually referred to as "a disgruntled office seeker." Chester Alan Arthur, Garfield's vice president, had built his own career on patronage hackery; yet upon succeeding to the presidency, Arthur, in the spirit of the times—and no doubt sensing the urgency of decreasing future assassination temptation—began to dismantle the spoils system. The Pendleton Act, the 1883 law that created the Civil Service, was a conscious effort to create an elite, predictable, patronage-proof bureaucracy like those in Europe.[5] The architects of AMERICRAT built a paper empire of procedures that might seem triplicate laughable today; yet at the time, the prospect of replacing crooks with dedicated professionals who would make public service their career, regardless of which party ruled, seemed like a great advance.

Creation of AMERICRAT

Even before Garfield's death, three significant forces contributed to the desire to bureaucratize the U.S. government.

First, as is so often the case, war triggered the expansion of state power. From 1861 to 1865 Americans were witness to the greatest cataclysm of U.S. history; when it ended, Uncle Sam's terrible swift sword was ready to remake the United States. If government power could be used to end slavery, people reasoned, then surely it could be used to emancipate people from poverty and despair. Domestic reformers had been particularly inspired by the Civil War accomplishments of the U.S. Sanitary Commission; in the years after Appomattox, good-government crusaders combined with muckraking journalists to improve schools, prisons, orphanages, and asylums.[6]

Second, German cultural influence on America was arguably at its strongest in the late nineteenth century. Germans were the largest bloc of immigrants coming into the United States from 1850 to 1900, accounting for nearly a third of total immigration;[7] even today, they are the most numerous ethnic group in America.[8] Along with beer and bratwurst, Germans brought over Bismarckian politics. Wisconsin, the most German-influenced state in the union, was not surprisingly a leader in the introduction of continental-style social reform. At the turn of the century, the Badger State's laboratory of democracy in Madison was at the forefront of social policy borrowed from BUREAUCRAT across the Atlantic, including the creation of unemployment insurance and worker's compensation. The first Socialist in the U.S. Congress was from Wisconsin; Victor Berger, born in Austria, emigrated to Milwaukee and was elected in 1910. What became known as the "Wisconsin Idea" illuminated the nation; one professor at the University of Wisconsin counted thirty of his students who went off to Washington to work on the New Deal.[9]

The prestige of German intellectual life was at its peak in the late nineteenth century, ranging from woozy Hegelianism, which had influenced the New England Transcendentalists, to the German university system, which would provide the model for the restructuring of American higher education. Richard T. Ely, one of the founders of the American Economics Association in 1885, was typical of intellectuals who felt they had more to learn from Germans than Anglo-Saxons. Ely studied at the universities of Halle and Heidelberg in Germany, where he came to admire the Bismarckian "corporatist" alternative to the laissez-faire that was predominant in the United States and Britain. Returning to America, he radiated with Hegel's idealized faith in government: "We regard the State as an educational and ethical agency whose positive aid is an indispensable condition of human progress."[10]

Yet there were more down-to-earth reasons why American intellectuals came back wide-eyed from the Kaiser's Germany. As historian James Allen Smith writes:

Ely and other Americans who witnessed the creation of the German welfare state were greatly impressed by the status of German professors. These professors had close ties to political leaders and civil servants and played advisory roles in policy areas as diverse as agriculture, trade, social welfare, and labor.[11]

A government that promised power and prestige to the intellectual was likely to win his support.

Further Germanic influence came from early Marxists, refugees from the failed uprisings of 1848. Karl Marx himself supplemented his income as a foreign correspondent for the *New York Daily Tribune*. He was fascinated by American utopianism, such as at Brook Farm, the short-lived Massachusetts commune.[12] However, though Marxisant ideas resonate to this day, Marxism itself never became a significant political force in America. Conditions were never desperate enough to inspire large numbers toward a foreign-based ideology that preached atheism and violence.

The third and most significant precipitator of AMERICRAT was the reformist Progressive movement, which gained momentum after the Civil War. Progressives believed that "good government," as conducted by career public servants, could provide an honest alternative to BOSS. They also saw the need to do something about the widening inequalities resulting from industrial boom on the one hand and waves of immigration on the other. Progressives volunteered themselves to mediate wisely between the greed of the rich and the rude passions of the poor.

Samuel Haber captured Progressivism's essence in the title of his study of the era, *Efficiency and Uplift*. If Americans were mostly immune to the seductions of Hegelianism, they had ecstasies of their own. Haber writes that the Progressive Era was "a secular Great Awakening, an outpouring of ideas and emotions in which a gospel of efficiency was preached without embarrassment to businessmen, workers, doctors, housewives, and teachers, and yes, preached even to preachers."[13]

Many Progressives relied heavily on the works of Frederick W. Taylor, who coined the phrase "scientific management" in 1911; he made a career studying every motion made by man and machine in an effort to wring maximum productivity out of the factory. Taylor was the paradigmatic "efficiency expert," the first of the much-made-fun-of fussbudgets with whistles and clipboards who once loomed large in popular culture; an image of "Taylorism" is found in the factory tyrants hectoring Charlie Chaplin to work harder in the 1936 film *Modern Times*. Taylor once declared: "In the past man was first; in the future the system will be first."[14] In his way, he was a Synoptic who dreamed of solving the labor question—strikes, syndicalism, and the threat of socialism—with his One Big Answer of industrial harmony. He claimed that "scientific management is not any efficiency device"; rather, it "involves a complete mental revolution" of workers, managers, and owners alike.[15] Judith Merkle, in her book *Management Ideology*, puts Taylor in the tradition of the French utopian socialist Saint-Simon:

> Taylor saw science as a moral system taking the place of a dying Christianity in the new industrial order. The machine, with its universally imposed discipline, was the most visible symbol of that new moral order.[16]

Scientific management seemed to offer more tangible benefits as well. In 1914, one Taylor disciple estimated that "inefficiency" in American industry cost the nation $105 billion annually—this in a year when the entire output of the United States was $38.6 billion.[17] Taylorism seemed to blend with Marxism, which in those pre-Bolshevik days offered the promise of unlimited plenty through better management of economic assets.[18]

Naturally, politicians were intrigued by the prospect of plentiful capitalism preempting socialist revolution. President McKinley had offered Americans "the full dinner pail," but he was killed by a self-proclaimed anarchist in 1901—the third president to be assassinated in thirty-six years. Meanwhile, Socialist Eugene V. Debs saw his vote totals surge tenfold in a decade, reaching an all-time high of 6 percent of the nationwide vote in 1912. Yet just as Bismarck preempted Marxism in Germany with his welfare state, so American Progressives—from Theodore Roosevelt to Wisconsin governor Bob LaFollette to the *New Republic's* first editor, Herbert Croly—sought the orderly and peaceful "reconstruction" of American society along more efficient and uplifting lines.

Robert H. Wiebe, in *The Search for Order*, writes that the period from 1870 to 1920 witnessed the birth of "a managerial government

. . . derived from the regulative, hierarchical needs of urban-industrial life."[19] Progressive thinking applied the new tool of bureaucracy to everything from industrial relations to partisan politics to social work. Reformers of the time had every confidence that AMERICRAT would prove not only more honest but more efficient than BOSS. Thus the socialist mayor of Milwaukee straight-facedly set up a government "Bureau of Efficiency and Economy,"[20] while in Washington, President Roosevelt established the government-reforming Keep Commission in 1905. During its four years of existence, the commission addressed civil service and contracting issues.[21]

Progressives, believing in "merit," propagated all manner of tests and licensing procedures, measuring and rating everything from IQ to aptitude for medical practice. They believed they could use their expertise, as one writer put it, to mediate between "two enemies . . . risen like spirits of darkness on our social and political horizon—an ignorant proletariat and a half-taught plutocracy."[22] Reformers who unabashedly saw themselves as "social engineers" and "technocrats"; they were operating under the immutable laws of the new science of management.

From AMERICRAT emerged administrative bodies such as the Food and Drug Administration (1906) and the National Park Service (1907), as well as activist trustbusting, such as the breaking up of the Standard Oil Company in 1911. Teddy Roosevelt even bolted the Republican Party to run on the Progressive Party ticket in 1912. Yet the grand slam for Progressive politics came in 1913, the first year of Woodrow Wilson's presidency, with the establishment of the Federal Reserve, the Federal Trade Commission, the direct election of U.S. Senators, and the income tax. Subsequently, Wilson, impressed by the ability of the federal government to mobilize the nation for world war, let slip his vague belief that management, if not ownership, of the American economy must eventually pass into the public sector.[23]

Progressivism was knocked back to the political periphery beginning in the late 'teens, amidst the popular backlash against overweening Wilsonianism, at home and abroad. But even the normalcy-seeking, Babbitt-era Republicans remained influenced by Progressive ideology; Presidents Harding and Coolidge wanted a government strong enough to secure a businesslike regime that could also break strikes and stomp

Bolshevism. Indeed, they were more pro-business than pro–free market, as evidenced by their toleration for cartels and their hikes in competition-reducing tariffs.

The last of this line was Herbert Hoover, "The Great Engineer," elected president in 1928 in one of the major landslides in American history. Hoover had made an entrepreneurial fortune in the private sector, but he was a technocratic bureauphiliac at heart. In between his humanitarian relief work in postwar Europe and his service as secretary of commerce, he had found time to conduct a Taylorite survey entitled *Waste in Industry*.[24] In the wake of the 1929 stock market crash, Hoover's faith in managerialism over market forces led him to reject the antiprotectionist petition of more than 1,000 leading economists and to sign the Smoot-Hawley Tariff in 1930, which raised excises on imports by as much as 100 percent, further depressing the economy.[25]

AMERICRAT: Early Upgrades

Franklin D. Roosevelt proclaimed during the 1932 presidential campaign: "New conditions impose new requirements upon government and those who conduct government."[26] However, much of the New Deal was not so much new as an Upgrade of the AMERICRAT 1.0 Program developed during the Progressive era. Roosevelt had served in the Wilson administration, and so it is not surprising that much of his New Deal was an expansion of Wilsonian Progressive ideas. The Roosevelt presidency will be dealt with in more detail in Part 3.

If Taylor's "scientific management" backdropped the Progressive era, James Burnham's *The Managerial Revolution*, published in 1941, predicted that in the bureaucratic world to come, "a different social group or class—the managers—will be the dominant or ruling class."[27]

At midcentury, it seemed inevitable that bureaucrats would occupy the commanding heights of the economy and society. However, not all Americans in the New Deal era were content to be mere managers; some romantics dreamt heroic Kushnerian dreams of bureaucratic earthly utopia. Synoptically Aspiring European fascists even had their American emulators and admirers, from General Hugh Johnson, chief of the National Recovery Administration, to Charles and Anne Morrow Lindbergh to the songwriter Cole Porter, who embarrassedly had to amend the pro-Mussolini lyrics of his song "You're the Tops."

In their book *Generations,* authors William Strauss and Neil Howe call the Depression-era children shaped by World War II the "GI Generation":

> Their personality has carried a strong "government issue" flavor . . . GI's have always regarded government as their benefactor . . . a generation content to put its trust in government authority.[28]

This cohort, the authors assert, "became the consummate mid-twentieth century 'technocrats' "; their predilection for planning made them become "the nation's greatest-ever economists, social engineers, and community designers."

Yet as we have seen, America escaped the devil Virus of totalitarianism that afflicted so much of the planet during the same period. The first reason was that Roosevelt was no radical; he was a democrat as well as a Democrat. He Upgraded the regnant bureaucratic paradigm, but he staunchly resisted radical, Viral mutations. Second, FDR and his moderation survived because the major undertakings of his presidency—from the Tennessee Valley Authority to Social Security to the Manhattan Project—were successful. In other words, AMERICRAT worked. But FDR was not merely lucky to inherit an effective Operating System; he worked to make it better, applying four significant Upgrades to AMERICRAT.

Upgrade #1: More Spending

The ideas of the British economist John Maynard Keynes were at the heart of the U.S. government's efforts in the thirties to revive the economy. Keynes theorized that the Depression allowed stagnant pools of capital to accumulate, doing nobody any good. It would be far better, he argued, for the government to stir up those pools with public works and deficit spending, putting more money in people's hands—thus increasing "aggregate demand" for goods and services and creating more wealth. Keynes may not have had all the answers, but his ideas were an improvement over the high-tariff policies embraced by Hoover after the Crash.

Ah, to be young and Keynesian at midcentury: one could do exactly what one wanted to do—spend billions building cities and saving the world—and be supported by an economic theory that said to spend still more, because spending was the route to riches. Keynes died in 1946, so nobody could ask the master whether deficit spending in an emergency might be different from endlessly increasing spending in good times as well as bad.

Looking back on those years, one can see that government spending filled in for the collapse of economic confidence. After the GNP fell by nearly half under Hoover, consumers and investors were too shell-shocked to spend and invest. Thus Keynesian policies worked because they filled the enormous slack in the thirties' economy. Such slack might not have been infinite—but nobody knew what the limit was. In 1929, federal spending accounted for less than 3 percent of GNP; a decade later, it rose to nearly 10 percent of national output; a quarter century after the Crash, in 1954, it accounted for about 19 percent of GNP. In that same year, the economy itself, as measured by inflation-adjusted GNP, was nearly double what it had been in 1929. One could conclude that if there was an upward limit on the capacity of the economy to bear the burden of larger government, it hadn't been reached yet.

Upgrade #2: Layering

All through his presidency, Roosevelt was famous for creating "alphabet agencies"—from AAA to NYA to WPA—and when they seemed no longer effective, he simply created further agencies on top of them to do the same thing better. This spirit of innovation predated by decades the pronouncement of management guru Peter Drucker: "Don't solve problems, pursue opportunities."

The same pattern of layering held for FDR's conduct of World War II. According to David Brinkley's *Washington Goes To War,* Roosevelt believed that the Washington myrmidons he had presided over during the thirties were incapable of managing the war effort, so he "insisted on creating virtually an entire new government establishment on top of what already existed." Roosevelt's idea was to recruit business executives—the so-called "dollar-a-year men"—to come to Washington and manage war production at the aforementioned salary. Thus a Democratic president entrusted the war economy to thousands of Republicans. This layering worked: the United States won the war with materiel, not manpower, overwhelming the Axis with an avalanche of weaponry, including 4,000 B-29 bombers, 57,000 tanks, and 4,000,000 Garand rifles.

One reason this layering strategy worked was that while the dollar-a-year executives supervised the bureaucracy, they were not bureaucrats themselves. As Brinkley describes it, "They had no civil service status and so could be fired at any time without ceremony or protests or hearings and appeals."[29] That sounds ruthless—but after all, America had a war to win.

Upgrade #3: Bottomlining

As with the dollar-a-year men, when the impossible had to get done immediately, AMERICRAT just did it.

As the historian Eric Larrabee recounts, when FDR wanted the best officers he could get, he didn't waste time with procedure and protocol. He picked George C. Marshall to be Army Chief of Staff over 34 more senior officers.[30] Marshall himself, when he needed help, displayed the same willingness to ignore the standard operating procedure that Roosevelt had displayed when picking him. In December 1941, he brought Dwight Eisenhower—who was just a temporary brigadier general at Fort Sam Houston in Texas—to headquarters to run army war planning, leapfrogging 350 more senior officers.[31] Soon, Ike was commanding the Allied Forces in Europe. Marshall understood that he needed someone with politico-military skills, not just the right amount of seniority.

Upgrade #4: The Hawthorne Effect

When all else fails, there's always the Hawthorne Effect.

The term comes from a series of work experiments at Western Electric's Hawthorne Plant in Cicero, Illinois, in the 1920s. Eager to improve productivity, researchers ventured to raise the illumination level on the factory floor and see what happened. Output rose for a while but then fell back to normal. So the company increased the lighting level again. Productivity went up again, but then again dropped back. Intrigued, the experimenters *reduced* lighting—and productivity went up once more. The lesson of the Hawthorne experiments was that almost any change in the work environment produces a short-term spurt of effort; workers are stimulated by the change and respond by working harder. The Hawthorne Effect is the organizational equivalent of adrenaline.

As anyone who has listened to a stirring speech knows, leaders can provoke adrenal responses, for better or worse. Roosevelt's famous words from his first inaugural, "The only thing we have to fear is fear itself," were for the better. It was a Hawthorne Effect speech, raising spirits—and economic activity—even before his policies had a chance to take effect. Indeed, FDR's confidence amid crisis was a tonic for both government and country. Michael Barone recounts the extraordinary output of the earliest New Dealers. One of them, Harry Hopkins, was given a simple command: get unemployed Americans off the hungry streets and into jobs. Hopkins was hired to run the Civilian Works Administration in early November, 1933. Three weeks later, 800,000 men were on the CWA payroll, and by December 7, that number had increased to 2 million. By January, 1934, that figure had grown to 4.25 million—fully 8 percent of the labor force.[32]

The Hawthorne Effect must always fade away, but FDR's activism—spending, layering, bottomlining, and Hawthorning—kept a sense of purposeful energy going for thirteen years.

AMERICRAT: Later Upgrades

Rooseveltians made the Upgrades to AMERICRAT 2.0 work. But not surprisingly, attempts to use the same Upgrades on the later version of AMERICRAT, 3.0, were less successful. Such is the law of diminishing returns: one can't make the same system work the same way when the environment is changing. AMERICRAT flourished in a time when Orson Welles could broadcast "War of the Worlds" and scare half the country out of its wits because folks were listening credulously. Today people would verify whether or not they were being attacked by Martians, switching over to one of the other 499 channels they had available— or go on the Net and to find out what the hell was going on.

From the AMERICRATic point of view, the midcentury's naive acceptance of new forms of authority and power was desirable—while it lasted. Yet Max Weber, once lauding bureaucracy as the great organizational advance of his time, nevertheless predicted, before his death in 1920, that a chilly gray bureaucratization would breed its own negation. Anticipating Herbert Marcuse and other New Left sages by decades, Weber predicted that regimentation and rationalization would cause "flight into the irrationalities of apolitical emotionalism . . . mysticism and . . . above all eroticism."[33] In other words, Weber foresaw the Beats and the Berkeleyites riding on the road to free polymorphous perversity, howling their protests against managerial America.

Indeed, the comfortable conformity of the GI Generation was first disrupted by the voices of the Beats, from Kerouac to Ginsberg. In the view of the nascent counterculture, big government and big business were equally oppressive; Americans were losing their yawping Whitmanesque souls for bureaucratically induced placidity and prosperity. Even before Vietnam, riots, Watergate, and the energy crisis sapped confidence in AMERICRAT, and the 1964 Free Speech movement at Berkeley took as its motto the command of the IBM punchcard: "Do not fold, spindle, or mutilate." Yet the counterculture of the sixties and seventies soon moved beyond beadshops, headshops, and bongshops. Hippies evolved into yuppies, and the rebellious "It is forbidden to forbid" ethos conquered the B-school, Brylcreemed stodginess of the flannelized business world. Thus the next door of perception was opened by capitalists-in-pony tails. From the Haight to the Village, easy riders, pushers, and hackers started a money sit-in. An ironic counterculture of getting rich was emerging, consciousness-rising toward a cyberworld of networks, knowledge work, and Mac Works.

"Postmodern" capitalism, like the rest of postmodernism, seeks to replace top-heavy rigidities with flexibility, interactivity, and maximum feasible participation. Postmodernites have grown accustomed to institutions in which vaporized chains of command have coalesced into what *Generation X* author Coupland calls "Power Mist"—namely, "the tendency of hierarchies in office environments to be diffuse and preclude crisp articulation."[34] All the "labor discipline" these firms need comes from bonuses and stock options for the elect and layoffs and temp status for the damned.

The point that James Burnham missed was that after the Managerial Revolution would come the Information Revolution, and this second revolution stormed the managerial bastilles of corporate America. Only in Washington was the Old Paradigm of AMERICRAT able to barricade itself in place.

When AMERICRAT was young, the way it did things made sense for the era. If people needed education, the easiest solution was to open schools and invite everyone to come and learn. If people faced poverty when they grew too old or ill to work, it made sense to give them the money they needed. Yet over the years, the culture shifted out from under these simple assumptions. As people grew more sophisticated, they wanted more choices and more options, and the old system could not keep up; in addition, the federal government undertook more functions, few of which it performed well. Failures of the Old Paradigm mounted up, from the C-5A transport to public housing to the Synthetic Fuels Corporation.

The result has been the basic two-tier system of the cyber-epoch: on the first tier, as we have seen, the government provides services, which are often free to the consumer, although expensive to the taxpayer; on the second tier, the well-off create their own surrogate government. This model today extends across society: anyone who ships via FedEx, studies for a test under the tutelage of Stanley Kaplan, or relies on a headhunter to find an employee/employer is relying on surrogates to do things AMERICRAT was set up to do—namely, deliver the mail, educate the young, and help people find work. Yet the appalling disjunction of quality between public and private has led to a cyberskewed flight out of the public square. As Elaine Ciulla Kamarck, director of Vice President Al Gore's reinventing government initiative, said once to her staff:

In the 50s, people's experience in the private sector and the public sector was likely to be similar. You'd have to go a bank between nine and three, you'd have to stand in a line, you'd have to deal with someone, and that was also the experience you'd have if you were getting a passport. Starting in the late 70s, the private sector discovered customer service with a vengeance. They started using computer technology to make things easy for people; the standout example is a bank ATM machine. And so while the private sector was knocking its brains out, the government just stood still. Today, if the government were a store, nobody would buy from it. If it were an airline, nobody would fly it.

When confronted with the shortcomings of the Bureaucratic Operating System, leaders first react by denying the anomalous results. After all, the BOS is a paradigm. As Kuhn argued, the upholders of a paradigm are usually "conservative" when it comes to the paradigm's conservation. Pillars of AMERICRAT forgot FDR's wisdom: "It is common sense to take a method and try it: if it fails, admit it frankly and try another— but above all, try something."

With this in mind, we can revisit the four Upgrades that we saw worked well for AMERICRAT 2.0 and see how they worked for AMERICRAT 3.0.

Upgrade #1: More Spending

In 1958, a decade after Keynes's death, John Kenneth Galbraith declared in *The Affluent Society* that Americans "must find a way to remedy the poverty that afflicts us in public services and which is in increasingly bizarre contrast with our affluence in private goods."[35] Galbraith's neo-Keynesian solution was spending more money:

> We can have good schools and well-paid teachers and ample and attractive housing and clean streets and sufficient and well-trained policemen and plenty of parks and well-supervised playgrounds . . . and they require only a willingness to tax and pay. Not many would now challenge the efficiency or morality of such outlays.[36]

Since the fifties, Americans had shown great willingness to tax and pay, yet it's apparent that social spending was not the cure-all that

Galbraith promised. After two decades of growing government, the happy policy of tax, spend, and elect broke down during the Nixon-Ford-Carter years. America suffered from the previously unknown phenomenon of "stagflation," in which both inflation and unemployment rose. Since then, Federal spending seems to have hit the ceiling of economic tolerance at around 22–24 percent of GNP.

Upgrade #2: Layering

Since FDR's time, the AMERICRATic way has been this: if the problem can't be smothered with money, it can be smothered with bureaucrats. Yet if layering worked in the war against the Depression, when AMERI-CRATS sat on problems and crushed them, it has failed in subsequent wars, such as the war on drugs. The job of director of the Office of National Drug Control Policy (ONDCP), a.k.a. the "Drug Czar," was created by Congress in 1988, apparently to convince the voters that the federal government was doing something. In the Bush years, ONDCP had a staff of 150 people to "coordinate" the drug-fighting efforts of the entire federal government. This bureaucratic ugly duckling had an impossible task from the start. The Drug Czar's *ukazy* were to command the efforts of the departments of Treasury, Defense, and Justice, even though the Czar himself was not of cabinet rank. Creating ONDCP was a bit of spin-conscious layering, a substitute for real action. The ONDCP-ocracy is the equivalent of fertilizer heaped atop the problem: a costly and smelly cover-up in lieu of the real work of weeding out the weak and failed antidrug programs scattered like crabgrass throughout the federal government. No wonder that, after a few years of decline, casual drug use is once again on the rise, while hard-core usage has continued to increase.[37]

Upgrade #3: Bottomlining

Government agencies today, from the Patents and Trademarks Office to the National Aeronautics and Space Administration to the Food and Drug Administration, never seem to get anything done. Yet why *should* they strive for the bottom line? What bad thing happens to them if they don't? Bottomlining works during genuine emergencies; otherwise nothing works.

During his presidential honeymoon, a cardigan-clad Jimmy Carter declared the energy crisis to be "the moral equivalent of war"; Washington mostly yawned. Carter asked for special "fast track" authority to bulldoze emergency programs for research and development through the bureaucracy, overriding rules and regulation, but Congress sat on Carter's idea. Critics on both the Left and the Right offered cogent criticism: if mere red tape was slowing down vital energy projects, then it should be snipped. But if the rules and regulations were useful, they ought to be enforced. Carter's only energy-policy "success" was not Bottomlining at all; it was Layering: he created another bureaucracy, the Department of Energy. And even though the DOE was new, it was old in spirit, a pastiche of bureaucratic body parts, sewn together so that Carter could claim some success from his 1977 "MEOW" speech. Even by Beltway standards, Energy is a poor performer.

More recently, we have seen a similar debate over enterprise zones: a Bottomlining approach to the economic revival of blighted areas. Yet if economic regulation is onerous, why repeal it only in certain targeted areas? In peacetime, there's little justification for policies that help people on one side of the street while ignoring those on the other side. Bottomlining should be reserved for true emergencies.

Upgrade #4: The Hawthorne Effect

Eventually, even the most frenzied agitation from the top can't keep bureaucratic waters from stilling and stifling. FDR was able to stir up the sludge of sedentary systems, and programs he focused on worked well. But in the five decades after his death, that sludge has resettled, cementing most AMERICRATic organizations into near uselessness.

The Hawthorne Effect is inherently artificial and thus impermanent. While great deeds can be accomplished with the right kind of leadership in the short term, in the long run, the system itself must be conducive to good performance; good ideas must be rationalized.

In Washington, one always hears noise about the "new and improved" policy or program for everything from procurement to public schools. Such hoopla is perhaps an invocation of the Hawthorne Effect; yet by now the main audience is not the bureaucracy, which is too far gone in its cynicism and retirement count-downing, but rather the public, which might be bamboozled once again into thinking that adrenalized words will somehow clear away the crud. But bureaucracies, like any human institution, have a finite life cycle, which the Hawthorne Effect can extend but not perpetuate.

Upgrades and Epicycles

Science provides a useful analogy to BUREAUCRAT's endless futile Upgrades: epicycles. In pre-Copernican astronomy, when the heliocentric paradigm was still dominant, those who fancied themselves astronomers faced a problem. As their telescopes and other devices got better, they could see more and more anomalies; a planet they were observing wasn't where it was supposed to be according to Ptolemaic theory. As we have seen, paradigms can be persistent, leading people to reject what they see in front of them because it doesn't conform to what they "know" to be true. So astronomers, rather than junk their paradigm, came up with the theory of "epicycles": the planets must be doing little loops as they orbit the earth. Celestial bodies, of course, are not given to somersaults—but the epicycle explanation enabled scientists to preserve their treasured geocentric paradigm for a little while longer.

AMERICRATic epicycles are as numerous as the planets, including the creation of more ombudsmen, inspectors general, and chief financial officers, all waiting to pick up "whistleblower" hotlines. Taken in isolation, each of these institutions may seem like a sensible response to a problem, but in the aggregate they represent a failed Upgrade; to incumbent politicians, their greatest value is as a source for headlines. Even the most troglodytic Old Paradigm politician can look like a reformer by collaborating with, say, the General Accounting Office to uncover "waste, fraud, and abuse" in some agency. The politician gets to hold a press conference, and then the whole panoply of hearings, investigations, and subpoenas begins—ending usually in some sort of epicyclic "reform" legislation. But there's just one problem: the "reform" is not reform at all, but merely another set of rules and regulations piled onto the back of AMERICRAT.

The most notorious practitioners of this type of camera-craving politics were John Dingell, the Michigan Democrat who chaired the House Energy and Commerce committee for fourteen years through 1994, and John Glenn, the Ohio Astrocrat, former chairman of the Senate Governmental Affairs committee. Routinely, Dingell and Glenn would haul in some hapless bureaucrat for public pillorying. Since such inquisitions dealt with symptoms, not causes, these media circuses could never be expected to produce much good; indeed, they caused harm. Fearful bureaucrats wasted taxpayers' time writing CYA memos to each other and hiding under their desks. The system was a perpetual PR machine that enabled pols to support big-government programs and simultaneously position themselves as critics of big government. Bureaucrats have their flaws, but they are rarely prone to the headline-making corruption that auditors and reporters like to look for. Mostly, they are guilty of bad judgment calls, on everything from the funding of research to the management of nuclear waste cleanup. Trapped as they are in the Bureaucratic Operating System, AMERICRATs frequently face lose–lose situations, having no good options to choose from. Thus they are sitting ducks for opportunistic bureaucrat-bashing.

Because of this climate of intimidation, it is hardly surprising that most efforts to instill "excellence" in government are a waste of time. One epicycle was Jimmy Carter's zero-based budgeting, which he touted in his 1976 campaign and abandoned thereafter. Another has been the business buzz-concept Total Quality Management. There's even a Federal Quality Institute, ready to dump a truckload of mantras, slogans, and posters on any federal department that wants to "do" TQM. Even in the private sector, TQM has always had its faddish, cultlike overtones, but at least in the business world it's possible to tell whether the bottom line has improved; companies know that if they don't do better they will be wiped out by the competition. By contrast, in the sanctums of the lifetime-tenured civil service, TQM is useless and irrelevant incantation. One thinks of Owen Glendower in Shakespeare's *Henry IV,* Part 1, who brags that he "can call spirits from the vasty deep." In response, Hotspur wonders, "but will they come when you do call for them?" Four hundred years later, we too wonder if the shades of quality, excellence, and peak performance can be summoned from the mists of Foggy Bottom.

Reinventing Government

When an Operating System is installed, not to decide is to decide: the existing mechanism remains in place by default. At one time the BOS software we call AMERICRAT was good enough to ensure that politicians who stayed within its bounds—roughly to the right of George McGovern and to the left of Barry Goldwater—were deemed suitable for election.

Yet in the last twenty years, that comfortable electoral calculus has changed. Outsider Jimmy Carter ran against the Establishment in 1976 and won. Yet as we have seen, Carter talked better than he governed; he was unable to deal with the increasingly glaring failures of the Bureaucratic Operating System. In the mid-nineties, after three of the last four incumbent presidents were defeated for reelection, survival-oriented politicians have had to take a closer look at the system they preside over.

Bill Clinton, a smart pol, could see that AMERICRAT was dysfunctional. Indeed, he campaigned against the accumulated failures of the federal government, from the deficit to welfare to health care. In 1992 Clinton promised to "revolutionize" government, saying that the middle class "paid higher taxes to a government that gave them little in return." Why? Because, he said, "Washington is dominated by powerful interests and an entrenched bureaucracy."[38] According to Clinton, the problems America faced could not be answered by either the Left or the Right, but rather by common sense.

One commonsensically smart thing Clinton did was catch the *Reinventing Government* wave. The authors of that 1992 book, David Osborne and Ted Gaebler, argued that the public sector must achieve a bottom-line mentality, loosening the most pinching of its internal rules and streamlining its overall operations. They summed it all up in phrases such as "customer-driven government" and "enterprising government,"[39] which they posed as sharp contrasts to traditional AMERICRAT:

The kind of governments that developed during the industrial era, with their sluggish, centralized bureaucracies, their preoccupation with rules and regulations, and their hierarchical chains of command, no longer work[s] very well . . . in the rapidly changing, information-rich, knowledge-intensive society and economy of the 1990s.[40]

One way to increase the effectiveness of public money, Osborne and Gaebler argue, is for policy leaders to "separate steering from rowing." As the authors explain it, policy managers should be free to "shop around for the most effective and efficient service providers," public or private.[41] Thus AMERICRAT "steers" policy, while various non-profits compete for the right to do the actual "rowing."

Clinton understood that once he was in the Oval Office, the buck would stop with him. So he recruited Osborne to work on the "Rego Initiative," known formally as Vice President Al Gore's National Performance Review. However, the Rego effort was crippled from the start, because Clinton had seemingly decided in advance not to rock the boat with Democratic majorities in Congress.

It was not surprising that the barons on the Hill liked the status quo; they had grown up with it and reinforced it. Thus the valiant band of Regoers was free to reinvent all the aspects of federal operations that no powerful lawmaker had an interest in preserving. Moreover, the Rego team was specifically charged with studying *means,* as opposed to *ends.* As such, the most important question of governance—the purpose of the state—was removed in advance from consideration.

Gore's report to the nation, on September 7, 1993, was a rare triumph for the administration. Gore himself subsequently launched his David Letterman career with his mocking of the federal procedure for buying ashtrays or, as the regs read, "Ash receivers, tobacco (desk type)." The Regoers made some progress on federal procurement reform, and yet Peter Drucker, who has spent a lifetime thinking about reinventing organizations, is harsh in his assessment:

In any institution other than the federal government, the changes being trumpeted as reinventions would not even be announced, except perhaps on the bulletin board in the hallway. They are the kinds of things that a hospital expects floor nurses to do on their own; that a bank expects branch managers to do on their own; that even a poorly run manufacturer expects supervisors to do on their own—without getting much praise, let alone any extra rewards.[42]

The inherent problem with government procurement is politicization; it is unlikely that federal procurers will ever actually "shop around" for anything more expensive than no. 2 pencils. Powerful politicians—typically, congressional committee chairs—will always insist that items more costly than pencils should be purchased from favored constituents and contributors back home. Civil servants know this; they know from painful experience that impolitic procurement means they could be keelhauled by wrathful legislators. So instead, being rationally risk-averse, they will keep following the path of least pain and resistance—no matter how blatant the waste. The porky predilections of congressional panjandrums, both Republican and Democratic, will always count for more inside AMERICRAT than some theoretical invisible hand in determining where government money goes.

So much for the idea that wise bureaucratic helmspeople can "steer" the ship of state away from the shoals of wasteful spending. Consider two of the most out-of-control programs in the federal government, Medicare and Medicaid. Both have been rising at 10 percent or more a year for decades; today the two programs together cost about $300 billion annually. They are "steered" but not "rowed" by Uncle Sam. That is, the government steers with its money, and the medical-industrial complex rows—all the way to the bank. As the Hudson Institute's Michael J. Horowitz points out, this steering-not-rowing policy has ballooned the cost of the two programs by a couple thousand percent each in just a generation. In a perverse way, bureaucracies already are "customer-driven"; it's just that the "customers" are often not the people who get the service but rather the people the government pays to deliver it. These are the customers who lobby the hardest to keep their good thing going. Once the American Medical Association figured out that "socialized medicine" would make doctors rich, it has become a most ardent proponent of Medicare and Medicaid.

Some might say that the problem of those two health programs was that for decades they were run virtually without controls, in a "cost-plus" manner—with the doctors billing Uncle Sam for any- and everything.

Indeed, as the government has cracked down in recent years, cost increases have slowed. However, more regulation creates the fiscal equivalent of epicycles as regulatees conspire to outfox the system.[43] Increased red tape also destroys the simplicity of the steering-not-rowing idea, leaving us with what many feared all along: a huge piece of American health care run by politicized as well as Post Officized bureaucrats.[44]

Two other groups, the seemingly disparate defense contractors and savings-and-loan operators, were also extravagant rowers for the government's feckless steerers; again, the taxpayers paid the freight. As with Medicare and Medicaid, the government set the policy—the purchase of bombers, the insurance of depositors—and then delegated that task to the private sector. Once again, the problem was not that government steerers themselves were on the take; usually, they were simply overwhelmed by the political pressure that rowers could bring to bear against them to keep the money spigot open, no matter what the "merits" of the case might be.

So Osborne and Gaebler's book is stronger on anecdotes than theory. Still, *Reinventing Government* made an enormous contribution; it broke the ice, suggesting to a disenchanted nation that imagination and entrepreneurship in the public sector could change the quality of government-as-usual. And even the Rego team deserves credit for starting the ball rolling toward the New Paradigm. Gore's group set in motion a plan to downsize the federal government by 250,000 bureaucrats, although that shrinkage begs the larger question: what is it that the other 2 million bureaucrats do?

Bugs in the BOS

Yet in the end, "reinventing" AMERICRAT is an Upgrade on a degraded Operating System. The root of AMERICRAT's problems is the Bureaucratic Operating System itself. Not only do the Upgrades no longer work, but the Bugs we saw in BUREAUCRAT are biting now worse than ever.

Bug #1: Parkinsonism

Columnist Carl Rowan echoes Parkinson when he observes that at the turn of the century, when nearly half of all Americans lived on farms, the U.S. Department of Agriculture had 2,019 employees and a budget of $2 million. Today, just 1 in 40 Americans lives on the farm, and the USDA has 100,000 employees, spending $60 billion.[45] So the ratio of agriculturalists to Agriculture Department employees has gone from about 2500:1 to 20:1. Or to put it another way, as the number of farms has dropped by more than half, the number of USDA employees has risen fiftyfold.[46]

Today, the U.S. military has almost as many senior officers as it had in 1945, when there were seven times as many uniformed personnel. The University of Minnesota's Paul C. Light calls it "the thickening of government," noting that since 1960, the federal government's Parkinsonian top-heaviness has swollen even faster than its spending; the number of deputy secretaries in the cabinet, for example, has increased from 6 to 21, the number of deputy undersecretaries from 9 to 52, and the number of deputy assistant secretaries from 77 to 507.[47]

The Clinton administration's plan to cut the civil service by 12 percent is admirable in its attempt to un-Parkinsonize the government, but in a competitive world, the cutting edge of de-bureaucratization is a fast-moving target; the Rego effort lags behind the dramatic restructuring that has taken place in what was once the mirror image of government: bureaucratic, corporatic America. In the past fifteen years, General Electric has cut its work force by almost half—and more than doubled its sales revenues.[48] Such tales are typical: from 1979 to 1992, the country's manufacturing work force declined by 15 percent—and output increased 13 percent.[49] This is a wrenching, painful process, but one must ask: what's the alternative?

Bug #2: Peterism

Today, the civil service's vaunted post-Pendleton nonpolitical purity and institutional memory have first coagulated and then petrified into a stony lack of accountability. When these qualities are combined with public-sector unionism, staffing and spending are locked into a stiff ratchet effect, where rollbacks are resisted to the last GS-12. Such stasis allows the Peter Principle—bureaucrats rising to their level of incompetence—to reign supreme under the closed monopoly of the Bureaucratic Operating System. Under Peterism, the federal government has not yet reached the status of Garrison Keillor's Lake Wobegon, where everyone is above average, but it has come close. *Forbes* reports that 99.8 percent of all federal middle managers receive merit raises. Of these, 35 percent are rated "outstanding" and rack up another raise.[50] If all these merit-badge-earning bureaucrats really have overcome Peterism, continuing to rise upward in their perfect sublimity, then St. Peter, at the pearly gates, will have a lot of company.

However, the Peterist Bug does not apply just to anonymous bureaucrats harmlessly shuffling papers during pea-lice inspections. Sometimes, it's a matter of life and death. Consider, for example, the Central Intelligence Agency: for $20 billion a year, America should be getting better brains. Yet after Aldrich Ames was revealed to have provided the Russians with enough information to blow nearly 100 U.S. agents and operations, 11 of his spook-superiors were given mere wrist-slaps.[51] The resulting furor cost CIA Director James Woolsey his job, but we are left to wonder how and why people move up at the CIA's Langley, Virginia, headquarters.

However, the most lingering and ineradicable cases of Peterism occur when garden-variety incompetence is grafted with hothouse hubris. Consider the career of Robert Strange McNamara, a paradigmatic AMER-ICRAT. He was one of ten U.S. Army Air Corps officers who sold themselves as a package to Ford Motor Company after World War II. As John A. Byrne wrote in *Whiz Kids,* the "methods of rational management they invented during the war—a system of tight financial controls that made quantitative analysis of every business problem essential"— seemed to provide all the answers.[52]

From Ford, McNamara was promoted to Secretary of Defense in 1961. That's when trouble began. After success as a junior officer and then as a corporate executive, McNamara hit his ceiling of competence. He brought his numbers-based, efficiency-minded approach to Washington with him—and then tried to make it work in Vietnam. As McNamara biographer Deborah Shapley writes:

McNamara was taught that the most efficient organizations were those in which workers obeyed: only men at the top had the right information to make decisions. The effect was to disempower foremen, engineers, craftsmen, and workers on assembly lines. Power flowed to those who spoke the new language of finance and used terms like "throughput," while knowledge at the bottom, held by those who did the work of the organization, was ignored. In Vietnam, of course, his need for throughput produced the body count.[53]

McNamara epitomized the wisdom: "If you're a hammer, the whole world looks like a nail." McNamara, having risen to his Peteristic level of incompetence, tried to hammer every human problem as if it were a quantifiable nail—and ultimately he hit America's Vietnam thumb.

Bug #3: Oligarchism

Oligarchs know that someone must rule, so it might as well be they. And they're happy to use state power to secure acquiescence from everyone else. Under AMERICRAT, perhaps the most powerful single group in politics today is the gaggle of public-employee unions. Individual teachers may feel frustration when they confront the challenge of educating children, but teachers' union officials feel mighty when they see politicians bowing down before them. From BOSS to BOS, the name of the ruling class changes, but the Oligarchic reality—someone has to be in charge—does not.

Although overall union membership is declining, the public-employee unions have grown. In the eighties, membership in the United Steel Workers fell by half, while the American Federation of State, County, and Municipal Employees grew by 22 percent; and AFSCME is on the verge of eclipsing the Teamsters as America's biggest union.[54] In 1959, membership in government employee unions was less than a tenth of total union membership. Today half of all union members are government employees and 80 percent of public school teachers are unionized.[55]

With unionized work rules as they are, public school principals can only rarely fire, suspend, or even discipline employees. The *New York*

Times reported that in the Empire State it costs an average of $194,520, spread over 476 days, to dismiss a teacher for misconduct, leading schools to ignore all but the most horrendous incidents.[56] Yet the steadiest stream of information many New Yorkers receive about the activities of their public employees comes indirectly from their own tax dollars; the ads that AFSCME Local 1000 purchases on the op-ed page of the *Times* regularly extol AFSCME members and denounce "privateers."[57]

Thriving because they still have a monopoly in their market, public employee unions dominate the politics of most big cities. As New York City labor leader Victor Gotbaum once boasted: "We can elect our own bosses";[58] that is, AMERICRATic unions can vote in more compliant bargaining partners: blank-check-signing politicians.[59] At the federal level, this new oligarchy received another boost in 1993, when Congress approved changes in the Hatch Act, permitting 3 million postal and civil service workers to become more active in politics. The provisions even allow federal employees to *manage* political campaigns while off duty. Although everyone has the right to be involved in politics, the direct involvement of tax-consuming bureaucrats in the election of tax-levying politicians further strengthens Oligarchy.[60] Moreover, the American Legislative Exchange Council disputes the notion that public employees are making a financial sacrifice for their public service; it found that federal employees are paid, on average, 50 percent more than comparable private employees, while state and local employees earn 36 percent more.[61]

Bug #4: Olsonism

As we have seen, Olsonism holds that in a democracy everyone eventually votes himself or herself a piece of the action, and so prosperity crumbles. The Olson Bug is rampant in America today, providing aid to the needy, to the nonneedy—and, most of all, to the greedy.

The economist Arthur Okun memorably said that society only transfers wealth in a leaky bucket. Today, that bucket is so leaky that some 85 percent of all domestic spending goes for the middle and upper classes.[62] One federal program, Chapter I of the Elementary and Secondary Education Act of 1965, sends federal dollars to school districts based on the number of poor students they have; Chapter I spent $6.4 billion in 1994, which funds were distributed to all fifty states and nearly all the nation's 15,000 school districts.[63] Yet one must wonder if only the poor were benefiting, or were almost all students, poor and rich alike, receiving program funds targeted specifically for the poor? Such arcane formula programs work like a lottery: the lotto-masters know that the trick is to make sure that many players win a little something. If people win two dollars for every three one-dollar tickets they buy, they feel like winners—even though they are down a dollar. In this case, where education money is siphoned by Washington and then sprayed back to all indiscriminately, many taxpayers' dollars have evaporated.

Yet as in a lottery, a few people win big under Olsonism. Author James Bovard paints this picture of Olsonized AMERICRAT:

> Farm subsidies . . . are the equivalent of giving every full-time subsidized farmer a new Mercedes every year. Annual subsidies for each dairy cow in the United States exceed the per capita income for half the population of the world. With the same $160 billion-plus that government and consumers have spent on farm subsidies since 1980, the U.S. government could have bought every farm, barn, and tractor in 30 states. The average American head of household now works almost one week a year simply to pay for welfare for less than a million farmers.[64]

Not only do farmers rake in billions, but the richest farmers take in the most; one study found that the cane-growing Fanjul family of South Florida receives $64 million a year in artificial profits, thanks to the U.S. sugar program.[65] Farmers with annual sales of more than $100,000 represent less than a fifth of the total agricultural population, but the fortunate fifth receive 71 percent of all direct federal payments.[66] Yet even these data understate the upward transfer of wealth. According to the *New York Times*:

> The Agriculture Department's $40 billion campaign to bolster crop exports, begun a decade ago to help beleaguered farmers, has instead enriched a small group of multinational corporations while doing little to expand the American share of the world's agricultural markets.[67]

In just four years, the USDA awarded $1.38 billion to four multinational corporations—two of them European.[68] Defenders of such spending might invoke Okun's leaky-bucket metaphor—such transfers to the rich are a byproduct of transfers to the poor—yet surely the nation can find a better way to help the needy. Economist Ed Rubenstein calculates that the average farmer collects $21,724 per year from the government, compared to $12,180 for the elderly or disabled and just $4,122 for the poor.[69]

Olsonism is more than unfair; it is dangerous to our economic health. Jonathan Rauch, author of the Olson-influenced book *Demosclerosis,* estimates that the total cost to the U.S. economy of all this parasitic "rent seeking" is between $300 and $700 billion a year.[70]

Bug #5: Information Infarction

The pathology of Information Infarction is that the government can never learn what it has to know to plan effectively. Complexity roadblocks the BOS.

The Administrative Conference of the United States once studied Uncle Sam's grant-making process. It found that the Department of Health and Human Services gave out 250,000 grants a year without adequate knowledge of whether the money was used well, wasted, or stolen; the report the ACUS wrote was given ample shelf-space in every dust-gathering cubbyhole in Washington. As always, the question remained: just how *would* HHS be able to ascertain whether all those billions of dollars were being spent to do actual good?

Former Bush administration official Charles E. M. Kolb says that the information-infarcted government must rely on the most primitive methods for measuring results—being content most of the time simply to ascertain that the checks were indeed cashed by the intended recipient:

> Right now, accountability means telling an accountant—be it an agency Inspector General or the Congress's General Accounting office—that the money was (a) spent, and (b) not misspent, in the sense of waste, fraud, and abuse. More qualitative inquiries—such as whether the money

did any good, or whether it achieved its intended purposes—are rarely, if ever, asked.[71]

According to Kolb, in its bureaucratic blindness, the government cannot see whether or not it is doing a good job with taxpayers' money. One result of this incurable infarct is that research programs with funny names—studies of screw worms, plant stress, or the monk seal—get blasted, when, for all we know, the scientists are working on arcane but nevertheless important tasks. Yet politicians and other posturers looking to score points with the home folks frequently attack scientific programs in the same breath that they attack pure spendthriftery, such as the Lawrence Welk museum in Strasburg, North Dakota; the Mark O. Hatfield Marine Science Center in Newport, Oregon; and the legendarily recurrent efforts of Senator Robert Byrd to transfer all non-nailed-down pieces of the federal government to West Virginia.

So the government struggles to find its glasses, signing blank checks to clever politicians. Meanwhile, the information- and media-drenched country moves toward new levels of on-line acuity that enable citizens to see more clearly how their money is being spent. AMERICRAT is behind now; even with "reinvention," it can never catch up.

We have reviewed the five Bugs that AMERICRAT shares with BUREAU-CRAT. However, we should note one further, final mutation in AMERI-CRAT that has changed the definition of American bureaucracy without really changing the way it functions: Vealocracy.

CHAPTER 6

VEALOCRACY

It might be argued that the two subjects of this chapter, the "Vealification" of the bureaucracy and the launching of "Orbital Bureaucrats," should together be viewed as the sixth Bug in the BOS. Yet, although the effect of Vealification and Orbitalization, as we shall see, has been mostly negative, these phenomena paralleled a positive social transformation: the decades-long movement toward racial and gender equality. Thus the changes we have seen in the past forty years are the result of forces far larger than BOS Bugs. This third chapter in the history of the Bureaucratic Operating System describes a massive, albeit mixed, Upgrade amid larger social transformation. We can view AMERICRAT 4.0—the final Upgrade—with ambivalence: on the one hand, few Americans would want to roll back the social gains made in the past few decades; on the other hand, the unintended consequences must be dealt with. As we saw in the previous chapter, the basic architecture of the current system is unsustainable; new thinking is needed. If we want to preserve our progress and still avoid the Cyber Future, it is a replacement, not another Upgrade, that is needed.

Pork: The Predecessor of Veal

When politicians spend government money to buy votes, it's called "pork," hearkening back to the nineteenth-century practice of ladling out goodies from the pork barrel. The Vealification process is a variant: the prime movers are no longer politicians but the voters themselves, frequently organized into special-interest groups or lobbies. It is they who pull the strings, jerking elected and unelected officials into giving them government money.

The first step in Vealification is that groups wrestle the government to the ground so that they can feed off it; the second step is the institutionalization of this process by corralling government programs, just as farmers lock up calves to turn them into veal. Thus when AMERICRAT spends money automatically, by entitlement formula— or even involuntarily, by judicial decree—we can call that "Veal"; the critters are the government agencies themselves, penned and helpless, continuously fattened up for fiscal slaughter to feed ravenous interest groups. How this Vealification process came to be is a long story, but it is critical to our understanding of what AMERICRAT has become.

Though the practice of pork politics has always been corrupt, for most of U.S. history it was sharply limited by the size of the government pork barrel. At the turn of the century, total federal, state, and local expenditures amounted to just 8 percent of GNP.[1]

By 1950, the government's percentage share of the economy had nearly tripled.[2] Journalist John Chamberlain, surveying the vast expanse of AMERICRATic interest groups, coined the phrase "broker state."[3] Yet the various cogs and components of the New Deal coalition worked well enough as long as their respective desires could be accommodated by the Spending Upgrade. However, the internal contradictions—not only ineffective spending, but also Bugs—within AMERICRAT were so great that such happy days could not continue forever.

An early diagnostician of the failed Upgrades and Bugs in the contemporary BOS was Theodore J. Lowi. His *The End of Liberalism*, published in 1969, described the government as "a gigantic prehistoric beast, all power and no efficacy."[4] Although hardly a conservative, Lowi saw that the government was growing beyond mere pork. He culprited "interest-group liberalism," which he identified as "the amalgam of capitalism, statism, and pluralism."[5]

Lowi's point was that interest-group demands had become so noisy and numerous that politicians could no longer satisfy them with more spending. Brokered government had grown so complex that legislators could no longer even comprehend the legislation they were voting for. In effect, they had to delegate the real power of rule making and interpretation to bureaucrats and, even more, to the courts. As Lowi observed, "Under present conditions, when Congress delegates without a shred of guidance, the courts usually end up rewriting many of the statutes in the course of 'construction.' "[6]

In 1935, FDR's Social Security Act, arguably the most consequential piece of domestic policy legislation in the twentieth century, was all of thirty-two pages long.[7] The 1956 Highway Act was just twenty-eight pages—and that was enough to get the interstate system built. Yet today, after three decades in which factions have multiplied like fruit flies, all buzzing around Washington, things can no longer be done so easily. The 1991 Intermodal Surface Transportation Efficiency Act, one of many subsequent, less far-reaching highway-building bills, bulged with ten times as many pages as the 1956 legislation.

And though it accomplished less, the 1991 act had to make room for all the pet causes and peeves that pressure groups and lobbyists could shoehorn in: concerns gamuting from historic preservation and erosion control to the encouraging of seatbelt wearing; from reductions in outdoor advertising and drunk driving to the hiring of Native Americans and the promotion of recycled rubber in making asphalt; from minority set-asides to the purchase of American-made iron and steel; from mandates for metropolitan-area planning to limitations on the use of calcium acetate in performing seismic retrofits on bridges.[8]

It's hard to imagine anything getting done under such circumstances. And yet the beat goes on: in two recent notable specimens of AMERI-CRATic aggrandizement—the Americans with Disabilities Act and the General Agreement on Tariffs and Trade—the letter of the law, plus the implementing language, swells into tens of thousands of pages of logorrhea. Nor does that word dump include the weight of lawsuits and the precedents thereby created, all cumulated into ever-heavier case law.

Thus the power of the government swells far beyond the power of the purse, into all the interfaces of private decision making: regulation and litigation steer as much wealth today as do fiscal appropriations. Only lawyers and lobbyists can love such brontosauri of bureaucratese: thunder-tomes that quake the earth whenever they're dropped. With little industry except that which the federal government attracts, Washington has grown rich off such bafflegab. On the theory that the closer one is to the money, the more one gets to keep, the number of trade associations based in Washington has grown at least tenfold in the last thirty years, while law firms from Seattle to Miami have found it profitable to open offices inside the Beltway. In his muckraking best-seller *Who Will Tell the People*, William Greider calls this government-inspired agglomeration the "grand bazaar," a place where nearly 100,000 white-collar wheeler-dealers traffic in the Beltway's two products: "the myriad claims on the federal treasury and the commercial rights and privileges that only the government can bestow."[9]

Of course, the coercion on Congress to just plain spend is still as intense as ever. Political scientist James L. Payne quantified this phenomenon; analyzing scores of witnesses before congressional committees, he found that the ratio of spending advocates to spending opponents was more than 100:1.[10] Big D.C. lobbying firms, such as Cassidy and Associates, mostly dispense with lobbying the Executive Branch and zero in on the real power: the twenty-five "cardinals" on the two appropriations committees in Congress. Cassidy's targeted tactics are the secret to its success; appropriators are increasingly brazen in their determination to "earmark" more and more of the $500 billion that passes annually through their committees. As just one tiny but typical example, Mark O. Hatfield (R-Oregon), the chairman of the Senate appropriations committee, set aside $12 million for the nursing department of the University of Oregon—and he carved brazenly those millions out of the Department of Energy's budget.[11]

Lobbying is often the most lucrative investment a company can make. Jonathan Rauch singles out Big Sugar: the growers who sweetened the pot of Senator Alfonse D'Amato (R-New York) and subsequently received a tax break worth $365 million—a 4 million percent return on their investment.[12] Hungering for such "returns on investment," PACs have poured more than $1 billion into the political system just in the past decade. Across the fifty states, lesser bazaars are also open for business in state capitals and city halls.

Yet it's not traditional porkbarrel spending, or even the brokering of New Deal–era interest groups, or even the stupefying complexity that Lowi described, that explains the unique bloating of AMERICRAT today; a real and radical transformation of the BOS has taken place in the past three decades. Old notions of logrolling, horsetrading, and backscratching have given way to the new political dynamic of Vealification.

The Great Society and Vealification

In the last three decades government bureaucracies have been turned into the organizational equivalent of veal calves, fat but unhappy, all wobbly legs and big tummies, well fed but trapped pitifully in place. The main function today of traditional bureaucrats is not to supervise, administer, or even manage. It is to spend money blindly, under the watchful eyes of interest groups armed with injunctions and consent decrees. AMERICRATs no longer have freedom of maneuver or movement; they are surrounded on all sides by the slats of litigation and injunction—and those slats are then reinforced by pressure from new interest groups and from the newly assertive public-employee unions.

Indeed, the judiciary today is the co-equal of the political system, forming the foundation upon which AMERICRAT rests. The architects of this legalistic Operating System were no other than the strategists of the Great Society. Those sixties apostles sought to shake up the "conservatism" of the Establishment, and they more than succeeded. Yet they sparked not only the explosive expansion of social spending but also the simultaneous contraction of the government's ability to enforce quid pro quo rules. Thus the Veal phenomenon: the government was plumper, but its employees had less power. Furthermore, although many Great Societeers set out to overturn bureaucratic hegemony, they ultimately reinforced the system. They rebuttressed the Old Paradigm by shifting the locus of AMERICRATic authority away from politicians to the courts.

The intellectual thrust of the Great Society was a furious critique of three reigning ideologies: Lowiesque interest-group liberalism, as practiced by aging New Dealers in Washington; big-city bossism, as practiced by Chicago's Mayor Richard J. Daley and his kind; and unreconstructed racism, as practiced by Mississippi senators John Stennis and James Eastland and others. That the avatars of these disparate ideologies were all Democrats underlines the intensity of the Great Societeers' attack; the young radicals went after their own party.

Meanwhile, the civil rights movement in the sixties was producing an unusual number of heroes who were likely to be Democrats but whose vision transcended partisanship, from Rosa Parks of the Montgomery bus boycott to John Doar and Burke Marshall of the Justice Department. The movement also had its martyrs, from Medgar Evers to the students Michael Schwerner, James Chaney, and Andrew Goodman to Martin Luther King Jr. himself. We should pause for a moment to recognize both their sacrifices and their achievements.[13]

The charisma of these civil rights heroes and martyrs, to use the Weberian term, spawned a moral as well as political revolution in America—a revolution that swept away centuries of institutionalized oppression. Yet it also created a new political structure that has had a mixed record of success ever since. As so often happens, the subsequent attempt to rationalize the charisma of heroes into a permanent replacement structure has proved disappointing.

Sargent Shriver and his Office of Economic Opportunity, created in 1964, was strongly antibureaucratic. Yet the Great Society suffered from its failure to develop a postbureaucratic model; its activists were too preoccupied with "speaking truth to power" to think carefully about the structure of the system they were speaking to. Reacting to the threat of spindling, folding, and mutilating by "corporate liberals," the credo of antipoverty warriors was "maximum feasible participation" of the poor; that is, OEO wanted to get resources out of the hands of politicians and bureaucrats and directly into the hands of poor people. Its goal was to "empower": to encourage spontaneity and creativity at the grassroots. The Great Society was impatient with "democracy" as practiced in the big cities and in the Deep South, viewing the power structures on both sides of the Mason–Dixon Line as unresponsive at best and racist at worst. When thwarted by the system, OEOers did not hesitate to confront the Establishment with direct action: mobilizing voters, mounting protests, staging sit-ins, and once taking over the office of the Secretary of the Department of Health, Education, and Welfare. The term "mau-mau," derived from the Kenyan rebels of the fifties, came into vogue during this time to describe the process of browbeating bureaucratic "flakcatchers" into submission. In its heyday, the OEO even funded Chicago street gangs in its quest for "authentic" community leaders.[14]

OEO was the sharpest blade of the larger Great Society buzzsaw that cut through what remained of Tweedism. Poor people no longer needed to abide by the whims of ward heelers to get help from City Hall; they could simply demand it. While such emancipation can be seen as a victory for justice and human rights, it had other effects as well. The death of BOSS broke down the sense of reciprocal obligation— the need to abide by community norms—that once went with government assistance.

OEO's effect on antipoverty programs was immediate and dramatic. Inspired by Great Society consciousness raising, the social-work bureaucracy shifted its orientation from support for the status quo to support for radical change. Whereas caseworkers were once seen as meddlesome snoops looking for reasons to boot people off welfare, during the sixties they redefined their mission. Thus, traditional work requirements and sanctions against illegitimacy were abolished or ignored in the rush to social justice.

Although President Lyndon B. Johnson began using the term "Great Society" in 1964, the high tide of high hopes for an end to poverty ran from 1962 to 1970. In the beginning was Michael Harrington's eye-opening, conscience-pricking *The Other America*. In the end was the leak of then–White House aide Daniel Patrick Moynihan's notorious "benign neglect" memo.[15] Yet in the eight years in between, the number of people receiving Aid to Families with Dependent Children jumped from 3.8 to 9.7 million.[16]

The ironic result was that the Great Society began with an attack on bureaucracy but ended with its reinforcement. Traditional bureaucracies were enlarged to handle the new duties of government, with the Great Society structures forming an additional layer on top of them. Yet, as we shall see, still more AMERICRATic formations were crystallizing.

The Rights Revolution: Charles Reich and the New Property

In some ways, the enormous expansion of welfare recipiency can be viewed as the final stage in the capture of government by interest groups: Olsonism, Bug No. 4 in the BOS, which we confronted in the previous chapter. That is, after the rich and the middle class discover the joy of politics, the idea of lobbying for government money then trickles down to the poor, who vote themselves whatever they can. However, as we shall see, the big winners of Reichianism were *not* the poor, finally getting their place at the table. Rather, the true beneficiaries were the middle-class service providers who took government money in the name of the poor and wound up keeping much of it for themselves. Hence the confusion in American politics for the past few decades: taxpayers blame the poor for allegedly gobbling up hundreds of billions of dollars for "welfare," but the truth is that those resources have in fact not been flowing to the poor at all, but to the nonpoor. In 1992 there were 37 million poor people in the U.S.;[17] in that year total federal state and local government antipoverty spending totaled $302 billion.[18] That twelve-digit dollar total works out to an average of $8,200 annually per person in poverty, or $32,800 for a family of four. Yet the median Aid to Families with Dependent Children payment is just $5,220 annually.[19]

But where's the money going, if not to the poor? In *The Enabling State*, authors Neil and Barbara Gilbert cite data showing how intermediaries have siphoned off much of that for themselves, all in the name of "service delivery"; government aid to private agencies went from virtually nothing in the early sixties to half of all the financial support such agencies received by 1980.[20] The Cato Institute calculates that in 1965, some seventy cents of every antipoverty dollar went directly to poor people. Today that share actually reaching the poor is around thirty cents on the dollar.

This profound change goes beyond the Olsonistic malady. It is part of the larger metamorphosis of government and society—a change driven not by voters and politicians, but by lawyers and judges. And it benefits not the poor, but the middle class.

Ever since the *Brown* v. *Board of Education* decision in 1954, many Americans felt that lawyers and activist judges were the truest, purist paragons of social justice. So a major objective of OEO was to put in place systems of legal representation for the poor. One such operation was California Rural Legal Assistance, which waged a protracted struggle with then-governor Ronald Reagan over the rights of farm workers. OEO was always a small program, beginning at $800 million in 1965 and peaking at $1.5 billion in 1970. However, it magnified its influence a thousandfold through the courts. Litigation was OEO's most lasting legacy; the quest for social justice through legal redress proved to be a big wave of the future.

The visionary theoretician of this rights revolution was Yale Law School professor Charles Reich. His article "The New Property," published in the April 1964 issue of the *Yale Law Journal*, is the most cited article in the history of that influential publication. Reich began his treatise by noting that the government had become a major source of wealth in America, brokering everything from farm subsidies to TV-station licenses to welfare checks. Yet such wealth transfers, he pointed out, inevitably came with strings attached: "the recipient of largess feels the government's power."[21]

The rich, on the other hand, have always been able to use their property as "a bulwark" against state power. Reich's goal was to guarantee that all Americans would have such a bulwark:

> Only by making such benefits into rights can the welfare state achieve its goal of providing a secure minimum basis for individual well-being and dignity in a society where each man cannot be wholly the master of his own destiny.[22]

Reich had a valid point, leading some perhaps to conclude that the answer was to roll back state power so that the government would have less sway. Yet Reich drew a different conclusion: since he assumed that big government would and should get only bigger, his idea was to sever the link between the gift and the giver—between "the new property" dispensed by the government and the power of government to judge and to dictate behavior.

Reich's article was a stew of distrust and trust: distrust in the government as it functioned in 1964 and trust in a utopian future brought about by government. Reich looked forward to "the highly organized, scientifically planned society of the future, governed for the good of its inhabitants . . . the best life that men have ever known." In his view, a further step toward paradise required the elimination of the tired distinction between wealth from the government and wealth from the private sector. His argument supported the ongoing trend toward eliminating invidious comparisons between, say, work and nonwork, or between legitimacy and illegitimacy.

Reich's thesis was half libertarian and half totalitarian; therein lies its appealing genius. On the one hand, people should be free to do what they want; on the other hand, the government should be big enough to guarantee that freedom by guaranteeing an endless gusher of no-strings wealth transfers. Not surprisingly, this line of reasoning struck a resonant chord in the sixties, as Americans struggled to reconcile the seemingly opposite values of big government and do-your-own-thing.

One critical Reich-influenced ruling of the Supreme Court was *Goldberg* v. *Kelly* (1970), which deliberated the circumstances under which welfare benefits could be terminated. Using Reichian language, the Court described public benefits as "new property" and, as such, these benefits were protected by the Constitution.[23] Just as the Fourteenth Amendment's due process clause required that anyone with "old" private property at risk get a full hearing, so "owners" of "new property," at risk—that is, those deemed by the authorities to be ineligible for benefits—were entitled nevertheless to a full evidentiary hearing, with an attorney present.

Goldberg, as well as the many decisions based on its precedent, set in motion the tidal wave of rights-based litigation that has inundated every public institution, just as Reich hoped—ranging from civil service job protection to the right to obtain a driver's license to immunity from corporal punishment in the public schools.

Far beyond the specifics of any particular law case came the feeling that only the courts could adequately distill the *Zeitgeist*, that new wind of liberation blowing across the planet. Yet the law is an imperfect distillery; Michael Horowitz, a former student of Reich's at Yale, calls *Goldberg* "the most anti-poor, anti-black, anti-community decision of my lifetime." He notes that the decision hastened the dismantling of all traditional sanctions:

> What the decision really did was impose on the poor a life that legal reformers wouldn't ever wish upon themselves. Most of American society lives in the world of contracts, in which individuals define their own environments and the means and rules by which they are to be governed. The rights revolution gave the poor "due process" rights which made wastelands of the public institutions upon which they needed to rely. Hence the gap between the private and public spheres: private schools expel students for talking back to teachers; public schools can barely expel students for shooting each other. Fancy co-op apartments evict people for playing music too loud; the Chicago Public Housing Authority can't even evict crack dealers. And ironically, reformers get warm feelings in their bellies for creating a legal regime and "giving" it to the poor.[24]

Today, hardly a city in America does not have a court order controlling the schools, homeless shelters, public housing, or mental hospitals—all in the name of "due process," "equal protection," or some other all-purpose legal crowbar. "Today, New York City is being run out of the courts," says Bert Pogrebin, a New York activist who has been working with Ralph Nader to set up a nationwide public-interest legal network.[25] Washington, D.C., labors under thirteen separate court orders and consent decrees.[26] In Morristown, New Jersey, Richard Kreimer was expelled from the public library because of his odor and his habit of following people around and staring at them; he sued. After the ACLU went to bat for Kreimer, not for library patrons, a judge awarded him $230,000.[27] Admittedly, such suits are few, but how many does it take to dissuade the workaday guardians of public normality—in this case, librarians—to look the other way when trouble comes into the reading room or other public places?[28] Indeed, federal law not only permits court injunctions against officials seeking to uphold order but also authorizes those interfered with to hold officials personally liable.

The rights revolution has also transformed the criminal justice system. In the interests of brevity, we can simply note that rights revolutionaries have taken the Fourth (against "unreasonable searches and seizures"), the Fifth (no person shall be "deprived of life, liberty, or property, without due process of law"), the Sixth ("speedy and public trial . . . impartial jury"), and the Fourteenth ("due process" again) Amendments and blended them into an elixir that for decades has paralyzed law enforcement. As with civil rights, the expansion of the rights of the accused has its heroic history, but another fact must be noted, too: violent crime went up 700 percent from 1960 to 1993.[29]

As we have seen, the actual crime wave has leveled off in recent years, leaving criminality at a fearful plateau, even as fear of crime climbs higher. Now that the prisons are full, a huge new arena for legal activism has opened up. Prison-rights litigants started with the Eighth Amendment ("cruel and unusual punishments") and then took it from there, and now forty-two states are under some sort of court order on prison conditions. In New Hampshire, judges supervising treatment for "troubled" youth forced the Granite State to spend $23 an hour for gymnastics instruction and $57,000 in cab fare for the transportation of a single family to and from court-mandated activities.[30]

In 1992, nearly a quarter of all federal civil suits were filed by inmates, with the total exceeding the number of federal criminal prosecutions.[31] The New York State attorney general reported that one-fifth of his department's resources were devoted to fending off such suits.[32] The vast majority of prison lawsuits are dismissed before even coming to trial, but they keep coming. One reason: there's money in them. The state of Florida was sued under the Religious Freedom Restoration Act of 1993 because it prevented white racist inmates from distributing their "religious" literature. Not only did the inmates win back their "rights," but the state of Florida was ordered to pay more than half a million dollars to the prisoners' lawyers.[33]

Bernard McCummings, having mugged an elderly real estate executive in a New York City subway station, was shot in the back and paralyzed. Then, serving two years and eight months in prison for the crime, he was awarded $4.3 million.[34] The indefatigable legal critic Walter K. Olson has accumulated a long list of such well-compensated criminals, including a San Francisco mugger who won $25,000 from a good samaritan who broke the mugger's leg during hot pursuit. Olson observes that such settlements lead to "defensive policing"; that is, police become risk-averse, because no city, and certainly no individual cop, can afford a million-dollar judgment.[35] The police also know that many of the people they arrest will be back on the streets the next day. In New York City, 91 percent of all juveniles arrested for misdemeanors never see the inside of a courtroom; they are scolded—not fingerprinted or otherwise recorded—and released.[36] That frustration, plus fear of litigation, leads many law enforcers to spend their time chowing down Bavarian Kremes in the precinct office. Yet such lassitude hasn't kept them from fighting for increases in pay and pension benefits: consider the "blue flus" that surged during the seventies and eighties. Indeed, as the psychic income of policing fell, the compensatory desire for real income rose.

In such multimillion-dollar cases as McCummings's, it should be noted that the lawyers for the plaintiffs were not always working pro bono; heady idealism has become crafty careerism. The same Ivy League law school grads who worked for free in the sixties went to work as staff attorneys for Legal Services in the seventies—and then hung out their own shingle in the eighties, working for a one-third, or even two-fifths, contingency fee.

The system has now been tilted to encourage such legal action. Hundreds of statutes explicitly authorize all lawyers to act as "private attorneys general" in the public interest. Lawyers who sue the government on behalf of a shallow-pockets client and win are entitled to "lodestar" hourly rates—that is, rates high enough to encourage lawyers to take "public interest" cases. Even the biggest, blue-chippiest firms, wondering what to do with underutilized associates, are not immune to such lucrative legalizing. And so the night-school-educated corporation counsel for some small town finds himself at the bottom end of a legal mismatch against a hotshot former law journal editor; of course, the town settles quickly. The settlement may be small, but a precedent is established, and the story resumes elsewhere.

Such an entrepreneurial subtext goes hand in hand with the fight for "social justice," broadly construed. After the National Endowment for the Arts defunded the celebrated performance artist Karen Finley and three other grantees in 1990, the fiscally challenged artists took the Endowment to court. Three years later, NEA paid the quartet a total of $26,000, which the court deemed they were "owed." In addition, each received $6,000 for, in effect, pain and suffering. Total: $50,000. But the big winners were the American Civil Liberties Union, the Center for Constitutional Rights, and the National Campaign for Freedom of Expression, which took home a total of $202,000 in legal fees.[37]

However, the money NEA spends in a year would cover the costs of the Social Security Administration for only a couple of hours. So it's little wonder that the Reichians have overhauled this deep-pocketed agency's operations, too. The Supplemental Security Income (SSI) program was begun in 1972 as a program spending less than $5 billion a year for the elderly and disabled. SSI now costs five times that much, but the most startling growth has been among two previously insignificant recipient categories: minor children and substance abusers. In both cases, lawyer firebrands touched SSI with their fire, and program growth has been conflagrating ever since. Today, lawyers advertise in newspapers and on TV, soliciting SSI cases. The breakthrough came in 1990, when the Supreme Court's decision in *Sullivan v. Zebley* expanded eligibility for children—a case brought by Legal Services.[38] Costs ballooned: in 1989, SSI served 290,000 beneficiaries under eighteen at a cost of $1.3 billion a year; five years later, SSI had inflated to 890,000 young recipients, and outlays had autopiloted to $5 billion.[39] Meanwhile, another category of SSI dependency was growing even faster; the number of SSI-receiving substance abusers quintupled in just three years, from 20,000 in 1991 to 100,000 in 1994.[40]

State and local officials generally looked the other way as SSI payments mushroomed. They reasoned that if Uncle Sam wanted to pump money into the local economy—and perhaps take some pressure off locally funded programs—states and cities had no cause to complain. When the state of Michigan, for example, terminated its state-funded "general assistance" welfare program, nearly a third of former beneficiaries went on to the federal SSI.[41]

SSI is a purer expression of Reichian-rights revolutionism than AFDC, since the program has always been cash-and-carry—no hoary history of bothersome social workers trying to change people's behavior.[42] Yet today, journalists have picked up on stories of homeless people putting their SSI payments on account at liquor stores, of parents coaching their children to misbehave so as to get "crazy checks." Thus driven by judges and lawyers—with federal bureaucrats merely along for the ride—the Social Security system may soon replace "welfare" as the income distribution mechanism of choice for those down on their luck, and SSI's cost may soon overtake that of AFDC.[43] Even if reform comes, SSI spending for children and substance abusers nevertheless will have plateaued at a funding level four or five times what it was just a few years ago.[44]

Thus mau-mauing for money has become institutionalized. Every politician and bureaucrat who denies people their "rights" now faces the threat of legal action—the full panoply of subpoenas, discovery, testimony—all with the legal-cost meter clicking away. Lawyers and activists, as befits their guerrilla-theater roots, usually know how to seize the media high ground with an effective "visual" or a snappy soundbite. Frequently they can point to some obscure statute or precedent and proclaim: "We just want Politician X or Bureaucrat Z to obey the law!" Their residual radicalism, combined with legal-eagling and media savvy, serves them well; they can flay "the system" by day, even as they drive home in their BMWs at night.

One of the pleasures of lawyering outside the strictures of AMERI-CRAT is lack of accountability—precisely what activists decry in government officials. While public officials struggle with disclosure forms and Freedom of Information Act requests, activists who are on the government payroll, but not formally in government service, are uninhibited about doing almost anything. What's private with them, such as the contingent income they receive from over 100 federal "fee shifting" statutes, remains private.

Orbital Bureaucrats

Few Americans realize that lawyers and ancillary activists have effectively privatized much of AMERICRAT's power in the U.S. today. We can call these new beings "Orbital Bureaucrats," because they transcend the dull old bureaucratic categories with their rocket-booster barristering.

In the post-Reichian, post-*Goldberg* world, the real power inside the government today is not held by GS-14s who car-pool from Rockville to their cubbyholes in the Federal Triangle, or even by members of the Senior Executive Service wearing tailored pinstripes and taking lunch at Washington's Federal City Club. From 1930 to 1960, government employment—federal, state, and local—doubled as a percentage of the civilian work force; yet in the last thirty-five years, even as the growth of public power has continued to accelerate, the percentage of the civilian labor force formally employed by all governments has increased only a fourth as fast, from 12.6 percent in 1960 to 15.5 percent today.[45] These modestly ramped employment totals reflect the continuing clout erosion of duly sworn public officials.

Indeed, the changes unleashed by Reich and *Goldberg* have left many AMERICRATs with their titles and perks intact, but with little to do except follow orders from a judge. Once-imperious AMERICRATs have learned that smart lawyers, working with activists and professional victims, *can* fight City Hall—and win. These Orbisters litigate rings around the police, the schools, the welfare bureaucracy, and public works. Some AMERICRATs, thus neutered of any policymaking role, have simply quit or retired. Others, less interested in exercising power than in doling out more money for unmet human needs, are delighted when their department is sued. Typically, after a half-hearted legal defense by the AMERICRACY, a judge orders the city or state to spend more for some specified program. Elected officials who oppose more spending are thus circumvented—although they are still charged with generating the revenues for their new government responsibilities.

If the percentage of old-time bureaucrats directly employed by the government has stagnated for four decades, the number of service workers who receive their support *indirectly* from the government— the New Class that includes all the litigators, consultants, and contractors—has risen enormously. Nobody knows how many of these exist, because they are scattered among the 32.3 million Americans engaged in what the Labor Department calls "managerial and professional specialties." But these semiprivatized Orbicrats are out there; we see their handiwork every day.

Thus the broad definition of AMERICRAT 4.0—the Old Paradigm that is in power today—must include Orbital Bureaucrats, those who fly high over the Veal pens they have helped create. Hundreds of billions of tax dollars flow into their tranche of Vealocracy. The Orbicrats who soak up this money operate many visible "private" social services: suicide hotlines, meals-on-wheels services, Head Start programs, midnight basketball leagues, methadone clinics, AIDS hospices, refuges for battered women, and so on. Every city has community leaders, most on the government payroll in one way or another, who lead the charge for more government spending as they attack "budget cuts."

Sometimes the cloud of buzzing Orbital Bureaucrats whirs so thickly over the Bureaucratic Operating System that Americans lose sight of who, in a democracy, is charged with setting policy. In New York City, homelessness policy has been driven for more than a decade not by politicians but by various court orders. This judicially driven subeconomy has become funding-flush, spending in 1992 an average of $18,000 per homeless person every year.[46] Real homeless people, of course, never saw that money, nor did Gotham's career civil servants. The real action was in the private sector, where recipients acting as intermediaries for government aid did well by doing good. One such social-service entrepreneur, Clint Cheveallier, president of Volunteers of America, earned over $215,000 in salary and benefits in a single year, while his organization received $198 million of its $269 million budget from city, state, and federal governments.[47] In Washington, D.C., the city government, hounded by lawsuits, has been in the process of disbanding its thirty-seven-employee Office of Emergency Shelter and Support Services and turning over responsibility for the homeless to a nonprofit group, the Community Partnership for the Prevention of Homelessness—along with $15 million a year in city funds."[48]

Drug treatment is equally Vealish. Dr. Mitchell S. Rosenthal, top executive of Phoenix House, a drug rehabilitation organization, was paid $260,000 in 1992. The top executives of ninety-six private, state-financed, nonprofit mental health organizations enjoyed salaries greater than that of the New York state mental-health commissioner. One-third of the state's mental-health budget, a total of $1.4 billion, goes to such nonprofit groups.[49] In all, some 3,000 private groups in New York City receive a total of $3 billion a year from the city and another $4 billion from state and federal governments.[50]

This is how the new system works today in every big city in the country: with their showmanship, entrepreneurialism, and "independence," Orbitals prove to be far better advocates for the Oligarchic class interest in bigger government than mere bureaucrats could ever be. Orbital Bureaucrats have the best of both worlds: they pull strings, make deals, and get on TV; they agitate, litigate, and even run for office. But unless they win election, they never face salary caps.

Nor do they have to worry about performance, because they have the muscle to get what they want out of AMERICRAT without having to produce. The federally funded Job Training Partnership Act is mostly Veal, run with little regard to whether anyone gets trained for jobs. It is not fly-by-night hustlers who get the money; one New York City contractor is Goodwill Industries. In return for $372,000 in 1993, it "trained" eighty-five people, of whom twenty-one were placed in jobs. But ninety days later, only seven were working; that's $53,000 for every successful outcome. Nonetheless Goodwill managed to get that particular program refunded for another $300,000. Another Goodwill project, starting the following year in the Bronx, received a contract for $1.2 million.[51]

One reason this system has gone unchallenged is that the Vealification of government bureaucracy has also trapped or co-opted independent nonprofit groups. Having gone on the government dole themselves, these private Veal calves have experienced an ideological mind-meld with AMERICRAT 4.0. Since Karl Marx was right—situation determines consciousness—it is not surprising that private groups taking the king's shilling all of a sudden start seeing things from the king's point of view. Both sides of this new Veal transaction have ended up espousing the basic AMERICRATic idea that government-funded solutions are the best solutions. Boston University's Peter Berger calls this "the fatal embrace," leading to the death of the sturdy, voluntaristic problem-solvers that observers, beginning with Tocqueville, have so admired. Today, these little platoons have frequently become mercenaries, and America has been deprived of an alternative, antigovernment perspective on the failings of the AMERICRATic paradigm.

"Community leaders" as diverse as Jesse Jackson, the late Mitch Snyder, and Louis Farrakhan have all received, one way or another, government money for their work, from food distributing to homeless sheltering to public-housing patrolling. Their defiance of individual politicians and bureaucrats never extends as far as refusal to cash the checks that the AMERICRATic system provides for them. As we have seen, the Orbital organization Volunteers of America receives two-thirds of its budget from the government. Author William Tucker has found other "name" social-action charities in the Bureaucentric Orbit, including Catholic Charities, the largest nonprofit agency in the country ($1.2 billion out of a total budget of $1.9 billion), and Planned Parenthood ($312 million out of $446 million). Tucker estimates that the 550,000 "private" charities in the U.S. collected $40 billion in 1993 from the government.[52]

With this much money to entice them, the orientation of traditional nonprofits has shifted from spontaneous problem solving to the more calculating process of making sure that their funding for the next year will be renewed. Old and new groups both find it worthwhile to hire full-time grantspersons, each scanning the horizon for government RFPs—Requests For Proposals. Then they hire lobbyists to keep the money flowing. And so the animating impulse of the charitable organization changes; professional fund-suckers eventually drive out the founding do-gooders, and as the organization expands, each client's individual life outcome matters less. Since bureaucrats are now the real customers, heartwarming stories of redemption must be supplemented by impressive stacks of statistics. As one close observer of this process, Father Richard John Neuhaus, puts it, "More people are 'helped,' but fewer lives are changed."

It is easy to see why "volunteer" groups and "charities" that depend on government money would Orbitalize into willing, even eager, collaborators in the cause of more government. Yet it is harder to understand why large foundations, with piles of their own money, such as Rockefeller and Ford, have also become cheerleaders for more government. Once upon a time, private philanthropy saw itself as a rival to the state, offering its own sometimes idiosyncratic vision of social and moral uplift. Andrew Carnegie, who gave away $325 million before he died in 1919, built libraries and subsidized teachers' pensions when dominant elites fretted that "feeble-minded" foreigners would never be able to learn. The Rosenwald family backed civil rights in the 1930s, when the federal government was distinctly uninterested. The Danforth family underwrote university chapels all across the Midwest.

In the past few decades, however, even the richest foundations have been swept up in the bureaucentric World Spirit, seeing themselves today as complementers of government, not competitors. In creating the foundation that would be named after him, Henry Ford stated his philanthropic credo: "a chance and not charity" adding—"I do not believe in giving folks things. I do believe in giving them a chance to make things for themselves."[53] Yet as has been well documented, the Ford Foundation, nudged along by such leading liberals of the day as former University of Chicago president Robert Maynard Hutchins, moved not only to the left of the founding Ford but also to the port side of the considerably more centrist Henry Ford II, who resigned from the board of his family's foundation in 1977.

The Ford Foundation was an early supporter of "educational TV," creating an infrastructure that could learn to lobby the government for direct funding; eventually the federal government indeed assumed responsibility for the new Public Broadcasting System. Even more dramatically, Ford helped pave the way for the Great Society with its "Gray Areas" and "Great Cities" grants programs in the late fifties. After the election of John Kennedy in 1960, many foundation staffers joined the new administration. In the words of one chronicle, "The great desideratum was now in sight: turning Ford's experiments into a federal program."[54]

Today, the Robert Wood Johnson Foundation and the Henry J. Kaiser Family Foundation have the same idea in a different field; both are major players in the push for Old Paradigmish health care reform. The whole culture of foundations today mirrors the government; they are the little givers, while Uncle Sam is the Big Giver. Most large philanthropies are not only ideologically indistinguishable from AMERI-CRAT, they are also bureaucratically Bug-ridden.[55]

Yet if economic justice is, in Reichian terms, a property right, then "meeting human needs" ought not to be a matter of charity, but rather a matter of entitlement. Such thinking cuts against the whole idea of voluntarism, to be sure; why should one volunteer one's time or money if the government is paying or taxing others to perform the exact same mission? Thus the tradeoff: foundations have greatly advanced Old Paradigm ideologies, but in doing so they have lost their separate and distinct souls. Now they are just the little legs on the great AMERICRATic millipede.

Having never come to grips with this problem, George Bush's "points of light" volunteer program was therefore a predictable failure. Bush wanted Americans to give their time, but he offered no new reason why they should. He urged them, in effect, to be auxiliaries to the government. Had he been willing to invoke real spirituality or religious zeal, so that people felt that they were saving souls and not just satisfying stomachs, he might have been able to elicit a charitable great awakening—although such action would have put him at cross-purposes with the philanthropic establishment. Yet since Bush was left with only namby-pamby exhortations, the best result he could hope for was a Hawthorne Effect surge, followed by subsidence, which is what happened. According to a Gallup survey, Americans' contributions of both time and money *declined* from 1989 to 1993.[56] Voluntarism will never be restored to its past glory as long as it is seen as merely ancillary to the "real" work done by government.

More recently, the Clinton administration's AmeriCorps program deliberately sought to further blur the distinction between voluntarism and government. The program was launched in the spirit of the Peace Corps, but in fact it was mostly a low-wage jobs program for social activists. In 1994 it spent $300 million to fund 20,000 young people in "national service," the first installment of a projected $1.5 billion over three years. Yet AmeriCorpsters are not volunteers at all. They are merely low-paid Vealcrats, working for private social-action agencies across the country, from the Red Cross to Habitat for Humanity to the Association of Community Organizations for Reform Now (ACORN). AmeriCorps workers help further cement the big-spending "partnership" between the public and private sector that is the essence of AMERICRAT 4.0.[57] And so what of the 80 million other volunteers across the country, including an estimated 2 million of college age? Who is subsidizing them? Paid voluntarism is more than an oxymoron; it is a golden apple of discord thrown on the table of traditional mediating institutions.

Thus the Great Society has come full circle. What was once a radical critique of interest-group liberalism has itself been seduced, subsidized, and institutionalized into a new form of Oligarchic status-quoism.

The same Orbital phenomenon occurs at the federal level. Few taxpayers realize that in 1994 the federal Energy Department had 160,000 people on its payroll—and yet only 20,000 of them were federal employees. The rest were contractors, hired to do everything from constructing nuclear weapons to cleaning up the residue. One might argue that such privatization is cheaper, but the contract employees averaged $120,000 a year in salary and benefits, compared to $90,000 for the average federal employee.[58] It may be true that the contractors were more productive, but the woeful history of the Energy Department belies the boasts of bureaucrats, both Orbital and motionless.

Nobody really knows how much money flows to Orbital Bureaucrats. But we know this: the total government share of the economy has grown to 34 percent of GNP.[59] Every category of spending, except for interest on the national debt, has been substantially rendered into either pork or Veal. This money—more than $2 trillion in public-sector expenditures—creates the gravitational force that keeps activists in the Bureaucentric Orbit. No matter how much public-sector entrepreneurs may denounce the government, they always hover close to the honey.

The reader may regard Orbitalization as a form of privatization, which of course it is. Indeed, in every one of these areas, the government could be said to be "steering" while the private sector "rows." But as with Medicare and Medicaid doctors—who have been rowing government health care for the aged and indigent to the tune of about $300 billion a year—this kind of privatization has more in common with the operations of defense contractors and savings and loans than with truly competitive free markets.

Why AMERICRAT 4.0 Failed

The crusaders of the sixties thought that their new vision would sweep across America, mobilizing everyone to overturn the hated Establishment. As we have seen, Charles Reich provided an intellectual framework for that vision, enabling litigants to paint themselves as following in the footsteps of Jefferson and Lincoln, securing the blessings of "due process" and "property rights" for all.

Yet a political revulsion against the Great Society was evident as early as the 1966 midterm elections, which installed in office such disparate backlashers as Republican Ronald Reagan and the ax-handle-wielding Georgia Democrat, Lester Maddox. The narrow victory of

Richard Nixon in 1968, followed by his landslide reelection over George McGovern in 1972, must be taken as further evidence of the failure of Great Societeers to change the thinking of the Silent Majority.

The negative response to the Great Society was partly based on racism and reaction. Yet much was motivated by a sense of reality; the new programs didn't all work as promised. Few Great Societeers foresaw such unintended consequences as the soon-to-come explosion in underclass dependency and crime. Furthermore, crusaders of the era had no idea that urban public education and public housing, for example, would collapse under the load of rights-responsibilities that lawyers and judges piled upon them.

The Great Society model of maximum feasible participation included three basic flaws.

First, it emphasized *preparing* people for work as opposed to actually *hiring* people to work. This "services" strategy was in part a compromise with those in the Johnson administration fearful of the cost of a New Deal–style jobs program, but it also reflected the ideology of the New Class of social-service providers; they were more interested in politicized "empowerment" than in apolitical employment. Yet we now realize that people are more likely to learn by doing—on the job—than by sitting in a classroom.

Second, Great Society activists had little appreciation for private-sector economic activity in cities, at either the micro- or the macrolevel. At the microlevel, within neighborhoods, the work of "informal" entrepreneurs—the store owners, petty landlords, jitney drivers—received little sympathy from the Antipoverty Warriors; this potential class of community leaders shriveled during the sixties. At the macrolevel, OEOers were mostly unconcerned about the decaying business climate and the flight of whites, along with their wealth. Cities such as Newark and Detroit, which suffered the most dramatic losses of capital and confidence, were devastated in the sixties; other big cities have been merely in a state of long-term decline. It would be unfair to pin the cities' downward fates exclusively on the Great Society, but it is true that the only growth industry in many such places has been the social-service bureaucracy. The Great Society vision of "maximum feasible participation" of the poor briefly spurred a liberating Hawthorne Effect of community enthusiasm, but eventually the same top-down system hardened around the ankles of the weak and the powerless.

Third, Great Society thinking destroyed something that it didn't even notice: a community's implicit Operating System. As we have seen, Reich and the other prophets of the rights revolution had their own legalistic vision of what a great society would be, imagining what we might call a "Legal Operating System," an explicit system of rights safeguarding. What was lost in the process was the implicit Operating System of community, the cluster of unspoken, assumed responsibilities as well as rights. James Q. Wilson has written that a neighborhood starts to fall apart when the first broken window goes unrepaired, yet in the ripeness of Reichianism, all too often rights revolutionaries rushed only to the defense of the accused window breaker. As a sense of helplessness rose, communities declined and eventually disintegrated.

Alfred North Whitehead once said, "Civilization advances by extending the number of important operations which we can perform without thinking about them." Civil society is an implicit Operating System. The necessity of traditional mediating institutions, such as religious and fraternal organizations—even the much-maligned Tweedy BOSS—was simply never considered during the rush to create the Great Society.

Heavy gavels can change people's lives, but since judges rarely see the gossamer strands of the implicit Operating System, they usually ignore that system and what it does for society. It's beyond the scope of judicial decrees to create or restore the cohesion and morale of a people; that's a job for grassroots democratic leadership. But since Great Societeers deliberately set out to subvert local elected officials, it's not surprising that they, too, had a hard time restoring a sense of community in blighted areas.

The family is another implicit Operating System. As long as the family was intact, few AMERICRATs gave it much thought. Now we realize that two-parent families are the best possible social workers. In the absence of parental influence, it isn't easy for sex educators to persuade boys and girls to abstain from sex before marriage, nor for harried English teachers to instill moral principles. And so we are forced to hire more cops and case workers to try and repair damage done by earlier government actions. Yet we know that we can never afford enough cops or caseworkers to restore the lives and communities that were shattered when the implicit Operating System that held them together was crushed.

Meanwhile, AMERICRATs missed the most remarkable success story of the past few decades: the fact that millions of immigrants, from Asia, Latin America, and the Caribbean, came to our shores and flourished. Why? Because they brought with them intact implicit Operating Systems that sustained them when so many of the incentives put in place by the Bureaucratic and Legal Operating Systems encouraged them to do the wrong thing.

The difficulty we face today is how to help people regain the Operating System that would help them move ahead. The decadence of AMERICRAT has crippled millions; so now what do we do? Precisely because the Reichian rights revolution was waged in the courts, not at the ballot box, AMERICRAT 4.0 is resistant to political therapy. Moreover, as that revolution became institutionalized, it inevitably became "conservative."

Today, the Reichian revolutionaries control much of the system they once despised. And their attitude toward bureaucratization has changed now that they Orbit above it; they have made their peace with the Establishment, proving the old maxim: "Where you stand depends on where you sit." As idealism cooled, cynicism and careerism congealed around the legal and political structure of Vealified AMERICRAT. No central cabal of Reichians exists. It's not necessary; hundreds of activist groups, many funded by the federal Legal Services Corporation, already see the world through similar lenses. And they are further united by the steady and sometimes profitable nature of their work, lawyering everything from housing and prisoner rights to the environment and reproductive freedom; all will fight to preserve the essential framework of AMERICRAT 4.0.

AMERICRAT 4.0 is not bureaucracy as Max Weber envisioned it; yet the essential features of the Bureaucratic Operating System—delegated and diffuse management along hierarchical lines, leading to stubborn, institutionalized opposition to new thinking—have not changed at all. The result is that institutional impetus will drive AMERICRATs to keep going across the Big Muddy, into further failure. As they do, the very people that the Orbitals are sworn to help will be hurt the most, because they are the least insulated against misfortune. If the poor remain in the coils of AMERICRAT 4.0, the gap between what the Bureaucratic Operating System does—and what could be done to ready them for the global market—will grow painfully wider.

As we have seen, AMERICRAT 4.0 does not enjoy the popularity of its predecessors, AMERICRATs 1.0, 2.0, and 3.0. Yet with government money suffusing once-independent private groups, it is little wonder the current system enjoys the near-unanimous support of so many political players, in and out of government.

Politics by Other Means

The reach of the rights revolutionaries extends to the private sector as well. The so-called litigation explosion—tripling the percentage of lawyers per million in the last three decades and quintupling private civil suits—has been amply documented elsewhere. However, one might infer from the title of an excellent critique, Philip K. Howard's *The Death of Common Sense: How Law is Suffocating America*, that this litigatimania is the result of some sort of collective temporary insanity.[60] Nothing could be further from the truth. The endless rights revolution may be bad for America, but as a Garrett Morris character on *Saturday Night Live* used to refrain, the litigation explosion has been "bery, bery good" to some key players. Private litigation threatens to create an entirely new layer of rights-based oversight that nobody voted for— more bricks in the wall, more slats in the pen. Three decades ago, avant-garde legal theorists concluded that the greatest challenge they faced was the equitable distribution of the resources that society had piled up. Reichianism held that every citizen in this, the richest country in the world, was entitled to a life of dignified well-being; it was an ideology of benefits without costs, with little thought given to what would later be called the "supply side" of the economy—the factors of production from which wealth actually comes.

Downloading the same *Zeitgeist* file as Reich, law school professors began to break down the old restraints against excessive tort litigation—

that is, compensatory damages for accident or injury. As legal scholar George Priest points out, the roots of the litigation explosion are cosynchronous with Reich's "New Property" article:

> During the four year period 1960–64 . . . the law addressing product-related injuries was irrevocably shifted to a course that, by the end of the decade, would render contract law obsolete and leapfrog existing negligence law entirely. The liability of manufacturers for product-related losses was vastly increased and the obligations of customers vastly diminished.[61]

Decades later, Abram Chayes of Harvard Law School made no effort to conceal the desire of reform-minded lawyers to use the courts as an instrument of redistribution: "We are attempting to secure redistribution of our goods and power from those that have to those that have not."[62] In 1987, Peter Edelman, a well-connected Washington lawyer who would go on to become a senior official in the Clinton administration's Department of Health and Human Services, put the Reichian argument boldly: "Court intervention becomes essential" because, he argued, "legislatures left to their own devices have not provided adequate economic protection for individual citizens."[63]

The Reichianization of the Private Sector

We have seen how lawyers turned the public sector into Veal. We shall now examine a few examples from the private sector.

This is the new frontier in legal activism: the campaign to Vealify the private sector, not through democratic politics, but through the courts. What we are seeing is, to paraphrase the Prussian military theorist Karl von Clausewitz, politics by other means.

The most obvious example of lawyer-leveraged policy is health care, malpractice having been a major contributor to the explosion of health care costs. More malpractice suits were filed between 1977 and 1987 than in all previous U.S. history.[64] New York officials have estimated that awards against hospitals and doctors in the Empire State have increased 300-fold in a generation, or 30,000 percent.[65] Malpractice premiums amount to $6 billion a year,[66] and "defensive medicine" costs another $25 billion.[67] It's said that the malpractice "crisis" has crested; if so, someone ought to tell doctors in New York, where malpractice premiums are still rising at 15–20 percent a year, to the point that Long Island neurosurgeons pay $130,532 annually in malpractice insurance.[68] Nationwide, tort lawyers are raking in an estimated $17 billion a year in contingency fees.[69]

The United States has launched an asbestos cleanup that could cost up to $200 billion,[70] mostly driven by tort lawyers who have been turned into tycoons along the way. One such is Peter Angelos, a workaday Baltimore attorney who hit the jackpot in an asbestos settlement and then, in 1993, wrote out a check for $175 million to buy the Baltimore Orioles.

At a time when AMERICRAT is throttling nearly everyone, including itself, in red tape, the plaintiff bar has found the one sure Gordian-knot cutter: the profit motive. Once again, the Orbitals fly high above the "terrestrial" bureaucrats, reaching for the contingency-fee constellations. The Equal Employment Opportunity Commission, run along old-fashioned, nonprofit lines—after all, it is a government agency—sloughs into the swamp of backlog; pending cases have doubled since 1990.[71] So who wants to wait for the bureaucrats when he or she can retain a contingency lawyer and sue right away? A single law firm, Saperstein, Goldstein, Demchak, and Baller, of Oakland, California, has won $600 million for its clients in bias cases just since 1992. Class-action lawsuits for alleged employment discrimination jumped 30 percent from 1993 to 1994.[72]

But the greatest costs come not from lawsuits, but from the fear of lawsuits. Every big corporation, blanching under the severe gaze of the Equal Employment Opportunity Commission—as well as the even beadier glare of "Title VII" antidiscrimination lawyers—has some sort of affirmative action program in place. The so-called "diversity industry"—consultants, auditors, facilitators—that has grown up in response has become a multimillion-dollar business.[73]

What will be the next big case that overturns some sector of the economy? The boggle of possibilities includes repetitive stress injury and carpal tunnel syndrome, sex harassment, wrongful termination, shareholder rights, and any other swamp of injustice that Veal barristers

can imagine themselves profitably draining. Many who clearly understand the danger of command-and-control economics turn a blind eye
toward torts. They see them as a private-sector phenomenon, not the
attempt to leverage state power into lawyer-enriching redistribution.
Yet regulatory zealots must look with admiration at the ability of private-
sector entrepreneurs who are not only redistributing an enormous
amount of money but getting rich doing it.

The legal critic Peter Huber estimates that the "tax" of private litigation
costs the U.S. economy up to $300 billion annually—steeply increasing
the price of many products and driving from the market many health
services and medications.[74] One expert calculated this "tort tax" on a
variety of common products: from 18 cents on a $6 baseball to $2 on a
$40 ski-lift ticket to $191 on a $578 doctor's fee for a tonsillectomy.[75]

The tort bar has moved the pursuit of social justice—and the seeking
of income transfers—into the private sector. Thus the private body of
lawyers has become more than Orbital Bureaucrats, a kind of privatized
virtual government. In the civil justice arena, with few agreed-upon standards, the caprice of a jury is all that stands between a corporation and
a financially crippling judgment. Indeed, tort lawyers are far more feared
than terrestrial 'crats; any business would rather be fined $100,000 by
OSHA or EPA than sued for $30 million by a high-powered tort lawyer
on exactly the same charge. Some defend these vast income transfers as
a part of social justice, even though upper-middle-class lawyers are raking
off a third or more of these contingency-fees transfers. Such "overhead"
makes traditional civil servants look like paragons of efficiency; even by
the sloppy standard described by Arthur Okun, the half or more of legal
wealth-transfers that disappear under the rubric of "transaction costs"
make litigation a very leaky bucket.[76]

It is likely that at least some of the excesses of the rights revolution
will be peeled back, belatedly, by the political system. However, because
the Reichians have been so effective at changing the terms of the debate—
and because the neo-Reichian tort lawyers have been so effective at working
the political system with status quo–maintaining contributions to both
parties[77]—it is far from clear whether real reform will get far. Any but
the most mundane political tinkering will be immediately denounced as
"depriving people of their rights." The Reichians have proved smarter than
conventional business lobbyists in the past, and so they have good grounds

for optimism that their Orbit over the U.S. economy will continue. Furthermore, simply stopping the Vealification of the private sector from progressing further is not the same as reversing it.

The final and perhaps most enduring irony of the rights revolution is that the group that has most profitably embraced the Reichian entitlement ethos is not primarily the poor or minorities; it is the elderly. From the Gray Panthers of two decades ago to the National Committee to Preserve Social Security and Medicare today, senior citizens have proved to be the most effective players in the game of squeezing AMERICRAT. In 1960, entitlement spending for those over sixty-five accounted for 2.4 percent of GNP; now it is 7.7 percent. Per capita entitlement spending on the elderly amounts to more than $11,000, compared to barely $1,000 for children.[78] Seniors vote more than they litigate, but they have created their own Veal pen for "their" programs, which dwarf everyone else's; Social Security, Medicare, and other federal retirement programs cost $577 billion in 1995, nearly 40 percent of all federal outlays.[79] Seniors groups are so strong—the American Association of Retired Persons has 33 million members and a staff of 1,200, including an executive director, Horace Deets, who earned $286,000 in 1993— that they have even forced the government to subsidize its own Vealification: the AARP received $85.9 million, about a fourth of its budget, from the federal government in 1993.[80] Also in 1993, the National Council of Senior Citizens received $68.7 million from the Department of Housing and Urban Development and other federal agencies—96 percent of its total budget.[81]

Legally, no government money can be used to lobby the government, but one lesson of the last thirty years is that all funds are fungible; anything that strengthens seniors' groups, including government subsidies, also strengthens their political leverage over their own subsidizers.

Systems of any kind tend to degrade over time; physicists call it entropy. Bugs accumulate, people figure out how to cut corners, and eventually a go-through-the-motions lowest-common-denominator mentality prevails. And as the original purpose is forgotten, reflexive self-perpetuation becomes the only goal.

The Bureaucratic Operating System has had a life cycle, from youthful vigor to mature effectiveness to aged obsolescence. In the absence of a hope-instilling or awe-inspiring grand plan, society lapses into malaise, the Big Fear, the sense of being on the wrong track. Trapped inside our old policy paradigm, our efforts are skewed; the clocks run backward, and water flows uphill in a Twilight Zone of lost horizons. Yet incremental reform, marginalia scribbled on the sacred scrolls of our government text, leaves the Bureaucratic Operating System intact. Like the enormous black monolith in Stanley Kubrick's *2001*, AMERICRAT may endure for political eons. Indeed, politicians with no sense of the larger forces at work in paradigm fall will have no impact on its hulking dominion; like the apes in the film, their screeches will go unheard.

Yet eventually, the Bureaucratic Operating System will join pterodactyls and Ptolemaic astronomy in the tomb of extinguished entities. Running the BOS on the scale it now occupies is a doomed strategy. It simply cannot deliver the sort of flexibility and accountability that we expect in the new, just-in-time, continuous-processing, total-quality-management world.

The Reich revolution shortened the way to the Cyber Future. If public institutions are dysfunctional, then Americans—including the litigants who have crippled the public sector—will purchase a privatized world that works just for them.

But until we give up on Upgrades and embrace a new way of thinking, the logic of the obsolete BOS will deform American life in tragic and perhaps permanent ways. The issue is paradigms, not personalities. Good people in a bad system will make bad decisions; the menu determines the meal.

We can't expect people inside the system to change it. What MIT's Rebecca Henderson calls the "embedded architecture" of the system—the organizational skeleton, the channels of communication, the accumulated culture and accreted habits—militates against any change from within.

So change must come from without. But before we can consider a New Paradigm replacement for the Bureaucratic Operating System, we must study how such change has occurred in American history—through a series of Big Offers—and the new alliances the nation will need to bring that change about.

PART 3

THE BIG OFFER

CHAPTER 7

THE BIG OFFER IN AMERICAN HISTORY

Having examined the history of the Bureaucratic Operating System, its old successes and newer failures, we can now turn to a more urgent question: how do we replace our obsolete political model with one that will work for all Americans today?

The answer will inevitably have its roots in the American political experience. A look at how political change has occurred in the past will help us envision a viable plan for the future. U.S. history can be thought of as the story of a leader and a party coming to power by making a "Big Offer" to the voters—a new idea, a new direction. If voters accept the offer, partisan loyalties realign, and a new majority coalition is created. The Big Offer party is then charged with implementing the new program. For as long as the Offer "works," the party stays in power; yet eventually the Offer decays and is replaced by a better one. In a Kuhnian sense, each Big Offer can be thought of as a "new paradigm"—a new model for political problem solving. Its history is important for providing clues about the *next* Big Offer.

A century and a half ago, Alexis de Tocqueville wrote admiringly that Americans

131

consider society as a body in a state of improvement, humanity as a changing scene, in which nothing is or ought to be permanent; and they admit that what appears to them today to be good, may be superseded by something better tomorrow.[1]

This pragmatic outlook is the key to our long-functioning democracy; Americans are always receptive to new thinking.

Yet only three Big Offers in U.S. history have succeeded: first, the American Revolution and the establishment of democracy; second, the presidency of Abraham Lincoln, which offered a unified country, free land for whites, and emancipation for blacks; and third, Franklin D. Roosevelt's New Deal. In each of these cases, after great political and social flux, a period of consolidation followed. The administrations of other great presidents—Jefferson, Theodore Roosevelt, Harry Truman—fall into this latter category: that of chief executives who cemented and expanded the coalition they inherited. Jefferson the President solidified the democratic ethos of the American Revolution; Teddy Roosevelt rejuvenated Lincoln's Republicanism; Truman carried on FDR's New Deal.

A Big Offer consists of four elements:

Vision. Leaders point the way to the promised land and, using universally understood words and imagery, describe for people what it will be like when they get there.

Audacity. Leaders who make Big Offers think big. They offer a platform bold enough to inspire people out of their apathy—and even out of their previous partisan affiliations.

Credibility. Big Offerers stay the course, keeping faith with those that elected them. To use the common argot, effective politicians "dance with the one that brung them," although they are allowed to add partners as the coalition enlarges.

Workability. Every big idea works in theory. But as Bismarck said, "Politics is the art of the possible." With the Big Offer, the question is not, "Will it play in Peoria?" but rather, "Will it *work* in Peoria?"

The Big Offer combines these elements into what Hedrick Smith, in *The Power Game: How Washington Works*, calls the "idea advantage."[2] Even the most hyping and bribing politicos and the most jaded and abraded reporters understand that ideas can be a powerful tool for electioneering. If it's a better mousetrap of an idea, people will beat a path to vote for it.

Paradoxically, once the Big Offer is inaugurated, the politicians who inherit it do not have to have any ideas at all. The paradigm-shifting, Big Offering leader has done that work already; subsequent politicians, operating within the new political paradigm, mainly have to read the script. Kuhn uses the term "normal science" to describe the plodding, day-to-day activities of ordinary scientists operating within a given scientific paradigm; they don't really expect to be heroes but just want to do their jobs. Similarly, most politicians have an unheroic view of themselves, simply aspiring to do the best they can and get reelected as much as they can. Thus we can define politics within the framework of a currently operating Big Offer as "normal politics"—and normal politicians, protected by their paradigm, go routinely about their careers. Yet eventually what Kuhn calls a "crisis" comes along, when old verities no longer hold true.[3] In such "abnormal" revolutionary periods, the crockery of political careers gets smashed.

Following Cicero's dictum that history illuminates reality, we can look back at American history to study the Big Offers of the past, with an eye toward the next Offer.

The Founders and the First Big Offer

The first Big Offer was the idea of the United States of America, the first nation founded on an idea. Even today, Americans carry the Founders' ambitious vision with them everywhere; *novus ordo seclorum*, a new order for the ages, is engraved on every dollar bill. The Declaration of Independence, the Constitution, the Bill of Rights, and George Washington's definition of the presidency as a majestic but not royal office— these idea-heavy documents and traditions Offered the prospect of a long-lived democratic republic.

Yet American democracy was not really secured until the presidential election of 1800. That was the year Jefferson defeated incumbent John Adams in a bitter contest. Adams stepped down as he was supposed to, proving that the new nation could peacefully transfer presidential power through its Constitutional mechanism.

Jefferson's ideal—decentralized democracy, widespread property ownership, and government-that-governs-best-governs-least—reinforced the distinctly New World notion that rulers ruled by the consent of the governed. Jefferson's idea of sturdy yeomen thinking and acting for themselves as equal stakeholders in the American Dream is at the core of our national identity. By the end of Jefferson's second term, the first Big Offer had become an unquestioned part of American civic culture, woven into the ideological fabric of all major political parties.

Abraham Lincoln and the Second Big Offer

By the 1850s, slavery, the great injustice left unresolved by the Constitution, had become the nation's most vexatious issue. The various fixes and compromises had not succeeded, leading to the electoral crackup in 1860, when Lincoln became president with less than 40 percent of the popular vote.

In spite of their small mandate, Lincoln and his Republicans came forth with the second Big Offer in U.S. history. It arrived in three parts: first, preserve the Union; second, establish a middle class of property owners across the West; and third, free the slaves. This offer can be summed up as extending the benefits of one free nation to everyone.

Lincoln's efforts to preserve the Union "with malice toward none" need no detailing here. But his special place in history rests on his ability to articulate not only magnanimity in victory but also justice in peacetime. Historian Garry Wills identifies one brief speech, the 272 words of the Gettysburg Address, as decisive in the transformation of America from a disparate aggregation of reactionary states into a unitary, forward-looking United States.[4]

The second part of Lincoln's Offer was the building of a business-minded, property-owning middle class. He signed the legislation that led to the Transcontinental Railroad. His Homestead Act opened millions of acres to penniless immigrants, converting peasants into burgers—and Republican voters—via the transformational experience of real property ownership. He established the Land Grant colleges and the Agriculture Department to benefit farmers. Lincoln signed new banking, tax, and tariff laws; historian James McPherson writes that his domestic legislation "did more to reshape the relation of the government to the economy than any comparable effort except perhaps the first hundred days of the New Deal."[5] As Lincoln said, his aim was "to elevate the condition of men—to lift artificial weights from all shoulders—to clear the paths of laudable pursuit for all."[6]

The third and most noble part of Lincoln's Big Offer was made to African Americans in 1863: freedom. "A new birth of freedom" can be thought of as Lincoln's Big Offer to blacks in particular and enlightened Americans in general. The Emancipation Proclamation was not popular among most northern whites at the time, but Lincoln gambled that he could hold on to white loyalty while reaching out to blacks and abolitionists. These two groups had heretofore felt distant from the war, which seemed to be fought over arcane constitutionalities; after 1863, their manpower and morale were fully utilized in what became a crusade for the soul of the nation. Nearly 200,000 blacks fought for the North in the war, while homefront opinion leaders moved strongly into Lincoln's camp. Abolitionist leader William Lloyd Garrison exulted: "Either he has become a Garrisonian Abolitionist or I have become a Lincoln Emancipationist, for I know that we blend, like kindred drops, into one."[7]

Yet if Lincoln belongs to the ages, he also belongs to his own time. Nothing is taken away from Lincoln's luster to assert that while his proclamation was an epochal moral moment, it was also a smart political move. The first Republican president was a Party man, seeking to build a broad-based political coalition that would reelect him and enable him to govern. He got one: the thirty-ninth Congress, elected in 1864, contained 145 Republicans and just 46 Democrats.[8] Yet even then, the sixteenth president needed all his political skills to pass the Thirteenth Amendment, abolishing slavery. As one biographer put it, "The art of logrolling, so masterfully employed by Lincoln in the Illinois legislature, proved equally effective now."[9] Lincoln did not live to see a postbellum peace "with malice toward none," but his offer left a strong majority coalition in place.

One bloc of voters that Lincoln won for his party was, not surprisingly, African Americans. Black Republicans represented southern states in Congress until black voting rights were snuffed out by the turn of the century. The first African American representative from the North, Chicago's Oscar De Priest, was elected as a Republican in 1928. Black loyalty to the GOP did not crumble completely until 1964, when the backlash-oriented candidacy of Barry Goldwater signaled a decisive break with the Lincoln legacy.

Like the American Revolution's Offer of representational democracy, Lincoln's Offer of perpetual union and freedom for all is forever alloyed into American political consciousness. The next Big Offer was to cement a new belief: that the federal government had a responsibility for the welfare of its citizens.

Franklin D. Roosevelt and the Third Big Offer

Franklin D. Roosevelt's Offer to the American people can be summed up in two words: New Deal. All the elements of a Big Offer were present: vision, audacity, credibility, and, finally, workability.

In the years prior to the Depression, the familiar Republican program of small government and big tariffs was in trouble; farm troubles in the Heartland were already abnormalizing American politics before the 1929 Crash. By 1932, the need for a new political and economic paradigm was apparent, but Hoover was blind to it.[10]

Roosevelt's famous phrase from his first inaugural—"the only thing we have to fear is fear itself"—epitomized FDR's enormous confidence in himself and in his country. But first he had to unify his own coalition. In the twenties, the Democrats had been deeply divided over such social issues as race, religion, and Prohibition.[11] The New Deal coalition was hardly a match made in heaven; it's hard to get communists and klansmen to walk down the same aisle. One wonders what words Congressman Vito Marcantonio, communist sympathizer from New York, and Senator Theodore Bilbo, racist rabble-rouser of Mississippi, might have exchanged as they passed each other in the Capitol—on their way to vote for the same piece of New Deal legislation. But vote together they did: the red flag and the white sheet flapping together in the same Roosevelt regatta.[12]

Much has been made of the ad hoc, improvisational nature of the New Deal. Yet the FDR coalition didn't stay together by accident. What united Democrats was the faith that AMERICRAT could work to improve the lives of "forgotten" Americans. Friend and foe alike were impressed by FDR's audacity; from the National Recovery Administration's Blue Eagle to the "Four Freedoms" speech to the GI Bill of Rights, Roosevelt thought big.

Some argue that the credibility of the New Deal Big Offer was actually cloudy, insofar as candidate Roosevelt was not entirely consistent about what he intended to do if elected in 1932. It is true that during that campaign he pledged to *cut* government spending by 25 percent.[13] However, everyone understood that FDR was going to take bold action to try to end the Depression, even if he had to improvise. New Deal historian William Leuchtenburg notes that "a fair amount of the New Deal had been foreshadowed during the campaign," citing Roosevelt's advocacy of public power development, stricter business regulation, centralized economic planning, and even reforestation as causes that the soon-to-be president raised during his campaign and for which he could claim a mandate.[14]

If the first three tests of a Big Offer are vision, audacity, and credibility, the fourth test is that the new plan works. Many have called the New Deal an incomplete success, even a failure; yet its bitterest critics often concede that it was an improvement over what came before. In 1929, when Hoover became president, unemployment averaged 3.2 percent. When he left office four years later, joblessness had risen nearly eight-fold, to 25.2 percent. In 1936 unemployment was down to 17 percent—still high, but at least the trend was downward.[15] Overall, the AMERI-CRATic system that FDR inherited and expanded passed Big Offer Test No. 4: it worked.

Like Lincoln before him, FDR was a believer in coalition politics. Unions, supported by a favorable legal environment, more than quintupled their membership from 1933 to 1945; by the end of World War II, one-third of American workers had been unionized, an all-time high.[16] The New Deal powered growth in the South and the West with new programs to provide cheap credit and electricity[17]—even as it made room for rising ethnic groups in the Northeast, particularly Italians and Jews, to participate fully in national politics. In many ways, the New Deal Big Offer was a pastiche: business cartelization, the minimum wage, agricultural price supports, and poor relief, with a spritz of soak-the-rich rhetoric. But in 1935 the New Dealers hatched a creature from a small egg that would grow up to be the Big Bird of the Big Offer: Social Security. When the nascent program was still pecking at the inside of its shell, Roosevelt predicted that so many people would one day stand under its protective wings that no Republican would ever be able to repeal it. He was right.

Like Lincoln, FDR had the benefit of an overwhelming coalition that would enact his agenda. Democrats outnumbered Republicans 322 to 103 in the Seventy-fourth Congress, which passed Social Security. But even those numbers understate FDR's congressional clout, since few Republicans wanted to vote against the New Deal. Thus the Social Security legislation passed the House 371 to 33.[18]

The New Deal pushed wide the gates of collective action. From the farms to the cities, old-line bosses sought to deliver crop support and poor-support for their constituents. Yet we can see stirrings of the Synoptic Aspiration as well. As we have seen, true-believing Synoptics—on the Right and on the Left—thought bigger than the New Deal. Why should the government content itself with dams and electrification when the real work of molding history was to be done?

Fortunately, Roosevelt was always a committed Democrat. His vision was the better management of the economy, not the reconstruction of society. The New Deal embraced Keynesianism, which, by the standards of the time, was a moderate policy. John Maynard Keynes believed that government action could improve the market, but he never contemplated using the government to replace the market. Roosevelt's technocratic "brains trusters" certainly thought they were smarter than the free market, but they never dreamed of taking America up the aspiring staircase to the Hegelian heaven of One Big Answer authoritarianism.

They didn't need to. Keynes's ideas were a success, politically as well as economically. Keynesianism elevated deficit spending to the lofty plane of "macroeconomics," providing an intellectual bodyguard to the New Deal Big Offer. Whereas porkbarrel spending had once been seen as crude redistribution aimed at buying votes, just about any government spending, after Keynes had provided the intellectual imprimatur, could be praised as economically essential pump priming. What we might call "vulgar Keynesianism" enabled the same old patronage purveyors to define themselves as paragons of prosperity, avatars of the new concept of "aggregate demand." These BOSSistic New Dealers were the same grafters they always were, but now the lift of a driving ideological dream made them seem almost honest. As Willie Stark pledges in Robert Penn Warren's Pulitzer Prize–winning novel *All the King's Men*:

> I'm going to build me the God-damndest, biggest, chromium-platedest, formaldehyde-stinkingest free hospital and health center the All-Father ever let live. Boy, I tell you, I'm going to have a cage of canaries in every room that can sing Italian grand opera and there ain't going to be a nurse hasn't won a beauty contest at Atlantic City and every bedpan will be eighteen-carat gold.[19]

Stark and the others won elections, because such Big Offering "worked." Fifty years ago, in vast stretches of dirt-poor America, people had almost nothing except the shirts on their backs; that first hospital or school or electricity line was a most tangible Big Offer. Economists might analyze Starkian spending in terms of "marginal utility"—citing, for example, the thirsty desert wanderer for whom the first gulp of water means more than the second, the second more than the third, and so on. The marginal utility of that first hospital or school in an area was extremely high. In addition, Stark types could rely on the greater efficacy of the Bureaucratic Operating System, which, when it was younger, had a higher correlation between inputs and outcomes.

And so the pattern was set for decades to come. AMERICRATic government would get bigger—and, as we have seen, Buggier—but it would never swell with the totalitarian Virus.

Most criticism of the New Deal focused on what Washingtonians today call "wefa"—waste, fraud, and abuse. Yet such was the momentum behind AMERICRAT that anti–New Deal vitriol was wiped like spittle off the glorious New Deal edifice under construction. Back then, government got the benefit of the doubt. In a famous passage from his 1936 acceptance speech, FDR waved away quibbles:

> Governments can err, Presidents do make mistakes, but the immortal Dante tells us that divine justice weighs the sins of the cold-blooded and the sins of the warm-hearted in different scales. Better the occasional faults of a government living in the spirit of charity, than the consistent omissions of a government frozen in the ice of its own indifference.[20]

FDR's successor, Harry Truman, had a follow-through plan: a bigger and better New Deal. He called it the Fair Deal. After World War II many predicted that the New Deal coalition would break up—ripped to the right by Strom Thurmond and his racist "Dixiecrats," lurched to the left by Henry Wallace and the pro-Soviet American Labor Party. From among these Democratic fragments, went the conventional wisdom, the old Lincolnian hegemony would return, having shaken the pall cast over it by Hoover's Depression. This forecast seemed on its way to fruition after the 1946 midterm elections, when the GOP won majorities in both chambers of Congress for the first time since the early thirties.

Yet Truman was serene, confident that FDR's Big Offer had changed America forever, that voters would remember those changes with gratitude in the upcoming 1948 presidential election. With one notable exception, as we shall see, Truman was no paradigmatic trailblazer; he was content to operate as a "normal" politician, working within the boundaries established by his predecessor. People looked forward to the expansion of the welfare state, viewing that task as Roosevelt's unfinished legacy. Was it big government? Sure it was. People wanted a government big enough to protect them from fascists and communists abroad and from capitalists at home. Truman saw this entrenchment of liberalism more clearly than most; that's why he kept his heady confidence while his fellow Democrats were losing theirs. As he recalled, "I knew that the people of this country weren't ready to turn back the clock—not if they were told the truth, they weren't."[21]

Paradoxically, Roosevelt, a New Yorker, had pointed the New Deal south and west, whereas Truman, a midwesterner, shifted the Democrats' center of gravity north and east. Many of the programs commonly thought of as "New Deal," such as federal aid for housing and education, were in fact "Fair Deal." Truman was hunting where the voting ducks were: in fast-growing urban areas, such as Detroit. And so the Democrats were no longer the Bryanesque party of the Plains and the South; by 1948 they were the tribunes of broad-shouldered big cities and their swelling minority populations.

Truman's major advance beyond the New Deal paradigm is one for which he will be honored forever. Truman integrated the armed forces in 1947 and included a civil rights plank in the 1948 Democratic Platform. Then-mayor of Minneapolis Hubert H. Humphrey was dispatched to deliver an electrifying civil rights address to the Philadelphia convention. Humphrey's speech—"The time has arrived for the Democratic Party to get out of the shadow of states' rights and walk forthrightly into the bright sunshine of human rights"[22]—caused southern delegates to bolt the building. The Dixiecrats reconvened in Birmingham, Alabama, and nominated Strom Thurmond as their presidential candidate. Truman was gambling that most southern Democrats would stay loyal to their ancestral party, even if it seemed to be going "soft" on race, and he was right: he carried seven of eleven Confederate states in spite of Thurmond. Meanwhile, the Missourian's liberal civil rights position diminished support for Henry Wallace's left wing fourth-party candidacy in the North.[23] As with Lincoln nearly a century before, Truman's most admirable undertaking, civil rights, had a firm foundation in practical, albeit high-risk, politics; he jeopardized the Solid South in return for a stronger base in the Northeast.

But Truman-era Democrats had more in mind than just civil rights; they wanted to take the next steps toward social democracy. As the Soviets were no longer seen as wartime allies but Cold War enemies, an anticommunist Left came to prominence in the late forties. As we have seen, Keynesianism provided the intellectual justification Cold War liberals needed for doing what their hearts were already telling them to do: build a democratic—and Democratic—cradle-to-grave welfare state. Fair Dealers in the forties were further inspired by another Briton, the new Labour Prime Minister Clement Attlee, who seemed well on his way to creating a nation fit for heroes,[24] beginning with the National Health Service.

Truman, eager to take America down the same womb-to-tomb path, became the first president to offer a serious proposal for national health insurance, on November 19, 1945—barely three months after VJ Day. He enunciated this furtherance of the Roosevelt Big Offer in universalist tones that echo today: "Everyone should have ready access to all necessary medical, hospital, and related services."[25] His plan was defeated in Congress, but the dream of health coverage for all—one big, holistic plan for everyone—has endured. To Democrats, national health insurance has been a cause based on calculation as well as conviction; they have believed that good numbers of votes are to be harvested in the course of doing good. From Truman to Clinton, one of the great cheer lines of the Democratic party has been "health care for all!" Just as the GOP collected generations of black votes based on Lincoln's Big Offer, so for decades did Democrats reinforced their popularity with their continuing Offer of universal coverage.

In the three years prior to the 1948 election, Truman staked his reelection chances on the unfashionable faith that America was still a liberal country. With only a few aides believing in what he was doing, Truman damned the GOP torpedoes and went full speed ahead with his Fair Deal agenda, from civil rights to health care to home rule for the District of Columbia. Truman reasoned that if the voters could see that he was fighting for them and their beliefs—while the GOP was fighting for the memory of Hoover—they would rally to his cause. In fact, the Republicans had grossly misread the message of their 1946 midterm victory. The GOP campaign slogan had been deceptively simple: "Had Enough?" With that polemical question, they had captured the votes of millions of New Dealers who may have been mad at some aspect of the Democratic administration but were not inclined, two years later, to unhorse the White House incumbent. And so the Republicans deceived themselves; an all-purpose appeal to disgruntlement may win midterm votes, but it does not bring a mandate for change in presidential direction. Reading in Colonel McCormick's *Chicago Tribune* that the New Deal was dead, Republicans rushed to bury it legislatively in the eightieth Congress of 1947-48.

So both Truman, who grasped the strategic situation, and GOPers, who didn't, agreed acrimoniously to disagree on just about everything.[26] Truman's goal was not to improve his legislative batting average in

1947; his aim was to hit a home run in 1948. And the Republicans obligingly threw him fat pitch after fat pitch. Truman didn't care if he struck out sometimes. He was playing to the fans, swinging to connect with the latent New Deal majority.

The president whistle-stopped 22,000 miles across America in the fall of 1948.[27] He presented the voters with a stark choice: forward with Fair Deal Democrats or backward with "do-nothing" Hooverite mossbacks. His "give 'em hell" strategy was not mere name-calling, but rather a strategy to rouse New Deal voters out of their torpor. Ironically, his opponent, Governor Tom Dewey of New York, was no conservative anxious to roll back the New Deal—all the more reason for Truman to ignore Dewey and zero in on the reactionaries in Congress who did want to roll it back.

Truman's calculated gamble paid off. Not only was he elected to a second term, but he won a smashing victory for the Democrats overall, a gain of eighty-four seats and control of both houses of Congress. His victory ratified the mandate for New Deal–style social programs, which were to shape the assumptions of the next six presidents. And though the long march to the left was derailed in his second term by the Cold War and the Korean War, the substantial bulk of the New Deal/Fair Deal program "worked," in the sense that even today people have no desire to repeal the social safety net of collective responsibility.

If the success of the first Big Offer was measured by the endurance of the Constitution; if the test of the second Big Offer was measured by the preservation of the Union, the expansion of the middle class, and the emancipation of slaves—then the test of the third Big Offer was the permanence not only of Social Security but of the collective sense that the federal government had a responsibility for the health, education, and welfare of all its citizens.

CHAPTER 8

RONALD REAGAN AND THE ABORTIVE FOURTH BIG OFFER

In 1980, Ronald Reagan made a new Big Offer to the American people. But that Offer was already tattering at the end of his second term, before being repudiated by his hand-picked successor.

As AMERICRAT aged into the 1970s, the big government of Roosevelt and Truman had grown bigger. Yet bigger was no longer better. "Bracket creep," spurred by the Great Inflation, nearly doubled the effective tax rate on median-income earners from 1965 to 1980; ordinary Americans were paying rates once reserved for the rich. Yet the Carter administration argued that still more tax increases were needed to cure rising prices.[1]

Compared to the falling-expectations, zero-sum "malaise" of the Carter presidency, Reagan's 1980 campaign was a clear channel of optimism. The three goals he outlined in his campaign—rebuild America's defenses, get government off people's backs, and cut income tax rates—were summed up in his theme: "Make America great again." If Reagan's Offer was easy to remember, so was his critique of Jimmy Carter's record: "Are you better off than you were four years ago?" Reagan won forty-four states in 1980, carrying with him the first Republican majority in the U.S. Senate since 1954.

Reagan started immediately to implement the three major planks of his platform. The first was readily achieved: defense spending, paying for everything from the M-1 tank to the B-1 bomber to the Strategic Defense Initiative, rose by nearly a third in real terms in his first four years. Less successful was his mission of "getting the government off our backs": he "RIFed" (the Washington verb form of Reduction In Force) a few midlevel bureaucrats and generally badmouthed the mission of domestic government. But the beating heart of Reagan's Big Offer was tax cuts. His "supply side" policy of across-the-board income tax rate reduction was the biggest single change the fortieth president made in U.S. domestic policy. However, as we shall see, in spite of all the dooming and glooming from his political opponents, little of the "Reagan Revolution" remained visible a decade later.

For a time, Reaganomics captured the popular imagination. From the late seventies through the early eighties, Republicans had the "idea advantage"—in the shape of the Laffer Curve. Economist Arthur Laffer had one key insight that was simultaneously profound and obvious: too-high tax rates discourage economic activity *and* generate less revenue for the state. Laffer argued that the marginal tax rate—the tax on the next dollar earned—was the key variable in determining not only economic activity but also the level of government tax revenues. It is the marginal tax rate that determines what the individual investor will do with a dollar. At some point, when rates get too high, rational capitalists will choose not to make the effort or take the risk to generate income, knowing that the taxman will take too much of what is gained. As Laffer put it, two different tax rates will both yield zero income for the government: a 0 percent tax rate and a 100 percent tax rate—since nobody will earn money just to turn it all over to the government. Somewhere in between, Laffer said, is the optimum rate at which government revenues will be maximized. For all the controversy the Laffer Curve generated, its logic rests firmly on a fundamental principle of economics: the law of diminishing returns. That is, if one pushes a given variable too far—in this case, tax rates—one winds up with less—tax revenues—of what one wanted in the first place.

Yet like so much of the dismal science, the curve has its cruel side: it is easier to soak the poor than it is to soak the rich. Those with high disposable income are the most flexible in their behavior; their investment decisions can be made in consultation with the finest tax-avoidance strategists, and they have the greatest discretion about how much taxable income they want to "earn." Before 1982, the top tax rate was 70 percent, but few millionaires ever paid tax at such a high rate—and that was Laffer's point. In a high-rate regime, people don't invest. Instead, the opposite of investment—consumption—becomes the optimum strategy. In effect, high living becomes a kind of tax shelter. Why invest if the government is going to take most of it? The higher the income tax rates, the more likely such IRS-thwarting consumption will turn conspicuous.

The other alternative for the overburdened rich is to lobby for loopholes. The money that can pay for the finest accountants can also hire the best lobbyists. For decades, this cycle of raising rates and ripping open loopholes led to a pernicious spiral, as the "interest group liberalism" that Theodore Lowi described brokered politically beneficent but economically inefficient deals between the rich and the powerful. Every few years a muckraker's report would explode over Washington, listing the millionaires who had paid little or no income tax. Such revelations were the natural consequence of complexity, but each would inspire a new wave of "tax reform." And so the dinner bell rang for the Beltway gravy train-riders; everyone with an interest in the shape of the tax code had to hire a lobbyist. Legitimate grievances—the poor paying higher effective rates than the rich, people with equal incomes paying grossly unequal taxes—were thus translated into the perpetuation of the lobby-loophole labyrinth. Thus the vicious cycle twisted over and over again: every "reform" would be logrolled into a regressive reaction.

Tax policy is as much a function of ideology as hard calculation. Levelers and redistributionists don't want to think about what will happen when their policies are enacted; they just want to hear themselves say, "Eat the rich!" When the British pushed their top income tax rate to 98 percent, it's hard to imagine they really thought plutocrats would sit still and pay tax at those confiscatory taxes. As author Anthony Burgess put it, the Left's goal was to make the rich scream. The rich screamed, all right—from their tax refuges in Switzerland or Monaco.

In the 1940s, American rates were almost as high, 94 percent, but their effect was minimized for two reasons: first, wars raged elsewhere, keeping capital at home; second, the miracle of loopholization swisscheesed the impact of those high rates. With the likes of Oklahoma senator Robert Kerr and Arkansas congressman Wilbur Mills—who rose from loopholing-as-usual obscurity to tidal-pool-dipping notoriety with stripper Fanne Foxe in 1974—running the tax bazaar, one should have expected nothing less. Yet as the rich finagled their breaks, the economy was the loser, investors making tax-driven decisions to put their capital into dry holes, slum property, butterfly tax straddles, and anything else that the Gucci-gulch group could finagle through Congress. The main victims of the high-rate regime were not the old-money Rockefellers, with their lawyers, trusts, and capital gains exclusions, but rather the unlawyered *nouveaux* earners, such as boxer Joe Louis, who lost his bout with the IRS in the fifties. Thus the U.S. entered into the worst of all possible tax worlds—unequal treatment of incomes, a bias against productive investment, and a steep penalty on American-Dreaming upward mobility.

The Laffer Curve offered a way out. A cut in tax rates, encouraging players to get back into the productive economic arena and eschewing either consumption or shelters, would disempower Beltway parasites and actually cause revenues to rise. The most notable convert to the new supply-side thinking was Reagan. The Curve squared with his own experience in Hollywood decades before; he understood that in a given year it didn't make sense for him to do another picture if he could keep only six cents out of every dollar he made. In 1981, he was finally in a position to translate this gut instinct into national policy. As his director of the Office of Management and Budget, David Stockman, wrote later, the tax cut was "one of the few things Ronald Reagan deeply wanted from his presidency. It was the only thing behind which he threw the full weight of his broad political shoulders."[2] Reagan's viscera, coupled with the cerebra of George Gilder, Jude Wanniski, and the *Wall Street Journal* editorial page, gave the GOP a powerful message: resurgent entrepreneurship would provide plentiful revenues for the Pentagon and those few missions the shrunken welfare state would continue to carry out. Congress voted to cut the top tax rate from 70 percent to 50 percent in 1981, then reduced it to 28 percent in 1986.

The Laffer Curve was not wrong, but it was vastly oversold. Tax rate cuts could not by themselves balance the budget and buy everyone a free lunch. Most Americans are workers, not investors. Those with surplus capital can play the tax-avoidance game; those earning money by their labor cannot. But below a certain income level, the Laffer Curve is invalid. When the tax on labor goes up, working people have to work harder—clocking overtime, moonlighting—just to make ends meet. So when income tax rates went down in 1981 and 1986, average Americans simply kept more of what they earned from the sweat of their brow, and government revenues declined accordingly; there was no Laffer Curve less-is-more magic for them. Moreover, the 1986 tax reform removed millions of working poor from the tax rolls. From the strict point of view of economic incentives, this reprieve from the taxman was a revenue "giveaway"—with no prospect of Lafferian tax revenue feedback.

As noted, the Curve's truth applies to capital, that quicksilver substance that can spill across income categories and national borders faster than one can say "1040." To the rich, declining tax rates meant that it was suddenly sensible to quit playing around with shelters and just invest. Thus as rates fell during the eighties, the share of revenues paid by the rich rose; the top 0.1 percent of taxpayers saw their share of income tax payments rise from 7 percent in 1981 to 14 percent in 1986.[3] Indeed, this century has taught us that markets deliver goods and services more efficiently than politics: the more de-politicization, the more efficiency. Reagan's reduction of tax rates—as opposed to widening loopholes or rebating tax payments—separated economic decisions from politics; investors looked to the market, not to the IRS, for their money-making opportunities. Such de-politicization disheartened lobbyists as well as Synoptic Aspirers, but it was a victory for freedom as well as economic growth.

As we have seen, a characteristic of a Big Offer is that its principles become subsumed into the permanent structure of U.S. politics. Just as Emancipation and Social Security endure, so Reaganized rates will be with us for a long time. Clinton raised the top income tax rate to 39.6 percent, but for all the rhetoricizing about repealing Reaganomics, few on the Left suggest taking rates back up to anywhere near the levels of even fifteen years ago. Laffer's name may be mud along the banks of the Potomac, but the basic logic is so inescapable that around the world income tax rates continue to come down.

As we have seen, the sovereignty of states has been Sorosized; government's ability to control its exchequer has been dethroned by the currency-trading global financial system and its millions of invisible hands. Presidents and potentates may view class warfare as a political winner at home, but it's an instant loser in the international arena of push-button capital flows. This same phenomenon is visible among the fifty states of the U.S., as governors strive to lower tax rates, knowing that a competitive disadvantage means money will migrate elsewhere.

What is true for cyber-era capital is also true for individual investors. *Forbes* magazine reports that in 1981, when tax rates were falling in the U.S. and the Soviet Union was on the move around the world, not one American gave up his or her citizenship. In 1993, with taxes on the way up and the Red Bear kaput, 306 Americans expatriated themselves; among those seeking asylum from the IRS were the heirs to the Campbell Soup and Dart Container fortunes. Knowing what its readers are interested in, *Forbes* adds that for a mere $200,000 an American zillionaire can find a new home in the Caribbean island of St. Kitts-Nevis, which has neither an estate nor income tax. These tax refugees won't be truly gone, to be sure; they'll still come to the U.S. to shop and ski, but the bulk of their fortunes will repose elsewhere.[4] Revealingly, the notorious "Rivlin Memo," listing every possible tax increase and spending cut that Clinton's OMB Director Alice Rivlin was considering in late 1994, did not even mention raising rich-soaking income tax rates.

Under Lafferian Reaganomics, the deficit grew, and yet real GNP expanded by a fourth. Reagan was the first president since World War II to leave office with both inflation and unemployment rates lower than when he took office. The "misery index"—the sum of the inflation and unemployment rates—had risen from 12.6 to 19.6 during Jimmy Carter's four years; it fell to 9.9 by 1988.[5] As a result, Federal Reserve Governor Lawrence B. Lindsey records: "Real income of the median family rose over $3000 under Reagan, after falling that same amount between 1973 and 1981 (the largest such retreat since the Great Depression)."[6]

Reagan's revolution had the potential to be the fourth Big Offer in U.S. history, based on a view of government totally different from FDR's. The underlying reality was a change of perception in the half-century since 1932; Americans were coming to see themselves less as grateful beneficiaries of government largess and more as victimized bill-footers. California's tax-cutting Proposition 13, passed by a 2:1 majority in 1978, projected the new attitude nationwide. Although the Golden State's Republican establishment had opposed the referendum, the national Republicans caught the wave. Two years later, they were in the White House. Reagan's 1981 inaugural set the new tone: "Government is not the solution to our problems; government *is* the problem."[7]

Beyond rate cuts, the most profound and permanent ingredient of the Reaganomics elixir was the indexation of tax brackets. For decades, the federal government had been a silent partner with inflation, because incomes went up while tax brackets didn't. This was a great system for incumbents. Elected officials did not have to vote for tax increases to enjoy more revenue. They could actually vote to *cut* taxes here and there, throwing a few bones to the populace, confident that the larger beast of bracket creep would still deliver meaty revenue year after inflationary year. Reagan thumbtacked creeping brackets—another permanent reform that few want to tinker with.

If FDR's Big Offer can be thought of as guaranteeing that people would get help from government spending, then Reagan's wannabe Big Offer can be summarized as guaranteeing that people would get relief from government taxing. If FDR Offered entitlement to tax "consumers" when most Americans were poor, Reagan's policies offered a reverse entitlement to taxpayers when most Americans were middle class.

This was as close as Reaganomics came to being a Big Offer. Middle-class Americans, those earning between $20,000 and $60,000, saw their share of the income tax burden fall from 67 to below 60 percent between 1981 and 1988.[8] Liberal academics Thomas Ferguson and Joel Rogers glumly concluded in 1986 that the Reaganites had hit upon "a surefire formula for holding on to [their] political support"[9] and predicted that Reaganism would predominate into the next century.

Yet Reaganomics fell short of Offerdom because the Republicans were only rarely able to extend their ambitious vision beyond the one macroeconomic issue of tax cutting. Reagan fixed some microeconomic distortions, such as eliminating energy price controls; this action, taken within days of his 1981 inauguration, ended the "energy crisis" overnight. Indeed, oil and gas price regulation, imposed a decade earlier by President Nixon, should be enshrined in textbooks as the perfect example of how price controls can not only cause shortages and long lines but also keep prices high by suppressing new supply. But Reagan and his copartners in governance for most of his presidency, speaker Tip O'Neil and Jim Wright, left many other microeconomic problems to fester, from the savings-and-loan fiasco to the agribusiness boondoggle to runaway Medicare costs.

Reagan had a domestic vision of reforming the welfare state, which consisted mostly of reducing it. Stockman wrote in his bitter memoir: "The Reagan Revolution, as I had defined it, required a frontal assault on the American welfare state. That was the only way to pay for the massive . . . tax cut."[10] The Reaganites did try; at one time or another Stockman and his OMB successors proposed wiping out the Small Business Administration, privatizing the National Institutes of Health, and chopping PBS and the National Endowments for the Arts and the Humanities. But while their hearts may have been in the Right place, they weren't able to use their heads to think through an effective spending-cut strategy.

For example, in May 1981, Stockman persuaded Reagan to propose a dramatic 23 percent slash in Social Security benefits. Whatever the economic merits of reducing entitlement spending, Reagan's direct attack on the core of the New Deal Big offer was a stunning political miscalculation. The Republican-controlled Senate voted 96 to 0 to reject the administration's proposal. Such a lopsided defeat demonstrated the difficulty Reaganites would face in launching a Stockmanian "frontal assault" on the welfare state. The congressional Democrats saw it as both ideological duty and political opportunity to defend the most popular legacy of the New Deal. Then in the 1982 midterm elections, Democrats made substantial gains, ending any Republican hopes that Reagan's popularity would translate into seismic 1934-type Congressional pickups for the party in the White House.

The battle between Reagan and his tax cuts and the Democrats and their spending programs framed the political wars of the eighties. The combatants at either end of Pennsylvania Avenue were evenly matched. The Republicans slammed Walter Mondale–style Democrats as tax increasers. Returning fire, the Democrats hit the Republicans on "fairness." Both sides had a bogeyman they could use to terrorize—and energize—their respective political bases.

Overall, people trusted Reagan to manage the economy; that's why he was reelected. Yet they wanted to be able to file their particular grievances with congressional Democrats; that's why *they* were reelected. This standoff was termed "gridlock," but what appeared to be a policy traffic jam concealed the slow forward crawl of the federal fiscal bulldozer. In no single year during the eighties did spending actually decline from the previous year.

Both sides exploited, in different ways, the concept of budgetary "baselines." Baselines are an only-in-Washington accounting concept that sets the starting point of the budget process at the previous fiscal year's budget level, plus increases for inflation, population, and "program growth." In the Stockman era, if the baseline presumption was that a program would grow by 10 percent in a year, Stockman could bargain the Democrats down to a 5 percent increase and still get credit for a 5 percent "cut." Tales of deep cuts gave Stockman bragging rights to Main Street Babbitts that he was indeed slashing "waste, fraud, and abuse," as well as to Wall Street savants that "deficit reduction" was on track.

Meanwhile, the Democrats would take credit with their constituents for a 5 percent increase in spending. But the Democrats had an additional advantage: they could blame America's ills on "ruthless Stockman–Reagan spending cuts"; they had command of heart-wrenching anecdotes of "people like us" being threatened with ruin by Reaganomics.

The obvious Republican counterattack—that conditions were worsening even as spending was increasing—was not an option, since that would have given away the whole fraudulent baseline game that Washington had been playing since the seventies. It would also have opened up an even larger issue: the fundamental failure of the social welfare system. And if that became the issue, then Reagan, as the leader of the country, would have been obligated to suggest not only small cuts but big reforms. This the Republicans did not feel confident to do.

Thus both sides chose to overlook the fact that spending was still rising. The Democrats gained too much from denouncing nonexistent cuts, and the Republicans were too interested in appearances to concede the spendthrift reality. The result: Americans "learned" that federal social spending had been "gutted" during the Reagan years, when the reality was just the opposite; such spending had almost *doubled,* from $303 billion in 1980 to $565 billion in 1989.[11] And so-called off-budget expenditures—outlays that the government arbitrarily chose not to acknowledge as expenditures—ballooned to $685 billion.[12]

Ultimately, Reagan and the Republicans emerged as the losers in this cynical game. The Reagan years were a steady spending spigot for the welfare state. Yet whether domestic spending rose 5 percent a year or 10 percent a year, the fact remained that problems were worsening, because the system wasn't working. Having taken credit for phony spending cuts, the Republicans had to take responsibility for worsening symptoms of social breakdown, from homelessness to infant mortality.

In his book *Dead Right,* David Frum argues that Reagan should have fought harder against spending.[13] But as we have seen, the frontal-assault strategy failed. Reagan could have made more of an issue out of the line-item veto, a spending cut tool enjoyed by forty-three governors, but a real debate would have required him to itemize specifically what he would veto. After the first few years, the Democrats had framed the debate so effectively that any reduction in the growth of government was a "cut" on the young, the poor, the old, the infirm.

Having given up their initial battle plan, the Republicans soon tired of the war. Strategies and maneuvers aimed at focusing the voters' attention on the true sources of trouble were never tried. About the "urban crisis," the Republicans said as little as possible, seemingly unable to summon up the intellectual energy to point out the obvious— that during the eighties, New York City, for example, had a Democratic mayor, a Democratic city council, and a Democratic governor upstate. Instead, the GOP just hid from the disastrous realities of gang violence, homelessness, and the underclass, which, regardless of their provenance, were challenging the conscience of the nation.[14]

What Reagan needed was a whole new intellectual arsenal that would have armed him with the idea advantage once again. Ideas for doing more with less abounded from the brows of "empowerment conservatives" like Robert Woodson of the National Center for Neighborhood

Enterprise, but the party as a whole never worked up much interest. Reagan's first White House domestic policy adviser, Martin Anderson, declared in 1980 that "The war on poverty has been won, except for perhaps a few mopping-up operations."[15] Later, the Administration grew more hostile to domestic innovation, which of necessity risked messy, un-Deaveresque confrontation with the Beltway Paradigm, instead it opted for simplistic split-the-difference AMERICRAT appeasement. Spurred to inaction by administration "pragmatists," the Gipper mostly lost interest in domestic policy reform after 1983. And the loss of the Republican-controlled Senate and the Iran-Contra affair in 1986 finished off what remained of his domestic leverage.

This intellectual and moral sloth was most evident in social welfare. Two intellectuals, one on the left and one on the right, helped reignite the debate over despair and dependency in the mid-eighties. Charles Murray's *Losing Ground* and Senator Daniel Patrick Moynihan's *Family and Nation*[16] helped persuade just about everyone that the status quo was unacceptable. Yet Reagan continued the Republican tradition of appointing get-along-go-along managerial half-a-loafers to high positions. His Health and Human Services secretaries—Richard Schweiker, Margaret Heckler, and Otis Bowen—were immune to the temptation to wage intellectual combat in the hope of changing the terms of the debate.

Domestic-issue confrontation was anathema to those Republicans who aspired someday to slip into the cozy culture of the Beltway, either as paid lobbyists or pro bono "wise men." Thus, with a few exceptions such as Jack Kemp and William Bennett, the GOP leadership drifted through the eighties.

It's a cliché that Reagan, the most conservative president of our time, nevertheless ratified the New Deal. That's seen as something of an irony. But the *real* irony is that Reagan ratified not just the worthy goals but the blundering bureaucratic technique—at the very moment when the world was headed away from bureaucracy. From *glasnost* to the leveraged buy-out, the great organizational wave of the eighties was restructuring and de-bureaucratization. If Reagan had possessed Truman's energy and zeal, he would have used the presidential proscenium to spotlight the contrast between increased spending and decreased results. Such leadership would have illuminated the structural disconnect—rising inputs, falling outputs—of the Bureaucratic Operating System. Reagan still might have lost the political fight against Tip O'Neill and the opposition-controlled House, but like Truman before him, one can lose a battle and ultimately win the longer war.

Having been an Old Paradigm–threatening politician in his first term, Reagan reverted to paradigmatic normality in his second and implicitly accepted the conventional definition of "compassion" as merely spending more money. It was Beltway business-as-usual, with Reagan mostly going along. He signed on to the misbegotten catastrophic health insurance bill in 1988; seniors, the intended beneficiaries, hated it, and the legislation was repealed the next year. He let farm support programs, backed by such prominent Republicans as Bob Dole of Kansas, grow as fast and green as chia pets. He pushed right-wing "big science" pork projects such as the space station, supported by Congressman Newt Gingrich, and the superconducting supercollider, supported by Senator Phil Gramm. Most egregiously, having been elected on a pledge to abolish two cabinet departments, he ended up creating one more, promoting the well-intentioned but poorly performing Veterans Administration to cabinet rank. And so the domestic conundrum continued—spending on social welfare up, social welfare itself down.

Reagan's Offer was great for those riding the stallion of unbridled capitalism. It wasn't so good for those trampled under the clumsy hooves of plodding bureaucracy—or paying for it. The Republicans assumed that if they expanded opportunity for entrepreneurs, the resulting swell would lift all boats. They were partially right; the number of black-owned businesses doubled during the eighties, to more than 400,000.[17] But for those tangled in the pathologies of the bureaucratic welfare state, the downward trend of the old order, already noticeable in the seventies, accelerated in the eighties. The public institutions of everyday life—cities, police, and schools—continued to decay. If Reagan did not, as his most outspoken critics claimed, actively undermine these structures, neither did he seek to reconstruct them to face new stresses.

The Department of Housing and Urban Development was severely Stockmaned, from $36 billion in 1980 to $15 billion in 1988[18]—but HUD remained HUD. The Reaganites may have wrung fiscal fluid out of the spongelike bureaucracy, but Housing Secretary Sam Pierce dedicated his tenure in office to moistening the beaks of his friends and cronies with what remained. The influence-peddled Pierce team simply piled illegal corruption on top of legal corruption.[19] After Pierce was washed away and new tides of lucre-liquid came flowing back, the absorptive capacity of the money-thirsty agency was undiminished.

The sense of unfairness that bubbled up from the failure of social welfare programs slowed and finally stopped the momentum of Reaganism. The resulting Republican lethargy was not only bad for the country; it was bad for the party. If the voters saw Republicans oversee-ing decline, then an obvious solution presented itself: elect fewer Repub-licans. The GOP lost its majority in the Senate in 1986—even before Iran-Contra blew up—and ended the decade with fewer seats in the House than when it began. Democrats elected in the eighties had no reason to fear Reagan. They defined the domestic problems on their terms: the programs weren't failing, they said; they were underfunded.

Meanwhile, the fallout from the rumbling detonation of the nuclear family blanketed the inner city in a new sinister snow. Crack cocaine first came to national attention in 1986, after the death of University of Maryland basketball star Len Bias. By the early nineties, the horrific *Clockers* culture of dealers, dopers, and drive-bys weighed, to use Karl Marx's desolate phrase, like an aching Alp on our consciousness.

As with any presidency, historians will write and rewrite the reality of Reagan. A century from now, his domestic legacy will likely be less remembered than his role as the commander in chief who presided over the climax of the Cold War. Such historiography would probably please Reagan, who, from his HUAC-testifying days as president of the Screen Actors Guild, saw himself first and foremost as an anticommu-nist. As one of his longtime political advisers, Charles R. Black, put it, "Reagan would wake up every morning and ask himself: 'How can I f—— up communism today?' "

However, in terms of the long twilight struggle against the federal behemoth, the net effect of Reaganism—as modified by the Democrats in Congress and the institutional conservatism of the AMERICRATic system—was barely a blip on the political oscilloscope. Reagan spent relatively more on defense and less on domestic programs than his predecessor, but the overall level of spending changed hardly at all: in 1980, total federal outlays as a percentage of GNP were 22.3 percent; in 1988 they were 22.1 percent.[20] The Tax Foundation calculates that during the eighties, "Tax Freedom Day"—the date by which the average person would finish paying federal, state, and local taxes for the year— moved from May 5 in 1981 all the way back to May 4 in 1989. And yet the federal debt nearly tripled, to $3 trillion.[21] John Makin and Norman Ornstein of the American Enterprise Institute are harsh: "His eight-year administration certainly lost the war against big government and high taxes."[22]

Richard Cornuelle, a leading theoretician of private voluntarism as an alternative to public bureaucracy, was even harsher:

> The so-called Reagan revolution was bogus—a disguised tax revolt. It was not an effort to repeal the service state but to preserve it—and to substitute debt or inflation for taxation as a way of paying its politically irreducible costs.[23]

So where's the rest of Reagan? His lost Offer is a lesson about what happens to politicians when they fail to develop a plan that meets the public's desire for a communitiarian whole-souledness, in addition to individual well-being. Even many anti-Reaganites might have preferred the higher middle ground of new ideas as opposed to the split-the-difference attrition politics of the eighties—but neither party thought much about that. The Republicans were not interested in rocking the boat they were captaining, while the Democrats were not interested in altering a propulsion system that had been pushing them ahead since the 1930s.

Reagan will go down as a political Shane, riding in to assure folks that no tax-increasing varmint would be able to erode their standard of living. However, like Alan Ladd in the 1953 film, he rode off into the second-term sunset, never looking back. He left a major bequest: confidence in markets and skepticism about government.

Reagan's legacy must also include the impression he made on younger Republicans, especially in the House of Representatives. Gingrich, Dick Armey, John Kasich, Chris Cox, and the other post-1994 GOP leaders can be equated with Joey, the boy in the film who calls out, "Shane! Come back!" at the end. Gingrich et al. were too young to have much effect in the eighties, but these neo-Reaganites came to prominence in the nineties.

Meanwhile in 1989, the chore of securing Fort Reagan fell upon the inadequate shoulders of Deputy Sheriff Bush.

CHAPTER 9

GEORGE BUSH'S FAILED LITTLE OFFERS

In 1800, 1860, and 1932, Big Offers were tendered and accepted. In each case, for decades thereafter, political practitioners could play by the rules of the Big Offer and prosper. Yet in the late eighties, as the distant thunder of the Cyber Future began to rumble the palaces of the Old Paradigm, George Bush, successor to the Reagan mantle, failed to notice that the foundations of his political throne were trembling.

Bush inherited what remained of Reagan's Offer—and then squandered it. In particular, he violated Test No. 3 of the Big Offer, which reads in part, "dance with the one that brung you." If Bush had kept his credibility with his own Republican support base, he not only might have restored the Reagan coalition but also expanded it. He might even have made his own Big Offer if he had thought anew and acted anew: combining "no new taxes" with a "kinder and gentler America." But he gave no consideration to the workings of AMERICRAT 4.0, even as it unraveled both American society and his own administration. Instead, he broke his promise and raised taxes, the effect of which was to better fund the BOS that was killing him. Bush traded away his Big Offer birthright for a mess of political pottage.

As we have seen, the Reagan Offer was emulsifying as early as 1986.

Bush won a comfortable victory in the 1988 presidential election against a weak opponent, but the GOP lost still more seats in that year's congressional elections. Such an ambivalent outcome was a sure sign that the voters were restless—and with good reason.

George Bush belongs to Strauss and Howe's "GI Generation," those born between 1901 and 1925. All their lives, the authors note, these men have been subsumed in team play and conformity.[1] From their early homogenizing experiences in the Boy Scouts, through the mass experience of World War II, through life in the white-collar suites or on the blue-collar line, GIs had a basic faith in top-down technocratic competence. By the eighties, that world had gone away; the long line of GIs had thinned and gone gray.

Once the youngest pilot in the navy, Bush had always been eager to serve. He was a war hero, but in peacetime, he was more of a servant than a leader. His nose-to-the-grindstone, eye-on-the-main-chance career equipped him to continue the Cold War abroad and big government at home, but when all that changed, he found himself trying to manage the unmanageable. Nobody had told him there'd be days like these.

The message of George Bush in the 1988 election campaign was preservation of the Reagan good times. The voters responded to Bush's stay-the-course campaign message with their own affirmation of the status quo. They voted Republican for president, thus hanging on to the shell of the Reagan Big Offer—specifically, no tax increase; meanwhile, they voted Democratic for Congress, counting on the latter to preserve the remnants of Roosevelt's New Deal Big Offer—chiefly, Social Security. The 101st Congress that Bush confronted in 1989 contained an eighty-two-seat Democratic majority in the House and a fourteen-seat majority in the Senate, the greatest Democratic numbers since the seventies. Bush was thus only the third newly elected president in U.S. history to face both houses of Congress controlled by the opposition.[2]

If the voters' confidence in Bush and residual Reaganism was mixed, the new president himself was equivocal and irresolute toward his own domestic policy. In 1988, candidate Bush was fed some tough lines ("read my lips, no new taxes"), some evocative lines ("kinder, gentler nation"), and some poetic lines ("a thousand points of light"). These worked well enough to get him elected, but once in office it became clear that to President Bush they were just that—lines someone else had written. He lacked respect for words and the ideas behind them. His notoriously weak and lazy verbiage was a leading aural indicator that he had little in mind; long before, he had dismissed the very idea of "the vision thing." Instead, he saw himself as an active crisis manager when needed and a passive in-box president the rest of the time. As Kenneth T. Walsh of *U.S. News & World Report* puts it, "Bush was there to make decisions in case some were called for."

As a vice president who succeeded a popular president into the Oval Office, Bush can be compared to Truman—although not favorably. Both inherited an ambitious political coalition; both were confronted by an opposition-controlled Congress. The big difference between the thirty-third and forty-first presidents was their understanding of their strategic situation. Disraeli held that every successful politician must know two things: himself and his times. Truman, secure in his own persona and accurately reading his era, felt comfortable in enlarging the legacy of his predecessor; under his guidance, the New Deal evolved naturally into the Fair Deal.

On the other hand, for all his proven physical courage and personal rectitude, Bush displayed the weaker character. To him, ideas were like dog whistles; he just couldn't hear the pitch. Loyal to the point of obsequiousness as Number 2 for eight years, he was possessed, when he finally got to be Number 1, by the political equivalent of Oedipalism toward the man who had bested him in the 1980 Republican primaries. But he repudiated the wrong parts of domestic Reaganism. The Gipper had cut taxes and neglected everything else; Bush, completely misunderstanding what was valuable about the Reagan legacy, *raised* taxes and neglected everything else. Reagan had an excuse: in the early eighties, he was busy dealing with communism and inflation. Bush inherited a stronger America and a strong economy, and yet he chose to carry on Reagan's complacency about a deteriorating system. Indeed AMERICRAT was eight years older and more obsolete in 1989; Bush punched out what remained of Reagan's Offer. In so doing, he demolished the political alliance he needed for his own reelection.

Another crucial distinction between Truman and Bush was the former's willingness to fight the good fight for his domestic policies. In his duel with the opposition-controlled eightieth Congress, Truman demonstrated that a president could win in the long run by losing in the short run. He had every confidence that big-government liberalism was the wave of the future; he eagerly showed voters the scars he suffered as he fought for them against a reactionary opposition. Thus he convinced the American people that he was their true champion. Bush, whose one sure contribution to *Bartlett's Familiar Quotations* is "voodoo economics," was not willing to wage a struggle for policies toward which he felt such ambivalence.

The lost horizon of the late eighties is that Bush could have constructed an attractive post-Reagan ideology out of the combination of cold-and-prickly economic policy ("no new taxes") and warm-and-fuzzy social policy ("kinder, gentler nation"). Naive White House aides theorized that President Bush might blend these two seeming opposites in a new-ideas crucible, out of which could come a gleaming alloy of reformist activism.

However, Bush didn't make the effort. His plan, such as it was, was much simpler: he would muddle through on domestic policy, steering to the right here and to the left there, depending on the current. Thus he hoped to increase social spending (prudently), while reducing the deficit (prudently), and even, promise notwithstanding, raising taxes (prudently). He thought he could assure his reelection—and his place in history—with his foreign-policy achievements.

From his first day in office, Bush proved to be careless about his campaign promises. Stepping into an intellectual bear trap in his inaugural address, he struck a premature note of compromise, telling his audience that the American people "did not send us here to bicker." Such lofty sentiments sounded good when spoken from the west front of the Capitol, but they communicated weakness of will to Senate Majority Leader George Mitchell and the rest of the Democrats under the Capitol dome. Those who loved the Reagan legacy and those who loathed it could agree on one thing: the profound ideological debate of the previous decade could not be papered over with Kennebunkport bonhomie. If Bush was unaware of the trivialized meaning of his own words, those on his left and his right were not. In the next four years, steel teeth from both directions would snap at Bush's feet.

"We have more will than wallet," Bush continued. With those words, he was accepting the Left's basic diagnosis: all that prevented America from becoming a great society was the government's chintziness—as opposed to, say, chronic systemic ineptitude. Thus for the next four years the battle raged between Democrats, who were unabashed in their support for more spending on everything, and the decidedly abashed Bush administration, which operated at an "idea disadvantage": accepting the premise of its enemies but conflicted and confused about what to do in response.

Bush and his top advisers were equally feckless about the fetters that held the unbundling Republican coalition together—the Reagan offer of a permanent, indexed income tax cut. After the 1988 election, Bush adviser Robert Teeter took a poll asking voters what they remembered of Bush's campaign promises. More than half could recall "read my lips," while none of the other recollections, including "education president" and "environmental president," scored higher than the low single digits. Incredible as it may seem in retrospect, Bush, OMB director Richard Darman, and White House Chief of Staff John Sununu did not anticipate the Republican firestorm that erupted after Bush's repudiation of the no-new-taxes pledge in the spring of 1990. His senior aides were themselves too little anchored in principle to think that anyone else might be so moored. The Bush administration's fight with the Right over the budget deal was not about ideas; it was a point of macho honor for Sununu in particular. Thus the only occasion when Bush battled over domestic policy was in a war against his own party when he repudiated Reagan's Big Offer of a permanent, indexed tax cut.

The Bush experience will go down as a valuable political science lesson: if a politician stakes his or her candidacy on one big promise, he or she had better not break it. White House aides joked that Bush could have deeded Kuwait to the Iraqis, imposed mandates for furloughed prisoners to date debutantes, and picked up first-dog Millie by her ears and swung her overhead—and still have been in better shape with his Republican base than after he broke his no-new-taxes promise. If the political story of the 1980s was the face-off between the dueling Offers of Roosevelt and Reagan, the story of the early nineties was Bush's collapse after he violated his political trust.

Oblivious to the central tax tenet of the Reagan Big Offer, Bush then tried to fill the resulting ideological void with lots of Little Offers, mostly to the Left. He signed legislation concerning civil rights, the disabled, and the environment—and yet nobody noticed a surge in support for Bush as a consequence. The only way he could have successfully synthesized conservatives and liberals around such social crusading was by Offering new ideas that lifted old disputes to new intellectual heights. Some fresh thinking amidst the red tape was evident in the 1990 Clean Air Act, which contained "emissions trading" provisions that allowed companies to buy and sell the right to pollute within an overall proscribed limit. But such fragile blossoms of market-sensitive creativity, sprouting up from the wasteland of regulatory overkill, were an endangered species.

If Bush had kept the Reagan coalition intact, he might have been able to raid disaffected Democrats and carry them back into his own camp with Little Offers of liberal gesturing. However, once the tax deal fractured his conservative base, he lacked the political leverage to crowbar loose anyone else's supporters. He was still enough of a Reaganite to antagonize the Left, but he wasn't effective enough to win the allegiance of the pragmatic middle.

Bush's "thousand points of light initiative" ranks as a Tiny Offer. Peggy Noonan's original thought had much merit: an attempt to get outside the paradigm of spending more money and hiring more AMERI-CRATS in what had become a diminishing-returns effort to improve the commonweal. Once in office, aides labored long into the night in their Old Executive Office Building cubbyholes to adduce a grand exegesis for Bush's pointy endeavor. Bushies chirped that the Boss didn't say "one big point of light"; he said "a thousand points of light," suggesting that he possessed a Tocquevillean, even Hayekian, appreciation of the value of voluntarism, diversity, and experimentation within the social-market context. However, the whole program was misconceived; the White House's plan was to pay bureaucrats to persuade taxpayers to volunteer their time, too. For all its kindly intentions, the points-of-light initiative was a thin noblesse-oblige icing on the stale cake of the Old Paradigm of bureaucracy.

Some in the Bush White House were opposed even to Little Offers. Sununu had a unique approach: No Offer. On November 9, 1990, in one of the most stupefying statements in modern political history, the

White House chief of staff proclaimed: "There's not a single piece of legislation that needs to be passed in the two years for this President. In fact, if Congress wants to come together, adjourn and leave, it's all right with us. We don't need them."[3] Call it just another delectation in a feast of ironies—that the self-proclaimed highest-IQed man in the White House would say something so dumb.

In spite of it all, if things had been going well for the country, Bush would have cruised to reelection. But mindless managerialism atop a senescent system is a game plan for disaster. Bush tried to practice normal politics in a time of snowballing abnormality. The Administration, having bragged that it was against the idea of new ideas, let its political muscles attenuate as its brain atrophied. Thus it was ill prepared to deal with its declining fortunes after the euphoria following Desert Storm.

In 1991 hopes were high for an "Operation Domestic Storm"; this was the fanciful notion that Bush would piggyback a Jack Kemp–like new-ideas empowerment agenda onto his levitating popularity. But instead of a ringing call for an activist, postbureaucratic, problem-solving government, Bush came back with more-of-the-same crime and highway legislation.[4] And in a display of cynicism notable even by Washington standards, White House aides "backgrounded" reporters, letting them know that the president would expend only enough energy on his domestic agenda to avoid being criticized for not having one.[5]

Higher spending eventually pulled inside out the GOP bag of budget tricks—caps, freezes, sequesters, balanced budget amendments, tax checkoffs. In the end Bush not only lost his presidency but also the battle against federal taxing and spending. From 1989 to 1992, annual tax revenues rose $100 billion, while spending rose $238 billion. In that same period, spending as a percentage of GNP rose from 22.1 to 23.3 percent.[6] Milton Friedman judges the record harshly: "Bush's policy was exactly the opposite of Reaganomics: higher tax rates, more regulation, more government spending."[7] Bush might have had an excuse if greater spending had gone for the greater good. But nothing was kind or gentle about the way the Old Paradigm tank clanked across the landscape. From the Cyber-Economy to Hypercrime, the evidence swelled: America was on the wrong path.

By the summer of 1992, far from being illuminated by the light of new thinking, the Bush administration was suffering mental blackout. Having traded away the aces of the Reagan Big Offer, the president found himself with a busted flush. With every domestic option foreclosed by some deal, firewall, or secret treaty, Bush found himself Gulliver-like, tied to the status quo by a thousand Lilliputian strings. Yet the voters didn't care about explanations for his passivity. All they knew was that he was as remote from their daily lives as the nearly invisible economic recovery that had officially begun in early 1991.

Pat Buchanan first smashed the shoes on Bush's clay feet; Perot and Clinton stomped each toe. Bush's towering poll ratings had scared the usual-suspect Beltway Democrats from running in 1992, but those presidential hopefuls with outside-the-Beltway olfactory sensitivities could smell vulnerability in the dry rot of a dozen years of Republican executive-branch incumbency. Perot came out of nowhere to assert that both parties and their respective Offers were no longer playing in Peoria. The Republican and Democratic wings of the political class, Perot said, had more in common with each other than with the people. Clinton talked the same talk, averring that he had entered the race because both parties were "brain-dead."

In the fall of 1992, preppy Republican Bush began comparing himself to earthy Democrat Truman. Bush spelled Truman's name right, but that was as far as he got. Since he had laid none of the ideological groundwork that Truman had put down prior to 1948, Bush's Truman allusion was illusion. It was denounced by none other than Harry's own daughter, who said her father would certainly have voted for Clinton.[8]

As Bush's campaign traveled and unraveled, it became apparent that the sole basis for the Truman analogy in the president's mind was that Truman had won a second term. Bush had no sense of the idea advantage that had lifted the Missourian into a second term. His analysis was simpler: "Harry Truman ran as an underdog just as I am." When Bush had to acknowledge that he had voted for Republican Thomas E. Dewey in 1948, Barbara Bush rose to her husband's defense: "The point is that Truman came from behind."[9]

After four years of ducking confrontation with the Democrats, Bush was finally willing to fight. But he had so little understanding of the war of ideas that he picked disadvantageous ground upon which to make his last Custerian stand. By the end of the campaign, he had a new target: the press. He was reduced to waving a bumper strip reading "Annoy the Media/Re-elect Bush." Such is hardly the stuff of a Big Offer; voters like to think that a presidential election is about more important matters than settling scores with Dan Rather. Meanwhile, the Bush campaign staff denounced Clinton with backfiring fax attacks. Its mix of Spiro Agnew–style thesaurus-driven vituperation ("Sniveling Hypocritical Democrats") with plain old name-calling ("Slick Willie") further eroded what remained of Bush's claim to a second term. And so the president lost, as heedless of the reasons for his defeat as he had been four years earlier of the cause of his victory.

Big government remained comfortably in place through twelve years of Republican antigovernment rhetoric. The voters failed to recall the words of an earlier Republican, John Mitchell, who said, "Watch what we do, not what we say." Making government slightly smaller or slightly bigger made little difference as long as the Bureaucratic Operating System controlled the hard drive. For more than a decade the Republicans got the fun of being in the White House, sitting behind big desks in comfy chairs; yet with every year that went by, their power decreased as problems worsened.

In 1992, Bush had lots of responsibility but little power. He was punished at the polls both for the failures of conservatism—the deficit as well as the widely broadcast intolerance expressed at the Houston Convention—and also for his failures to keep faith with conservatism: breaking his pledge on taxes as well as hiking spending and regulation. But the stone irony of his defeat is that he was also blamed for the embedded failures of the exhausted New Deal paradigm. Bush will surely be the last president to "govern" on the presumption that the Bureaucratic Operating System can hold together for two terms. It's not his fault that the termited system sagged while he was standing on it, but his four years of ignorance were not blissful for the American people. Having chosen to stand pat while the idea advantage slipped away, Bush let his domestic legacy all but disappear.

Unconscious of the great *Zeitgeistal* zephyr that was simultaneously activist and antibureaucratic, Bush tried to cling to the Same Old Thing. Thus he flunked all four Big Offer criteria: he himself dissed vision; he reserved his audacity for overseas; he buried his credibility with his broken tax pledge; and he allowed the recession, the deficit, and the furious national mood to answer the question of whether or not he could have made the Reagan Offer work.[10]

Yet future historians will likely ignore Bush and look instead at such starkly defined archetypes as Reagan, Clinton, and, lastly, Ross Perot—honchoing his millions of disaffected middle-American militants. Perot's 19 percent of the vote was the highest third-party total since Teddy Roosevelt's Bull Moose run in 1912; his strong candidacy demonstrated the extent to which both the New Deal and the Reagan Offer had disintegrated.

History will record the following irony of the Reagan-Bush years: America confronted overseas collectivists head-on and defeated them, helping to liberate the erstwhile "Second World"; yet the albatross of BOS was left to stink and rot around the necks of middle-class and poor Americans at home. The world was made safe for the privatized cyber-economy, even as AMERICRAT gangrened the public sector. After Reagan, the domestic deluge hit Bush; he was totally unprepared for the arrhythmic bump of the reformatted, core-dumped, snow-crashed, dog-deletes-dog nineties. Content with the fading certitudes of the Old Paradigm and heedless of its crumbling, Bush was not ready for the first shocks of the Cyber Future—and so he fell hard.

Clinton has been more aware of his place in history, mindful of the need to repair the internal contradictions within his own coalition. Yet he, too, has proved unable to reconcile what he inherited of Roosevelt's Big Offer with the reality of the near-twenty-first century.

CHAPTER 10

BILL CLINTON'S FAILED BIG OFFER

If Bush was a fizzled Truman, then Clinton is a failed FDR.

In the 1992 campaign Clinton made many offers to the American people. Unlike Isaiah Berlin's hedgehog, who knew one big thing, Clinton was a fox, who knew many things, including many ways to catch voters. His best remembered appeal was, "It's the economy, stupid!" But Clinton also promised to retool the work force for the twenty-first century, using government as the "catalyst." He was a "New Democrat" who would win back the Reagan Democrats by bridging traditional liberalism and conservative values with "third way" thinking. He would not only "end welfare as we know it," he would "reinvent government." Even so, he would "put people first," providing "health care that can never be taken away." Finally, he said he would raise taxes on the rich to restore "fairness," cut taxes for the middle class, and reduce the deficit. Moreover, he promised a fast FDR-like start, beginning his administration with "an explosive 100-day action period," promising "a legislative program ready on the desk of Congress on the day after I'm inaugurated."[1]

Given that overload of Offers, it was little wonder that the president-elect had trouble deciding what to do when he got to the White House.

The two months from November 1992 to January 1993 were consumed in sorting out his promise plethora. Did Clinton receive a mandate for New Democrat I? Or was it New Deal II?

The data from the 1992 elections were ambiguous. Clinton won just 43 percent of the vote, and yet the Republicans gained eleven seats in Congress, scoring their first congressional gains in eight years; those results should have portended that Happy Days weren't here again. Yet the ding-dong-Reagan-and-Bush-are-dead euphoria in Washington led the Clinton "dream team" to hallucinate about the size of its mandate for change. Thus miraged, Clinton made his historic blunder: having run as a de-bureaucratizing, reformist New Democrat, he was snared by AMERICRATic Old Democrats. And so Clinton, in partnership with Hillary Rodham Clinton, chose to make the wrong Big Offer: European-style national health insurance.

The political rationale for health care as the flagship of the Clinton presidency came from pollster Stanley B. Greenberg, who was certainly the contrarian; at a time when most people were saying "limit government," his message was "expand government." Greenberg's roots may have been New Left, but he pitched his nineties argument to Clinton on pragmatic, partisan terms; he had a plan, he said, for overturning the Republican hegemony. The first step was winning back Reagan Democrats. Their parents had been lifelong-loyal to the party of the New Deal Big Offer, and yet as Greenberg put it, the new generation had drifted away from their ancestral party, as it seemed to be preoccupied with "special pleading" on behalf of minorities.[2]

In 1990 Greenberg laid out his case for a big-government Big Offer in the pages of a liberal journal, *The American Prospect.* "Democrats need to rediscover broad-based social policy," he wrote, "that sends a larger message: Democrats are for 'everybody,' not just the 'have-nots.'" This declaration formed the crux of Greenberg's thesis: if the Democrats offered help only to the "truly needy," then nonneedy Americans would feel left out and turn resentful. But if the Democrats made the government a friend and helper to all, whether they needed help or not, then all would be grateful: "To recreate a rationale for electing Democrats the party must once again become the party of government."[3] Clinton read the essay three times.[4]

Practical-minded Democrats could see the political payoff from offering 100 million people a new entitlement. Once the health care ratchet had clicked, government care could be a tower of power for the party of government. Democrats knew that Britain's National Health Service was so popular that even Margaret Thatcher couldn't roll it back. The NHS was to the British Labour party what Social Security was to Democrats—and here was the Democrats' chance to build a second social citadel.

On a higher level, the holistic oneness of "global" budgets and "universal" health care and, best of all, a "single payer" system appealed to Synoptic Aspirers; the Clinton plan was another step closer to the Promised Land. As Bob Woodward described the odyssey of health care architect Ira Magaziner: "He had moved from utopian agitator to business management consultant," but, through it all, he was perpetually "a man for grand designs."[5] Even before the plan was released, its larger purpose was noted; Cathy Hurwitt of Citizen Action spoke of the social redemption inherent in the health care cause: "The whole purpose of reform should be to build social solidarity. Everybody should be in these alliances."[6]

Finally, there was the Hillary factor. Ample evidence exists that the First Lady supported a single-payer plan all along. Yet she evidently made the calculation that the administration should not attempt the long march to the medical Jerusalem just then; it should settle for a shorter hop.[7]

Indeed, the Clintonians prided themselves on their hard-nosed, *realpolitik* approach. Their plan was designed so that big insurance companies, who already dominated managed care, could also dominate the proposed health care "alliances." To the Clintonians, this corporate co-optation was clever; their plan wasn't big government, they could say, it was a public-private partnership. Just as bureaucratic AMERICRAT was Orbitalized in the sixties, so the aborning Clinton plan would create a Great Society–type Vealocracy out of national health care. Sure enough, the largest insurance companies—Aetna, Cigna, Met Life, Prudential, and The Travelers—played footsie with the Clintonians all during the health care debate. It was the small insurance companies, gathered into the Health Insurance Association of America—and left off the Clintoncare gravy train—that formed the hard kernel of opposition.

The further decision was made not to sell the plan on its merits at all—but instead to sanctify the mission with the halo of Hillary hagiography. In 1993 an adoring media presented Hillary's efforts as an Anita Hill–avenging affirmation of the changing role of women;[8] with the help of her Hollywood-glam A-Team, she wafted upward on the wings of a worshipful press, air-cushioned not on the substance of the plan but on the substance of her image.

All these wishing stars—the Democrats' need for a magnetic issue, the Left's yearning for a Grailic quest, women's desire for a place in the policy sun—constellated in Clinton's first year.

Greenberg's prescription, moreover, can be seen as the antithesis to Reagan's tax cut. In a way, the Reagan Offer and the Clinton Offer were "programs": one designed to deliver incentives for growth, the other intended to deliver health care; only time would tell which Offer the voters thought the more valuable.

Such was the Clintons' devotion to "health care that can never be taken away" that the administration short-shrifted the New Democrat agenda—notably, "ending welfare as we know it." The middle-class tax cut was also round-filed. Middle-class voters, having been burned by Bush's broken tax promise, probably never thought Clinton really meant it when he said he would cut their taxes. But it was a bit much for Clinton to turn around and seek to *raise* their taxes as soon as he took office. It is true that Clinton's higher income taxes soaked only the rich, but he proposed other tax hikes as well; his excises on energy, including the now-forgotten "BTU tax," would have cost the average car-driving family $500 a year. That latter tax hike was defeated, but it did not go unnoticed, contributing to Clinton's chasmic credibility gap.

Throughout 1993, the accumulation of personal wobbles and policy waffles weakened Clinton's clout, leaving him in a junior-partner relationship with the Democratic majority in Congress. And so the sound of the White House changed; no more saxing populist riffer—the new noise was that of a lilting Beltway choirboy. Clinton backed down on tough campaign finance reform, cuts in congressional staff, and the line-item veto. Other New Democrat planks, such as "reinventing" government, were Elba-ed aside to exile in the office of the vice president.

For a while, it seemed as though Greenberg's plan to engineer himself and his boss a place in political history was well on track. Had the Clintons managed to get their plan out the door in the spring of 1993, as originally intended, they might have been able to wreak political transubstantiation through their faith in Hillarian miracles.

To those who complained that the Clintoncare plan was a sloppy slice of procrastinated pie-in-the-sky, Greenberg urged patience; the Big Offer had to be delectable enough to get people's attention. While Chef Ira labored with the recipe for this mother of all health pies, Greenberg restated his Big Offer argument to *New York Times* reporter Robert Pear, the Boswell of the health care saga:

> I've argued all along that it's very important for every American to have a stake in health care reform. I've encouraged people to think bigger rather than smaller. There is an enormous opportunity here . . . A bare-bones program won't excite the imagination of the public.[9]

Unfortunately, Greenbergian theorizing couldn't provide the stuffing of a plausible proposal; it took the White House ten months just to announce even the broad outlines of Clinton's Big Offer.

Nevertheless, the first course of Clintoncare was well received. On September 22, 1993, the president spoke to Congress and the country, brandishing a mock "health security card." Polls showed better than 2:1 support. It seemed as though a new entitlement—a New Deal for health care—was in the offing. What the Clintonian health carers had attempted was the simultaneous expansion of access and contraction of cost, assuming bureaucratic enforcers would cost-control the big square peg of demand into a small circle of supply.

Right-wing ridiculist P. J. O'Rourke observed, "Santa Claus is a Democrat"; the only catch, he added, is that "there is no such thing as Santa Claus."[10] Eyeing Clinton's health care gift to the nation, he judged it to be as inedible as a lump of coal. "If you think health care is expensive now," he grinched, "wait till it's free."

By the time the full plan was served up in November, enthusiasm had cooled. With all its red tape and price controls, the Clintons' stew smelled suspiciously like bureaucratic big-government leftovers. Nostalgic New and Fair Dealers found much to savor, but many Americans saw something less appetizing. They agreed with Senator Phil

Gramm (R-Texas), who said that the administration wanted to "tear down the greatest health care system in history and reinvent it in the image of the Post Office."

Instead of a health care Offer that everyone could understand—the original Social Security bill, as we have seen, was just 32 pages—what emerged from the White House boiler room was not the vindication of the vision of Stan Greenberg; Rube Goldberg was more like it. The plan was a 1,342-page parody of a panacea: 240,000 words describing a trillion-dollar package that included a $2 billion line-item just to pay for more agencies, bureaux, and commissariats. The public's response was to worry about the threat of AMERICRATic authoritarians at the head of the health care table.

Big business had hungered for the Clinton plan early on, thinking it would consist mainly of controls on corporate health care costs—along with giveaway garnishes that permitted automakers, for example, to lay their older-worker health care costs on the government. Yet all these Stephanopoloid spinarios were ferociously fact-checked by conservative blue-pencilers; the Heritage Foundation estimated that the original Clinton plan would have overrun its budget by $800 billion before the year 2000. Magaziner provided instant rebuttal: "By 1998," he blithed, "everyone is paying less."[11] Yet the critics gained ground, pointing to the federal government's track record in a previous health venture, Medicare. In 1965, that new health program for senior citizens was projected to grow to an annual cost of $9 billion a quarter-century later; in 1990, spending clocked in at $67 billion—and has more than doubled since then.[12] At this point, even the corporate bureaucrats whom the Clintons thought they had co-opted didn't stay that way when confronted with contra-indicators.

As we have seen, Big Offers rest on four legs: vision, audacity, credibility, and workability. Bill, Hillary, and the Democrats had plenty of the first two attributes, but numbers three and four proved to be tough sleds, as molehills of doubt multiplied into mountains of disbelief. It was the Clintons' misfortune that Americans had been burned so many times by state secrecy, from the Pentagon papers to the Watergate transcripts, that people now wanted to read the fine print.

The nosy journalism of Pear and other inquiring minds rooting around for truffles of truth was too much for Ms. Clinton. Speaking for every policymaker who ever dreamed of his or her own "Get Smart"-like cone of silence, she complained about "the overly information-loaded society."[13] She saw that public scrutiny led to skepticism. Just as the church lost power in the fifteenth century when Gutenberg started printing Bibles, allowing people to read Scripture for themselves, so the Clintonian clerisy found itself on the losing side of a policy reformation, as people studied the once-forbidden, now-translated texts.[14] Any info-empowered Protestant today can nail critical theses to the White House gate—or its e-mail address. The result has been the ebbing of the Clintonian creed, leaving behind, finally, an aridly wonkish existentialism. Echoing Kierkegaard, Linda Bergthold, codirector of the White House task force that developed the plan, admitted that the dollar estimates were, after all, "a leap of faith."[15]

Sensing the doubting trend, the First Lady stepped in, seeking to interpose her own forceful persona between the plan and its disbelievers. She recalled pointedly that FDR "didn't have to describe every jot and tittle" of his Big Offer.[16] "When Franklin Roosevelt proposed Social Security," she complained,

> he didn't go out selling it with actuarial tables and books of regulations. He basically said, "Look. Here's the deal: You pay in; you're taken care of." . . . If he'd had to have been pressed to the wall saying, "Well, what about the spouse who didn't work, and what about somebody who only worked 20 quarters instead of 24 quarters?"—I mean, we would never have had Social Security.[17]

Health and Human Services Secretary Donna Shalala also saw the health care cause in epochal terms that transcended nitpicking. "Thirty years from now," she intoned, "we won't be judged by whether we got the subsidies right or the caps [on costs] right . . . We'll be judged by whether we got the best health care in the world."[18]

Yet the American people were deciding they didn't want the Clintonians Offering them health care. Polls showed the shift: Americans were worried about too much government involvement in health care.[19] As CNN analyst Bill Schneider put it, the Clinton health care plan was beheld, in the public eye, as just another income-transferring social program.

What went wrong? The rise and fall of Clintoncare is a tale of high hopes laid low by the tyrannical gravity of reality. The Clintons were impulsed by the semi-Synoptic faith that Washingtonians could achieve mastery over political science—as well as human nature. It was the old story of Frankenstein, or, for the younger set, Jurassic Park. Put simply, nobody is smart enough to think through all the intended and unintended consequences of such a humongous undertaking. For nearly a year, Magaziner, the mad scheming scientist, had practically lived at 216 Old Executive Office Building, beseeching the ghosts of Bismarckian BUREAUCRATs past to help him fabricate something that could live and breathe in these new times. In that corner chamber, Magaziner's 1,000 bureaucratic Igors cobbled together a creature, using body parts exhumed from dead Democratic health care plans and harvested from living donors in Western Europe. With angry peasants clamoring at the gate, Magaziner blithely insisted that his beast, still cold and flat, would soon walk, talk, and possess a warm bedside manner. Yet the final creation didn't so much run amok as lie still, no matter how many times Magaziner elevated the slab into the dark and stormy night, hoping that lightning would strike.

Dr. Magaziner's creation never took a single step. On July 23, 1994, the *Washington Post* headline blared, "Clinton Plan Is Officially Laid to Rest." Senator Max Baucus (D-Montana) ventured a terse pathology report for the putrefying product: the Clinton plan, he said, "smacks of excess government and the smell of socialism."[20] House Speaker Tom Foley (D-Washington) said that nothing with Clinton's name on it could pass;[21] Republican strategist William Kristol echoed: "The fate of health care reform is now out of the hands of Bill and Hillary Clinton."[22] For a few weeks, the Democrats attempted to assemble their own critter, but on September 26, 1994, the last man in the lab, Majority Leader George Mitchell (D-Maine), threw down his jumper cables.[23]

After the plan's fall, even the left-of-center *New Republic*[24] was moved to comment that the Magaziner operation mixed the "worst management consultancy blather with paleoliberal ambition," the presumption being that "complex social problems are amenable to totalizing intellectual solutions and that democracy is an obstacle to implementing them."[25] Or, as Robert J. Samuelson wrote epitaphically, "The real undoing of 'reform' was its utopianism."[26]

In a time of diminished expectations about government, Bill Clinton came across as a weak and untrustworthy leader, while Hillary Rodham Clinton seemed an undimmed Synoptic disciple. She seized upon obvious concerns about access to coverage as an excuse to go beyond problem solving to redesigning one-seventh of the U.S. economy—the equivalent of using the space shuttle to transport commuters. As *U.S. News & World Report*'s Gloria Borger put it, the Clintonians were "crusaders," embarked on a "moral project"; any opposition was viewed as "heresy."[27] Had they been less grandiose in ambition and more content to "salami" the health care problem a slice at a time, they might have succeeded. But from Savonarola to the Sandinistas, crusaders are not compromisers; they want it all.

As the gurney wheeled away the formaldehyded remains of the Clintons' Aspiration, the postmortem finger-pointing began. Some Clinton supporters blamed the Health Insurance Association of America's "Harry and Louise" TV ads; yet the Clintons had been preaching from the presidential pulpit for two years, and they had mounted their own costly ad campaign—which was more like Thelma and Louise sailing off a cliff, out into the ether of public mistrust, down upon the rock-ribs of the Republicans. Magaziner's own pathology report was closer to the truth. He cited "the general mistrust of government," although files autopsied from the Magaziner *Schloss* also revealed internal truth-butchering. One Ira-crat described his day's work: "We sat around the table making guesstimates of the savings to be realized. It was an appropriate exercise for April Fools' Day."[28]

The *Wall Street Journal*'s Paul Gigot dealt harshly with the Clintons' vision, writing that the administration "chose entitlement expansion over anti-entitlement reform."[29] The problem was that the Big Offer of entitlement expansion to the middle class meant getting money from the middle class. Bribing voters with other people's money is standard practice; bribing people with their own money is a harder trick. Clinton tried to finesse this difficulty by calling the health care payroll tax—up to 9.5 percent—a "premium" to be paid by employers, but even official Washington couldn't swallow that locutionary lozenge. Nor could ordinary people paying a third to a half of their income in taxes fail to realize that the money for a payroll tax ultimately comes out of employees' pockets.

One recent study of the workers' compensation program casts light on this burden of payroll taxes. Economists Jonathan Gruber and Alan B. Krueger showed that 85 percent of workers' comp insurance costs were reflected in lower wages, noting also that the same results would likely hold true for the larger issue of health care:

> Given the similarity between workers' compensation insurance and many proposed employer-mandated health insurance plans, our findings suggest that a large share of the employers' cost of meeting health insurance mandates may be borne by employees.[30]

In other words, employees would end up paying for what they were getting. Even if the best things in life are still free, things from the government are not. Many Americans concluded that they should have more say over their health care than the Clintons could offer.

A big political market exists for health care reform, but today the perception that any such reform automatically entails "government takeover" blocks the sale. When the Clinton plan was revealed to be what it was—a giant tax increase, probably intended all along to reconfigure quickly into a Synoptically satisfying single-payer system—it was doomed. A similar crash-and-burn fate befell California's Proposition 186, which called for a single-payer system financed by big tax increases: it went down to a 3:1 defeat in November 1994.

In contrast to the New Deal/Fair Deal days, AMERICRATsters had no great reservoir of good will to draw upon when they needed to drench the populist prairie fires of bureauphobic Limbaugh-lash. In our time, the dream of Bigger and Bigger Government no longer has much appeal, except maybe to those who work inside it. Former Congressman Vin Weber (R-Minnesota) expressed strained sympathy for the times-misreading Chief Executive: "Clinton must feel cheated. All he was trying to do was push familiar Democratic nostrums, but the public wasn't buying."

Everyone agrees that the Clintonians are a smart bunch; they may have more after-tax disposable IQ points than the two previous administrations combined. So we come back to the question that everyone asks about professors: How can people so smart be so dumb? With intellect comes hubris; perhaps that's why the Clintonians weren't interested in more modest health-caring mechanisms, such as insurance reform or health care IRAs. Having waited a lifetime to move the big levers of power, they were not about to cut their fiefdoms into pieces and distribute the power back to states, let alone individuals. In Big Offer terms, the essence of the idea advantage goes to Test No. 4: workability. In their zeal to solve all of America's health problems in One Big Bang of an answer, the Clintonites lost sight of the need to develop a health care plan that would function here on earth.

The 1994 Election

Even before the Big Offer of Clintoncare crashed, Greenberg had bailed out. In August 1994, with Republicans campaigning against the "Clinton Congress," Greenberg advised Democrats to distance themselves from Clinton and his unpopular, unraveling Offer.[31] As Republican pollster Bill McInturff gloated, "The term 'government-run' kills support for national health insurance," because "no Baby Boomer believes that 'government-run' is synonymous with quality and efficiency." Toward the end of the 103rd Congress, it was the Republicans who were anxious to have a vote on the plan, so that they could say "nay," while the Democrats were desperate to avoid having to say "yea." The Clintons' bill never came to a vote on the floor of either chamber. All that congressional Democrats, sniffing doom, wanted to do was get home and mend fences with the voters. Thus the Clinton plan was not so much gridlocked to death by the Republicans as sabotaged by the Democrats. Before Bob Dole could wheel up the heavy howitzers, congressional Democrats had already dropped wooden shoes into the plan's fragile mechanisms.

The *Washington Post*'s David Broder observed from the campaign trail: "Health reform, the biggest lobbying and policy battle of the past year in Washington, has virtually vanished from the midterm campaign."[32] Fearing the political drag of the White House, Democrats hid their health care duds and donned police blue. Mandy Grunwald, who rose to earned fame as Bill Clinton's 1992 ad maker, described the MO of her 1994 campaigns: "We have filmed cops or jails or boot camps in every state we're working in."[33] In other words, the Clinton Big Offer: R.I.P.

For most of his first two years in office, Clinton had displayed a curious complacency about the bulk of his support base. All through 1992, he was the tribune of the "forgotten middle class." But incumbency blunted his common touch. The bright-line dichotomy between the hemispheres of what he said and what he did blotted out what remained of his believability. Clinton claimed the government had shrunk, and by the narrowest measure of the number of bureaucrats on the payroll, perhaps he was right. Yet one study found that the number of civil servants employed in active regulation, as opposed to clock-watching contemplation, rose in the first year of the Clinton presidency to 128,615, the highest level ever. Another easy measure of Uncle Sam's net intervention is the number of pages in the Federal Register; in 1993 this compendium of red tape jumped to the highest level since 1980, the last year of the Carter Administration,[34] and 1994 showed another increase.[35]

Maybe Clinton truly didn't know that the Old Paradigm was acting as it always did—taxing or subsidizing everything that walked, flew, grew, or oozed. Like Bush before him, he seemed content to ride the preexisting system wherever it took him, up or down. In the last few weeks of the 1994 campaign, as it became clear that the Democrats were on the road to nowhere, the president pricked up his populist ears. Having flirted with entitlement cuts both as governor and president, he was now reduced to waving the bloody shirt of the Social Security issue.[36] He campaigned hard for such paleoliberals as Mario Cuomo and Teddy Kennedy, provoking titters when he called the Bay State solon, a veteran of thirty-two years in the Senate, an "agent of change."[37]

William Kristol of the Project for the Republican Future put his finger on the state of the Clinton Democracy: "It turns out there is no 'new' Democratic Party. Gone is all that heady 1992 talk of rethinking liberalism and reinventing government."[38] By older measures, the economy did well in the first two years of Clinton's presidency; 5 million new jobs were created. Yet many American families with both spouses working thought that the economic recovery was making the government better off, not them. According to a *CBS/New York Times* poll, only 18 percent of Americans thought that the next generation would enjoy a higher standard of living.[39] Clinton's own Secretary of Labor, Robert Reich—who, as we have seen, wrote a nonfiction cyberscenario in *The Work of Nations*—redefined the middle class as the "anxious class." Clinton himself conceded that crime was "a gnawing fear" undermining the national sense of well-being.[40] Falling incomes, rising fear of crime: people could see the Cyber Future.

In the 1994 midterm elections, spin smashed up against these realities. The Democrats lost eight seats in the Senate and fifty-two seats in the House, the worst defeat for the White House party since 1946. Clinton, having given activist government a bad name in his first two years, was forced to concede that the American people "don't like it when they watch what we do here." Guru Greenberg spun the defeat into a new but unpersuasive web: while Clinton feels "very upset," he weaved, "he feels liberated from Congressional leaders that helped drag him down."[41] This must have come as a shock to the vast bulk of congressional Democrats who faithfully supported Clinton policies, even unto the end.

Historians will wonder what the fate of the forty-second presidency would have been had Clinton used his first two years to reengineer government for real, instead of trying to steamroll national health care. Had Clinton spent 1993–94 accumulating credibility on the issue of government management rather than dissipating it, his presidency, not to mention prospects for health care reform, would have been different.

Clinton badly miscalculated what Ross Perot and his populist supporters wanted. We know now that "the deficit" was not the focus of Perotista concern; it was just a marker for larger dissatisfaction over big government. Clinton had raised taxes on the theory that higher taxation would reduce the deficit and push down interest rates. Taxes went up, but so did spending; indeed, the Clinton Administration strongly opposed the Penny–Kasich spending-cut bill in 1994. The deficit went down because of strong economic growth, but interest rates went up; they were higher on Election Day 1994 than on Election Day 1992. With the entire logic of the Clinton economic plan turned upside down, the voters gave Clinton little credit for economic recovery.

Perot said repeatedly during the 1992 campaign that the government comes *at* the people, whereas we want a government that comes *from* the people. Yet Clinton never tamed the Democrats' Old Paradigm appetite for centralization. At the time of the 1994 elections, it seemed as though every federal department had some scheme for rules, quotas, mandates, or lawsuits in the offing. On his good days, Clinton was aware of the problem, but on bad days he was never able to stand up to the internal institutional impetus for more bureaucratic power. As journalist Joe Klein puts it, if Clinton had campaigned in 1994 with a Reagan-era $600 toilet seat, assuring the taxpayers that such abuse would never happen in the new era of government reinvention, the 1994 outcome would have been different.

Clinton: Eisenhower Republican or Gorbachev?

If Clinton is not FDR II, then what is he? He himself may have provided the answer: Eisenhower II.

In *The Agenda: Inside the Clinton White House,* Bob Woodward reports that Federal Reserve Board chairman Alan Greenspan got to Clinton in December 1992 and so terrified him with scenarios of reelection-denying Carter-style inflation that the president restrained his impulse to "invest"[42]—that is, "spend." The new president felt so pinioned by Wall Street's interest rate anxieties that, with the conspicuous exception of his health care initiative, he inadvertently found himself presiding over an incrementalist, small-"c" conservative administration.[43] As his $16 billion neo-Keynesian economic "stimulus" package was going down to defeat in the spring of 1993, a red-faced Clinton complained to his cabinet that "We're all Eisenhower Republicans"—adding bitterly, "We stand for lower deficits and free trade and the bond market. Isn't that great?"[44]

Clinton may have been on to something, analogywise. Unlike his predecessor Truman, Eisenhower was nonideological. Ike's implicit message to his party was that it had lost the battle against New Deal liberalism; his presidency was derided by conservatives as "me-tooism" and "dime-store New Deal"—which of course it was. Yale's Stephen Skowronek suggests that Clinton's role in history will be to reconcile the Democrats to the post-Reagan reality, just as Eisenhower's "Modern Republicanism" helped the GOP accommodate itself to the New Deal.

Skowronek says that presidents who come to power as challengers can take one of two leadership postures: they can "renounce and repudiate the predecessor," or they can "incorporate the commitments of the previous establishment" into their agenda. Skowronek's verdict: "Clinton may have hoped to do the former; he's going to end up doing the latter."

Does Clinton want to be a "Modern Democrat," delivering the sad news to the party faithful that hoped-for happy days are never coming back? Surely not, although he seems to prefer conciliation to conflict; he was the first president since Millard Fillmore not to veto a single bill in his first two years as president.[45]

Clinton tried to placate all sides: spend a little, save a little, reinvent a little. But after the "stimulus" package and his health care Offer were rejected, he was left with no significant spending increases, no significant reform, no significant anything.

The Bureaucratic Operating System Clinton presides over is recognizable as AMERICRAT, but Upgrades have left it so deformed that it can barely keep its distended torso upright on its Vealic little legs. In the nineties, the ever-fattening Vealocratic Operating System has been undoing Clinton, just as it undid Bush. Clinton's political instincts tell him to change, but institutional Democrats dissuade him; this course of prudence and compromise is floating the president closer to the same falls that Bush went over in 1992.

Another, more recent, parallel for Clinton is Mikhail S. Gorbachev. Both men represented a new generation of reformers, keenly aware of their mandate to overcome domestic stagnation. Popular at first, both were soon stymied. The Old Guard in both parties claimed it was being betrayed by even minimal reform, while the opposition, its appetite for change whetted, demanded that the new leaders move faster. Amidst the acrimony, the quality of life in their respective states declined. More and more people concluded that the problem was the system itself. But both leaders shrank from genuine *perestroika*.

Nearly a year into his term, Clinton recalled the fading rationale for his candidacy:

I got into the race for president because I was very concerned about the direction of my country, a direction that had been underway for 20 years under the leadership of people in both parties in Washington with forces that are beyond the reach of ordinary political solutions.[46]

But like Gorbachev's communist party, Clinton's core constituency—the Iron Triangle of traditional Terrestrial Bureaucrats, Orbital Bureaucrats, and congressional Democrats—is the essence of the governmental system he presides over. The Old Paradigm is destructive to the commonweal, but it's the only order the Clinton administration knows.

Like Gorbachev before him, the danger for Clinton is this: having loosed the idea of change, he will not be able to keep up with the demand for more change. In 1938 a Harvard professor named Crane Brinton published an insight so deep and yet so manifest that it instantly became part of the conventional wisdom. Few have read Brinton's *The Anatomy of Revolution*, but everybody understands his point: revolutions don't occur when things are getting *worse*; they happen when things are getting *better*. Rising expectations fuel ferment—and then explosion.[47]

Gorbachev wanted to end the institutionalized hypocrisy and cynicism of the Brezhnev-era *nomenklatura*. But when he saw that his own Communist Party was the obstacle to *glasnost*, he backed away from reform—only to be swept away by the tide of history. Clinton's dilemma is similar. Real change would rend his governing coalition, but crazy-gluing over the cracks in the old system with more money assures Clinton of a Gorbachevian fate at the hands of an American Boris Yeltsin—or even, as the Cyber Future gyres closer, an American Vladimir Zhirinovsky.

As we have seen, the three Big Offers—in 1800, in 1860, and 1932—have come every sixty or seventy years. Each Offer depended on a new political model: a new paradigm. Could these intervals be the political equivalent of a Kondratieff Wave, the long cycle of boom and bust, hypothesized by the Russian economist Nikolai Kondratieff in the twenties?[48] We need not believe in some sort of political Halley's Comet, whizzing through our political galaxy every so often to bring change. Instead, it is reasonable to think that a Big Offer, like any other human enterprise, goes through a cycle of wax and wane.

The Old Paradigm is clearly waning. And with it will go the two parties as they are now configured.

PART 4

A THIRD PARTY
AND THE NEXT
BIG OFFER

CHAPTER 11

THE DEMOCRATS

Having witnessed the foreshadowings of the Cyber Future, having examined the rise and slow fall of the Bureaucratic Operating System, having looked at Big Offers and how they have changed America for the better in past times of crisis—we are now ready to consider the potential of the two parties to make the next Big Offer, the one that will save us from Blade Runnerization.

The Jeffersonian and AMERICRATic Traditions

The original Democratic-Republican Party,[1] founded by Thomas Jefferson, stood for something revolutionary: small government. In his first inaugural address, in 1801, Jefferson listed some of America's many blessings, then asked this question: "What more is necessary to make us a happy and a prosperous people?" His answer:

A wise and frugal government, which shall restrain men from injuring one another, shall leave them otherwise free to regulate their own pursuits of industry and improvement, and shall not take from the mouth of labor the bread it has earned.

At the time, it was the opposition Federalists, with their aristocratic longings, who stood for the then "conservative" idea of statism. Three decades later, the descendants of Jefferson, the Jacksonian Democrats, elected Old Hickory to the White House; Andrew Jackson was loyal to the Jeffersonian Offer, even to the point of opposing such necessary— and inevitable—modernizations as a central bank. The original quasi-libertarian Jeffersonian Democracy mostly expired with the three losing presidential candidacies of William Jennings Bryan, in 1896, 1900, and 1908. As we have seen, Woodrow Wilson, the first Democrat to win the White House in decades, accelerated the bureaucratization of American politics. Franklin D. Roosevelt finalized the transvaluation of the Democratic party's essence; New Deal Democrats were the unquestioned masters of the Bureaucratic Operating System.[2]

That was long ago, in the days when the president was proud to call himself "liberal." As AMERICRAT aged, it was Upgraded, with Spending, Layering, Bottomlining, and Hawthorne Effect-ing; as we have seen, the early Upgrades worked far better than the later ones. Also more manifest were the five Bugs in the Bureaucratic Operating System: Parkinsonism, Peterism, Oligarchism, Olsonism, and Information Infarction. As with any human institution, the BOS life cycle devolved—from enthusiasm to cynicism, from energy to entropy.

Defeat in 1980: The Democrats' Divided Response

Yet in a two-party system one party can flourish, in spite of its weaknesses, as long as the other party is in worse shape. In the early and midseventies, Watergate was only the most glaring Republican disaster. President Richard Nixon had virtually conceded his domestic policy to the BOS; the steep upward momentum of spending, regulation, and Vealification during the Great Society continued and even accelerated during the Nixon years. The intellectual emptiness of the GOP in those days was summarized when Nixon, the first president ever to impose wage and price controls in peacetime, declared in 1971, "I am a Keynesian."

Keynes wrote his *General Theory* in 1936; by the seventies, the best days of Keynesian economics were behind it. So Nixon was not only a "me-too" Republican, but a belated one at that. With opposition of such small intellectual caliber, the Democrats looked like big guns. Indeed, when Jimmy Carter was elected in 1976, incoming House Speaker Tip O'Neill, surveying his 292–143 seat advantage in the ninety-fifth Congress, wondered aloud whether Gerald Ford would go down in history as the last Republican president.

However, the Democrats had their own appointment in political Samarra in the late seventies. Although they controlled every major government institution in the Carter years, the policy tools they knew how to use—tax increases, more spending, more regulation—all proved counterproductive. The real problem confronting America wasn't Republican leadership; it was the off-kilter *kybernan* of the Old Paradigm, which was steering America into a stagflationary dead end. The Bugs in the BOS were not only chronic but progressive. They weakened the body politic with every passing year, undermining the political prospects of anyone who could be tarred with incumbency. And so Carter lost, the fourth "failed" president in a row.

The 1980 elections were bad news for the Democrats, but the losses were not distributed equally. The Democrats lost the White House and control of the U.S. Senate, but in O'Neill's House, they retained a 51-seat majority. After the 1982 election, their majority bulged to a comfortable 104 seats, effectively ending the Reagan Revolution.

So the Democrats went through the eighties experiencing two different states of consciousness. At the national level, they suffered bad karma, carrying just seventeen states in three presidential elections; in the struggle for lesser offices, in Washington and across the country, their electoral karma was sublime. The Democratic majority in the House continued to grow in the eighties, and the party won back the Senate in 1986.

Not surprisingly, these two different sets of experiences led to two different responses. Democrats who concerned themselves about the presidency and the larger public agenda felt the need to change and rethink; congressional Democrats and their more parochial allies—those focused on a particular region, cause, or constituency—felt little pressure at all. The first group wanted new ideas; the second group was content with the old ways. Although the second group is less interesting, we can consider it briefly, since its enormous mass displaced so much of the new-thinking effort.

The Ehrenhaltians

Traditionally, the strength of the Democratic party was its diversity or, more accurately, its flexibility: its chameleonlike ability to blend in with the local political terrain. From near-feudal southerners to near-socialist northerners, the Democrats were all things to all voters. The price they paid for this heterodoxy was intraparty fractiousness. It was Will Rogers who said he was not a member of any organized party: he was a Democrat. These cleavages were deep, and yet strong leadership—and the New Deal Big Offer—kept the party working together until the Carter era. Even through the Reagan years, the Democrats retained their strength as a congressional party.

In his brilliant 1991 book *The United States of Ambition*, Alan Ehrenhalt described the process that seemed to guarantee the Democrats their congressional majorities even as the Republicans dominated the national political debate. Put simply, the Democrats had the better candidates; whereas the Republicans came across as rigid and politically gauche, the Democrats were supple and graceful in their political practitioning.

As Ehrenhalt demonstrated, the Democrats in the eighties achieved an unprecedented degree of professionalism. Vietnam and Watergate had once galvanized idealists into Democratic politics, and yet by the eighties, the motivation was more careerist. Coming then into the arena, wrote Ehrenhalt, were men and women "who had devoted their lives to the business of campaigning and did not need the fervor of an issue to sustain them"[3]; their personal belly-fire was enough. This new crop of Democrats was tireless and perpetually hungry; for most, being a member of Congress was the best—in some cases, the only—job they had ever held. As true children of the television era, they were glib, smooth, and soundbiteful. We can call them "robocandidates," or "Ehrenhaltians."

Since Ehrenhaltian Democrats had little agenda beyond ambition, they quickly slipped into the groove of the BOS once they got to Washington. As AMERICRAT continued to march to its own bureaucratic drummer, Ehrenhaltians were frequently forced to vote for programs that put them to the left of their constituents. However, being the superior pols, Ehrenhaltians were able to skate over this troublesome detail with better "homestyle" politicking. To further cinch their seeming-lifetime sinecures, they "reformed" the campaign finance laws so as to snuff out challengers; they ballooned their staffs and franked themselves to the hilt, burying their Republican challengers under avalanches of money,[4] constituent service,[5] and mail.[6]

Thus did the Ehrenhaltians survive the Reagan Revolution. Democrats representing liberal states and districts felt free to confront the Republican White House, while scores of their colleagues, whose numbers made the Democrats the majority, played a cagier game of I-agree-with-the-president-when-he's-right-and-disagree-with-him-when-he's-wrong survivalism.[7]

Ehrenhaltian electoral surefootedness was a mixed blessing. On the one hand, canny Democrats could cling to power; on the other hand, they could also cleave to outmoded thinking, even as the storm gathered. Clinton's election spelled the end of the Ehrenhaltian majority. With a Democrat in the White House, Democrats in the Congress could no longer find shelter from the gusts of ideological accountability in the lee of loyal-oppositiondom. Forced to vote yea or nay on high-profile, ideologically charged items on the Clinton agenda such as health care, the Democrats were finally exposed in unflattering ideological relief to the folks back home. So when the electoral storm of 1994 squalled up, the Democrats, burdened by institutional and ideological dead weight, could not dodge the voters' lightning bolts.

The Neoliberals

If defeat in 1980 convinced many nationally minded Democrats of the need to do something, the even bigger defeat of Walter Mondale in

1984 underlined the urgency of *perestroika*. The enormous excitement generated in 1984 by Colorado senator Gary Hart's primary challenge to Mondale helped introduce a new word to Americans: "neoliberal."

The neoliberal stars of the eighties were a generation younger than presidential candidates McGovern, Carter, and Mondale. Besides Hart, they included Michael Dukakis and Paul Tsongas, the governor and senator from Massachusetts; New Jersey Senator Bill Bradley; and Richard Gephardt and Al Gore, congressmen from Missouri and Tennessee. Neoliberalism owed a debt to the New Left of the sixties, which, as we have seen, was in part a rebellion against New Deal–era broker-state liberalism.[8] Hart had electrified younger Democrats in 1974 when he said, on his way to victory against a Republican incumbent, "We're not a bunch of little Hubert Humphreys." A decade later, he summed up the new neoliberal thinking: "What is changing are not principles, goals, aspirations or ideals, but methods."

Randall Rothenberg's 1984 book, *The Neoliberals: Creating the New American Politics*, provides a window into the neoliberal movement at its apogee. Rothenberg's key supposition was that out-of-power Democrats had the luxury, as well as the necessity, of rethinking the old relationship between goals and techniques. Or, as Bradley put it, "You *do* find a group here trying to think through the problems of the eighties, who see that the traditional Democratic responses really had their origins in the thirties and are not going to meet those problems."[9] Gephardt sounded positively Jeffersonian in his devolutionary determination:

> I would get rid of government in health care. I would get rid of government in education to a much greater extent than we have. I would discharge those responsibilities either to the private sector or to the states.[10]

In the eighties, the neoliberals seemed to be on the verge of a genuine alternative to Reaganism: combining venerable liberal ends with new market means. Charles Peters's plucky *Washington Monthly* was the best expression of neoliberal thinking: "We still believe," Peters wrote in 1983, "in liberty and justice and a fair chance for all, in mercy for the afflicted, and help for the down and out," but that desire led Peters to challenge the AMERICRATic status quo, not defend it. Criticizing entitlement spending, he took dead aim at the heart of the New Deal Big Offer:

> We want to eliminate duplication and apply a means-test to these pro-grams. As a practical matter the country can't afford to spend on people who don't need it . . . we don't think the well-off should be getting money from those programs anyway—every cent we can afford should go to helping those in real need.[11]

In opposition to the neoliberals were the "paleoliberals," the old-time Democrats who believed that Mondale was misunderstood—along with those Democrats in Congress who quietly realized that they themselves were better off with a Republican in the White House, not a Democrat with whom they would have to share intraparty influence.

Indeed, in the smoky rooms of Washington powerbrokerage, the light of the neoliberals proved ephemeral.[12] One leading "neo" was lost to the Circean call of expedience; when Dick Gephardt said he wanted to shed just about every responsibility the federal government has taken on since Jefferson's time, he was only a junior congressman from St. Louis. As a backbencher, Gephardt could afford to freethink. But when he got hungry for the presidency in 1988, he carbo-loaded on paleoliberalism. Trying to bulk up his appeal to Old Paradigmsters within the party, he buffed himself into a Japan-bashing protectionist as well.

Yet the wind of history blew against Gephardt; he lost the Democratic nomination to Dukakis, pedestalized in Rothenberg's neoliberal pantheon as a "tough, no-nonsense" Massachusetts Miracle-worker.[13] Dukakis, however, was defeated by George Bush after being portrayed as just another cuisinarting, belgian-endiving, arugula-waving north-eastern liberal presiding over a falling-soufflé economy. Yet even in defeat, Dukakis won 4 million more votes than Mondale had in 1984 and carried ten times as many states. Opinion-leading Democrats concluded that they might win the White House next time with an even newer kind of Democrat.

Pro-Business Democrats

Another piece of the Democratic comeback plan was a more "pro-business" orientation. The Democrats had always had their share of fatcats and fatcat factotums; from FDR's commerce secretary Jesse Jones to Lyndon Johnson to Lloyd Bentsen, Texas Democrats in particular had shown a special knack for wheeler-dealering.

Yet after Carter's defeat, the Democrats resolved to try harder. Seeing that the national party labored under an "antibusiness" image, Tsongas engineered a pro-business overhaul of northern Democrats. In a celebrated speech to the Americans for Democratic Action in June 1980, Tsongas had warned that efforts to raise taxes and regulation on corporations were harmful; such attacks on employers were being felt by employees.[14] The event that triggered his ideological reassessment was the 1979–80 Chrysler bailout.[15] The Massachusetts senator came away from that experience with a new vision, one which he would nurse along for a decade. Preparing to run for president in 1992, he issued *A Call To Economic Arms: Forging A New American Mandate*, in which he called for "strategic investments" as part of a new "national economic policy."[16] How did Tsongas define his ideology? "Pro-business, some would call it. And so it is. Aggressively so."[17]

With these words, Tsongas ironically summoned up the ghost of Jefferson's great Federalist nemesis, Alexander Hamilton, whose 1791 *Report on the Subject of Manufactures* has been an inspiration to American interveners, paternalizers, tariffers, and planners for two centuries. Tsongas argued that America had neglected this Hamiltonian heritage and the time had come to reclaim it: "Industrial policy is what Japan has. It is what Germany has. It is what we must have as well."[18]

Yet the key distinction that industrial policymakers, from Hamilton to Tsongas, have chosen to overlook is the difference between "pro-business" and "pro-market." There's nothing new about "pro-business" policies designed to help countries, as well as individuals, get rich; "mercantilism" was the name given to the potpourri of ad hoc fixes that were tried over the millennia to achieve this goal. The basic idea of mercantilism was that a country should sell more than it bought, so that it could hoard the differential. This trade strategy may have seemed sensible, but its practical application has always led to inside-dealing cronyism that restricted commerce and depressed the general standard of living. This self-defeating visible hand was what Adam Smith rebelled against; anti-mercantilism was at the core of his *Inquiry into the Nature and Causes of The Wealth of Nations*. Smith's treatise was so persuasive that it triggered a worldwide commercial revolution against the aristocratic economics of his time. Yet enemies of free trade and free markets, on both the Left and the Right, have still preferred to remain glutinated in neomercantilist policies, because these policies provide political power, as well as free lunches, to well-connected courtiers and contributors.

The Tsongas Tsynthesis, based more on politics than economics, attracted Democrats for three reasons:

First, it got the party off its anticorporate "limits to growth" jag of the seventies. Once again, Democrats proclaimed, they were the big-fisted party of boom, advocating even more growth than the incumbent Republicans. Of course, one of the luxuries of being out of power is that a party can promise anything.

Second, the Tsongas pro-business program offered the prospect of uniting the various factions of Democrats around their hardy-perennial ideas, big BOS government and the spending Upgrade. Even Republican businesspeople jumped on the industrial-policy bandwagon; there has never been a shortage of broad-minded bipartisans ready to receive a subsidy check. All the while, the Democrats could play Uncle Sugar, dispensing tax breaks and subsidies, keeping only their fair share for their own political needs. Former California representative Tony Coelho, The Man to See in the Reagan-outliving Ehrenhaltian Congress, was a master of such crony capitalism, in which corporate America PACed Democratic campaign coffers in return for political preferences.[19]

Third, the vast ambition of the pro-business agenda—to make America more like Japan or West Germany—fired the smoldering Synoptic embers in the hearts of Aspirers such as Robert Reich and Ira Magaziner. Reich co-authored a book on the Chrysler bailout[20] and then joined with Magaziner to write *Minding America's Business*, a paean to European-style industrial policy.[21] Once more, Hegelians were yearning for a heavenly holism: an economic plan that united quasi-capitalists and quasi-socialists in one blissful *koan*.[22]

The Tsynthesis bound Democrats together, but since Republicans ruled the White House, it was never bestowed upon the nation. So in the eighties, America saw entrepreneurs, not professors, leading the high-tech revolution. The biggest lesson to emerge was that the true policy mantra for encouraging economic activity is not planning, or infrastructure, or even capital, but rather humility—a genuine modesty about which industries and which products will flourish in the real world. The ultimate truth is not One Big Answer—but simply the fact that nobody knows; even the best and the brightest, sitting in an their office suites, aren't smart enough to identify the "sunrise" industries still over the horizon. The most eggheaded technocrats never guessed that Steve Jobs and Bill Gates, starting out as teenage college dropouts, would lead the personal computer revolution; no one heard of these micropreneurs until they emerged from their garages. Even Jobs and Gates didn't realize what they were doing; they were too busy doing it. If industrial policy had been in place for the past two decades, the bulk of "strategic investment" in computers would have gone to IBM or Burroughs or Honeywell—to subsidize the creation of better mainframes. Of course, since politics soon intrudes on even the most academic discussions when money is involved, such "investment" would have been Robert Byrded; instead of the thriving Silicon Valley in California, we'd have a well-financed but noncompetitive "Vacuum Tube Valley" somewhere in West Virginia.

New Democrats

Tsongas won the 1992 New Hampshire primary but stumbled on the way to the New York nominating convention. Besting him was Bill Clinton, who, as chairman of the Democratic Leadership Council, had honed a winning message that combined neoliberal smarts, pro-business savvy, and populist schmooze in one triumphal package.

Clinton began as a dark horse, but his thoroughbred idea-spinners proved to be Triple Crown material. Reich, Magaziner, and much of the resumé-ready Kennedy School faculty were on board early; the opinion-leading press corps came next. Once Clinton looked as if he might actually win, he attracted more Democrats, new and old, who were tired of losing presidential elections. And thus many paleo-Democrats clambered aboard, including the National Education Association and the American Federation of State, County, and Municipal Workers.

Clinton even enticed a slew of Republican-leaning tycoons and CEOs in 1992. As governor of Arkansas, he had been unabashedly pro-business, as his tight relationships with Wal-Mart, Tyson Foods, and the shadowy Stephens investment house all attested.

Clinton's most engaging modality was "New Democrat"; his themes of reciprocal responsibility, reinventing government, and national service were attractive to a Bush-fatigued nation. Yet Clinton soon found that it was easier to sell these newish ideas to the country than it was to his own Democratic party.

Could anyone have ever found a way to accommodate academics, business, and labor—New Democrats and Old—all under one party standard? Clinton, at least, couldn't do it; by 1994, the coalition of two years earlier was a sundered memory, much to the consternation of some of its cheerleaders. The late columnist Hobart Rowen complained in the *Washington Post* that business wasn't rallying to the Clinton cause, even though "it would be hard to match Clinton's series of overtures to business, starting with his commitment to industrial policy." Rowen reminded the recalcitrant that Clinton's " 'partnership' role to promote exports . . . has had the president himself and Commerce Secretary Ron Brown playing the role of adjunct salesmen."[23]

Thirty years after Mario Savio's antibureaucratic "free speech" movement, twenty years after Gary Hart's shot at Hubert Humphrey, ten years after Rothenberg's book highlighting the movement, the neoliberal/New Democrat reformation had been worn down by the reality that the Democratic party had not changed.[24] It was still the party of AMERICRAT, first, foremost, and seemingly forever.

The NEA, the Democrats, and EDUCRAT

In 1976, a new power came to the political front-and-center: the National Education Association, which has since become the biggest single pillar of paleoism; it has fossilized the forces of educational reform inside the Democratic party. The NEA had been gaining power for years, as poor-but-genteel schoolmarms were professionalized—and unionized—into a hard-knuckled organization assuming the vanguard leadership mantle once worn by the United Auto Workers. But the NEA's break into the bigtime came after it endorsed candidate Jimmy Carter early in the 1976 primaries. President Carter returned the favor, establishing the Department of Education three years later; DOEd became the juiciest chunk of Veal in the whole federal stockyard. The NEA has been tightening its tentacles ever since; it has created its own variant Operating System for education, which we can dub EDUCRAT.

EDUCRAT is now bigger than the NEA's 2 million members, bigger even than the total of 3.2 million people who work in the 15,000 public school districts across the U.S.[25] Indeed, the EDUCRATic machine includes trade associations, think tanks, and schools of education.

Yet EDUCRAT has been a mixed blessing for the Democrats. It's a source of political strength, but it's also a liability: as long as EDUCRAT remains in place, education will continue to decline. Critics point out that America spends more than $240 billion a year for public elementary and secondary schools, more than any other country in the world. For that money, America should have, as Ross Perot would say, a "world class" educational system; yet the EDUCRATed Democrats say little except "Spend more!" However, as long as the system of neo-Bismarckian bureaucratic monopolies stays in place, higher per-student spending will have little or no impact on student performance. Indeed, in the decade after President Reagan announced that poorly performing schools made America "a nation at risk,"[26] spending per pupil rose a full third in constant dollars.[27] Yet since 1965, average Scholastic Aptitude Test scores have declined so much that the Educational Testing Service changed the scoring of the exam, rather than report more downward results.

EDUCRATs understand that their system is held together by politics, not achievement. That's why the NEA, as well as the American Federation of Teachers, has become deeply immersed in politics—to protect its privileged position. EDUCRAT grew so strong inside the party that it was virtually immune from criticism, except from the pesky neoliberals.

Peters and the neos critiqued the public schools for their unionized bureaucracy, credentialism, and pedagogical obscurantism.[28] Yet the neoliberal prescription—merit pay, teacher testing, and an ill-defined stab at de-bureaucratization—was modest relative to the problem. The neoliberals were still Democrats, committed to living within the parameters of the Bureaucratic Operating System.

The overall timidity of the education debate within the Democratic party offended radicals who remembered the sixties, when idealists and activists sought to subvert the dominant paradigm. Los Angeles public interest lawyer Roy Ulrich asks: "If progressive women are pro-choice when it comes to their bodies, why are they anti-choice when it comes to their children? Why have we not heard from progressives on the school choice issue?" He answers: "Democratic officeholders have their own interest groups that they are beholden to . . . One such group is the education Establishment which is a major contributor to Democratic campaigns at all levels."[29]

One New Democrat who for a time ventured from EDUCRAT dogma was Bill Clinton. In 1990 he wrote to state representative Polly Williams, an African American Democrat from inner-city Milwaukee, praising her bureaucrat-busting private-school choice plan:

> I am fascinated by that proposal and am having my staff analyze it. I'm concerned that the traditional Democratic Party establishment has not given you more encouragement. The visionary is rarely embraced by status quo [sic]. Keep up the good work.[30]

Someone must have tattled on Clinton's off-the-reservation ramblings, because soon after, William Jefferson Clinton's neo-Jeffersonian notion of "power to the people" completely disappeared. As the NEA-endorsed candidate in 1992, Clinton faithfully mouthed the anti-choice NEA line; today, federal education policy is effectively dictated by the de facto Department of Education at NEA's 16th Street headquarters.

The Democrats' Need for a New Paradigm

The voters will always admire energetic optimism more than doleful cynicism or slothful complacency; one of the most attractive features about Clinton in 1992 was that he spoke to hopes, not fears. Like Marlon Brando in *On the Waterfront*, Clinton couldda been a contender in the battle for new ideas; instead, he sold himself out to the AMERI-CRATs and the EDUCRATs—and got a one-way ticket to Old Paradigm Palookaville.

Clinton was unable to break the dead grip of AMERICRAT and EDUCRAT, and the Democrats paid the price at the polls. By the midnineties, government and problem-solving were no longer seen as synonymous; they were seen as opposites. Even Al Gore and his tiny team of reinventeers could chip only flakes off the Gibraltar of bureau-cratic obsolescence.

Charles Peters, with his unerring sense of the bureaucratic imperative, was blunt: "The number-one goal of the typical bureaucrat is to protect his job." Applying the skewering insight that marginalizes him in his own party, Peters added:

> Deep in the bureaucrat's DNA is the awareness that if his agency attains its goal of, say, eliminating the energy crisis or solving the farm problem, the elimination of the agency and his job would follow. So the civil servant quickly learns to master the tools of make-believe—memoranda and meetings—so that he can appear to be busy while accomplishing little if anything.[31]

Contemplating the state of the Left on Labor Day 1994, the *Washington Post*'s E. J. Dionne, Jr., observed:

> The real problem for liberals and labor is that many of their leaders have let Americans forget that their whole reason for existing is *not* to create bureaucracies, enhance government power, inhibit change in the marketplace or redistribute somebody else's money.[32]

As we have seen, the definition of bureaucracy is "rule by offices"; it's no great surprise that office holders so persistently insist on "a role for government" in just about everything. Indeed, as the Democrats AMERICRATify into the party of the "gerunding" professions—teach-ing, nursing, social-working—it's natural that they insist, as a matter of class interest, on a substantial tax-paid role for people like themselves.

In November 1994, the voters caught on to the congressional Ehren-haltians, finally figuring out that their own Democratic lawmakers were part of the Washington gang supporting tax increases, health care sovietization, and pork-rinded crime bills.

Yet even after the midterm elections, the Democratic party has resisted rethinking. Indeed, since some of the more forward-looking Democrats, such as Tennessee's Jim Cooper and Oklahoma's Dave McCurdy, were defeated, the shrunken party's center of gravity has shifted Old-Paradigmatically. Yet the Democrats still have cause for complacency; even after losing both houses of Congress, they neverthe-less comprise two-thirds of all elected officials nationwide. It may seem obvious that the party can't survive too many more 1994-type debacles; yet reduced to minority status for the first time in four decades, Demo-crats in the House robotically reelected the survivors of the previous "leadership team" to carry their banner in the 104th Congress.

Many in the party hew to the view that the voters had a tantrum, a political colic attack; so the best thing to do is let the people have their big burp—and then pat-pat them back into the Democratic column in 1996.[33] Others declare fealty to the Old Paradigm because that's simply who they are. As one San Francisco supervisor put it in the wake of the 1994 election, in which city Democrats, bucking the national trend, actually scored gains: "We're conservative about our liberalism."[34]

What these responses have in common is that they forfeit any pretense of national leadership. Mark Mellman, a savvy Democratic pollster, was right when early in 1995 he outlined a plan for the Democrats to beat a strategic retreat, all the while looking for tactical opportunities: "Cuts in student loans, cuts in school lunches, and cuts in Medicare transform the debate, from one about general principles to a debate about spe-cifics."[35] In other words, the Democrats win when a given issue is particularized as "helping people"; the Republicans prevail when the debate is generalized, as in "big government," pro or con.

Mellman's approach can inflict casualties, but it concedes the idea advantage to the opposition—just as Nixon, in the early seventies, threw a Republican cloak over the Great Society.

Can the Democrats abandon what journalist Jonathan Rauch calls their "obsession with government"? Will the party sworn to help the middle class continue to defend a system in which, according to the Tax Foundation, the median two-income family paid more than 40 percent of its income in federal, state, and local taxes? The party that was once proud to represent the horny-handed sons of toil is now far more effective at protecting the interests of Oligarchic AMERICRATs; pollster Gordon Black discovered that nearly half of the 1992 Democratic convention delegates were employed by the government in some way.[36] Richard M. Daley, the three-term mayor of Chicago and son of the late six-term mayor, said recently of his party,

> The Democrats are the party of Washington. They are the party of the bureaucrats. They are the party of the special interests. They are the pro-tax party.[37]

It didn't have to be this way. Had the Vanderbilts figured out that they were in the transportation business, not the railroad business, a prosperous Vanderbilt Airways might be flying today. Had IBM determined itself to be the company of cutting-edge cybernetics, not just mainframes, Packard Bell and Gateway 2000 might be subsidiaries, not market-share-gaining rivals. Similarly, had the Democrats learned to defend their humane goals, not their bureaucratic institutions, they might have been able to slough off AMERICRAT and then EDUCRAT.

If the American Left lets itself be permanently linked to the failed status quo, then a hard rain is gonna fall. Or, as the pallid daughter said in the movie *Addams Family Values*: "Be afraid. Be very afraid." The Bureaucratic Operating System has broken down; the Democrats have no choice but to hearken back to their Jefferson-Jackson political roots. The greatest Democrat of this century, Franklin D. Roosevelt, proclaimed: "New conditions impose new requirements upon Government and those who conduct government."

With a wad-shot Clinton in the White House, with the Ehrenhaltian remnant in the Congress and EDUCRATs holding sway in the hinterlands, the prospect for a Democratic renaissance seem dim. And so the burden of leadership—and the challenge of fending off the Cyber Future—may well shift to the Republicans. Ready or not.

CHAPTER 12

THE REPUBLICANS

The dilemma of conservative ideology has been frequently posed as the unresolved wrestling match between the Culturalists and the Economists. Culturalists, such as William Bennett and Pat Robertson, are seen as a tag team, knocking heads with Economists such as Jack Kemp and Milton Friedman. But another split in Republican thinking—between Movement Conservatives and Republican Regulars—is equally significant.

Economists versus Culturalists

It's true, as Bennett and Robertson say, that dysfunctional "family values," spread across all strata of society, underlie some of the nation's most pressing social problems. From Murphy Brown to the stereotypical "welfare mother," single women struggling to raise children loom large in our popular and political culture.

Yet the phenomenon of single parenthood is a paradox of prosperity as well. People live longer and travel more; they are less content to spend a lifetime with one spouse, especially when they can flip on the

TV and see hardbodies on faraway beaches having fun, fun, fun. For many, the moral monopoly of tradition has been broken. People are free now—free to find their true selves, free to abandon their families. And they can afford to: U.S. per capita GNP is around $25,000. Enough money sloshes around the private sector to ensure that most people have the resources, in personal savings, rich uncles, or siblings with extra bedrooms, to survive family trauma. Yet as the writer Peggy Noonan has observed, it's hard for the media and political elites to talk about the sanctity of the family unit when so many of them, too, are divorced.

In such a socioeconomic environment, the power of big government to strengthen the family looks pitifully small. Republicans in particular, if they truly believe in limited government, should accept limits on government's efficacy, even to accomplish things they favor. David Blankenhorn, indicting American society for contributing to a "culture of fatherlessness," concludes, in his book *Fatherless America*, that only a spiritual revolution, a great awakening of paternal feeling—"the re-creation of fatherhood as a vital social role for men"[1]—can save America.

Yet as Dan Quayle discovered, Americans don't like to be lectured to, certainly not by politicians. Richard Weaver, a conservative hall-of-famer for his book *Ideas Have Consequences*, warned nearly half a century ago: "We must avoid . . . the temptation of trying to teach virtue directly, a dubious proceeding at any time and one under special handicaps in our age."[2] Today, America is even more diversified, multicultured, and 500-channeled; it's hard to imagine any politician, no matter how pure or well intentioned, saying much of anything that wouldn't generate an equal and opposite reaction from somewhere.

So if preaching is best handled by preachers, what role is left for government in shaping the culture? How can society create the circumstances in which people make better personal choices and stand firmly by them? The most realistic answer is to focus on the economic side of reform—not because culture is less important, but because the government is better at leveraging explicit economic Operating Systems than implicit social Operating Systems.

So the Republicans should start humbly, with the political equivalent of the Hippocratic Oath: first, do no harm. Tellingly, the cultural crisis is most acute where Vealocratic government intervenes the most: in the lives of the poor. When government taxing and spending policies favor nonwork, the usual result is not only less work but also the loss of a work ethic. Phil Gramm spoke for the Economists when he said, "We're going to try to deal with the collapse in morality by changing a system that has corroded the values of our people."[3]

The government can also address other family disincentives built into the economic system. Among the socially counterproductive distortions that crept back into the IRS code after the 1993 tax bill was the "marriage penalty": the additional income tax paid by a man and a woman simply because they are married to each other. The National Bureau of Economic Research reported that a family of four, with a husband and a wife each earning $50,000 a year, would have to pay $4,348 more in tax than if the man and the woman were not married.[4] Tax considerations won't have much effect on behavior in Manhattan and Hollywood, but reducing Uncle Sam's bite on matrimony would send a pro-marriage message to Heartland America.

From a partisan Republican point of view, the Economists have another advantage: practical politics. Whereas the Culturalists tend toward Spenglerian doomsaying, Kemp-style Economists offer Rotarian hopesaying—and as we have noted before, the American people would rather vote their hopes than their fears. Some might say that Kemp gets carried away with his relentless upbeatitudes, as when he says, "If the Republican Party would replace urban socialism with urban democratic capitalism—access to capital, credit property, education, job training and ownership—I believe we could turn the inner city of East Harlem or East LA into another Hong Kong."[5] Yet across the country, GOP mayors and governors have been most successful when they pushed Economistic restructuring: tax cuts, school choice, and incentive-based welfare reform.[6]

Movement Conservatives versus Republican Regulars

For a half-century after the New Deal, the Republicans, even when they were the minority, seemed to be the Old Guard. Most GOPers of that era—the Deweys and the Tafts, the Bushes and the Michels—were united in their reflexive commitment to preserving what they could of Lincolnian postbellum America. After all, for most of this century, it was their institutions—property, business, traditional Main Street/mainstream Protestant values—that were under assault from the Left.

Yet as the New Deal Big Offer ripened, the burden of "conserving" the status quo began to shift, from the Right to the Left. It became the Democrats who pledged to maintain AMERICRAT and the Bureaucratic Operating System. Jimmy Carter and Walter Mondale were both defeated in part because they seemed more anxious to defend the past accomplishments of liberalism than to talk about making things better in the future. In 1992, Clinton seemed "new" because he sounded determined to change that retrodynamic; yet as we have seen, he too was trapped in the gravity field of the Old Paradigm.

Beyond the divide between Culturalists and Economists—as well as the generation gap between "Young Turks" and "Old Bulls," or even between the "People's" House and the slower-moving Senate—lies the fault line between Movement Conservatives and Republican Regulars.

In the spirit of their hero, Ronald Reagan, the Movement Conservatives see themselves as the wave of the future, not the past; they are little interested in conserving anything we see today. Reagan may have called himself a conservative, but he was in fact half-radical and half-reactionary: aiming to go forward into a better future—based on the Golden Age past—by demolishing the present. It was Reagan, not Carter or Mondale, who dreamed, in radical Tom Paine's words, of "beginning the world over again."

The Movement's ideological identity transcends loyalty to anything so prosaic as the Republican party. Indeed, in the seventies, when the GOP seemed hopelessly thralled by Ford-type Regulars, Movementers flirted with forming a true-believing third party. Reagan's ascendancy in 1980 made such talk of secession moot; yet even today, the Movement is quietly contemptuous of the Regulars, whom they view as mere drones, more interested in country-club camaraderie than in storming the barricades of liberalism.

The Movement is defined by cutting-edge positions on guns, God, and government; it keeps its national consciousness raised via Rush Limbaugh, the *Wall Street Journal*'s editorial page, and a variety of party-bypassing pressure groups, such as the National Rifle Association, the

Christian Coalition, and Americans for Tax Reform. The Maximum Leader is House Speaker Newt Gingrich. For a man of the Right, Gingrich is extremely sparing in his references to traditional conservative icons such as Aristotle or Adam Smith but is unstinting in his citations of modernizing twentieth-century technocrats such as Peter Drucker and W. Edwards Deming. Gingrich owes less to Russell Kirk, author of *The Conservative Mind*, than to Captain Kirk, leader of the starship *Enterprise*.[7] Gingrich paid his dues, after a cyberfashion, orating to an empty House all through the eighties, with only C-SPAN cameras watching. They all laughed then; today, dozens of former cable-TV junkies are serving with Speaker Gingrich in the Congress.

The Movement, blessed with the gift of agenda-setting articulation, exudes a Victor Hugo-esque confidence that no one can stop ideas—their ideas—whose time has come. And they are convinced that the Old Paradigm will not stand. The greatest challenge they face, as we shall see, is what to replace it with.

By contrast, the Republican Regulars are less interesting. Just as a fish never thinks about water, so Regulars lack ideological self-awareness; they are too willing to go with the flow of the Old Paradigm. Regulars like to think of themselves as pragmatic problem solvers, but that really means they serve the conventional wisdom. As Keynes wrote sixty years ago, practical men, believing themselves immune to any intellectual influences, are usually the unwitting slaves to some dead economist or philosopher. George Bush inherited the shambles of previous Big Offers and discovered what happens to in-box managerialism in a hard-drive-crashing environment. Today, GOP Regulars—actually, the right wing of the Old Paradigm—still seek to boot up the Bureaucratic Operating System. What Regulars lack in passion they make up for in numbers; they are the bulk of the party, literally its rank and file.

Yet Movementers are right to claim credit for the Republicans' massive 1994 election triumph; it was the Contract with America that cut a clear channel to victory through the apathetic clutter of talk shows and soaps suds. While polls show that only a fraction of voters knew the details of the House Republicans' Contract with America, people were aware that the Republicans had some sort of shake-'em-up plan, and that was good enough to attract the swing Perotistas and give the GOP its best midterm election results in half a century. The Movement encompasses oft-antipodal Culturalists and Economists, but in 1994, uniting in a common commitment to attack-activism, both found a deeper unity in anti-Arkansasism.

1994 and Beyond

The strength, as well as the weakness, of the Movement-inspired Contract with America was its neo-Reaganism. Reagan may have altered world history, but his domestic political Big Offer faltered; when he left office his party was well short of the numbers or agenda it needed for realignment into majority status.

Gingrich was a remarkable leader of the opposition in 1993–94—all the more remarkable because he was in fact Number 2 in the minority Republican hierarchy at the time. His rise was powered by the Movement, the flying wedge of vanguard ideologues. The Contract with America was Gingrich's soundbited distillation of what he knew from a lifetime of plotting and thinking; the Contract will be remembered as the most effective vote-vacuuming partisan manifesto in modern times.

That is no small achievement. If journalists emphasized the failures of the Contract's "100 Days," dwelling mostly on the defeat of such high-profile sideshows as the Balanced Budget Amendment and term limits, the judgment of history will likely be different. Other enacted reforms, securing property rights against "takings" and immunizing local governments against unfunded mandates, will spill out their ramifications for decades to come.

As for the lowering of the long-term trajectory of government spending in the wake of the Contract, we can consider just one provision: the enactment of the line-item veto. Ronald Reagan said that the greatest regret of his presidency was that he lacked this tool for spending control. It's an irony that Bill Clinton, no enemy of government spending, may be the first president to wield the item veto.

Yet the Republicans had not yet taken control of the 104th Congress when Jesse Jackson said that the GOP had declared "war on the poor."[8] It's true that if the Republicans decide to wash their hands of the Other

America, the American dilemma of poverty and racism won't go away; what remains of the middle class will just continue to pay for a slightly downsized welfare system that serves people with smaller portions and even lower quality. And other problems, from crime to prison costs, will continue to replicate, spiraling America toward the Cyber Future.

So long as the Democrats remain in the White House, the Republicans should have the easier task; they can exercise power without responsibility for the state of the union. However, when Clinton is reduced to asserting, to a skeptical country, that he is "relevant," the Gingrichian Contractors will likely feel obligated to fill the Washington power void. But to succeed in that goal, agenda-setting Movementers will have to overcome the pitfalls that have snared both the Culturalists and the Economists in the past.

GOP Traps

The Republican hurdles on the road to majoritarian realignment include one genuine moral quandary as well as two traps. First, they must reconcile the seemingly irreconcilable: the party's deep division over abortion. Second, they must overcome the lingering feeling that they are Culturally intolerant on gay rights and, at an international level, chauvinistic toward foreign trade and immigration. Third, they must resolve to do better on two closely related Economic failings: a perception of unfairness and the consequent ineffectiveness of the Republican agenda.

Emptying the Backpack

Bob Teeter, the respected pollster-turned-frustrated Bush campaign manager, complained in 1992 that the GOP could be likened to a hiker with a knapsack, picking up bricks along the way. Every time the Republicans adopted a difficult-to-defend position—such as the absolutist no-exceptions "Human Life Amendment," support for assault weapons, or mandatory school prayer—it was as if they had picked up another brick and put that deadweight in the knapsack. Eventually, the Republicans couldn't move; their backs broke. Defeat in 1992 offered the GOP the chance to empty out its overloaded pack, losing the mostly Culturalist bricks it had and provisioning itself with better intellectual trail mix for the nineties, yet the temptation is always present to stock up once again on bricks.

The social-issue showdown so many Culturalists had girded their loins for finally took place at the Houston convention, where it seemed to many Americans that the ayatollahs were in ascendancy. Pollster Gordon Black, who earlier noted the government dependency of Democratic conventioneers, found that 47 percent of the delegates to the 1992 Republican convention considered themselves "born-again Christians."[9] Since the Religious Right was the last loyal linchpin of the Bush-busted Republican confederation, it had the president by his broccolis in Houston. Robertsonian platform-writers pushed the erstwhile Planned Parenthood activist to the ideological edge of the earth, writing a right-to-life plank that called for a ban on *all* abortions.[10] The activists' exertions brought victory in the verbal battle of the August convention but helped bring about defeat for the GOP in the November election. In the words of Dan Quayle, "we scared off the party's moderates and some independent voters."[11]

Abortion

Virtually all Republican political professionals privately admit that the abortion issue is an albatross around the neck of the GOP. However, abortion is such a profound ethical concern that it is unfair to categorize it as a mere trap that foolish or mean-spirited GOPers stumble into. Armstrong Williams, an African American radio talk show host, speaks from the heart when he asserts that abortion is "the great moral issue of our day"; he goes on to compare abortion to the Holocaust and slavery, issuing a stern warning to the GOP not to abandon the defense of "the foremost Constitutional right, the right to life."[12]

Yet it is still true that the "hard core" right-to-life position favored by most Movementers is a serious detriment to GOP electoral prospects. To Republicans who say that the mission of the party must be to fight for life, the late Lee Atwater had the right answer: distinguish, he said, between ideologies, which tend toward the monolithic, and parties, which must be inclusive. In a free country, people are entitled to their opinions, but in a democracy, to win majorities, parties must be "big tents." Atwater's goal was to "catch" voters agreeing with the GOP— to take advantage of similarities, not to find differences. Haley Barbour, Chairman of the Republican National Committee, echoes the point: "A fellow who agrees with you 80 percent of the time is your friend and ally, not a 20 percent traitor." Yet American wariness about the GOP's ultimate true intentions has given the Democrats one of their best issues: defending a woman's right to choose. Indeed, Barbour is as wary as a scalded dog when the question of including abortion in the 1996 GOP platform arises.[13]

In the pages of *National Review*, conservative intellectuals William Kristol and George Weigel offer a more solid strategy. After a thousand words of throat-clearing designed to reassure pro-lifers, Kristol and Weigel get to the point: "Taking account of current political realities," the GOP must undergo "a strategic redeployment in the matter of abortion."[14] The Republicans don't need to be *the* pro-life party; they simply must be *more* pro-life than the Democrats. Thus they can reflect both the antiabortion beliefs of Catholics and evangelical Protestants and the pro-choice beliefs of libertarian free-enterprisers. Kristol and Weigel are both pro-life, but their argument is not intended to change people's soul-felt beliefs; it is intended to warn Republicans of the practical consequences of their actions.

The Republicans followed the Kristol–Weigel line in 1994; Gingrich's Contract with America was a secular document, a carefully crafted continuation of the GOP's less-government stance—a focus-grouped flock of tax and spending cuts targeted to the yuppie libertarianism of swing suburbanites. Such repositioning of Republicanism worked for a while; Ralph Reed, director of Pat Robertson's Christian Coalition, said at the beginning of 1995 that his top priority was the enactment of the Contract. This alliance of Park Avenue and the trailer park beckoned the GOP with the prospect of dominating American politics for a generation.

Then came the inevitable: the social-issue spark that ignited the passions of the Movement. The kindling in question was Dr. Henry Foster, Clinton's nominee to be Surgeon General. His initially confused accounting of his own record as an obstetrician front-and-centered the issue of abortion. Say good-bye to cool and cerebral discussions of the flat tax; say hello to hot and visceral wrangling over teen sex. Reed was a changed man; loin-girded for Armageddon, he declared that the Republicans must write a pro-life platform and nominate a pro-life ticket in 1996.[15] The shrinking sound that GOPers heard was the folding of the once-inclusive "big tent" of Republicanism—as Reed and his Religious Right allies sought to exclude from national-ticket consideration pro-choicers with attractive ideologies and geographies. Specifically bulls-eyed were New Jersey governor Christine Todd Whitman and California governor Pete Wilson. Democratic spin doctors were already composing their attack riffs: "Republicans Dance to the Anti-Choice Tune of Fundamentalists." And so the tax-and-spend debate that the Republicans can win threatens to be replaced by the fire-and-brimstone brouhaha that the Republicans always lose.

Was this unfolding of events the fruit of some grand plan by the Democrats to drive the Republicans "off-message"—to divert the Republicans from their strongest issues, economic growth and reducing the size of government, and toward their greatest vulnerability, the "below the belt" issues of sex and privacy? Clinton is probably not that clever, but he may be that lucky.

The Republicans were historically the party of Episcopalians who supported contraception and abortion in part to help suppress the Catholic population. Yet in the two decades since the Supreme Court's *Roe* v. *Wade* decision legalized abortion, the GOP has been demographically transformed by two pro-life groups fleeing the Democrats: Catholics and southern evangelicals. Yet if their goal is victory, the new Republicans must be careful. Pro-choice Senator Arlen Specter of Pennsylvania is probably not destined to be the next Republican president, but he is right when he says to his fellow GOPers, "If abortion stays in the platform, we will give Bill Clinton his best chance—and perhaps his only chance—to be reelected." It remains to be seen whether a Republican leader can emerge to synthesize a compromise that enables the GOP to stay together and also win elections.

Yet the next great leader of the Republican party must also find a way to extricate the Republicans from two traps: its frequent, gratuitous hostility to gays and what might be called its "nasty nationalism."

Trap #1: Intolerance

The GOP has been called the Christian Party, which makes many Republicans proud and many Americans fearful. The irony is that this double-edged perception is not even accurate. According to one exhaustive study, New Agers are among the most Republican of religious groups—vastly more Republican than Catholics and even more pro-GOP than such traditionally Republican Protestant denominations as Methodists and Christian Scientists.[16] Yet the GOP, for all its professed determination to displace the Democrats as the majority party, sometimes seems determined to antagonize potential voters such as gays and minorities.

Anti-Gay Rights

Los Angeles retailer Mark Hoffmann is one of many registered Republicans who were so repelled by the Houstonized GOP that they could not bring themselves to vote for Bush in 1992. Hoffmann, who happens to be gay, voted for Perot.

Conservatives and Republicans, before they open their mouths on gay issues—and lose more votes—should pause and ask themselves a question Mario Cuomo once posed: "What if someone in your family were gay?" Cuomo's point reached new poignancy for the Right when the grandson of Barry Goldwater, the son of conservative activist Phyllis Schlafly, the daughter of Bush's Commerce Secretary Robert Mosbacher, and the sister of Newt Gingrich all came out of the closet.

Gay political power is here to stay. Mobility and prosperity have concentrated gays and their wealth in highly visible financial and cultural power centers. New York City and San Francisco—and lesser-known locales, such as Northhampton and Provincetown in Massachusetts—have in effect become lifestyle enterprise zones. This is a sharp change from the past, when closeted gays and lesbians—"confirmed bachelors" and "spinsters"—lived lonely, isolated, politically unconscious existences in small towns. Today's urban clustering-by-affinity heightens gay political and economic influence. The gay community is now able to elect its own representatives, who in turn can leverage their way into larger coalitions.

Yet the current coalition that most gays find themselves in offers little in return. Their alliance with the Old Paradigm Left is held in place by fear and loathing of Senator Jesse Helms, not by objective mutual interest. The *Advocate*, a leading gay magazine, quotes New Yorker Christopher Lynn, a lifelong Democrat who endorsed Republican Rudy Giuliani's 1993 mayoral candidacy:

> For years I've been active in city politics as a Democrat, but in recent years I have been genuinely concerned about the ability of the city to survive. My life partner and I bought an expensive apartment, and we want to stay here. David Dinkins was a swell guy with great positions on our issues, but I felt that Giuliani had more to say on all the other issues that matter to me.[17]

Mayor Giuliani, who ran on a law-and-order platform, won 31 percent of self-identified gay voters. That's not a lot, but it's an improvement from his gay-vote catch four years before. New York City's first Republican leader in a generation says: "There is no reason why the party shouldn't appeal to gays and lesbians in the same way it does to all Americans."[18] Rich Tafel, national director of the gay Log Cabin Republicans, slammed pundit and presidential wannabe Pat Buchanan for criticizing Giuliani's pro–gay rights stand: "If Pat Buchanan were a true Republican, he would spend a lot more time working to liberate families of New York from high taxes, spiraling crime and Democrat corruption rather than trying to punish Republicans who disagree with him on gay rights."[19] Tafel has a point: the failures of the Old Paradigm, nowhere more visible than in the big cities, present an opportunity for the GOP to reach out to urban constituencies.

These basic issues exceed the symbolism of "gays in the military" or whatever other cause sends a crowd spilling out into highly visible but unrepresentative media magnets such as Christopher Street. Books by gay conservatives—*Coming Out Conservative*, the autobiography of ex–William Buckley associate Marvin Liebman, and *Stranger at the Gate*, from Mel White, a former speechwriter for Jerry Falwell—suggest that if the Right quit castigating voters, it would reap a thresher full of votes currently plowed under or left fallow. And from the point of view of the Right, such snubbing is actually worse than simply neglecting a potential harvest. In politics, unlike business, defeated enemies don't go out of business and disappear; they still show up on the next Election Day to give the opposition candidate their franchise.

Log Cabinites make the point that Republicans don't have to do anything positive to attract gay voters; they just have to be consistent in the application of their limited-government philosophy. The proof that this live-and-let-live principle can reap results comes from the *New York Times*'s exit polls. In 1992, Republican Congressional candidates got 23 percent of the gay vote. In 1994, Republicans won 40 percent, an increase of 17 points, far more than the 4-point increase in the GOP vote overall.[20] This gay upswing does not suggest that gays are suddenly all becoming Republicans, but it suggests that "Houston" abnormally suppressed the gay GOP vote.

To get gay votes, the Republicans need not invite RuPaul to sing the national anthem at their next convention. They simply need tolerance, an allowance for different strokes for different folks. Even Cultural Republicans ought to reconsider how much morals policing they want to see, knowing that every cop in the bedroom is one less on the street. Steve Gunderson, elected as a Reagan Republican in 1980, was for years coy about his orientation, but in 1994 he didn't object when the *Advocate* headlined him as "Our Third Openly Gay Congressman."[21] Gunderson is now unapologetic about his politics as well as his sexuality, asserting that the Republicans "seek a strong national security to allow maximum liberty and opportunity for each individual."[22]

A unifying GOP leader will not seek to impose a Greenwich Village solution on Utah, or vice versa. He or she will show both gays and straights that they are better off in a constructive alliance for choice, markets, and empowerment than they are when locked in a mutually destructive antagonism.

Nasty Nationalism

The Republican Party has a chance to be the majority party based on a new paradigm of new ideas and inclusivity—although apparently that's not what every Republican wants. The great white hope for the Old Paradigm Right is Pat Buchanan, calling for aggressive "Americanism." One might call it patriotism, and yet it is the sort of in-your-face nationalism that has become the refuge for those seeking to wrap their prejudices in the American flag.

Nationalism once marched mostly with militarism; the two are still in formation, but the new alliance on the right wing of the Old Paradigm is nationalism and protectionism. Buchanan ardently opposed both the North American Free Trade Agreement and the General Agreement on Tariffs and Trade. Yet protectionism has been so discredited as an economic theory since the disastrous Depression-deepening Smoot-Hawley Tariff that we must look elsewhere for the true wellsprings of its support. The real appeal of protectionism is xenophobia: fear of anything foreign. Buchanan and his nativist comrades-in-arms are hostile to imports, immigrants, internationalism, and anything else that smacks of cosmopolitanism. Buchanan wrote in 1994 that GATT was "un-American."[23] Going further into bare-knuckled nationalism, he pushes his isolationist ideology in the most provocative possible terms.

Buchanan makes little effort to hide the ugly undertones of his ideology. He uses "culture war" and *kulturkampf* interchangeably, giving his audiences a choice between American-style conflict and its German cousin. In case anyone misses his point, he calls his platform "America First," the motto of Nazi-honored Charles Lindbergh and other appeasers of the thirties. No less a conservative luminary than William Buckley opined that Buchanan was an anti-Semite.[24] Indeed, after the GATT vote, Buchanan accused internationalists of propagating the "Great Myth of the twentieth century"; he surely knows that his formulation echoes the title of Nazi propagandist Alfred Rosenberg's 1930 anti-Semitic tract, *Myth of the 20th Century.*[25]

The Mexican peso plummet of late 1994 was a bonanza for Buchanan. Whatever the merits of the issue, he seized the I-told-you-so ground, using the moment to describe the situation in terms not heard from a presidential candidate in years. He described "transnational companies, the Big Banks, the One Worlders," as a conspiracy against "Middle America." Fortunately, he added, "economic nationalists" stand atop the *Kultur*-ramparts, ready to rain unquenchable hellfire on the cosmopolitan "power elite."[26] Characteristically, Buchanan has taken an argument over economic policy into an edgy crypto-discussion on ethnicity; he relishes every word as he rips into Clinton's Mexico policy, which he derides as little more than a payoff to "the friends of Robert Rubin and Alan Greenspan," noting that America needs Reaganomics, not "Goldman Sachs-onomics." Such words are dynamite, but exploding the contemporary Republican party seems to be Buchanan's minimum objective.

Trap #2: Unfairness/Ineffectiveness

If some Culturalists fall into the hole of intolerance, the Economists sometimes trip into the trap of seeming unfairness, which in the past has also rendered them ineffective. It follows that if the Republicans can solve the fairness problem, they will accomplish more.

Since GOP economics today is Reaganomics as redacted by the Contract, we should reexamine David Frum's point in *Dead Right* that the Reagan–Bush Republicans failed in the fight against Big Government; today, Frum says, conservatives should try again. Indeed, the new generation of Republicans should prove their fairness—and thus enhance their effectiveness—by "ceremoniously and ostentatiously decapitating" programs that benefit GOP constituencies, including shipbuilders, military-industrial complexers, and the Vealtors orbiting NASA. One piece of low-hanging fiscal fruit that a truly cost-conscious GOP would have plucked long ago is the National Endowment of Democracy. The $34 million-a-year entity is bipartisan, but its staunchest support has come from nostalgic neo-Reagan-Doctrining Cold Warriors. Yet in the words of *CBS News*'s Eric Engberg, the NED mostly exists today "so D.C. insiders can see the world."[27] The NED may only account for 1/50,000 of the federal budget, but leadership consists of small gestures as well as big strokes.

In the same self-abnegating spirit, one might ask why the triumphant Republicans didn't begin the 104th Congress with some true Capitol Hill belt-tightening. The GOP lawmakers noisily cut committee staffs by 30 percent, but they didn't touch their own personal staffs; the latter are the busy bees who do all the constituent service and write all the letters that turn incumbents into a new species: Republican Ehrenhaltians. Indeed, the defeat of term limits in 1995 underlined the fact that Republicans are just as eager as the Democrats to make public service a lifelong entitlement. Having shown no interest in sending themselves home, they also displayed no eagerness for exemplary shared-sacrifice dieting: the Republicans neither cut their generous pay—$133,000 a year—nor their even more munificent pensions.[28] And whatever of the promise to sell off a House office building as a 1994 "Christmas present" for the American people? Perhaps some Movementers, having stormed the Washington pleasuredome, are already finding themselves seduced by its Xanadunic gratifications.

Having done little to demonstrate a willingness to de-feather its own nest, the congressional GOP then proceeded to cut spending—on the poor. In a remarkably inept bit of positioning, let alone morality, Republicans managed to kick off their 1995 spending-cut crusade, not with slashes in subsidies to corporations, but rather with reductions in school lunches. Whether the policy was defensible or not, what Washingtonians call "the optics" of that policy were flawed.[29]

Perhaps the single most execrable upward income-transfer in all of BOS is federal subsidies to agriculture. According to Republican Pete DuPont, former governor of Delaware, "The average farmer is twice as rich as the average taxpayer and earns about 25 percent more each year"; he adds that two-thirds of the subsidies "go to the largest 15 percent of all farms."[30] Yet only days after the 1994 election, Gingrich was already backing and hoeing on agricultural subsidies; with Kansas's Pat Roberts, the new Republican chairman of the House Agriculture Committee, looking over his shoulder, Gingrich retrograded about "level playing fields"[31] for U.S. farmers in the international market— always code for the continuation of welfare for Agro-Americans.

On such issues, Gingrich hardly stands out from the herd, but that's the point: the 1994 elections were supposed to spell change from government-as-usual. The history of the 104th Congress would have been different if more Republicans had taken the tack of Indiana senator Dick Lugar. As the new chairman of the Agriculture Committee, farm-stater Lugar earned respect as well as attention by broaching the subject of eliminating agriculture subsidies.[32]

GOPers did away with budgetary baselines in their own calculations, but they were unable to break the "baseline mentality"—the fiscal equivalent of the old Soviet Brezhnev Doctrine—which assumed that the state had first claim on resources, no matter what else might be happening in the U.S. economy.[33] Many Republicans were Finlandized. Before the 100 Days of the Contract were up, they were reduced to defensively bleating: "We're not cutting spending; we're cutting the rate of spending increases." The Republicans were hindered because they were trying to serve two objectives; they wanted to cut government spending overall while protecting their own particular constituents. The Republicans would have been more effective at deficit reduction if they had been both more rigorous and more fair.[34]

Crude gaffes made by would-be welfare-cutting Republicans—in which they repeatedly analogized poor children to animals[35]—hardly helped the GOP cause, but their real problem was structural, not rhetorical. In part because they were not willing to impose sacrifice on themselves and their friends, the Republicans lost the moral high ground on the issue of welfare reform; they could no longer offer a comprehensive critique of a system that costs more than $300 billion a year and yet leaves poverty on the rise. And so when the opposition accused the Republicans of wanting to take bread out of children's mouths to give it in the form of tax cuts to the rich, the party was thrown on the defensive. Thus did unfairness lead to ineffectiveness.

Without thinking through the secondary and tertiary ramifications of what they were proposing—and without taking time to make tangible to the public their own vision of what a Gingrichified welfare program would look like—the Contract Republicans tried simply to ram spending cuts through Congress. Yet author Richard Cornuelle explained thirty years ago why frontal assaults on spending don't work: "The starvation strategy ignores the fundamental force behind government's growth"[36]—which is that unmet human needs continue to arise amidst the widening circle of American compassion and collective responsibility.

Past attempts to lop off programs foundered over the basic question: "What will you replace them with?" As detailed earlier, the Stockmanesque head-on strategy—chop, slash, and gut—met a Pickett's Charge–like rebuff. With the exception of the Clinch River breeder reactor and a few other programmatic odds and ends, Reagan's spending-cut offensive never captured much territory, despite appalling political casualties. America may be more conservative today than it was in 1981, but not so conservative that it will sit still for blanket repeal of the New Deal Big Offer.[37]

Gingrich has always been careful to say that America must "replace" the welfare state, even though many of his supporters would say "abolish" it. Yet much of Gingrich's talk is either careless or else deliberately provocative; the Georgian gives new resonance to the word "polarizing." Activists adore him for his tell-it-like-they-think-it-is rhetoric; when he dichotomizes America into "McGoverniks" versus "normal Americans," when he accuses Democrats of "despicable demagoguery," when he labels one reporter "a remarkably foolish person" and the media in general "shameful" and "socialist"—he rises to the high pedestal once occupied by former vice president Spiro Agnew, the Bambino of Republican press-bashing. It is true that many newspaper editorialists are, as he says, the "mortal enemies" of neo-Reaganism, but Lincoln was correct when he said that the best way to conquer enemies is to make them friends. And as with Lincoln more than a century ago, the only way to overcome foes with friendship is through an idea-advantaged Big Offer. It is that knowledge edge which the Gingrichified Republicans forfeited in 1995, at least in the area of social welfare. The speaker's fate will ultimately be determined by something he should know well— Newtonian physics, which posits that every action creates an equal and opposite reaction.

Gingrich has seen that the Old Paradigm cannot stand, but he hasn't given shape to a new paradigm that might replace the Bureaucratic Operating System.[38] Most likely, America will get beefy tax cuts and watery domestic reform; the policy equivalent of "mystery meat" will be left bobbing in the transparent gruel of spending recisions. And what remains of the Bureaucratic Operating System will remain, defaulted in place till the next economic or social shock.

For years to come, the fall of every sparrow from the sky will be blamed on "Gingrich spending cuts." As plutocrats as well as paupers proliferate in the cyberizing nineties economy, this decade will likely bring a second anti-eighties backlash. Yet the continuing William Gibsonization of society guarantees that the disparities of the nineties will be even more spectacular than they were in the time of Trump. And a much higher baseline of pathology—the nationwide illegitimacy rate has nearly doubled since 1980—virtually guarantees that the Republicans will be marked as Scrooges causing ever-greater skews.

As we have seen, the phenomenon of income disparity has been so overwhelming in recent decades that it rose not only during the great inflation of the seventies, but also during the tax cutting of the eighties and the tax increases of the nineties. Looking ahead, we can spy this megatrend: with the Republicans running Congress, and perhaps soon the White House, which is more likely to improve: the investment climate for billionaires, or the life prospects of welfare recipients?

The most idealistic Movement Republicans will try to bring markets, empowerment, and entrepreneurship to the poor; the worst will simply want to unplug the iron lung of the Old Paradigm. Democrats, locked in their fatalistic mind-set, will resist everything—and stop many things. Meanwhile, the traditional Republican enthusiasm for cutting taxes on capital will get out in front of their untraditional interest in reforming the welfare state, and the focus of GOP attention will revert back to the business of business. Thus the RPM of the money wheel will accelerate: the top quintiles of the country will benefit enormously; those below will continue to be ill served by rip-off bureaucracies.

Without the leaven of new leadership, the American people will then face a cruel conundrum: Old Paradigm institutions deserve defunding, but poor people trapped within them deserve a better deal, too. In the past, there would have been alternating Schlesingerian cycles of liberalism and conservatism, with public purposes coming along just in time to mitigate private acquisitiveness. That may yet happen, but the vision of the cyberpunks tells us that in the future there will be no countervailing swing toward redistribution—because the social contract will have crashed.

The Republican Window of Opportunity

As the self-styled "revolutionary" party, the Republicans have the chance to take history into their hands and reshape it for the benefit of all. Yet they seem determined to sail in two directions at once.

From one direction blows the wind of history—the great gust of de-communization, de-socialization, and de-bureaucratization that is blowing across the planet. If the Republicans could set their sails to harness that great force, it would carry them far.

From the other direction blusters hot air. Intolerance, unfairness and ineffectiveness still dog the GOP. The Republicans have spent so much time in the past year offering insults and imprecations that they could lose their window of opportunity; a critical mass of Americans are coming to view the GOP as little changed. And so America is indeed left with a neo-Reagan Small Offer: spending cuts without transformation, politics without the hope of a unifying, idea-advantaged new-paradigm-inspired Big Offer.

If the Democrats were still emitting brain waves, the Republicans would face trouble. But as we have seen, the historic edge of the Democrats— their Roosevelt-era idea advantage—has been overwhelmed by the gear-grinding failure of the Bureaucratic Operating System. All the Democrats' Ehrenhaltian apple-polishing has come to naught, because hustle can't overcome the fact that Democrats are still championing more government at more cost. Clinton's ideology of empathy cannot repair the faltering BOS.

The Republicans hope that the Democrats go the way of the British Labour Party in the early eighties: a shrunken coalition, bobbing leftward. The Democrats hope that the Republicans, drunk on their own dogma, Savonarola-ize themselves. Both dreams may well come true. But it's possible to imagine an America in which anti-Democratic votes do not benefit the Republicans and vice versa, leaving the U.S. with something previously thought to be mathematically impossible: two minority parties.

Today, neither party has the intellectual or moral stature to make a Big Offer to the nation. The problems aren't the result of bad people; they are the result of a bad paradigm. Overcoming the embedded architecture of the Bureaucratic Operating System will require more leverage than either party currently possesses. If the haywire BOS remains in place, then the Cyber Future looms, like a gravid cloud, growling in thunder and flowing our way.

The Republicans may discover that the real battle they face in the nineties is not against the Democrats, but rather against the forces pushing American society as we know it toward breakdown. As Gingrich himself said when riding triumphantly into Washington, "If this degenerates into the usual baloney, then America will move to a third party."

Chapter 13

A Third Party?

Lord Palmerston, the nineteenth-century British prime minister, said, "We have no eternal allies and we have no perpetual enemies. Our interests are eternal and perpetual, and these interests it is our duty to follow." Interests—the goals we have for ourselves, our families, our communities, and our country—last forever, while simple partisan and political affiliations change to suit those interests.[1]

In the four chapters on the Big Offer, we saw how past presidents have made Big Offers to the American people. In the previous two chapters, we've seen how both the Democrats and Republicans, who in the past have each been able to assemble Big Offer coalitions for constructive change, may fall short of wanting to make—or being able to make—a New Paradigm Big Offer.

With the Old Paradigm of the Bureaucratic Operating System dug in like a Texas tick, the next Big Offerer will need a gargantuan pair of tweezers to yank it out. But for constructive, healing change, the next Offer must not only remove the parasitic paradigm; it must balm the wounds that remain. To do all this, mere majorities will not suffice. The leader who brings forth a New Paradigm will need a huge mandate—a wave of popular support for his or her program, made manifest by supermajorities in Congress. This has been the pattern in American history: Big Offerers have enjoyed enormous working majorities. Such grand political alliances necessarily bring together voting blocs that were previously indifferent or even hostile to each other; different pieces of partially collapsed Roosevelt and Reagan Offers could yet become building blocks of a better political architecture. But nothing can be built without a plan.

Gergenism

What won't work is a lowest-common-denominator process, as in let's-paper-over-our-differences. Former Reagan aide David R. Gergen joined the Clinton White House in the spring of 1993 to bring a measure of centrist bipartisanship to the administration. While Gergen brought maturity to Clinton's bratpack, he notably failed to change the intellectual or ideological cast of his new colleagues.

"Gergenism" failed not because of Gergen but because it was plan-less—doomed because it was predicated on the notion that ideas don't much matter, that profound ideological differences can be overcome through a little negotiation and a lot of spin.

In the absence of a clear vision, a mandate for change becomes mere motion, an endless circulation of flecks and specks. Remember the 110 congressional freshpersons of 1992, the newcomers who were going to clean House? They were going to be the gridlock-busting, perk-ending, campaign-finance-reforming, special-interest-curbing Young Turks of the 103rd Congress, who would reduce the deficit and never bounce a check. Here's what happened: 99 of those fabled frosh suckled a total of $15 million from political action committees during their campaigns, then snarfed another $1.2 million from PACs after the election.[2] From that raveningly inauspicious beginning, they were tempting targets for the Washington political elite. *Roll Call*, the Washington weekly, damned the new class with understatement: "In the end, most freshmen behaved like their more senior colleagues."[3] None of their signature causes—not even the inclusion of Congress under the laws regular Americans must abide by—were enacted into law in 1993–94. And so the system lived on for two more years. Indeed, most politicians, possessed by their perks and power, want to muddle through for a few decades until they can retire into lawyering or lobbying. Individual incumbents may be replaced—including eighty-six members of the 103rd Congress in the 1994 elections—but as long as the system that shapes them remains entrenched, their replacements will look just the same: meet the new boss, same as the old boss.

Milton Friedman emphasizes that the established political Operating System overrides parties and personalities. As he said in a 1993 speech to the libertarian Cato Institute:

> We sometimes think the solution to our problems is to elect the right people to Congress. I believe that's false, that if a random sample of the people in this room were to replace the 435 people in the House and the 100 people in the Senate, the results would be the same. With few exceptions, the people in Congress are decent people who want to do good. They're not deliberately engaging in activities that they know will do harm. They are simply immersed in an environment in which all the pressures are in one direction, to spend more money.[4]

Indeed, only the rarest and most dogged visionary can change embedded architecture. Thus Gergenism could never succeed beyond superficial Gridiron Dinner bonhomie. Phony consensus works no better than "gridlock" because both leave the Bureaucratic Operating System intact. Former congressman Tim Penny (D-Minnesota), retiring in disgust at the age of forty-three, said that the current two-party system offers only expansion or contraction of the same old stuff. Yet there is a third alternative, he points out: replacement of the system.

A Third Party?

In U.S. history, the failure of the two major political parties, be they Whigs and Federalists or Democrats and Republicans, has meant opportunity for third parties to spring forth. In the wake of the 1992 presidential election, in which Ross Perot's 19 percent of the vote was the highest share for a third-party candidate since 1912, it seemed as though a "radical middle" party, or movement, might emerge.

In their 1994 book *The Politics of American Discontent: How a New Party Can Make Democracy Work Again*, pollster Gordon Black and political scientist Benjamin Black cite 1992 exit polls showing that 36 percent of the electorate would have voted for Perot if they had thought he could win. Today as many voters identify themselves as "independents" as partisans of either party; 63 percent say they would support a third party in the future.[5] Arguing for a party of "radicalized moderates," the Blacks write:

> The failures of the two-party system have created a chasm in the electorate: a large group of voters distinctly different from partisan Democrats and Republicans. These voters are liberal or moderate on social issues, profoundly conservative on fiscal issues, and disturbed by the loss of their democratic influence.[6]

Indeed, frustrated by the two parties, many activists in recent years have devoted themselves to nonpartisan Perotian "direct democracy" crusades—pushing for term limits, tax cuts, environmental protection, even "death with dignity."

Yet in the 1994 midterm elections, most third-party candidacies fizzled into single digits. Although Angus King, an independent, won the governorship in Maine, the most noteworthy independent candidates of 1994 turned out to be either millionaire egomaniacs or single-issue obsessives—and they lost. Alaska and Connecticut elected independent governors in 1990, both of whom were replaced by major-party candidates in 1994. Most insurgent movements end this way: they get co-opted into one of the major parties. Thus the Democrats absorbed most of the populists in the 1890s, while the Republicans absorbed much of George Wallace's support in the 1960s. In 1994, perhaps two-thirds of 1992 Perot voters switched to the GOP.

Democrat David Boren of Oklahoma gave up a safe Senate seat in frustration over the joint failure of the two parties to deal with the nation's problems. He saw no future for the Democrats, but he couldn't bring himself to be a Republican. He posed the current political crisis in an ominous historical context: we will see, he dired, "more change and upheaval in the politics in this country than at any time since the Civil War."[7] The current political crisis is indeed reminiscent of the

1850s, when the familiar partisan Operating System dating from Jefferson's day finally crashed; the two major parties, Whigs and the Democrats, could not between them find a peaceful solution to vexing problems. During that period of failed, single-term presidents, a variety of third and fourth parties emerged. The Republicans, founded in 1854, were one such new party; the GOP's 1856 presidential candidate, John C. Frémont, won 33 percent of the vote, behind Democrat James Buchanan but well ahead of the candidate of the expiring Whigs. In the next four years, the Whigs collapsed completely. Abraham Lincoln was elected president in 1860 in a four-way race.

We can breathe an historical sigh of relief that it was Lincoln who won—and not another newbie candidate, John C. Breckenridge of the breakaway southern Democrats or John Bell of the Constitutional Union party. Today, journalist Ronald Brownstein foresees a window of opportunity for a third "Toyota Party" to surprise-attack the Democrats and Republicans, just as the Japanese automakers divebombed Detroit out of its daydreaming. Such lightning-bolting may be inevitable, but it is risky. A look back at the last five third-party candidates who won more than 2 percent of the popular vote since World War II—Perot, John Anderson in 1980, George Wallace in 1968, Strom Thurmond and Henry Wallace in 1948—suggest that the two major parties haven't been so bad, relative to these available alternatives. But that's not much of a compliment.[8]

History may tell us that the baton of leadership will inevitably fall to the ground, but it can't tell us the precise identity of who—if anyone—will pick it up. All the *Zeitgeists* and tectonic plates of history cannot overcome for-want-of-a-nail imponderables; yet it is possible to identify areas of possible alliance, places in our politics where a new Big Offer coalition might come together.[9]

Alliance Issues

Military strategists know that attackers need a 3:1, 4:1, or even 5:1 ratio of attackers to defenders to overcome a fixed position. Using a more peaceful analogy, business strategist Peter Drucker has observed that a new technology cannot displace an established technology—

with its installed base of plant, equipment, training, personnel, and satisfied customers—unless the innovation is ten times more cost-effective than its predecessor. Drucker's point is that not until the advantages of change are blindingly obvious can one overcome the inertia of current operating procedure.

Drucker's dictum explains why most people can feel that the partisan political system we have today doesn't work—and yet be unwilling to leap to the paradigmatic equivalent of the next lily pad. Voters don't yet see any tangible reason to justify the jump. That's the obligation of the Big Offer–making leader: to outline a future that will work, so that overwhelming majorities want to follow his or her lead.

For our purposes, we can stipulate that no profound change in the system will occur until the reform forces have amassed a 4:1 advantage. Such an 80 percent coalition need not agree on everything—it needn't even all be in the same party—but it must agree on the big things. As we have seen, Lincoln enjoyed enormous congressional majorities when he was making his Big Offer; so did Roosevelt when he made his. Thus familiar politics-as-usual, no matter how it is dressed up, cannot be the basis of a Big Offer. In 1992, all three candidates said they wanted "change," but none of them could muster more than 43 percent of the vote. And in 1994, remembered as a triumph for the Republicans, the GOP won exactly half of the nationwide vote. Percentages in the forties and fifties can never launch a Big Offer. Until a given debate is seen as an "80:20 issue," the odds are that the normal checks and balances, plus the abnormal sclerosis of the contemporary system, will stymie all progress.

The Big Offer must be like a magnet, so powerful that the iron filings of the electorate come streaming toward it, and amidst the heaps of votes, people within the new array will surely notice that some of their fellow filings are unfamiliar. That's what the New Paradigm Alliance, if there is one, will be like: lions, lambs, sugar, spice, and puppy-dog tails, all rolled into one supermajoritarian Alliance. Only such an eclectic melange can yield up a total of 80 percent. But it takes leadership and vision to shape that "Megalliance" into an effective political force. The current generation of political leadership looks more like polarizing 51 percenters than Big-Offering 80 percenters.[10]

In the New Paradigm world, the two parties would realize that the

crude cleavages they represent are harming the country—and why, as
E. J. Dionne, Jr., puts it, Americans hate politics. If neither party by
itself can get to 80 percent, then perhaps ad hoc bipartisan coalitions,
such as that for the North American Free Trade Agreement, would
spring up.[11]

To escape permanently from the 51 percent trap, both genders and
all races and creeds need to be attracted into a new Alliance. But what
is needed even more is a synthesis of new thinking: an upwardly
spiraling fusion of radical conservative dialectic. We need the spirit of
radicalism to spearhead the New Paradigm, but we need the best of
conservatism to provide order and context.

Kuhn's theory of "paradigm shifts"—long periods of intellectual
quiescence followed by a burst of intellectual ferment, then another
period of aging and settling—embraces both the conservative and radical worldviews in its explanation of how advances are made. The title
of his book, *The Structure of Scientific Revolutions*, contains words that
are oxymoronic: "structure" and "revolution." Paradigmatic transformation—or, in our terminology, a Big Offer—leads to consolidation, to
the creation of a new establishment; both are necessary parts of the
unending process of progress.

At least four issues exist around which new Alliances can be made:
personal security, personal responsibility, the value of the family, and
a sense of community. These issues are old and new, but as we shall
see, they are already attracting Left and Right, radicals and conservatives.
Properly presented, they could help strong and strange coalitions to
form an 80:20 Megalliance that would propel the New Paradigm Big
Offer.

Alliance Issue #1: A Sense of Personal Security

Americans think that crime is one of the two or three most important
threats to our way of life, and yet the Bureaucratic Operating System
is foolishly creating criminals even faster than it is apprehending and
incarcerating them. The government subsidizes substance abuse and
illegitimacy, among the factors most strongly correlated with antisocial
behavior. An Alliance to fight crime could be built around eliminating

what were once called "the root causes" of crime—not mere economic poverty, but the entire understructure of perverse incentives that channel people out of the mainstream. A supermajority would rally behind a candidate who proposed a comprehensive crime-fighting approach, offering nonpork prevention as well as deterrence: the guarantee of a job for everyone, along with a crackdown on those still skulking the streets with malice aforethought.

We can already see the beginnings of a new Alliance, based on a fuller understanding that the "roots" of crime are not only dysfunctional families but also the dysfunctional Operating System that creates them. The Right has begun to acknowledge that society, at least parts of it, *is* to blame for criminal behavior. In 1994 Newt Gingrich went so far as to blame Susan Smith's drowning of her two boys in Union, South Carolina, on a "sick society."[12] When even conservatives "blame society" for pathological behavior, an informed Alliance is possible. With one eye on the intransigent evil within human nature, the other looks toward dealing with crime in an anticipatory way. That means guaranteeing the core elements of the middle-class lifestyle—personal empowerment, a good education, and, above all, physical safety. Gingrich says to his fellow conservatives: "If we care that an eleven-year-old black girl says the Pledge of Allegiance every morning in school, then we ought to care about what happens to her during the rest of her day."

The Left, for its part, has recently been asserting that some crimes deserve real punishment after all. Liberals may be stereotyped as bleeding-hearts, but increasingly their chests run dry in regard to domestic violence and "hate crimes." If the Left can agree that hate crimes are to be severely punished, then it's a slippery slope down to the conclusion that *all* crimes merit retribution. Feminists have always supported tough treatment of antiabortion vigilantes. When Paul Hill, the Florida preacher who killed an abortion doctor, was sentenced to die in the electric chair, groups such as the National Abortion Federation and the National Abortion and Reproductive Rights Action League welcomed the death penalty for its deterrent effect.[13] As T. S. Eliot wrote, sometimes the end of all our exploring is to arrive where we started and to know it for the first time.

Today, women's groups are expanding their horizons to include a broader definition of gender-inspired violence that comes—after all is said—to resemble the traditional definition of crime. Patricia Ireland, president of the National Organization for Women, calls for tougher sentences for men who kill women, complaining that women who kill men get fifteen- to twenty-year sentences, whereas men who kill women get two to six years.[14] Since at least 90 percent of violent crime is committed by men, a feminist-led antiviolence campaign would inevitably produce stringent incarceration strategies: lock 'em up. In other words, former antagonists might reach common ground; women of the Left leading "take back the night" crusades are potential allies of Conservatives wanting to sweep the streets of hoodlums and restore civic virtue and order. A tiny bow in the direction of sexual-identity politics is not too high a price to pay for safer streets.

Another bloc in a possible supermajority anticrime coalition is gays; "Pink Panther" groups patrolling their neighborhoods are only the most visible gay anticrime crusaders. These new activists may have first come together to guard against gay-bashing, but they inevitably become a bulwark against people-bashing of any kind. In Salt Lake City, when Judge David Young reduced the sentence of a killer of a gay man to just six years, a gay leader responded angrily: "Judge Young has said that it's OK to kill faggots." His voice, typical of a new outspokenness, has helped raise national levels of consciousness. Citizens of all orientations are realizing the need for a greater fairness in the judicial system. Significantly, the same judge has come under fire from NOW for being too lenient on crimes against women.[15] Thus the potential Alliance: anyone who believes in the rule of law—pro-choice and pro-life, straight and gay—can unite around the idea that violence is a form of intolerance and hatred.

Alliance Strategy #2: A Sense of Personal Responsibility

An equal part of any successful crime-fighting strategy must be incorporating a sense of personal responsibility into society's Operating System. People believe in it, but the system doesn't. The survey firm of Mellman and Lazarus has done exhaustive polling on "values," concluding that America's strongest value was "being responsible for our actions."[16] Yet for years, the values of our system have been disconnected from our values as people. Politicians who would follow their own teenage daughters around with shotguns nevertheless preside over a system that presumes the total helplessness of other people's teenage girls. And as any parent knows, young people usually live up to what's expected of them. Today, government policy has encrusted around irresponsibility. Corporate subsidies, welfare, public housing, no-fault litigation, and lax child-support laws all spit in the face of the heartfelt belief that the rich and the middle class, as well as the poor, need their moral fiber improved with a little more self-reliance.

Today, both Right and Left claim to be grappling with "values"; yet neither side is getting anywhere close to the 80 percent critical mass needed to effect real change, because the Left has let itself be talked into opposing "hegemonistic" mainstream values and the Right has been detoured into a "traditional family values" agenda, spearheaded by antiabortionism and homophobia.

Since the time the revolutionary French guillotined their king, conservatives have brooded about what people freed from religious tradition would do with their freedom. Fearful of the rabble's incipient majoritarianism, many rightists resigned themselves to their status as "the remnant," awaiting the revolution from rural redoubts. A newer generation of conservatives, led by James Q. Wilson, now sees that morality can be regenerated, because it springs from within. Of course, conservatives will have to accustom themselves to new manifestations of spirituality and to new religious patterns not fitting into older systems; New Age believers may not perform their liturgies in Latin, but from the sociological point of view, they demonstrate all the criteria one could hope for in a renascent moral sense. The Right has anguished over the unraveling of a traditional religion-based social fabric; yet it should not overlook the determination of individuals to knit it together again. Moral values can be woven into a new cloth, into a new tapestry of decency and ethical concern.

For their part, radicals of the Left were too optimistic about the good that would come of liberation, of emancipation from the old. In her 1969 Wellesley commencement speech, young Hillary Rodham said that her generation was searching for a "more immediate, ecstatic and penetrating mode of living."[17] Soon she was at Yale Law School, home to Charles Reich, whom we noted earlier as the author of "The New

Property." In 1970 Reich penned the rad-classic *The Greening of America*, in which he contended that modern industrial society had sucked the juice out of our Whitmanesque mystical vision. At the same time, Reich pointed the way up the metaphysical staircase: we were ascending, he wrote, to Consciousness 3: "This means a 'new head'—a new way of living—a new man."[18] Some elements of society were vastly improved by the era's radical critique of tradition and authority; minorities, women, and gays have more life choices now than they once had. However, as most sixties radicals Big Chilled into an Ob-La-Di Ob-La-Da lifestyle—with safe sex, marriage, children, and the usual middle-aging allotment of Proustian remembrance—they realized that what they had sought liberation from was not the friendly fascism of "Amerika," but the process of life itself. New head or no new head, reality was hard to escape from. Liberation remained elusive.

So a potential Alliance might be forged among old believers, new believers, and aging Boomers. The common denominator is a sense of personal responsibility: honesty, integrity, and uprightness. The Cultural Right, looking deep within its traditional heart, and the New Age, drawing upon its leftist and libertarian influences, can agree that character counts.

Yet government, as we have seen, can be more effective at expunging virtues than inducing them. The tax burden on families has brought about a sense of fatalism among many Americans. According to Stanford's Paul Krugman, an average family was paying a higher share of its income in taxes at the end of the eighties than at the beginning; higher Social Security taxes blotted out lower income taxes.[19] Reaganomics segued into Darmanomics and then Clintonomics, leaving working families more burdened than ever. Casting aside his promised "middle-class tax cut," Clinton in his first two years tried to convince Americans that good economic policy could be based on "fairness"—defined as tax hikes on the rich. Yet as Hayek observed, the real purpose of soak-the-rich taxes is not to cut taxes for everyone else, but to make everyone else feel better about paying high taxes, too.[20]

High taxation, combined with the trends of the cyber-economy, leave the middle class with little choice but to work harder; family and community life suffer as a result.[21] The Heritage Foundation calculates that the total federal tax rate on families with children has soared from

2 percent in 1950 to an all-time high of 24 percent in the 1990s. With the real value of the personal exemption having fallen by some 70 percent since the forties, the average family is running harder on a treadmill. Heritage's William Mattox coined the phrase "family time deficit": working harder and spending less time with children—to pay for government.[22]

President Clinton says "work organizes life." Yet cybertechnology disorganizes work, and taxes to fuel the Bureaucratic Operating System loot its worth. The work ethic is part of the moral sense, but it is being deprogramed out of people by various government disincentives, such as high taxes on labor and high subsidizing of nonlabor. So while an overwhelming majority of Americans believe that work is the way to the American Dream, the system invalidates that belief—and even militates against it.

Alliance Issue #3: A Sense of Family Values—And the Value of the Family

For most of human civilization, few have disputed the wisdom encapsulated by Aristotle: "Man by his nature is even more meant for marriage than he is for political association, in proportion as the family is earlier and more necessary than the polis." Yet for much of this century, the family has been under heavy assault from modernity; it has been deracinated by Madison Avenue pop culture mongers as well as steamrollered by ivory-towered social reconstructors. Through it all, the sinews of familial loyalty have strained but not snapped. Today, the recent political fracas over "traditional family values" aside, the value of the family, preferably intact and nuclear, is not in much dispute anymore.

Yet state power is still devaluing the family. The institutionalized inertia of the government makes it a lagging indicator in the current debate. For example, the taboo against out-of-wedlock birthing was based in part on the frank recognition of the economic non-viability of family fragmentation in a harsh world. Most Americans seem to agree with Charles Murray's once-heretical *Losing Ground* thesis: that the current welfare system has achieved a first—making single motherhood a viable life choice for poor women. One who says he agrees is Bill Clinton.[23]

Clinton was elected just as consensus crystallized around Murray's argument; his campaign promise to "end welfare as we know it" by "moving people from welfare to work" capitalized on this new mood. Indeed, Clinton echoed Dan Quayle when he weighed in with these words to a church group: "You shouldn't have a baby before you're ready. And you shouldn't have a baby before you're married."[24]

If Dan Quayle and Bill Clinton can come together at the rhetorical level, albeit not on a substantive level, then a new reform Alliance is possible. The burden of proof has now shifted; the Old Paradigm—dominated welfare system, having failed to accomplish its ameliorative mission, must now step back to allow other possible solutions.

Alliance Issue #4: A Sense of Community

In Shakespearean tragedy, when the Great Chain of Being—that is, the Cosmic Operating System—is disturbed, shattering storms roll over the heath, portending chaos and doom. In our time, what David Halberstam has called "the covenant of the culture" has been rent apart; yet some brave and good souls are trying to glue it back together.

Mutual respect, a sense of shared purpose, even manners and politeness—these virtues flourish among people who feel kinship to each other. In big cities, people struggle to create the urban village, as Anna Quindlen has observed:

> Look at New York. People turn the big city into a series of villages to make it manageable—the village of your office, the village of your building or your block, the village of your neighborhood association . . . Almost all programs I see that are working on social issues are small and community-based.[25]

Quindlen echoes a long line of contemporary left-of-center thinkers who have stressed the importance of small institutions. Perhaps the best known is Jane Jacobs, whose *The Death and Life of Great American Cities*, published in 1961, alerted America to the dangers of barbaric

Brasilia-type totalism in the name of "urban renewal." Other works in this gentle tradition include E. F. Schumacher's *Small is Beautiful: Economics as if People Mattered* (1973), and Kirkpatrick Sale's *Human Scale* (1980).

America needs streets, these authors say, that are safe as well as yeasty, to lure people off their couches, out of their malls—and in from the Internet. Robert Nisbet wrote *The Quest for Community* four decades ago, when the Left was still anxious to pour cement and plow virgin fields in the name of progress. The medievally conservative Nisbet warned in 1953 of the unintended consequences of large-scale modernization, issuing an Aristotelian admonition: "Individuals who are not bound together in associations, whether domestic, economic, religious, political, artistic, or educational, are monstrosities."[26]

From the opposite ideological pole comes another believer in community, Amitai Etzioni. Hailing from the Left, Etzioni and his allies in the new Communitarian movement seek to resuscitate the ancient conservative idea that society is an organism with a legitimate interest in its own self-preservation. In his book *The Spirit of Community*, Etzioni sees hopeful signs of "the new *Gemeinschaft*," a revived sense of customary rights and responsibilities that is neither oppressive nor hierarchical.[27] Such thinking was the essence of Edmund Burke's organic conservatism, although the mechanistic Left derided it as reactionary rationalizations for feudalism. In spite of this yin-yanged intellectual pedigree, Etzioni has become a major force in the fight for sanity on "quality of life" issues, such as drunk driving and vagrancy.

Democrats Elaine Kamarck and William A. Galston—both currently back-burnered in the Clinton White House—suggest that we need "tolerant traditionalism": a deliberate oxymoron designed to umbrella an old–new mix of community values, from crime watching to recycling.

New Alliances

If the goal is to unify Left and Right, radicals and conservatives, in a new Alliance that bypasses the failed policies of the past, we should look to those groups, such as African Americans, that are most ill served by the partisan status quo. A Big Offer that served this disadvantaged group would help create a new Alliance—as would Big Offers that served gays and, perhaps surprisingly, public school teachers.

Such an alliance could be compared to a pyramid. At the top would be a leader or leaders with an agenda that every block in the base supports. At the bottom, the different blocks, or blocs, could be so far apart from each other that they would rarely notice how different and disparate they are. If they wanted to win, they wouldn't be looking for the mote in each other's eyes but rather would concentrate on their zone of agreement; they would look up to the apex of the pyramid and focus on a shared vision.

As Americans clutch for every ethical straw, some surprising huts of Alliance may spring up. An article by Jon Meacham in the *Washington Monthly* blared: "What the Religious Right Can Teach the New Democrats." The author allowed that religious conservation is "really right" on teen pregnancy, welfare dependency, divorce, values, and community service. "These are Religious Right favorites," he says—"old-time moral causes that are now *progressive* causes." From his vantage point on the neoliberal left, Meacham throws rocks on the Right's "obsession with homosexuals and abortion" but then tosses a bonbon: "There's a fairly sensible cultural vision and a not unreasonable policy agenda that's as neoliberal as it is fundamentalist."[28] Given that 39 percent of Americans identify themselves as born-again or evangelical Christians,[29] some sort of dialectical accommodation between old antagonists is a necessary aspect of any Alliance.

So the potential for either Alliance or antipodes exists, depending on the quality of leadership. A leader, instead of emphasizing areas of disagreement, such as gay rights, could focus on areas of agreement, such as community values. Good leadership, calling for a new Alliance, would then arrange the blocks of the pyramid so that questions of sexual orientation are pushed toward the base—on opposite sides of the pyramid. This is how Roosevelt kept the New Deal coalition together: communists and klansmen were part of the same superstructure, but they rarely rubbed elbows. Similarly, pro-choice and pro-life movements could be arranged away from each other at the base—as areas of agreement, such as personal security, form a crown of consensus at the top of the pyramid: an unblinking eye of Alliance.

No rule says that one of the two existing parties can't adapt consensus goals into a new Alliance; yet their failure to do so suggests that at best one or both need a spur, while at worst they need to be replaced. Three potential Alliance groups are African Americans, gays, and public school teachers. A Big Offer that touches on them directly could pull each group into a New Paradigm Alliance.

African Americans

Those most victimized by the Old Paradigm are African Americans. Jesse Jackson says that more young blacks are imprisoned in the "jail-industrial complex" than are enrolled in college. The most deleterious effects of the failures of the bureaucratic welfare state—the breakup of the family, the collapse of public housing, the erosion of public safety, the failure of public education, and the cyberskew of job prospects and earnings—have come down hard on the heads of blacks.

More than two decades ago, John Rawls's *A Theory of Justice*, one of the most important philosophical treatises in postwar America, argued that the true test of society should be the condition of those worst off within it. By this theory, the Old Paradigm must be judged a miserable failure. Yet poverty-stricken African Americans, given their position at the bottom of the well, also have the most to gain from a paradigm shift: the healing of their families, the safety of their streets, and better futures for their children.

After Clinton took office, a curious complacency set in. The new line was that conditions in the underclass may be bad, but they weren't as bad as they had been under Reagan and Bush. The existing social-service-ariat seemed to have settled into the smug view that the current welfare system is the best that America can afford. Yet as Michael Meyers, African American executive director of the New York Civil Rights Coalition, declared:

> All the institutions we developed for the purpose of influencing the mainstream have become moribund, dysfunctional, and self-destructive. We've been so content with getting set-asides, carving a special program for our own, that we no longer engage the mass of the American people

in dialogue—if anyone doesn't agree with the civil rights groups they are written off as ideologues, called bigots.[30]

The effect of the 1994 elections was merely to hasten the demise of dysfunctional institutions, already doomed by their own ineffectiveness.

The progressive coalition of the future must therefore seek a newer deal for blacks, pulling together the threads of entrepreneurship and discipline into a new texture of opportunity and uplift. Jackson declares: "The strongest weapons against welfare despair and crime would be business development, jobs and education."[31] Observing that "the engine is capital formation," he adds, "welfare is the caboose."[32] Capital formation, work, and learning are the building blocks of an Alliance pyramid. Who will make a Big Offer based on these issues?

Echoes of part of Abraham Lincoln's Big Offer, the 1863 Homestead Act, ring through Jack Kemp's advocacy of private ownership of public housing units. The Homestead Act can be a powerful analogy, because that long-ago policy helps us understand the nature of true empowerment—that is, ownership and sovereignty. A half-century later, the Bolsheviks "offered" the Russian people "peace, land, and bread"; yet the peasantry quickly discovered that they owned nothing at all, that the Red Commissars wielded far more power over their lives than White aristocrats ever dreamed of. Only when the government truly transfers the tools of equity and ownership—the twentieth-century equivalent of the forty acres and a mule that blacks have been waiting for since 1863—will the nation be Offering African Americans the same power accessed by earlier immigrants to the economic mainstream. And so the line of thinking about economic development that extends from Booker T. Washington to Marcus Garvey to Malcolm X will be extended further.

Another step in this process is moral and spiritual revival, initiated not from above, but from below. Authentic life-changing fervor does not emanate from bureaucrats; African Americans will flourish only in the same way other Americans do: from the rooted flowering of a vibrant civil society. In contemporary urban America, true social and cultural revitalization will sometimes affront mainstream belief; the challenge the majority faces is discerning the familiar in the unfamiliar. The twentieth-century version of Methodism, the soul-saving movement that inspired and uplifted the English underclass, is Afrocentrism. An Afrocentric morality can provide abstemious inspiration, just as John Wesley's sermons in the open fields once stirred the English working man; descendants of the pharaohs would behave according to a noble tradition. Frederick Douglass observed more than a century ago:

> It has been the fashion of American writers to deny that the Egyptians were Negroes and claim that they are of the same race as themselves. This has, I have no doubt, been largely due to a wish to deprive the Negro of the moral support of Ancient Greatness and to appropriate the same to the white race.[33]

White participants in the new Alliance will note the conservative, even prudish, social byproduct of Afrocentrism. In the words of Dr. Khalid Abdullah Tariq Al-Mansour,

> The role of racial and cultural pride is to organize the masses of people around a history and a heritage who lend themselves to a sustained frontal attack against feelings of inferiority, illiteracy, alcohol/drug/gambling dependency, lack of discipline, destructive spiritual values but promotes self-sacrifice and educational/economic initiative.

Then Mansour adds the kicker: such racial pride will enable African Americans "to duplicate the successes of such countries and people as Japan, Korea, Malaysia, Singapore, Taiwan, Hong Kong, etc."[34]

What tools need to be transferred? The most significant resource kept out of the hands of black parents is the public schools. Only when African American parents, not bureaucrats, control their own schools will an education revival be possible; so far, buds of hope have mostly been stomped by the knee-jerk negative reactions from the Old Paradigm, both Left and Right. The educational equivalent of the Homestead Act will be the full voucherization of the schools. As we have seen in EDUCRAT, the dollar numbers are enormous: an average annual per-pupil expenditure of $6,000. "Community control" has been a ruse to maintain the power of the Old Paradigm; no true revolution was ever led by the ruling class. Whoever presents African Americans with the tangible possibility of getting true control of the money that schools have misspent in the name of their children—he or she will have made a Big Offer so enormous that African Americans would scoop it up at once.

Another piece of the Big Offer is work. One particular Old Paradigm alliance, the axis between organized labor and the bureaucracy, rested on a sinister entente that limited minorities' access to that *sine qua non* of the American Dream: a job. Since the New Deal, organized labor has supported social welfare programs—so long as the political system enforced regulatory requirements that kept minorities from competing with unionized workers. One flagrant example is the Davis–Bacon Act, a federal law since 1931. The act requires that every public construction contract in excess of $2,000 pay the "prevailing wage" to workers on that contract. As applied, the law has led to scandalous abuses: electricians in Philadelphia are paid $38 an hour for Davis–Bacon projects, compared to $16 an hour for private-sector work.[35] Such wage-fixing schemes effectively force contractors to use unionized labor at the expense of others who might do the work more cheaply. The law was specifically intended to keep minorities from underbidding white labor; its effect is no different today. The Clinton administration sought to scale Davis–Bacon back. Not surprisingly, the Old Paradigm–controlled Congress blocked even that tentative reform. Full repeal of Davis–Bacon is an archetypal New Alliance issue, since opening jobs to minorities would also save the taxpayers $600 million a year.[36]

Movie director Spike Lee's *Do the Right Thing* is remembered as a parable about violence and misunderstanding, but it also touches on themes of economic self-reliance. Lee told *Rolling Stone:* "All I'm saying is that black people for too long haven't really thought of owning businesses. That's the key. Because when you own businesses, you have more control and you can do what you want." Lee was asked point blank: are you a capitalist? "Am I a capitalist? . . . I've always tried to be in an entrepreneurial mode of thinking. Ownership is what's needed amongst African-Americans. Ownership. Own stuff."[37] One of his later films, *Malcolm X*, showed its hero not so much as an anti-white revolutionary but rather as a pro-black missionary, an enemy of dependence and an apostle of empowerment.

The spirit of Malcolm has been fused to the ghost of Dale Carnegie in the person of black businessman George Fraser. His book *Success*

Runs in Our Race: The Complete Guide to Effective Networking in the African-American Community radiates with the power of positive thinking. The basic message is that the business of black America is business. Fraser points out "the great need for African-Americans to own their own businesses to ensure job security."[38] In search of an Afrocentric rationale for capitalism, Fraser conjures up a medley of Harriet Tubman and "the new Underground Railroad," Kwanzaa, and African village lore.

So why are so many African Americans falling behind? One reason is that the Bureaucratic Operating System grinds down upon their upward mobility. In *The State Against Blacks* Walter Williams outlines the many ways in which occupational licensing regulates poor people out of their chance to earn a living, from barbering to plumbing to trucking.[39] Forward-looking mayors, such as Stephen Goldsmith of Indianapolis, have been working to open up employment and entrepreneurship. Goldsmith's city now permits cab drivers to cruise the streets for passengers; the old system required radio calls, which benefited the big white firms which could afford the infrastructure of advertising, radios, and dispatchers. While "conservatives" such as Clint Bolick of the Institute for Justice have been litigating to overturn these oppressive rules, "progressives" have been generally silent. One has to wonder what Malcolm X would think of the current arrangement of political Alliances, in which the poorest and the blackest have to go the richest and the whitest for permission to earn a living.

We see glimmers of hope, but only glimmers. In 1993, conservative supply-siders, led by syndicated curmudgeon Robert Novak, flirted with the Congressional Black Caucus over the issue of a capital gains tax cut. The potential Alliance was clear: more entrepreneurship meant not only more entrepreneurs, but also more tax revenue for everything else. Novak asked Caucus chairman Kweisi Mfume (D-Maryland) whether the door was still open to such negotiations. Mfume responded:

> It's still open . . . We are not looking necessarily at old methods to try to win on behalf of the people we represent. We're trying to find new ways of doing it. And if that means new coalitions, then so be it. Now I know that's out of form for some members of our party, but we believe at this particular point in time, that people are hurting so bad in this

country, and want to see action so bad, and are so tired of Republican vs. Democrat, that they want to see whatever works. And if that works, trying . . . to bridge the gap, then we're going to pursue it.[40]

The Congressional Black Caucus missed the deal when it had the chance—that is, when it controlled a score of committee and subcommittee chairmanships. Today, with African American Democrats in Congress shut out of the majority for the first time in forty years, blacks need to be players in both political parties.

One new voice is J. C. Watts, who became the second black Republican elected to Congress in modern times in 1994. Watts laments that "black people have become irrelevant in American politics, taken for granted by one party and rightfully ignored by the other." Yet Watts pointedly refused to join the Congressional Black Caucus, saying "my father brought me up to be a man—not a black man." Watts, who represents an overwhelmingly white district in Oklahoma, says he looks forward to the day when race is as incidental to American human relations as religion. Many will consider Watts to be a wishful thinker, even though he is merely restating the dream of Martin Luther King, Jr.

For the forseeable future, the Democratic party is likely to remain the home to most African Americans. Yet that fact puts a special burden on black Democrats to form an Alliance with Watts and his party for the overall benefit of black America. Fortunately, there are signs that this is happening: echoing Palmerston a century ago, Mfume said after the 1994 elections, "We don't have permanent friends or enemies, just permanent interests."[41] Such words offer hope that a new Big Offer— as well as a New Alliance—is possible.

Gays and Lesbians

Even more than African Americans, gays and lesbians have been regarded as among the nation's most radical groups. Self-proclaimed "Queers" purposely perpetuate the image—claiming that their orientation is an act of rebellion, signing every 54-point manifesto calling for the elimination of hegemonism and age-of-consent laws, insisting that AIDS is a government conspiracy. These radicals may be the most visible, but they do not represent a community that is varied and eclectic. Rich Tafel of the Log Cabin Republicans believes that gays must rethink their alliances: "The 1994 elections are the end of the Stonewall Generation" of gay political leaders; the time has come, he asserts, for leadership that can work with straights to advance a broader agenda.

A Big Offer to gays and lesbians would include not only eliminating antigay ordinances, but also sanctioning a stance as radical to the Religious Right as Afrocentrism is to both the Cultural Right and the Cultural Left: legalized gay marriage. Gay marriage would ally the radical and the conservative; it would allow gays to preserve their current liberation, but it would encourage them to share in the conservative vision by joining the ranks of stable, bourgeois, monogamous America. Such a ball-and-chain opportunity might seem dreadfully dull to some, but the AIDS plague has reminded many that the deadly limits of the liberationist vision are not imposed by Jesse Helms, but rather by biology. In a world of limits, the beckoning of kith and kitsch—of Ozzie & Harry, Lucy & Ethel—might not seem so bad after all.[42]

Gay marriage is not a prospect in Sarasota or Salt Lake City, but it is an issue in West Hollywood and the West Village. Once again, the genius principle of federalism provides the answer: different strokes for different folks. All that's needed is for Culturalists of the Left as well as the Right to keep cool while the Ninth and Tenth Amendments, reserving power for the states and people respectively, permit this issue to be resolved at the local, not national, level.[43]

It's an irony that many conservatives, who emphasize biology and inheritance, choose to view homosexuality as some sort of fad brought on by cultural decadence and legal license. Radicals, on the other hand, who like to believe that all sex roles are the result of socialization, find themselves arguing that homosexuality is immutable, not something that could be "cured" by faith or therapy. This disconnect is an indicator that vision and politics are out of alignment.

As with every group, both radicalism and conservatism have been evident among gays and lesbians. But after a sobering decade, the conservative vision is on the upswing. The biggest factor has been AIDS; the plague drenches American culture, leaving its indelible, melancholy stain and profoundly changing behavior patterns. Larry Kramer, the playwright and founder of ACT-UP, shrewdly chose *Playboy* to deliver his epitaph to the hedonism the magazine celebrates: "I don't know if sex will ever again be as it was in the Sixties and Seventies—even if AIDS is cured." Hugh Hefner seemed like a radical three decades ago when he launched his editorial crusade for the "Playboy Philosophy" of sexual liberation. Soon, American culture surpassed him. Everyone from the Village People to Madonna pushed the edge of the social, and then the epidemiological, envelope. Kramer is no prude, but like Richard II, he has a sad tale to tell of the death of friends: "The body should be able to do what it wants and enjoy what it wants to enjoy. But it would appear that mother nature doesn't allow that."[44]

When a gay activist invokes "mother nature" as an argument for restraint, we know that the gyre of time is turning round—and that gays are looking toward the conservative vision with more respect. Those who turned the West Village and The Castro into "liberated zones" are now achingly aware that Randy Shilts, a self-described conservative,[45] was right when he sought early on to close the free-love bathhouses of San Francisco. At the time, radical gays were saying that AIDS was a hoax dreamed up by homophobes to push them back into the closet. A quarter million AIDS-related deaths later—including his own—Shilts has been vindicated: the band can't play on. The "gay lifestyle" denounced by televangelists and direct mail kings is fading. According to a 1994 survey by *The Advocate*, "80 percent of the men say that if they had to live without sex or without love, they'd live without sex."[46]

Singing the song of those taken from them, gays and lesbians are creating their own lore of remorse. The pink triangle, the red ribbon, and poignant memoirs assure that AIDS will have a prominent place in American historiography. The Quilt is the greatest testament to the emerging conservative vision of gays. Made up of patches from the lives of the dead, it evokes a Burkean sense of obligation and duty to the memory of those who have passed on.

Gabriel Rotello, the former editor of *OutWeek* magazine, participated in the April 25, 1993, march on Washington—while imagining that his dead gay lover was marching with him:

There's something in all of us, straight and gay, that moves us to want to make a meaning out of death. It's why Lincoln resolved that the fallen in Gettysburg should not have died in vain. It's why Churchill, as bombs rained death on the British, proclaimed it their finest hour. They know that it's not death that has meaning, really—it's what the living make of it. AIDS, like some misguided cavalry charge, may have begun as an accident. But that accident is now our finest hour. It is forcing . . . a new birth of freedom. And I have no doubt that unfinished work to which we are now dedicated will long endure and will bind us to our posterity, gay and straight, just as, last Sunday in Washington, it bound the living to the dead.[47]

No one can dispute that this one gay American takes the long historical view that is central to the conservative vision.

So both Republicans and Democrats have a claim on gay consciousness. The liberating vision we know; the conservative vision we will see more of in the future. The human instinct to settle down, to put down roots, is manifesting itself in gay enclaves. Gays will never be monolithically conservative; yet many yearn to tie into a conservative vision of community. As we have seen, with a little bit of tolerance, Republicans can win gay votes. Having separated from blind lockstep with the Democrats, gays are now in a position, as Palmerston said, to look out for their permanent interests—for someone who will defend their space against street criminals as well as Jerry Falwell.

Today, the most likely Big Offerers of gay marriage are the Democrats. Two Democrats, Eddie Basha of Arizona and Karen Burstein of New York, ran statewide in 1994 pledged to support gay marriage; both lost. Yet thirty-nine openly gay candidates were elected to lesser office.[48] Eventually, a pro-gay marriage Democrat will make a breakthrough for gay rights, although the national Democratic party is likely to move away from such controversies in the wake of its 1994 trouncing.

The Republicans have two choices. First, they can go with the Big Mo flow of their 1994 victory and maintain their semiofficial homophobia—and watch as the Democrats sew up the gay vote for another generation. Second, they can do a "Nixon goes to China" and make the Big Offer themselves. So how could a conservative be for gay marriage? The point is not that the Republicans must embrace "the gay lifestyle"; the point is Alliance, based on a universalist principle of tolerance.

Looking back at his life, from closeted teenager to HIV-positive activist, Larry Kramer thinks of might-have-been: "Who's to know what would have happened if we had been gently allowed our rights, allowed to marry? . . . Could we have learned about intimacy and physical pleasure without so much death?"[49] Andrew Sullivan, editor of the *New Republic*, argues that the institution of gay marriage would actually advance the conservative cause: "It would foster social cohesion, emotional security, and economic prudence."

Whether one likes it or not, gay marriage is on the national agenda. Domestic-partnership laws are springing up in cities across the country, responding to the rise in the number of opposite- as well as same-sex relationships. In California, where an estimated 5 percent of the households consist of unmarried couples, the sponsor of domestic-partnership legislation argued that it "strengthens family values." Nevertheless Republican Governor Pete Wilson vetoed it.[50]

In the 1994 movie *Four Weddings and a Funeral*, Gareth, mourning the death of his lover, remarks that Matthew had always liked funerals better anyway: "It was easier to get excited about a ceremony he had a remote chance of being involved in."

Gareth's eulogy for his life partner includes these lines from Song IX ("Stop all the clocks") of W. H. Auden's "Twelve Songs":

He was my North, my South, my East and West,
My working week and my Sunday rest,
My noon, my midnight, my talk, my song;
I thought that love would last forever: I was wrong.[51]

Are these words radical? Are they convention-breaking, tradition-upheaving? On the contrary, they form a threnodic paean to emotional stability, to day-in-and-day-out devotion, to lifelong commitment.[52]

Bruce Bawer's thoughtful book *A Place at the Table: The Gay Individual in American Society* exemplifies the conservative vision within the gay community. Lamenting that Americans "equate homosexuality with the gay subculture—an entirely different phenomenon," Bawer contends that America nevertheless "is basically a tolerant nation." He adds: "A misunderstood and persecuted minority's best chance lies not in sowing antagonism but in attempting to sow understanding." Such understanding could be reaped by a New Paradigm Alliance.[53]

Teachers

Unlike African Americans and gays, public school teachers seem to have done well under the Old Paradigm regime. The number of school-aged children has barely budged since the fifties,[54] but real per-pupil spending has more than tripled during that same period.[55] And as the number of teachers doubled, the student–teacher ratio fell from 27:1 to 17:1.[56] Yet teacher salaries have not kept pace. They increased by a fifth during the EDUCRAT boom in the eighties, when education "reform" consisted mostly of spending more money, but have been flat during the nineties.[57]

Today, the average American public school teacher earns a little less than $36,000 a year. By contrast, Japanese teachers make $44,000, Swiss $53,000.[58] U.S. teachers would naturally like to catch up, but they haven't been able to—in spite of their enormous political clout, particularly inside the Democratic party. Even with the Democrats resurgent in 1993, the NEA reports that teacher pay raises were the smallest in a quarter-century. The 1994 elections spelled the end of the era in which the political system rewarded failure with higher appropriations; the most likely outcome over the next few years is spending cuts, at least in the rate of future increase, leaving salaries to lag further.

So school teachers face a two-part multiple-choice test; they can fight, or they can switch:

Fight—Teachers can fight for more money from the Old Paradigm spigot. As witnessed by the Oligarchic subjugation of the Department of Education, EDUCRAT retains its Brezhnevian grip on the party. The unions boast that they have defeated a score of voucher votes in the past twenty-five years. So the "fight" option is familiar, calling for a bitter blood-sweat-and-tears struggle against all school choice plans—in the legislatures, in the courts, in referenda.

Yet none of these political victories can resolve what's at the heart of the NEA's problem: people no longer have faith in the educational product that bureaucratic monopolies can deliver. People are as willing as ever to spend money on education, but they aren't willing to spend it on the NEA. As John Golle, the president of the entrepreneurial private firm Education Alternatives Inc. put it, "American citizens spend

$236 billion each year to educate more than 40 million children in public schools." Golle added, hand-rubbingly: "Unlimited opportunities abound."[59] In other words, someone will eventually crack the pecuniary piñata of EDUCRAT, and all the money will tumble out of reach of the NEA; it cannot preserve its island of bureaucracy in the swirling sea of the market, so American teachers are stuck, unless they try something new.

Switch—Rather than play a losing political game, the teachers could get back to teaching and maybe get ahead in the process. Most teachers want to teach. Yet in the current climate, they may feel that their prime objective is to keep their jobs, and thus they fall into their present-day negative alliance with the barons of the Old Paradigm. What's lost in this endlessly escalating process of politicization is what teachers want to do in the first place: educate.

Since it's EDUCRAT itself that is now defective, no Upgrade will suffice. What teachers will benefit from is a New Big Offer: school vouchers to parents, or some similar charter-school-type mechanism.

Before that Big Offer happens, the teachers can make their own Big Counteroffer: let them run the schools for real, let them make the decisions, and let them reap the rewards of success or suffer the consequences of failure. If the teachers stopped thinking like bureaucrats and started thinking like either entrepreneurs or true altruists, the paradigm shift in education would come sooner.

School choice might not solve all the problems of American elementary and secondary education, but it would solve the biggest problems the teachers face. As we have seen, total spending for public K–12 education has gone up enormously; yet teacher salaries have just inched up. Where's all the money going? Bug No. 2 in AMERICRAT is Parkinsonianism: busywork expands for bureaucrats; from 1960 to 1984, the number of nonclassroom personnel grew ten times faster than the number of classroom teachers.[60] Today, of 4.6 million public school employees, just 2.4 million are teachers.[61] According to one study, less than a third of educational expenditures trickle down to the classroom.[62]

A hypothetical example illustrates the opportunity to de-bureaucratize the schools profitably. Consider the economics of a typical school with 1,000 pupils. On average, the government spends $6,000 per child; doing the multiplication, we find this school's total to be $6 million. As we have seen, the national average student–teacher ratio is about 17:1. Thus our average school has 59 teachers; we can round the total up to 60. According to the NEA, public school teachers in the U.S. earn an average of $35,723 a year; with a benefits package, the total annual compensation per teacher might be $42,000. Sixty teachers times $42,000 equals $2.5 million. But we just saw that the school spends $6 million. Can chalk and Tater Tots really be that expensive? Where did the other $3.5 million go? That's the dirty secret of the decadent Bureaucratic Operating System; the teachers, who think they're benefiting, are in fact losing. Bureaucracies can be reasonably effective at stopping outright thievery, but just because the money is spent legally, that doesn't mean it isn't wasted.

Bureaucracies are not good at efficiently marshaling resources toward a bottom-line objective. So $3.5 million spills around with no particular purpose, financing layer upon layer of mandarins and myrmidons, all with their commensurate share of computers, curricula, and corner offices—and with little reaching in the classroom. But since it's nobody's money, nobody cares.

Imagine what would happen if the sixty teachers at our average school decided really to take history into their own hands, creating a new form of employee ownership. That is, they make a profitable Alliance, an Employee Stock Ownership Plan—an EDUCRATic ESOP. Eyeing that $6 million in cash flow, this "nifty sixty" starts its own school: call it the New Paradigm Academy, or NPA. Taking what they know about educating kids, the teachers are now free to use any combination of technique and technology to offer a better education package to parents, in exchange for their $6,000 voucher. Assuming they keep 80 percent of their students—this is freedom of choice— the employee-owners of NPA still have a cash flow of $4.8 million a year. Of course, if they build the education equivalent of a better mousetrap, the sky's the limit. Either way, there would be a lot of room for pay raises and profit sharing above the old level of $36,000. Few Americans would begrudge teachers twice their salaries—if kids got educated. Teachers could be millionaires, and no one would mind. What Americans really hate is getting ripped off. Of course, people act for many motives other than income maximization; nothing in this scenario would prohibit a bunch of abstemious soul-saving Mother Teresas from giving the money back to the community in some way.

Such an arrangement would pit the teachers against the administrators, school boards, and possibly their own union. And not every teacher collective would be successful. Such competition-driven success and failure is the way the market works—and also the reason the market works.

Yet some teachers would hang back; they would worry that to "voucherize" the schools on affluent Long Island, where some property tax–enriched schools spend as much as $15,000 per year per child, is not the same as voucherizing schools in Texas's impoverished Rio Grande Valley, where the per-pupil expenditure is perhaps a fourth or a fifth as much. As we have seen, the Old Paradigm uses these statistics, what it calls "savage inequalities," to excuse the failure of the public schools. One might consider the obvious rejoinders: first, the kids on Long Island probably aren't getting their parents' money's worth for their schools; second, Catholic Schools in South Texas do a better job with even less money; third, schools in the big cities spend substantially more than the national average and yet deliver an inferior product.

Nevertheless, the goal is more equality of opportunity—and so the New Paradigm must face up to the charge of inequality.

A grand compromise for a New Paradigm in education might be an equalization of per-pupil funding, on at least a state-by-state basis—so long as that funding comes in the form of a voucher to the parent. If the national average per-pupil expenditure is $6,000, that figure could be the target, adjusted for different states' cost of living. Since this is a free country, we could not stop parents, one way or another, from supplementing vouchers with their own money. But we could stop the insidious tax-subsidy scheme that currently undergirds the lavishly funded Old Paradigm. Since local schools are mostly supported by property taxes, and since property taxes are deductible from one's income tax, all Americans end up chipping in for $15,000-a-year public schools; other taxpayers have to make up for the revenue lost from this shelter. Thus we have a sneaky semivoucher system for the rich: they can "spend" their money on the schools via their tax-deductible property taxes. An honest voucher system could eliminate this tax-expenditure prop for the Old Paradigm.

Does this brief sketch work out all the kinks? No, but difficulty of implementation should not be an excuse for inaction. The plain fact is that markets work better than bureaucracy. The poor suffer the most under bureaucratic socialism, but the workers don't do very well, either.

De-bureaucratization can come in two ways: either through rational reform or through cyberconvulsion. Neither of the two parties has fully come to grips with the need for a replacement Big Offer. Instead, blinkered by their old paradigm, the parties look at the bleeding patient—and prescribe leeches. The big difference: the Democrats use big leeches, the Republicans use small leeches. Neither approach leads to a cure. The interests of America would be best served by two parties moving energetically into the information age. To do so, the Democrats would have to abandon their tradition of depending on bureaucrats, and the GOP, which has an edge in terms of its willingness to revamp the Bureaucratic Operating System, would have to rethink its determination to go its own polarizing way. The challenge America faces is too immense for just a 50 or 60 percent coalition. Until that 80:20 point is reached, as David Byrne sings, we're on the road to nowhere. And if the two parties continue to fail, a third party will emerge—for better or worse.

Yet anyone who aspires to lead America must understand that mere majorities are insufficient; new leadership is needed to unite Americans around positive issues. The challenge is to identify the Alliances that create the largest possible coalition on the side of progress. Three groups in particular—African Americans, gays, and public school teachers— are good candidates for the New Paradigm. Today these groups may want nothing to do with each other; the leader's task is to show them how they can all find a safe place on the pyramid of Alliance.

Americans are waiting for the farseeing leadership that will bring them a Big Offer that will solve their most pressing problems.

PART 5

THE NEW PARADIGM BIG OFFER

Chapter 14

THE NEW PARADIGM BIG OFFER

This book contains five visions.

First, we've seen what others predict will happen if present trends continue: a Cyber Future of shrieking separation of high-tech wonders and low-tech horrors, a staggering inequality of incomes, and a harrowing fear of crime—the death of the American Dream.

Second, we've seen what has happened in the past: the creation of a paradigm of government—the Bureaucratic Operating System—with high hopes a century ago, degenerating since into a dangerously leaning tower of privilege for the few, overlooking failure for the many. Kushner's oldest living Bolshevik could be speaking for all of us when he asks: "The Great Question before us is: are we doomed? The Great Question before us is: Will the Past release us?"[1] The Soviet Union could never escape its virulently Viral version of BOS, but the American experience offers some hope.

Third, we've seen how in the past, America has been saved from crisis by new Big Offers, the political equivalent of paradigm shifts. In 1862 Abraham Lincoln counseled his fellow Americans to "think anew, and act anew"; he had the idea advantage, as well as the moral high ground. Seventy years later, in the midst of another deep crisis, Franklin

D. Roosevelt told the American people that "new conditions impose new requirements upon Government." Roosevelt, too, seized an idea edge—one that worked to the benefit of a dejected nation. Yet the last Big Offer, the New Deal, is an inappropriate model for the future, because bureaucracy is the problem, not the solution.

Fourth, we've seen how the two parties have both failed to pull together a Supermajoritarian Alliance that can overcome the dead hand of the Old Paradigm; as we have seen, Big Offers cannot be made with bare majorities. Seemingly unlikely Alliances must be formed to include groups that have not always benefited from the American Dream— and yet share a desire for self-determination and improvement. So we have considered the possibility of a third way, or party, or movement, noting that while an inchoate "market" exists for a reformist radicalism, courageous leadership is still required to pull its different strands into a political force.

The fifth and final vision is a manifesto of the New Paradigm: an open letter to anyone—Democrat, Republican, or other—who thinks that things can't continue, that something has got to give, that there has to be a better way. If we can break with the Old Paradigm and chart a New Paradigm course, here is what we might see:

An America where people can get rich, but nobody is poor. An America where entrepreneurship is rewarded, but wage-work is respected as well. An America that trades freely with the world but empowers its entire labor force to compete. An America that esteems traditional values but looks with live-and-let-live tolerance upon those with their own codes. An America where choice in the bedroom is paired with choice in schoolroom. An America where the vital idea of community is adaptive and evolutionary, not static or backward-looking.

Thus we present a manifesto, a call for a new Big Offer to the American people: a genuinely new politics that is entrepreneurial and empowering, compassionate as well as hard-nosed, yet mindful of the Jeffersonian dictum that government is best when it governs least.

The New Paradigm Big Offer contains these elements:

First, a stronger commitment to prosperity, based on a more efficient and equitable system of taxing and spending, including entitlement reform.

Second, a new emphasis on federalism and government decentralization, including privatization.

Third, a greater dedication to the empowerment of all Americans—in health care, in education, in the workplace.

A Stronger Commitment to Prosperity

"The central political fact today," states Robert Shapiro of the Progressive Policy Institute, "is the stagnation of workers' real incomes." From 1950 to 1970, average incomes doubled in real terms; yet from 1970 to 1990 they barely grew at all.[2] This collapse in income growth has made the American middle class the "anxious class": sometimes sullen and fatalistic, sometimes mad as hell, but no longer content to be the cash cow for the Bureaucratic Operating System. Americans may not know the numbers, but they know in the their bones that their standard of living cannot continue, let alone rise, if they don't save more, invest more, make more, and export more. Americans no longer fear the Russians, and Western Europe is burdened with even more BUREAU-CRATs than we have home-grown AMERICRATs; the real challenge is from the four points of the world—any place that can produce things better, cheaper, or faster. So the Big Offer that makes a commitment to the well-being of all Americans will have to begin with incentives to private-sector wealth creation.

Taxes

The income tax Operating System—we call it the IRS—started out simple and small in 1913, with a top rate of 7 percent on what would be almost 7 million of today's dollars. Rates went up as high as 77 percent during World War I, then down to 25 percent in the twenties, then up to 94 percent during World War II, then down to 70 percent in the Kennedy–Johnson years, then to 50 percent under Reagan. The top rate settled in at 28 percent in the late eighties, but that didn't last.[3] Now it's back up to an effective rate of 44 percent, when various tax-hiking gimmicks are factored in.

After eighty years of Upgrades, the income tax system is pocked with anomalies that reduce growth, revenues, and fairness. Every special-interest-driven break, from accelerated depreciation for business to the home mortgage deduction, has a motivated constituency. Such tinkering pleases politicians, who find it easier to take credit for a specific loophole than for the overall commonweal. Yet it is precisely the common good that is Bugged by this process; we all have read of mailroom clerks paying more in taxes than the profitable companies they work for. Congressman Sam Gibbons of Florida, ranking Democrat on the Ways and Means Committee, says that the 5.6-million-word income tax code is so inefficient that the process of collection costs the economy a third of what's collected—more than $200 billion a year.[4]

In the wake of the 1994 elections, the new Republican majority in Congress will surely fix a few economic inequities and inefficiencies, but the Contract-bound Republicans have committed themselves to so many other tax tweaks that the net result will be an even more epicycled and complicated system. In isolation, it's hard to argue against tax credits for dependent children, dependent adults, and adopted children, but the cumulative result of all these breaks is to erode the tax base, which inevitably impels money-hungry politicians, of either party, to keep rates high.

Thus the triple whammy: first, high rates reduce investment and growth; second, they encourage baroque loophole-seeking, which further exacerbates the unequal treatment of different kinds of income; third, the system gets ever more burdensome, shifting 6 billion person-hours yearly out of the productive economy and into the parasite economy of accountants and lobbyists.[5]

To prosper in the twenty-first century, America must escape the cul de sac of manipulating loopholes and tax breaks altogether and climb to a higher place of de-politicized efficiency. When the nation does that, not only will the pool of capital dramatically increase, but so will the ultimate sense of fairness in the system. Two different strategies lead down this path: the flat tax and the progressive consumption tax.

A Flat Tax

In 1986 the Washington establishment made a rare move in the right direction, toward low rates and simplicity, but it turned out to be a false start. That year's bipartisan tax reform created just two rates, 15 and 28 percent. The combination of lower rates and fewer loopholes forced many previously well-loopholed plutocrats to pay taxes to the IRS for the first time. Unfortunately, the 1990 and 1993 tax increases took us back toward complexity, creating a less efficient and less fair tax code. In 1992 Ross Perot struck a chord with audiences when he held up a blank piece of paper and demanded that the current tax system be junked so that America could start over. Today, that radical idea seems positively prudent; little of the current system is worth preserving.[6]

Taxes on capital are likely to be counterproductive when that capital is mobile. People can scan the planet for the best venue for their money and push-button it overseas, confident that in the cybercapitalist world far fewer commissars or caudillos threaten expropriation. Relative to the world, high U.S. taxes deter investment in American productivity.

Unfortunately, U.S. tax rates stay high mostly to make room for unproductive loopholes. Dubious upward-tilting tax expenditures include the home mortgage deduction, which is available to homeowners with mortgages of up to $1 million. It's nice that America encourages the ownership not only of homes but of *big* homes; perhaps Uncle Sam should take an equally kind view toward investment in productive assets. Furthermore, benefits of the home mortgage deduction are highly selective; it grants a tax subsidy with a total value of $51.3 billion, and yet only 21 percent of families take advantage of it. A closer look at who gets what reveals the gross disparity: of families making less than $10,000, just 0.1 percent take the deduction, for an average of $258; of families making over $200,000, 71 percent take the deduction, for an average of $8,348.[7]

Some might say that the solution is to close that particular loophole;

yet the goal of the New Paradigm is not to engorge the government, but rather to encourage scarce capital to go to its highest and best use as determined by the market. And the best way to achieve such optimal use of capital is for the government to stop playing favorites.

The Progressive Policy Institute's Shapiro has concluded that the U.S. taxes capital more heavily than any other country and that these taxes have contributed significantly to the stall in our national standard of living. The goal of the flat tax is not to make sure that the rich pay less; it is to make sure that those with capital are not discouraged from investing. The flat tax also promises simplicity and the de-politicization of economic decision making.

In 1994, Perot's fellow Texan, House Majority Leader Dick Armey, proposed a 17-percent flat tax that would sweep away tax breaks and preferences, enabling most people to file their returns on a postcard. Long before Armey's proposal, White House Chief of Staff Leon Panetta, then a congressman from California, proposed a 19 percent flat tax in 1982. "If we don't do something to simplify the tax system," Panetta said, "we're going to end up with a national police force of internal revenue agents."[8] A decade later, Jerry Brown endorsed a flat tax in his 1992 presidential campaign.

Yet the Old Paradigm, both its right and left lobes, has dismissed the flat tax. Why? Elites naturally see the national interest as best defined by people like themselves. Aside from the usual Leftist knee-jerkers and nonideological loophole-loving lobbyists, who both like the status quo, other groups have also opposed change. For example, charities like high tax rates, which make it cheaper for upper-bracketeers to give them money. Yet Americans should know that the deepest opposition to rate reductions comes from those with an intellectual stake in Big Government; the current high-rate regime is really about power. So long as people must spell "tax relief" using the letters W-A-S-H-I-N-G-T-O-N, the dream of One Big Answer on the Potomac is not yet dead. We can discern the faint wheeze of the Synoptic Aspiration in the desire of those who would use the tax code to run either industrial or social policy out of the nation's capital.

A more mundane objection to the flat tax is this: to keep it from turning into a tax increase for those with low incomes, proponents must exempt income at the bottom—so much that the flat tax ends up losing substantial amounts of revenue. Armey's version included a huge personal exemption: a $26,200 personal deduction for a married couple and $5,300 per child. Thus a family of four earning the median income would pay nothing.[9] The Clinton Treasury Department produced a study showing that such a plan would "cost" the government $244 billion a year. We can be suspicious of this number, which was released during the 1994 election season; indeed, anyone familiar with the fates of various rosy scenarios touting "declining deficit paths" over the past few decades should know that all these numbers are at best guesses and, at worst, advocacy dressed up as "data." Yet proponents believe that a flat tax would unleash a Hong Kong–like boom in the U.S., with the government also standing to benefit from the resulting revenue gusher; the small island colony has a 15 percent top tax rate.[10] A possible compromise would be to raise the rate a little: Hoover Institution scholars Robert E. Hall and Alvin Rabushka have proposed a 19 percent flat tax.[11]

The beauty of the flat tax is that it taxes all income only once, at the same uniform rate. While such simplicity has vast appeal, the flat tax would create a serious perception problem if enacted. More forms of corporate income would be taxed, and fewer exemptions and deductions would be permitted; yet to avoid the double taxation of capital, such moneys would not be taxed as they went to investors. In other words, millionaire coupon clippers would pay nothing—the theory being that the firm from which they received the money had already paid tax for them—while working stiffs would still suffer a 17 or 19 percent bite in their paycheck. Opponents call the flat tax a "wage tax," although as we have seen, the accusation is incorrect, because every dollar gets taxed at some point along the fiscal food chain. Moreover, an extraordinary degree of public education would be required to correct this and other misperceptions.[12]

A Progressive Consumption Tax

Another idea is to do away with the income tax completely and to tax consumption instead. A consumption tax is distinct from a national sales tax or value-added tax, in that it is imposed not at the point of sale but rather on that portion of income which is not saved or invested. With a consumption tax, investment is tax-free; what's taxable is high living. As we saw in our earlier discussion of the Reagan years, higher taxes on capital can turn unproductive consumption into a kind of tax shelter.

The best Big Offer on taxation is a system that no longer taxes capital formation at all. To administer a consumption tax, the IRS would ascertain income, exempt that which is saved and invested, and tax the remainder. Such a tax could be made as progressive as the current income tax, or more so. From a strict investment-incentive point of view, it doesn't much matter at what rate consumption is taxed. Indeed, if the two political parties could agree that productivity-boosting investment capital should be sheltered, they could still wage a vigorous debate over the optimum tax burden on Rolex and Rolls-Royce consumption.

Such a solution would leapfrog the current trench warfare, in which "higher rates" and "lower rates" ebb destructively across no-man's-land. The New Paradigm argument is that what Americans want is a tax system that works for them—a system that maximizes overall economic growth.

The progressive consumption tax is already an Alliance issue: Senators Pete Domenici (R-New Mexico) and Sam Nunn (D-Georgia) have their own bipartisan proposal, combining both growth and progressivity; one version sets the rate on consumption at zero for the lowest earners and raises it to 45 percent, beginning at $80,000 of consumed income. In the words of the cosponsors, a progressive consumption tax offers "simplicity, efficiency, equity," while boosting net national savings and international competitiveness.[13] Yet conversion to a progressive consumption tax would be complicated, creating arcane new missions for the IRS.[14]

No magic bullet will miraculously heal the current tax system. However, a New Paradigm tax system, as it emerges, must retain three principles:

First, a repudiation of the Washington idea that economic policy should be made by the members of the Senate Finance and House Ways and Means committees in conjunction with an electron-cloud of lobbyists and fixers.

Second, the realization that those with capital are infinitely more likely to stash their money in unproductive tax shelters when the top rate is in the forties than when it is zero.

Third, the recognition that the poor are the biggest losers from the slow economic growth that results from an unfriendly domestic investment climate in an increasingly capital-friendly world.

Spending

Any consideration of government spending must begin with the oft-overlooked question: "What do we want to get for our money?" Most Americans believe that they are not getting their money's worth, because neither the form nor the function of government has kept up with the times. Yet the New Paradigm Fiscal Offer must be fair to all, including the poor. It must offer all Americans the reasonable prospect of being better off four years from now.

If we acknowledge that AMERICRAT 4.0 no longer works, we still face the challenge of sorting out the necessity and efficacy of governmental functions. A New Paradigm leader can apply two tests to the government.

The Drucker Test

Twenty years ago, Jimmy Carter campaigned for president on a promise to enact a hot new idea in public policy: "zero-based budgeting." It seemed like a great idea; every fiscal year, the government would start with a blank slate, and advocates for each program would have to rejustify its continued existence. It was a great idea, but it never happened—not in Carter's presidency, nor in any subsequent administration.

Jonathan Rauch has said that the government never starts from a blank slate, adding that it has lost the ability to learn from trial and error—and to eliminate the error:

The end result is that, with rare exceptions, *we are stuck with everything that the government ever tries*, including some rather bizarre things.[15]

In the dark night of our Old Paradigm souls, we have so far not escaped from the nightmare of the past. Yet clearly, we need a bankruptcy mechanism, so that every so often we can start from a zero base and cleanse ourselves of our past AMERICRATic sins.

Fortunately, we have what can be called the Drucker Test. Thirty years ago, management seer Peter Drucker said that effective executives "slough off the past that has ceased to be productive" by asking themselves and their people: "If we did not already do this, would we go into it *now*?"[16] In a fast-changing world, no human institution can withstand a rigorous Drucker Test without modifications to meet shifting circumstances. Indeed, every day brings new information that makes plain the obsolescence of the old ways.

Yet since every government program, just like every cost center in a business, has a constituency that swears by its vital necessity, real determination is needed to recalibrate or amputate a function that does not meet the Drucker Test threshold. This test is not an answer in and of itself; it is merely a way of thinking about what government should look like at each step of the way.

So with the Drucker Test in one hand, we need the Lindsey Test in the other.

The Lindsey Test

A standard joke runs: "We're not getting all the government we're paying for—thank God!" Yet as the deterioration of the Bureaucratic Operating System worsens, the basic services we depend on are jeopardized.

Americans are confused: is the real problem too much government— or incompetent government? And what of the deficit: how harmful is it? Federal Reserve Board Governor Lawrence B. Lindsey offers a sensible explanation: "People don't worry so much about the deficit; they worry more about what they're getting for their money."

The real issue, Lindsey says, is not spending; it is the *rate of return* we're getting on our spending. He cites studies showing that in the last forty years, the rate of return, adjusted for inflation, on private investment has averaged about 10 percent a year.[17] Yet as we transfer money from the private sector to the public sector, the rate of return declines:

> It matters little whether the government taxes that money or borrows that money. Either way, the private sector must forgo activities that would have yielded that 10 percent return on investment.

Not every private dollar is invested, because people want to consume as well; acquiring food and shelter can be a higher priority than growing one's nest egg. Yet the question remains: Can the government "invest" our surplus capital better than we can by ourselves? Sometimes government does: the Fidelity Magellan fund could never have defeated Hitler or built the interstate highway system.

But does every government program generate 10 percent a year in direct or indirect benefits? Supporters of specific programs produce studies to backstop their flacks and lobbyists. The Department of Labor estimates that mandating 1.5 percent of payroll for on-the-job training would cost $21 billion a year but yield $63 billion in new economic activity and 2.5 million new jobs over three to five years.[18] The Children's Defense Fund offers an even better deal; according to its prospectus, "Our nation can't afford *not* to give every child a good quality early childhood foundation when, according to new research, every dollar invested saves more than $7 in later years."[19] Other programs come with even bigger claims: The Rural Electric Co-ops claim 7.5:1. One NASA study claims 8:1.

Wouldn't we all want to "invest" money and get back 300 percent or more? There's only one problem: the facts might not be as the advocates of government "investment" aver. Since there's no Securities and Exchange Commission to guard against political scams, we have to depend on our own common sense to tell us that we can't spend ourselves rich.

Worth scrutinizing is one typical study, a report by the California Department of Alcohol and Drug Programs (DADP) that offers a suspicious degree of precision: the $209 million the Golden State spent on treatment in 1991–92, it claims, yielded $1.5 billion in savings from reductions in crime and health care costs. In the words of DADP Director Andrew M. Mecca, "Treatment is very beneficial to taxpayers," offering a "$7 return for every dollar invested."[20] Mecca exulted: "This is what I call slam-dunk evidence!" On the east coast, Alan Leshner, director of the National Institute on Drug Abuse, echoed his fellow rehabilitator in Sacramento: "Most people don't believe treatment works," he conceded—but answered quickly: "They're wrong. That's why a study like this is so important." Yet we should bear in mind that DADP paid $2 million for the study, conducted by two research firms which randomly sampled substance abusers in treatment and asked them if they had committed crimes or otherwise done things that would cost the taxpayers money. Obligingly enough, the samplees said that they had done fewer costly things since entering treatment.[21] Is it only cynics who find it suspicious that bureaucrats with an obvious "class interest" are able produce studies—at taxpayers' expense—that demonstrate the worthwhileness of their work?

Lindsey offers an elegant explanation for the deterioration of national competitiveness: we're taking dollars earning 10 percent out of the private sector and putting them into the public sector, where most of those dollars earn substantially less and, in some cases, "earn" at a negative rate. Thus the same AMERICRATic system that made government spending a good investment a generation or two ago is now manifestly—and quantifiably—obsolete. The public sector now squanders capital that might have been well invested in the private sector today—or in the public sector yesterday.

So long as the U.S. underinvests in true investments and overinvests in plain old spending, it doesn't matter whether the government borrows or taxes the money for its continuing binge. Until Americans can come up with an effective, post-bureaucratic system for collective action, the money they spend on government will serve nobody well.

The Lindsey Test—that is, calculating whether or not government spending is yielding a better return on investment than capital left in the private sector—should be put out in the open, where everyone can do his or her own assessment. Indeed, the only way to apply the Lindsey Test is to compare one investment to another. Thus we are left with experimentation, trial and error, and choice and competition as the only way to discover the optimum solution.[22]

Few dispute today that markets are more efficient than politics, but that truth still leaves the question of social justice. The challenge the New Paradigm will face is bringing the benefits of the market to those whom capitalism has ignored and government has failed to help.

Every Man and Woman an OMB Director

The general proposition that unites most Americans is that government is too big and spends too much.[23] The Congressional Budget Office's *Reducing the Deficit: Spending and Revenue Options* provides ready reference; in 361 pages, it lists enough spending-cut options to make everyone feel like OMB Director for a day, choosing among various options: from canceling the C-17 transport plane (saving $7.7 billion over five years) to charging federal employees for parking ($530 million) to freezing Social Security and Railroad Retirement cost-of-living allowances for a year ($47.7 billion).[24]

In 1992, all three presidential candidates claimed they would find ways to reduce federal spending and the deficit; of the three, Bush was the least credible. As we have seen, domestic spending rose steadily during the dozen years of Republican rule. Yet as president, Clinton showed little interest in spending restraint; Al Gore's "reinventing government" exceeded the low expectations with which it began, but it has hardly reinvented the leviathan.

Furthermore, to the Clintons at least, the Rego effort was begun as mostly a smokescreen for their larger agenda: enlarging government with a Big Offer on health care. So it is little wonder that few Americans gave the administration credit for reinvention; as *U.S. News*'s Ken Walsh puts it, whatever the true accomplishments of Gore's Rego, "people still think there are five million more bureaucrats hidden out there somewhere, all wasting money."

Beginning in 1995, the new-majority Republicans have made a crusade out of spending cuts, but they are in constant jeopardy of forgetting a basic rule of budget cutting: the sense of sacrifice must be shared. The 80 percent Alliance would come from those who believe government is too big—and also those who believe that spending and deficit reductions ought to be fair.

We can divide our discussion of spending cuts into two categories: discretionary spending and entitlement spending.

Discretionary Spending Cuts

The paradox of discretionary cuts is this: the tempting and easy cuts are small; it is the hard and uninviting cuts that offer big savings. This paradox is not an argument against making the easy and tempting cuts; it's an admonition that the hard and uninviting cuts must be made as well. Discretionary spending cutters must beware of two snares:

First, not getting beyond symbolism. Cutters could eliminate federal funding for every limousine, naughty art exhibit, public TV station, chinchilla ranch, and midnight congressional payraise, and the total savings would barely amount to a rounding error in the budget of the Department of Health and Human Services.[25] Newsworthy anecdotes about wasteful spending fire radio talkshow outrage, but it is the chronic and hard-to-visualize outgoes that add up, such as the $300 billion Uncle Sam absent-mindedly spent on the S&L bailout. Fairness requires that the nonneedy make sacrifices before the needy; the yipes of the defunded middle class must not deafen the New Paradigm Big Offerer to the droning sound of Big Government continuing to crank out payments to every class and category of people. A spending-cut strategy that is plush in symbolism will be threadbare in actual deficit reduction.

Second, doing only what's easy. The natural spending-cut strategy— to take the path of least resistance, focusing on "soft" targets and bypassing "hard" targets—may work in military strategy, but it fails as a spending-reduction strategy. Good generals know that victory comes from striking at the weak spot in the enemy line: the exact opposite of a "fair fight." Yet if the goal in war is to assemble overwhelming force against a soft target, the goal in domestic policy is to assemble overwhelming force against a hard target. The "easy" spending cuts can be made at the expense of weak groups, such as the poor, the young, and the unregistered.[26] Yet precisely because such groups are weak, they are less likely, despite common misperceptions, to enjoy big spending on their behalf. Thus there is less money to be saved by slashing them. John J. Pitney Jr. of Claremont-McKenna College points out that all means-tested—that is, targeted to the needy—spending in fiscal year 1996 could be eliminated, and Uncle Sam would still be in the red. So that reality forces cutters, if they're honest, to look toward nodes of "hard" spending. True leadership, that which would convince the vast majority of the American people that a new Big Offer of limited government is in the making, would build credibility by zeroing in on, and perhaps zeroing out, the hard targets. An Alliance-making leader would lead by example—first sacrificing his or her own constituents' pet spending programs to the greater good of fiscal discipline.

The New Paradigm Big Offerer could begin his or her budget-cut expedition with agricultural subsidies, the Alaska Power Administration, and Amtrak and end somewhere on the alphabetical backside of the Veterans Department, water subsidies, and West Virginia. Everyone has a little list of cuts, or even a big list. The key to long-term success is making the cut list fair. Politicians should articulate their spending-cut principles in advance, so that the voters can give them a mandate. If spending surgery is done in an above-board process, even those who are about to get cut won't be able to say that their voices weren't heard. One attractive spending-cut package is the "Green Scissors" report, released jointly in 1995 by the Friends of the Earth and the National Taxpayers Union Foundation; that report targets "wasteful and environmentally destructive subsidies," some dating all the way back to 1872. Green Scissors seeks to cut thirty-four programs, saving the taxpayers $33 billion.[27] We will consider other templates for spending cuts later on.

One workable mechanism for executing cuts is the Pentagon's Base Closure Commission. As with any government program, military bases have their knee-jerk political defenders, anxious to protect every job back home. With the military budget scheduled to fall by 40 percent in real terms from 1985 to 1997, something new was needed to overcome gridlock. Enter once again Dick Armey, the Texas Congressman, who in 1988 invented the legislative equivalent of the tank to override the dug-in opponents of rational Pentagon downsizing. Armey set up a Defense Base Closure and Realignment Commission, the members of which were appointed by the president and confirmed by the Senate. The process worked well. The Secretary of Defense submitted a list of proposed reductions, on which the commission held public hearings;

the commission then voted on a package of cuts and sent the list to Congress. Congress could vote yea or nay on the entire package, but it couldn't amend it. So far, the Base Closure Commission has overseen three rounds of cuts, reducing the domestic base structure by 15 percent, with an annual savings of $6 billion.[28]

The commission has been popular because it followed principles of overall fairness, not case-by-case logrolling. The public got big defense savings, and members of Congress got insulation from adverse reaction back home to unpopular cuts. Solons could noisily oppose the individual provisions that affected their constituents and even vote against the commission's findings; yet they were secure that there wouldn't be enough "no" votes to derail the total reduction package.

Armey's idea had a big advantage: it worked. The base-closing model provided an across-the-board comprehensivity: the feeling that we're all in this together—that the individual sacrifices were made for the greater good. The Pentagon, which accounts for only about a sixth of total federal spending, could be seen as the fiscal guinea pig for the rest of the federal government.

When John Kasich (R-Ohio) took over as chairman of the House Budget Committee, he found that Uncle Sam funded 9 export promotion programs, 22 child abuse programs, 163 job training programs, and 300 economic-development programs. One must ask: What are the chances that all these programs are equally effective? Since they obviously cannot be of equal worth, it makes sense, from the point of view both of saving money and of improving services, to start phasing out the poorest performers.

Kasich and Senator Connie Mack (R-Florida) have suggested an overall Spending Reduction Commission modeled after the Base Closing Commission.[29] Certainly just as much fat and featherbedding can be found at DOE or DOT as at DOD. Yet since the newly dominant Republicans will find themselves affected by the same D.C. culture of spending that mesmerized the Democrats, it would be in their political interest, as well as the national interest, to create such a spending-cut commission.[30] The Kasich–Mack plan is a great idea—except for one thing; it specifically excludes from cutting consideration the biggest piece of the budget: Social Security.

Entitlement Spending Cuts

The "real money" in the federal budget is in entitlements and other programs that benefit mostly the middle class. As we have seen, Social Security was the heart of the New Deal Big Offer; today, it's the hardest of the hard budget targets. Much of the Bureaucratic Operating System has crumbled, but Social Security still hums along, getting bigger every year. Its grip is so strong that even Ronald Reagan couldn't flex back its fingers. Yet just because Social Security is popular, that doesn't make it fair. Workers who put in a few hundred dollars in FICA taxes over their entire careers now take thousands of dollars out of the system every year. Stanford economist Michael Boskin has calculated that a worker who retired in 1980 will, in the course of an actuarial lifetime— that is, in the length of time he or she is expected to live—receive a net transfer of wealth of $63,000 in 1994 dollars, whereas a worker retiring in 2025 will suffer a net wealth loss of $48,000. Former Commerce Secretary Peter Peterson writes: "Most currently retired Americans receive Social Security benefits that are two to five times greater than the actuarial value of prior contributions, by both employer and employee." Peterson adds that the Medicare payback is five to twenty times greater.[31]

How long will it be until this fiscally inverted pyramid topples? The answer to that question depends on the willingness of young and poor workers to pay the taxes needed to support the old, regardless of whether seniors need the money or not. The Committee for a Responsible Federal Budget reports that one-third of Social Security beneficiaries have incomes greater than the median family income. Meanwhile, millions of working families, all paying FICA taxes, have incomes below the median.

Recently Congressman Joe Kennedy II, a liberal Democrat from Massachusetts, called for means-testing entitlements, arguing that non-needy people should get back only what they put in.[32] Yet for the most part, both parties are complicit in this great generational injustice. Democrats know that their single best vote-getting issue is Social Security; Republicans, having been burned in the past, most notably in 1982, now go to elaborate lengths to avoid rousing the ghost of Claude Pepper, the legendary champion of full-throttle Social Security. And so Americans slave to the grind: the overtaxation of work provides for the oversubsidization of leisure.

Nobody wants seniors to sink into poverty, but neither should Americans impoverish their children and grandchildren to augment retiree Ross Perot's wealth. With real wages already declining, one should ask why a recent college graduate earning $400 a week faces a 15 percent chomp out of his or her paycheck just to pay Social Security and Medicare taxes.[33] The payroll tax crept up steadily during the Reagan years, and there's no reason to assume it won't keep going up as the retired population swells. Merrill Lynch has calculated that today's teenagers will pay 37 percent of their lifetime earnings in taxes, compared with 23 percent for those born at the turn of the century. The Wall Street firm estimates that the lifetime tax rate for a new worker today could go as high as 82 percent, largely because of retirement costs.[34]

So far at least, Generation X seems more resigned than riled, but that may change. As Lawrence Lindsey says, "There'll be an election one of these years which will be waged on the issue of payroll taxes, pitting workers against beneficiaries."

The New Paradigm Big Offer must save the country from age war; it must be a plan for all Americans. Supermajority Alliances can be built only on appealing and enduring principles, such as fairness and equity. Entitlement spending currently consumes half the federal budget, up from less than a quarter of the budget in 1963. More than a third of federal outlays—about $550 billion in fiscal year 1996—go to Social Security and Medicare. The essence of unfairness is to cut everything else and leave those two programs intact.

What to do? The solution may be a variant of Nixon-goes-to-China. Perhaps only a Democrat can repair the Democratic Big Offer. If so, then Senator Bob Kerrey of Nebraska may be the Nixon for the nineties, convincing Americans that it is possible to reduce Social Security and Medicare spending without throwing the elderly into the snow—or, since so many retirees now live in Florida, the sand.

Kerrey chaired the Bipartisan Commission on Entitlement and Tax Reform, which released its final report in December 1994. He did the unusual in Washington; he looked beyond the next election. What he found was this: in the year 2001, the Medicare Hospital Insurance program, currently funded with a 2.9 percent payroll tax, will become insolvent.[35] In that same decade, as the oldest Boomers start to retire, the ratio of workers to retirees will fall by 40 percent, from 5:1 to 3:1. By the year 2012, projected outlays for entitlements and interest on the national debt will consume all tax revenues collected by the federal government. And by the year 2030, spending for Medicare, Medicaid, Social Security, and federal retirees will consume *all* federal tax revenues.[36]

The recommendations of Kerrey and his cochair, former Senator John Danforth, were swept off the table, not because they were wrong, but because they were right. Yet the Nebraska Democrat and the Missouri Republican had reached across the aisle of partisanship, contributing to an informed dialogue that could be the basis for future reform.

So the first element of the New Paradigm Big Offer on entitlement reform is to do what Kerrey and Danforth did—tell the truth. Decades of misinformation about Social Security need to be overcome. Back when the federal government was trusted, people were told that they would enjoy a cradle-to-grave welfare state. Included in that Roosevelt-Truman-era message was the fiction that they had their own Social Security account.[37] Half a century later many senior citizens sincerely believe that they are only getting back what they put in, plus interest. Kerrey suggests a national on-line entitlement database. David Frum suggests appending to each Social Security check an honest financial statement, itemizing each beneficiary's lifetime contributions and receipts.[38]

The second element of the Big Offer should be cuts in program growth. If just 5 percent of private-sector retirees get cost-of-living allowances added on to their pensions every year, why should 100 percent of Social Security recipients get such raises, regardless of the condition of the overall economy? A one-year COLA freeze would save $40 billion. Denying all entitlement payments to those earning more than $100,000 a year would save $46 billion over five years.

A third element is raising the retirement age. When Bismarck selected 65 as the retirement age in 1889, the average life expectancy in Germany was about 40 years.[39] When Social Security became law in 1935, life expectancy in the U.S. was 64. Today, life expectancy is close to 80. Yet even small changes can save money. The retirement age is already scheduled to rise to 67 in the year 2027; moving that target age forward by two decades, to 2007, would save $60 billion.[40]

A fourth element is taxing all entitlement benefits; that would save $250 billion over five years.[41] Peter Peterson has an even better idea: an "affluence test" to guide the spending-cut process, targeting the truly unneedy. According to Peterson, in 1991, 25 percent of all federal entitlements went to households with annual incomes of more than $50,000.[42] As he archly observes, the government could do a fairer job of distributing wealth by throwing it out of an airplane. Applying Peterson's affluence test would reduce outlays by $250 billion over five years.[43]

Such spending cuts and tax increases would take us only part of the way. After decades of being told that Uncle Sam would take care of them, millions of elderly Americans are at least as dependent on the government as anyone on AFDC. The next Big Offer will have to rethink the whole issue of saving for retirement so that people no longer reach sixty-five with little or nothing except their Social Security. However, caution and persuasion must not be confused with procrastination—because, as we have seen, the unmet needs of the nation can't wait.

The high concept of entitlement reform must be to encourage people to save more so that the government can spend less. Reducing taxes on both labor and capital as outlined above will help, but such tax relief must be accompanied by a stern warning: there's not enough money in the world—or in America, at least—to pay for people's old age if they don't save on their own.

Kerrey and Danforth made a dramatic step in that direction, suggesting a 1.5 percent cut in the Social Security payroll tax, coupled with a forced-savings plan that would funnel 1.5 percent of income into a mandatory individual retirement account. Given the extreme delicacy of the entire Social Security issue, such incrementalism is useful—as long as America begins to move in the right direction.

Forced saving in lieu of taxation is not a new idea. Since 1955, Singapore has required most employees to contribute into its Central Provident Fund: a forced savings plan. Yet unlike Americans in the Social Security system, Singaporeans retain direct ownership of their CPF account. They can withdraw some of their money for specified purposes, such as purchasing a home or buying life insurance. And

Singapore workers can withdraw all their money upon disability or retirement; upon death, CPF accounts remand to the worker's heirs.[44] Chile adopted a similar program in 1981, and a half-dozen Latin American countries have followed suit. We can learn from others' experience, perhaps maintaining a two-tier system for a while: a basic minimum benefit and, on top of that, money from the worker's own IRA.

A transition will not be easy; we have a $6.7 trillion overhang of future liability for the current Social Security system. That future debt will have to be paid, regardless of what we do to revamp the system today. That's not an argument against reform; it's a reminder that reform will be as arduous as it necessary. Fortunately, Americans, wielding their calculators and Quicken financial software programs, are much more able to handle their financial affairs than they were in a less literate age.[45]

The New Paradigm leader will begin with a basic confidence that senior citizens are ready to do their bit, that they are merely waiting for a credible figure to ask them to take part in shared sacrifice. America needs an ask-not John F. Kennedy to exhort the GI Generation to one last expression of the spirit that brought the nation shining through the Depression, World War II, and the Cold War. They've done it before, and they can do it again, for their own grandchildren. Yet nobody wants to jump into the void alone; such reform and retrenchment must be bundled into an overall Big Offer.

A New Emphasis on Federalism and Privatization

Enhanced prosperity from a fairer and more efficient tax system, as well as from limits on government spending, will address many, but not all, of the problems America faces. Such measures by themselves do not address the challenge of reengineering and restructuring the bureaucratic state. If the object were only for the government to lose weight, we could just as easily cut an arm or a leg off the federal behemoth. The better goal is to replace the Bureaucratic Operating System with a New Paradigm Market Operating System that works. Success in this undertaking would cement in place a long-lasting political coalition.

Thus the second phase of the New Paradigm Big Offer: federalism and privatization, two tools for downsizing and rightsizing the government into efficiency. After that, only a small number of elite Samurais, as we shall dub them later on, would remain in public service to carry on the remaining vital missions of government.

Federalism

"Federalism," a word coined by the eighteenth-century statesman Edmund Burke, refers to the distribution and separation of political power. The *Federalist Papers*, written by Alexander Hamilton, John Jay, and James Madison, were published in 1787–88 to persuade the people of New York State to ratify the new Constitution. In Federalist #45, Madison, discussing the relationship between the states and the federal government, declared that states would "have the advantage." Indeed, he added, "were the Union itself inconsistent with the public happiness," he would say: "Abolish the Union."[46]

The Bill of Rights, ratified shortly thereafter to rectify gaps in the Constitution, includes the long-neglected Tenth Amendment, which reads in its entirety:

> The powers not delegated to the United States by the Constitution, nor prohibited by it to the States, are reserved to the States, respectively, or to the people.

In his first inaugural in 1801, Jefferson called state governments "the most competent administrations for our domestic concerns and the surest bulwarks against anti-republican tendencies." The idea that state authority was prior to federal authority dominated political thought until the Civil War; the idea of "states' rights" continued well into the twentieth century.

Yet in modern times, when the headrushing Synoptic ideologies of the Right and Left were described as "the wave of the future,"[47] the old Newtonian checks-and-balances mechanism of the Founders seemed too slow for the new era of factory turbos and bureaucratic dynamos.

From the 1930s to the 1960s, it was believed that America's greatest domestic objectives—from Keynesian pump-priming to interstate highways to integration—could be fulfilled only from Washington.

Yet the persuasiveness of that argument began to diminish in the seventies. One reason: Uncle Sam's expertise at fine-tuning both society and the economy came into question; riots, inflation, and gas lines seemed chronic and incurable. Moreover, the states were no longer seen as the bastions of troglodytic reaction and unreconstructed racism they had been before the Supreme Court's "one man one vote" decisions of 1962–64; these rulings ended gerrymanders that had reinforced rural power to the detriment of urban power. In addition, the Voting Rights Act of 1965, sending more people to the polls—white as well as black—put an end to rustic rotten-borough hegemony. Today, seventeen African Americans represent congressional districts in the Old Confederacy. And in the past few decades, states have "professionalized" their governments; almost as many graduates of Harvard's John F. Kennedy School of Government work for state and local government as go off to Washington. This bureaucrat-diffusion is surely a two-edged sword, but at least the feds can no longer bedazzle and befuddle their state counterparts with the latest technocratic jargon.

In 1982 Ronald Reagan's "New Federalism" proposed a swap: the federal government would take over Medicaid, and the states would assume the burden for welfare. Although Reagan pushed hard, his proposal went nowhere in the Congress; people didn't trust the Republicans to administer the exchange fairly. Yet the federalist idea keeps resurfacing—because the Upgrades to AMERICRAT keep failing.

Just as Democrat Bob Kerrey opened the door to real entitlement reform, so another Democrat, Alice Rivlin, may be seen to have played a Nixonian role, piercing the bamboo curtain of centralized bureaucracy. In her 1991 book *Reviving the American Dream*, she argued:

> The proliferation of federal programs, projects, offices, and agencies in so many parts of the country made the federal government increasingly unmanageable. It resembled a giant conglomerate that has acquired too many different kinds of businesses and cannot coordinate its own activities or manage them all effectively from central headquarters.[48]

Rivlin counted some 500 federal categorical programs, each with its own rules and regulations,[49] making the now-obvious point that all 500 could not possibly be managed well by the D.C. Beltway's central processing unit. Whereas most Washington policy mavens are better at describing the problem than proposing solutions, Rivlin was quite specific in itemizing what ought to be de-conglomerated back to the states:

> The federal government should eliminate most of its programs in education, housing, highways, social services, economic development, and job training.[50]

Rivlin hasn't been as blunt lately;[51] she is now director of the Office of Management and Budget in the Clinton administration, which has shown little enthusiasm for federalism or anything else that might devolve Washington's power. Yet other Democrats are picking up on Rivlin's theme. Governor Ben Nelson (D-Nebraska) recalled that when he took office, "I wondered why I had been called governor, as opposed to administrator, or branch manager, because most of my budget and my priorities were established by mandates from Washington."[52]

No rational reason calls for the federal government to siphon $25 billion from the fifty states to Washington, only to turn around and slosh it back across the country, building highways between Anytown and East Anytown. But that's what the Department of Transportation does for a living—as this centralized sloshing process is also hijacked by politics. In 1994, Senator Byrd of West Virginia, then chairman of the Appropriations Committee, snagged fully 52 percent of "highway demonstration projects" for his state, which has less than 1 percent of the U.S. population.[53] No lawmaker will likely ever match Byrd's brazen porkery, although in the 104th Congress, many bacon-hungry Republicans, lean from their years in the wilderness, will surely try. Indeed, now that GOPers oversee the money-sloshing committees, they seem substantially less eager to punt the power out of Powertown.

To avoid the endless spoils-seesaw, the New Paradigm Big Offer must follow through on a basic nonpartisan principle: it must make a clearly stated commitment to federalism, with the specifics right on the table where everyone can see them. Only by acting in this above-board manner can the New Paradigm Offerer win the 80 percent mandate needed for genuine federalist reform. We can call it Rivlin's Razor.

Let's make a list of the fourteen cabinet departments, in the order in which they were created, and consider which ones are vital to the nation and which ones are eligible for the Rivlin Razor. First come

State
Treasury
Defense
Justice
Interior

The five above are "keepers"; they fulfill clear-cut missions for the nation. Total spending for all five departments amounts to $300 billion—not a small sum, but barely a sixth of total federal spending. While some areas of outlay could be beneficially reduced—and many functions altered or eliminated—we can say that from embassies and soldiers abroad to the currency, the courts, and Mt. Rushmore at home, a taxpayer-paid cabinet official will be needed to watch over them. That can't be said of the next three, possibly four, departments:

Agriculture
Commerce
Labor
Health and Human Services

Our purpose here is not to pick a fight with the past—that is, to reproach the original rationale for each department's creation—but rather to improve the future. These departments once had a purpose, but three of them—Agriculture, and Commerce, Labor—have now degenerated into slush funds for their various Vealy constituencies, costing the taxpayers more than $100 billion a year. Farmers can fend for themselves without the USDA, and capitalists are doing just fine; they don't need Commerce. Workers, as we have seen, are having a hard time, but the Labor Department is not the answer. As part of the abolition process, some programs can be spun off into small independent agencies, such as the Census and Labor Statistics bureaux; others can be consolidated and/or transferred elsewhere, such as food stamps or the Forest Service. But we must be clear: most spending line-items should be removed from federal purview and given to the states, if they want them. These range from farm price support programs ($10 billion a year, minimum) to job training ($20 billion) to the Commerce Department's ventures into special-interest-driven industrial policy, including the Advanced Technology Program, the Economic Development Administration, and the Travel and Tourism Administration ($800 million for all three).

Most federalists, from Madison to Rivlin, would say that the states should then be free to pick up these discarded federal programs. While it is unlikely that Kansas would tax just Kansans to further enrich its millionaire farmers, a federalist America should grant the Jayhawk State its right to do so.

Other functions, such as work training, are vital for American well-being and competitiveness; that's precisely why they need to be reinvented. The fifty states are already spending more than $200 billion a year of their own money on K–12 schooling; they all see the imperative, not only of learning, but also of preparing young people for a productive life of work.

The last department of this group, Health and Human Services, presents a more complicated picture. For decades, it contained four programs that are at the heart of the Old Paradigm: Social Security, Medicare, Medicaid, and Aid to Families with Dependent Children. In 1994, the Social Security Administration was spun off into an independent agency with a budget of more than $400 billion. This organization-chart alteration meant nothing in terms of SSA's operation, since, as we have seen, the real power over the agency rests with Vealifying lawyers and pressure groups. The remaining programs, Medicare, Medicaid, and AFDC, which together account for another $300 billion a year, pose a different problem; we will consider health care and poverty in more detail in the next section.

The following five departments, budgeted at a total of $150 billion a year, should be disposed of quickly, not because their works are unworthy, but because their functioning at the federal level is wasteful and counterproductive:

Housing and Urban Development
Transportation
Energy
Education
Veterans Affairs

A few functions deserve rescue, or at least reshuffling. The Federal Aviation Administration, which is part of the Department of Transportation, has a vital purpose, although its job needn't be performed by bureaucrats; many countries, from South Africa to Switzerland, have turned their air traffic control systems over to the private sector.[54] Other programs might not be privatized, but rather "Samuraized": turned over to the Samurai bureaucrats we will soon examine.

As for the rest of the programs, expedience recommends a process of transition, such as converting the budgets of these five departments into "block grants" every year; that is, Uncle Sam could "cash out" these departments and send a prorated check to each state. The states today don't need federal G-People to tell them how to weatherize buildings or help kids go to college; they just need the money. Yet eventually, the foolishness even of this block grant process—sending money to Washington so that Washington can take its cut and then send most of the money back—will be so manifest that the states will decide just to keep the money for themselves in the first place.

The last department, Veterans Affairs, deserves special attention. On the exterior of its Vermont Avenue headquarters, a plaque quotes Lincoln's second inaugural address: "To care for him who shall have borne the battle, and for his widow, and his orphan." The VA—becoming the DVA in 1989 at the instigation of Ronald Reagan, in what was arguably his worst domestic blunder—has been sliding further downhill ever since. VA hospitals are so rife with abuse and corruption that less than 10 percent of eligible veterans use them, leaving nearly a quarter of its hospital beds unfilled. Yet the American Legion and other big veterans groups jealously guard the $37 billion-a-year DVA as is; they are Orbital Bureaucrats with American-flag lapel pins. Their solution to its chronic wasteful incompetence amounts to this: more funding for that wasteful incompetence. Yet the grip of organized veteranry is so strong that DVA could just as easily be renamed the Department of Veal Affairs. George Bush's Veterans Secretary, Ed Derwinski, a World War II vet and lifelong hawk, was drummed out of his job in 1992 because he dared to suggest allowing nonveteran Medicaid patients to use VA hospital beds that were otherwise going unused. The Legion and the other Orbitals buzzing around "their" department couldn't stand the thought of any intrusion, so they prevailed upon Bush to fire Derwinski. Since then, DVA secretaries have been better behaved, not rattling their Veal pens. Indeed, the Vealification of the DVA was completed when President Clinton named a veterans group lobbyist, Jesse Brown, to be Secretary of Veterans Affairs.

Uncle Sam might block-grant the $16 billion that VA hospitals spend each year, giving each state its share in proportion to its eligible veteran population, but devolving one giant soviet for veterans' health care into fifty little soviets is not the best America can do for those who have borne the battle. Here's a better idea: convert that $16 billion into vouchers for veterans. Thus we would not only bypass the veterans lobby in Washington, but also the lobbies that barnacle each respective state capital. The vouchers would go straight to each recipient, not to an AMERICRAT—empowering the veteran to seek the best available health care. Health care providers of all shapes and sizes would come courting, just as they do for anyone else with money to spend on health care.[55]

We can look at the other 2,000 or so federal entities with the same cold Rivlinesque eye: Is this agency necessary? If so, do we need it in Washington? Many regulatory agencies with a national mandate can meet this necessity standard, including the Environmental Protection Agency and the Federal Election Commission. Yet most, from the Small Business Administration to the National Endowments for the Arts and the Humanities, from the Public Broadcasting System and the U.S. Information Agency to the anachronistic Radio Free Europe, cannot. If we can agree that the size of the state must be limited, then surely the agencies that subsidize the nonpoor—entrepreneurs, artists, professors, and DJs—should be the first to go.

When we have finished, we are still left with the national debt, which costs $250 billion a year in interest payments. However, if the federal government can be shrunk by a third in the next decade—and by

another third in the decade thereafter—America should be in a position
to cut taxes further and eliminate the deficit and begin to pay down
the $5 trillion debt. And of course, interest rates would likely fall as
well. So in the postsynoptic era of No One Big Answer, what would
be the total size of government, federal, state, and local? We have no
way of knowing: if state governments once again mattered, then the
nation would, in Louis Brandeis's famous phrase, have fifty different
laboratories of democracy, each striving to find the right ratio of public
to private. The results of such experimentation would surely be uneven,
but the net result of diversity and experimentation would be greater
information about what works. As Kant reminds us, the actual proves
the possible.

Federalism thus foreshadows contemporary technology. A basic
point of cybernetics is this: one central brain controlling 100 percent of
computing power is not as effective as 100 little brains each controlling 1
percent of the total—all networked together. Thus the technological
justification for the Synoptic Aspiration collapses; we learn that One
Big Answer does not, in fact, "work." The Synoptics of the twentieth
century never much cared whether extreme concentrations of power
really would produce a better world; as we have seen, the real origin
of their Aspiration was spiritual and philosophical. Yet today's technological advances remove even the pretense that Synoptic politics is
based on anything more than power-lust.

For non-Synoptics, the good news is that in the era of the New
Paradigm, no tradeoff exists between decentralization and efficiency.
What works today is flattened, delayered pyramids and PCs, not the
hulking counting machines of AMERICRAT or the Vealpreneurship of
the Reichians. Moving decision-making authority away from the center
may decrease "control," but it increases intelligence. If government
functions are compartmentalized into manageable units, it will be easier
for policymakers to make continuous improvements as well as apply
the Drucker and Lindsey Tests. Federalism, a 200-year-old doctrine,
turns out to be the best antidote for the Synoptic Aspiration. Together
with twentieth-century technology, the genius of eighteenth-century
politics offers the best opportunity yet for all Americans to fulfill their
Dream.

Today, federalism is a cause for the Right, which sees the need to get power out of Washington. Conservatives have a point: it is all too easy for Beltway pressure groups to have their way with fellow Washingtonians in the legislative and executive branches. There's even a term for this E-Z lobbying approach: "one-stop shopping." However, one day soon the Left will wake up and realize that at least some of the values it most prizes, such as personal freedom and the right to be different, are best protected through the same federalist principle. Indeed in the past, progressive state and local governments have bypassed centralized conservative power, choosing to do their own thing on issues as diverse as the decriminalization of marijuana, experimentation with the RU-486 abortion pill, and gubernatorial permission for the deployment of National Guard troops to Central America.

Privatization

Recently the federal government auctioned off assets most Americans have not yet heard of—licenses to set up wireless phone networks—for $7.7 billion.[56] It's usually not that easy for Uncle Sam to raise revenue, but a more bottom-line approach to government can benefit both the economy and taxpayers. Privatization includes not only asset sales, but also "contracting out" services and even "buying out" functions so that government operators can continue under more efficient private management.

Privatization is least effective when it merely puts bureaucrats into profitable, private-sector Orbit. It works best when the privatized entity must compete in the market. In the same way that private defense contractors become wasteful if they know they'll get Uncle Sam's money no matter how poorly they perform, so any provider of goods or services will do the best job for the least money if rivals are offering similar goods or services. Vouchers are thus far superior to contracting out, because they work to break up monopolies, private as well as public.

Other forms of privatization include the buyout of "public" ownership, converting Oligarchically controlled institutions to private ownership, complete with enforceable contract rights. As we have seen, Singapore has been empowering its workers with their own retirement accounts for forty years; the same idea could be used to give ordinary people genuine control over the nation's wealth in the form of equity ownership. During the eighties, British Conservatives privatized every-thing from the phone and gas companies to Jaguar and Rolls Royce; they even privatized Heathrow and Gatwick airports. All in all, assets worth 41 billion pounds were transferred to the private sector.[57] Much of this transfer went to the workers, in the form of stock; thus wage slaves became stockholders. The number of shareowning Britons more than quadrupled, from 2.5 million in 1979 to 11 million in 1992.[58]

One irony of this historic redistribution of wealth was that the opposition Labour party, still lost in its BUREAUCRAT-worshiping Synoptic reverie, found itself opposing this empowerment program; it fought against this shifting ownership of the means of production to the proletariat with Swiss Guard intensity. It was the party of the Right, the party of Margaret Thatcher, that went to the barricades on behalf of the working class.

Meanwhile, this phenomenon has become worldwide, transcending party labels. Privatization has been embraced by free-marketeers from Russia to Argentina and by socialists from Spain to New Zealand. The net result: in the past decade, more than 10,000 state-owned enterprises,[59] valued at some $400 billion, have been sold off.[60]

Privatization has its ideological, anti-Synoptic side—but to most people its appeal is practical. Only the most die-hard AMERICRAT loyalist still claims that the Old Paradigm operates efficiently; anyone who has dealt with both FedEx and the Post Office knows better. When people control their own piece of the action—whether it be a voucher they can take anywhere or a share in a newly privatized corporation—they can control their own destiny; they are able to command efficiency and accountability.

E. S. Savas of New York City's Baruch College has documented the contrapuntal spiral of higher costs and lower service in state and local government, concluding that de-bureaucratization shaves an average of 25–30 percent off each function through streamlining and greater efficiencies. Another study by a New York state advisory panel came to a similar conclusion; the group identified New York State assets that, if privatized, would save taxpayers $10.5 billion a year. Prospects for privatization ranged from airports to bus service to bridges to recycling operations.[61] The Empire State's publicly operated Off Track Betting is currently unprofitable, leading an exasperated Rudy Giuliani to wonder why New York runs "the only bookie operation in history to lose money."

Andrew Young, the former mayor of Atlanta, writes that privatization not only helps the poor; it de-subsidizes the rich. City employees, Young recalls, once performed an undistinguished job of maintaining Atlanta's golf courses, playgrounds for the affluent. When Young privatized their groundskeeping, not only did the city save several million dollars which had previously gone to comfort the comfortable; the golf courses also became income generators. Young urges further privatization, calling it "a great windfall for Atlanta's taxpayers."[62]

Thousands of public services around the country have been recently privatized, from snowplowing to rodent control to hospital operations. Philadelphia has moved twenty-six functions from public to private operation since 1992, including nursing home operations, printing, and prison food services, for an annual savings of $25 million.[63] In the years to come, Americans will see more "heavy" privatization, divesting prisons, roads, and waste disposal out of the public sector.

To those who find this daunting, Savas points to the England–France "chunnel" for inspiration. As he puts it, "If a private consortium can design, finance, build, own, and operate a $12 billion, thirty-two-mile tunnel under the English channel, surely municipal infrastructure is child's play."

Typically, public employees and their unions are the strongest opponents of privatization. Their reasons are less intellectual than personal: they believe their jobs are at stake. In one well-known case, public employees blocked Los Angeles mayor Dick Riordan's plan to sell off LAX, even though the airport's privatization would have been worth billions to the hard-pressed city.

One answer is for New Paradigm privatizers to cut a special deal with public employees and their unions, as Thatcher did in England, giving them preferences and financial aid to acquire ownership of their enterprises. The same strategy should be tried in America. In a previous chapter—noting that the national expenditure per public-school pupil is $6,000 per child, for a total of $240 billion—we suggested that teachers would do better to lead the privatization parade, rather than resist until they are run over. Other public employees also sit atop enormous capital stocks of equipment, land, routes, and other assets; again, if they were to take a hard look at the numbers, they would see that privatization and divestiture could make them owners as well as employees—and quite possibly rich owners, at that. If rank-and-file wage earners—such as letter carriers, air traffic controllers, Amtrak conductors, and Tennessee Valley Authority workers—could unburden themselves of their power-oriented and Synoptic-Aspiring "leaders," they might see the chance to make a Big Offer of their own: privatization in return for ownership.

Such restructuring is never easy, but employee ownership can work because privatized enterprises with a profit potential can get better access to capital. Investors are always looking for high rates of return, and only efficient enterprises—the usual result of privatization—can promise adequate yields needed to garner new infusions of cash. Today, the dollars frozen in the Old Paradigm ice are so enormous that beneficial Alliances for privatization can be struck between employees, financiers, and taxpayers to melt down glaciers of obsolescence. Robert W. Poole of the Reason Foundation in Santa Monica, California, has found a trove of unrealized wealth that could be used to benefit both public employees and the public. Poole has identified $319 billion worth of one-time sales that could be made by the federal government, plus another $33 billion saved each year in government subsidies eliminated and new taxes collected from profitably privatized enterprises. Among the items to be sold: a $95 billion portfolio of loans to farmers, businesses, and students, and billions more for the sale of television and radio frequencies. That's just the feds; Poole identifies another $227 billion in state and local assets suitable for privatization.[64]

Progress is being made. Recently the Food and Drug Administration decided to turn over part of its testing operation to private contracts; the goal is both to speed approvals and to save money.[65] But the debate over the fate of AMERICRATic management will continue. In the political bout to come, the two paradigms, old and new, will square off. In one corner stands the Old Paradigm, composed mostly of those with an Oligarchic class interest in the Bureaucratic Operating System and a smattering of Synoptics; they will tout the good feeling they think people should get from collective ownership. In the other corner, flexing its muscles, stands the New Paradigm, seeking to make tangible to people the real monetary benefits of privatization.

Samurai Bureaucrats

Since the replacement for the Bureaucratic Operating System will still require bureaucrats, America ought to take more pains to see that the men and women in public service are, without apologies, the best and the brightest. As we have seen, one consequence of the Vealification of AMERICRAT 4.0 has been the demoralization of AMERICRATs. All but the most ardent libertarians would agree that public servants are necessary; yet a career in government offers few satisfactions to those who might seek to contribute their hearts and brains, as well as their iron-bottomed endurance. Thus we must consider ways to raise the prestige of government service. One suggestion is the creation of a post-*perestroika* class of civil servants: what we might call Samurai bureaucrats. These would be select guardians of the commonweal, named after the elite defenders of Imperial Japan. They would become peaceful warriors for good government and the public trust: men and women who derive job satisfaction not from their salary but from the feeling that they are doing a quality job at tasks their fellow Americans think are important and honorable. While America would never ask them to commit *hari-kiri* as a matter of duty, a New Paradigm nation would ask them to work enthusiastically within the shrunken but still vital Post–Bureaucratic Operating System.

Here are three rules for Samuraization: first, the mission must be important; second, it must be something that cannot be reasonably performed by another group; third, it must be kept clear and simple, allowing no "mission creep."

We can consider one example of a government organization that once possessed Samurai status and now clearly does not: the Postal Service, né the Post Office. When it was created in 1789, the Post Office was seen as a vital part of new-nation-building. It was run by patronage workers, but a great deal of ideology went into the solemn oath that letter carriers took to deliver the mail from sea to shining sea. The Pony Express exemplified the heroism of ordinary Americans called to glory by the Postmaster General. Recently, a special marker was erected to honor the memory of John March, one of five Post Office workers who went down with the Titanic rather than be separated from their mail duty.[66] That's good Samurai behavior.

That was also 1912. Why does the Postal Service exist today in the era of the fax, FedEx, and the Net? It's nominally privatized, so nobody goes to work for it out of any sense of calling or patriotic duty; it's just another job with good pay and bad working conditions. Indeed, the Postal Service wouldn't last long, at least in its present form, without its monopoly. The Congress and mail-Orbital Bureaucrats use their political leverage to keep the Vealified Postal Service intact because there's a market for the Postal Service's flesh in the wheeling-dealing, PAC-ing governmental grand bazaar. The main beneficiaries of the status quo are two interest groups: the 729,000 people who work for the service and the junk-mailers who like the artificially low third-class rates.

So the Postal Service falls short of our three rules for Samurais. First, its mission was once a matter of national security, but not any more. Second, its function can be carried out by others; indeed it already is. Third, its mission has "crept" to accommodate political pressures—from the promotion of workplace diversity to the mailing needs of nonprofits—so as to render the original organization almost unrecognizable.

The Postal Service began as a noble idea—to bind the new nation together through communication—but it has been so corrupted by the Bugs in the BOS as to be a candidate for the glue factory.[67] Yet other public servants have proven themselves capable of visionary thinking about how to link Americans together. The Internet grew out of the Defense Department; the Net will go down as one of the greatest gifts the government has ever bestowed upon the American people. Fortunately, no one had the bright idea of putting the Postal Service in charge of the Net.

Yet certain functions must be kept in the realm of the public trust. Having devolved, voucherized, privatized, or otherwise done away with most of the what the federal government currently does, the nation would be left with a substantial number of functions that should not be turned over to either private entrepreneurship or Orbital Vealcrats.[68]

History provides some cautionary tales. In the Middle Ages, one government activity that was frequently privatized, what could be called "tax farming," led to disastrous consequences. Typically, the king would put a duke in charge of a territory and let that subordinate use any means necessary to collect revenue from the territory. The duke would owe a certain amount to the king, but above that threshold, he could keep everything he raised. The process was sometimes so brazen that kings would auction off tax-farming rights to would-be revenue harvesters. The defects in this entrepreneurial system became obvious; as Max Weber noted, not only could the exploitation become ruthless, but also "the long-run yield capacity [could be] endangered."[69] Imagine what would happen today if IRS agents worked on commission.

Yet we can see echoes of rapacious tax farming in the activities of contemporary law enforcers. The Drug Enforcement Agency in particular has been accused of unseemly entrepreneurialism, targeting rich drug dealers and users so that it can benefit from the asset forfeiture that follows. In such situations, government employees don't personally acquire the seized assets—including cars, boats, and real estate—but drug enforcers are permitted, under current law, to retain or liquidate such property for the official use of their agency. It all sounds reasonable until we learn that kingpin-catching cops are riding around in Maseratis and speed boats.[70]

So the surviving functions of a reduced government should be in the hands of Samurai bureaucrats, not private corporations or Vealcrats. Using the terminology of *Reinventing Government* for these surviving missions, Samurais should row, as well as steer.

The New Paradigm won't change human nature, but it will change the environment in which federal employees exist, making them strictly performance-accountable for certain tasks. Today, federal service is looked down upon; if the government were de-conglomerated—if it conducted a few key functions well rather than a lot of functions badly—the prestige of public service would rise. Men and women do not live by paycheck alone; the nonmonetary incentive of service to community and country can be a powerful lure.[71]

Career federal employees in some agencies, such as the Office of Management and Budget and the Centers for Disease Control, are more effective because they already enjoy fairly strong Samurai status. The techniques they use to generate such esprit are no mystery: a strong institutional culture that emphasizes the common cause, clear-cut goals, and intolerance of poor performance.

The uniformed military, which makes a fetish of such things, is always mostly Samurai. In fact, one technique the military uses to maintain this status might be adopted by all government bureaucracies in the New Paradigm future. Military personnel move either up or out after a certain number of years—typically, four to six—at each rank. Whether enlisted or commissioned, deadwood is systematically chopped out of the armed forces; one cannot be a corporal or a captain forever.

If more civilian government employees are to achieve Samurai status in the eyes of the nation, they will have to adopt more of these rigorous techniques. Professionals take pride in their mission and their excellence in achieving it. Such honed honor is the Way of the Samurai; it gains respect because it merits respect.

Author Philip K. Howard suggests giving public servants the latitude to make decisions without the threat of lawyers and lawsuits hanging over them. As he puts it,

> No one has the ability to do anything. Democracy is as powerless as we are, because law has supplanted the decisions that made democracy important . . . We have invented a hybrid government that achieves nearly perfect inertia. No one is in control. No one makes decisions. Only the massive weight of accumulated laws keeps everyone in check.[72]

Howard's book, *The Death of Common Sense: How Law is Suffocating America*, should be included in the Samurai's kit. The author believes the law should emphasize goals and principles, not process and procedure, arguing that "The sunlight of common sense" more latitude, more accountability, more responsibility."[73] If a new Samurai system were given respect and prestige—if government service were dignified as the work of an elite few—the recruitment of skilled and honorable swordsmen and swordswomen for the Republic would be easy.

A Greater Dedication to the Empowerment of All Americans

Empowerment is based on a simple enough idea: that people are happiest when they can choose, think for themselves, be in charge of something. Thus we come to the third element of the New Paradigm Big Offer: extending self-determination to all Americans in health care, education, and work.

Health Care

The 1994 elections were the Waterloo of bureaucratized medicine. That the Democrats should suffer their worst midterm defeat in half a century in the absence of war or recession suggests that the American people were indeed fearful: of the increasingly Gibsonized economy of high–low dividedness—and, also, it seems, of government-run health care.

Universal health coverage is still a good idea. But hiring bureaucrats to run such a universal plan is a bad idea. As the critics of the Clinton plan never tired of pointing out, the restructuring of one-seventh of the U.S. economy required a fair degree of arrogance from the same folks that brought us the Small Business Administration, mohair subsidies, and public housing.

Now that the Republicans have their congressional majority, with the Synoptics in remission, the GOP has to figure out what to do with its power. After having turned 1994 into a referendum on Clinton's plan for "socialized medicine," the burden is on the GOP to prove that its better idea is not just more of the same—which is to say, more corporate domination of health care.[74] Some 60 percent of Americans are enrolled in a managed-care plan today, compared with a third a decade ago.[75] More remarkably, three-fourths of American doctors have signed some form of managed-care contract, agreeing to cut their fees and accept supervision in return for guaranteed access to patients.[76]

In the absence of legislation, the percentage of both patients and physicians enveloped in a managed-care plan will surely rise higher. This is good news for Aetna, Cigna, Prudential, and the other big insurers, but it's not clear that the American people like being "managed" by corporations any more than they liked the thought of being managed by the government.

Meanwhile, 40 million Americans are without health insurance, and health care costs, while not rising as sharply as they once were, are still going up at more than double the rate of inflation. The United States has the most expensive health care system in the world. And for that near-trillion-dollar expenditure, it gets a three-tier system: the rich get terrific care because they can use traditional indemnification-type insurance and supplement that with their own money; the middle class gets herded into health-maintenance organizations; the poor get government Medicaid, plus emergency rooms. The net result is that the U.S. has world-class treatment facilities that attract the rich from around the world—and at the same time the nation ranks seventeenth internationally in infant mortality and eighteenth in life expectancy.[77]

Meanwhile, health care costs continue to rise. And since the federal government pays a third of the national health care bill, the health cost issue affects prospects for deficit reduction as well.

Yet for all this outlay, the system still doesn't work well. Corporations have been able to muscle down their health care costs by corralling their employees in managed-care plans,[78] but the doleful phenomenon of "job lock"—people trapped in jobs they would otherwise leave for fear of not getting coverage for themselves or their families in their next position—will only worsen as more companies practice "adverse selection," screening out "undesirable" customers based on "preexisting conditions." Some 84 million Americans are said to have such preexisting conditions, ranging from cancer to AIDS. And better medical techniques will surely discover that all 260 million Americans have some sort of genetic predisposition that will eventually make them sicken and die.

So if the Republicans can't or won't address the two big problems of health care, cost and access, then the "health care crisis" will reemerge as a political issue. Indeed, in an NBC/*Wall Street Journal* poll, a full 70 percent of Americans said that the biggest problem they faced was unaffordable health care.[79]

In light of these realities, the two parties, representing the two ideological wings of the Old Paradigm, need to rethink their strategies.

The question for the Left is whether it aspires more to Synopticism than to health care reform. In other words, is the Left willing to decouple its treasured goal of national health insurance from the venerated technique of bureaucracy? If so, there could be an empowerment-based New Paradigm Alliance in the making.

For its part, the Right must resolve to do something about the plight of those suffering under the status quo. One can't stand pat on quicksand; costs will continue to rise, and access will continue to shrink.

So the way is clear for a New Paradigm Big Offer, aimed to create an Alliance based on something different and better than what America has now. The opportunity for an Alliance exists based on the one approach that has never been tried before: personal empowerment.

The Old Paradigm of Paternalism

No real reform of health care is possible as long as the existing health care paradigm dominates—that is, third-party payments. The percentage of health care costs that people pay for themselves has been declining for decades; today just 5 percent of all hospital costs are paid by the patient, and less than a fourth of all personal health care expenditures are paid for out of pocket.[80] The rest is paid by third parties, either public or private. To many, that seems like a blessing: who can afford such bills? But there is no free lunch, Americans are paying for health care as a society—nearly $3,500 per man, woman, and child, for a total of $884 billion in 1993, or 13.9 percent of GNP.[81]

Yet most of the reform plans one hears about, such as health alliances and managed competition, have something in common: they retain third-party payments. And so, for all their variation, they retain the basic conceptual problem: if people don't feel the cost of their medical bills, they have no incentive to restrain their health care consumption. As economists say, when the price of something goes toward zero, demand for that thing goes toward infinity.

Health insurance today has gone beyond the notion of "insurance" as applied to automobiles and property; what exists today is more properly thought of as "prepayment." Traditionally, "insurance" has meant indemnification for a specified loss. Thus damage to a car or home would be covered in the event of an accident or flood. But today, Americans have come to expect something more from health insurance: both indemnification for specified illnesses and coverage for nonillnesses, such as annual checkups and physicals. There's nothing wrong with this approach, in the sense that there's nothing wrong with buying auto insurance with a low deductible; it's just very expensive. Most people prefer to keep a high deductible in exchange for lower premiums, reasoning that they are better off paying for dents and dings out of their own pocket rather than filing for reimbursement with the insurance company.

Since much of today's health "insurance" is really prepaid coverage, Americans pay—or more likely, their employer pays, in their name—for coverage of predictable, recurring medical expenses. Again, such maintenance contracts are not unheard of outside of the health care field; many people pay in advance for appliance maintenance, for example. Yet usually, such contracts are written carefully, so as to discourage customers from calling the Maytag repairman every day.

Until recently, health insurance existed on a "cost-plus" basis: the patient went to the doctor, the doctor treated the patient, and one or the other sought reimbursement from the insurer. For decades, there were no real limits on health care consumption, and so for decades, health care costs outstripped the growth of the overall economy; the share of GNP devoted to health care more than doubled since 1960.[82]

As Phil Gramm archly put it, if grocery stores were run like health insurance—that is, one pays up front and eats for free all year—he would eat differently, and so would his dog. Gramm, never one to attribute behavior to the better angels of our nature, nevertheless had a point: with the combination of *prix fixe* and all-you-can-eat, people would consume a lot more steak and caviar, and so would Fido. This is an expensive way to run health care. Americans send their money to Washington or Hartford, and the public- or private-sector bureaucrats therein send it back to us—minus their middleman's cut.

The persistence of such wastefulness is a testament to the persistence of old ways of thinking. Three groups in particular like the system as it is:

First come the Synoptics and their cousins, the paternalists. Both retain a faith in top-down decision making, as well as a skepticism about the ability of ordinary people to think wisely for themselves about their own health care. The old theory was that third-party payment systems, overseen by technocrats, would see to it that the "right" decisions were made *for* people, not by them. In the days when AMERI-CRAT was young—when few understood such concepts as hygiene and sanitation—a clear need existed for expert intervention from above. Today, the Synoptic and paternalistic elites take a different view of the problem, which they now define as people consuming too much health care. Indeed, health care overconsumption may well be the "wrong" decision. But the elite solution is also wrong: top–down management, based on unjustified confidence in the elites' own competence.

The second group that likes health-care-as-usual consists of Beltway-centric lobbies with their hands gripped around the fiscal feeding tube. Every conceivable health care interest, from chiropractors to plastic surgeons to sperm bank operators to marriage counselors, seeks to make sure that its specialty is included in the "standard benefits package" people receive from their public or private insurer. So the interests go out and lobby—and win. In 1970, there were just forty-eight such "mandated health insurance benefit laws"; today, there are more than 1,000.[83] On the margin, each such add-on sounds good and costs little; cumulatively, this process threatens to give the American people what they want—at the moment the system goes bankrupt.

The third group that likes the third-party status quo is the gaggle of insurance companies and managed-care providers that profit from their stranglehold on the current system. But private-sector control of the Old Paradigm mechanism is hardly a panacea. Under the curent arrangement, individuals still have no reason not to consume as much health care as they can, but they no longer deal with a system willing to pass the cost explosion on to the rest of society. Now people are in an endless struggle with private-sector cost-control bureaucrats.

In spite of the corporate takeover of much of health care, the system still isn't working right. Costs are continuing to rise faster than inflation, as the first and second parties in the health care equation—patients and providers—conspire to milk as much money as they can out of the third parties.

Meanwhile, more people are being left out of the system altogether, turning them into public-health endangerers or emergency-room utilizers.

Seen in this light, the 1993–94 battle over health care—between Hillary Rodham Clinton and "Harry and Louise" of TV-ad fame—was essentially a struggle between the left and right wings of the Old Paradigm. The Left wanted government to act as the third-party payer, as did the Right, although the latter wanted private insurance companies to do the deciding. What united both was the presumption that central authority should keep control. The establishment's stubbornness on this fundamental point was part ideological and part financial. For every activist who dreamed of One Big Answer for health care, there was a lobbyist who liked the trend we're seeing now: millions more Americans being herded into the cost-cutting corrals of private insurers.

The New Paradigm of Empowerment

The inescapable reality of health care is that in the end, rationing must be effected. The passive-voice construction of the previous sentence echoes the difficulty in conversing candidly on this topic, because the issue at hand is life and death. Still, Americans will be forced to address this issue head-on eventually; they might as well do so before the country is bankrupt. The truth is that someone must do the rationing. Indeed, from the point of view of elected officials, it's only a matter of time before the power they've accumulated comes back to haunt them, as angry constituents target them for protest when the inevitable health care crunch occurs. Forward-looking politicians thus have lots of incentive to make a Big Offer: that pushes power and responsibility out of their offices. However, such power ought not to be automatically devolved to big insurance companies and their managed-care allies. Politicians in a democracy should not be seeking to push clients toward a favored business; they should seek to empower the individual, not corporate third parties.

The New Paradigm Big Offer asserts that the third-party-payer model offers no way out of this impasse. As Einstein said, no problem can be solved on its own level; so three things must be done to bring the problem to a higher level. First, patients must be motivated to think about not only their own care, but also the cost of that care. Second, health care must be de-politicized, so that paternalists and lobbyists no longer control health policy. Third, market forces must be allowed to generate the same savings and efficiencies they produce in other sectors of the economy.[84]

The American people are frustrated enough to consider such an Offer because it seems as though both parties have only half the pieces of the puzzle; voters want activism, but not AMERICRATs. The bureau-maniacal Clintoncare plan foundered, not because people didn't want reform, but because they didn't want Magazinerians running health care.

The only escape from the dead end of the Old Paradigm is an empowering voucher system for health care called Medical Savings Accounts (MSAs). The idea of a Medisave account—a tax-favored IRA for the purchase of health care, which people use to pay for whatever combination of insurance coverage and out-of-pocket expenditure they choose—has been kicking around for some time. The heart of the MSA idea is delayed gratification or, to put it another way, self-rationing.

The MSA approach is the ultimate in decentralization: bypassing the single-payer Synoptics, Magaziner-style health "alliances," and corporate oligarchy. We know that bureaucrats, public or private, suffer from Information Infarction; they lack the gyroscopic nuance needed to achieve balance in a constantly shifting environment. Our best hope is the collective judgment of 100 million American families, acting as sovereign health care consumers, minutely calculating what's best for them.

MSAs are already being used by companies ranging from Quaker Oats to *Forbes* magazine. Lest anyone think that these are only a capitalist tool, the United Mine Workers recently bargained for such a plan in its agreement with the Bituminous Coal Operators Association.[85] These MSAs combine a high deductible with catastrophic coverage. Typically, MSA-empowered employees pay all their health care expenses up to $2,000 a year; if they incur more than $3,000 in costs, the catastrophic coverage supplements their expenditure. The beauty of the system is that if employees stay below the $2,000 threshold, they can pocket the difference.[86] In addition to the micro-effect on personal behavior, MSAs would have two positive macro-effects: first, their IRA-like tax status would make them more attractive vehicles for savings; second, since they would be "portable," following their owners from job to job, workers would be more inclined to use them for long-term investments. For these two reasons, the too-low national savings rate would substantially increase.

Yet MSAs will never take off until the tax code treats all health care coverage equally. Currently, the cost of health insurance purchased by an employer is deductible to the employer and tax-free to the employee. This tax-sheltering encourages overconsumption of health care benefits in lieu of cash compensation. That is, a $3,500 health insurance plan is worth far more to an employee than a $3,500 raise—which might amount to only $2,000 after taxes. Conversely, under today's rules, MSA money that a healthy employee pockets at the end of the year *is* taxable, because the IRS sees it as ordinary income. But if this disparity in the tax treatment of income were ironed out—if the implicit subsidy for health care insurance and, ultimately, health care consumption were removed—then people could decide for themselves whether they wanted their compensation in the form of health insurance or income.

So we come to one of the most vehement objections to MSA plans: that people will spend their money foolishly. Even if we mandate the purchase of some sort of catastrophic coverage, the argument goes, people will opt for consumption now and forgo crucial health care expenditures for themselves and their children. Yet in the era of the New Paradigm, we are learning over and over that centralized institutions, no matter how smart the people in them may be, in fact turn out to be dumb and dumber; they just can't keep up with the fast-changing market, even as individuals learn to do so. Today, people acting in the marketplace—as they comparison-shop with the help of everything from computers to *Consumer Reports*—are better than their bureaucratic masters at looking out for their own well-being. And information is increasingly available: some forty states now collect data on health care quality, measuring hospital costs and mortality rates, the frequency of certain procedures, even the touchy issue of physician performance.[87] In 1995, the nonprofit, independently audited National Committee for Quality Assurance has issued a model "report card" for HMOs around the country. While the average HMO quit rate was 23 percent, the

NCQA found enormous variations in HMO quit rates—from 2 percent for the Blue Cross HMO in Rochester, New York, to 48 percent at MetLife HealthCare Network in St. Louis. Similar variations were found in twenty-seven other criteria examined by the NCQA, including immunizations, cancer screening, and length of hospital stays.[88] Knowledge is power, said Francis Bacon centuries ago; it is also the key to a healthier life.

Already, tens of millions of Americans are exploring alternative approaches to wellness and healing, suggesting that people are dissatisfied with the traditional practice of medicine. Empowering people further will only accelerate the ferment of new thinking and the creation of more alert health care consumers; people will have more reason to learn if they have the power to act on their own behalf.

The New Paradigm will not be built in a day. As a start, one might stipulate that withdrawals from an individual's MSA be limited to expenditures for either health care, including catastrophic coverage, or retirement, along the lines of Singapore's Central Provident Fund. A tax-sheltered MSA could supplement the type of forced-saving plan examined earlier in the discussion of entitlements. Like the CPF, the individual would retain ownership of the account and could bequeath it to his or her heirs.

So where would people get the money for their MSA? As we have seen, the total health care budget for the country works out to around $3,500 per person. So the money is already there in the system; the issue is distribution of that money among 260 million Americans. That's where MSAs come in: they are a better technique for securing equitable, empowering distribution. The New Paradigm Big Offer would be forthright; the goal is to empower everyone with an MSA. So for the currently uninsured working poor, the government could offer not just a tax deduction or tax credit for the MSA, but a "refundable" tax credit; in other words, the government would give them the money to set up an MSA. Then, once the money is in people's hands, as opposed to the government's, a natural pattern of consequence-conscious behavior would assert itself, just as happened when the landless became the landed after the Homestead Act. In the same spirit, MSAs would encourage labor mobility; making the MSA portable would minimize the danger of chronic European-style structural unemployment.

What about the chronically and terminally ill, those whom no rational insurer would ever sell a policy to? Here again, we must be forthright: maximum empowerment is the goal, but realism suggests that, especially during the transition period to an MSA system, not everyone will be empowerable. For example, current Medicare and Medicaid recipients should be encouraged to form their own MSAs, but it must be accepted that some people will always depend on health care directly financed by the government. The MSA will transform health care in the twenty-first century, not the twentieth.

So will America's health care costs continue to rise? Probably. The National Center for Policy Analysis estimates that an MSA plan would save $140 billion a year as true market forces streamline administrative costs out of the current oligopolistic system, but it is likely that any such savings would be overwhelmed by the inexorably rising costs associated with an aging population and the nation's unslakable appetite for technological and pharmacological "fixes."[89] In a free country, people get what they want, and Americans value longer life. Yet one advantage of MSAs is that they remove the god-playing temptation; de-politicized health care is also de-Synopticized health care. Not only would special interests no longer be able to hijack the One Big Answer gravy train—because there wouldn't be any such train—but there would be no health oracle declaring that we are spending "too much" or "too little" on health care. The U.S. would spend exactly the amount that people want to spend, based on their empowered decision making in the health care marketplace.

So how is all this paid for? We noted earlier that a New Paradigm goal should be to end the tax favoring of health care consumption. As we have seen, employees should not be taxed on the health care money they don't spend; it should be left to accumulate, tax-free, in their MSA. Furthermore, the self-employed ought to get the same tax break for providing health insurance for themselves as employers get when they provide it for their employees. Finally, having set some reasonable standard for an MSA—say, $3,500 a year—we should subject all health care expenditures above that threshold, including those in insurance policies, to taxation. This would deprive the rich of one of their most notorious tax shelters, one that allows them to enjoy all sorts of "therapeutic" pleasures—often little more than healthy vacations—as part of a gold-plated, tax-free health insurance plan. According to economist C. Eugene Steuerle, households with the lowest quintile of family income received $270 in tax subsidies for employer-provided health insurance in 1992, while those in the top quintile collected $1,560.[90] By closing this loophole, the New Paradigm Big Offer would soak the rich a little even as it dampened excess demand for health care.

In 1993 Bill Clinton identified a real problem and proposed a statist solution that would have made the problem worse. In 1995 health care is still in a slow-motion crisis, although the dominoes today are tumbling in the direction of corporate control. Yet the prospect of the private sector playing third-party heavy may cause people once again to look to government as the better alternative. So with the jaws of private- and public-sector control closing around them, Americans have no good option except to go forward to a new, more empowering system. And the nation stands ready to reward the New Paradigm politician who Offers to take it to a better Operating System.

Education

After the 1994 elections, the Clinton administration seemed to have got the message that the voters wanted a different, less bureaucratic approach to the delivery of social services. Members of the administration began to develop the ideas that candidate Clinton had hinted at two years before: the willingness to think anew, to use "conservative" market-oriented techniques to achieve liberal goals.

One new technique was vouchers. In December 1994, Henry Cisneros, Secretary of the Department of Housing and Urban Development, proposed vouchers for public-housing residents, using language reminiscent of his predecessor, Jack Kemp. With vouchers, said Cisneros, public-housing dwellers "will be able to make the choice as to whether they want to stay in places that are unacceptable or, in effect, vote with their feet and move to another location."[91] If Cisneros and the Clinton administration had sounded like that beginning in 1993, the 1994 midterm election results might have been different. Their belated embrace of empowerment suggests the outlines of a New Paradigm Alliance: the government retains a role in redistribution, but it not only gets out of the business of directly providing services; it also makes sure that aid goes directly to people, bypassing the usual bureaucratic brokers.

The same voucher policy, albeit in muted form, was advanced by Labor Secretary Robert Reich as he proposed "skill grants" for job training.[92] Then Clinton himself, in his speech calling for a "Middle Class Bill of Rights," proposed a new IRA savings program for college tuition.[93] He didn't use the "v-word," but he might as well have: anything that empowers people to be sovereign in the marketplace is a voucher of sorts.

As we have seen in a previous chapter, Clinton himself seemed interested in education vouchers as recently as 1990. Indeed, the Democrats have a long association with school vouchers and their cognate, tuition tax credits. Historically, a key cause for northern Catholic Democrats was aid to parochial schools. In 1869, New York's Boss Tweed succeeded in getting a voucher plan through the legislature in Albany, although the mostly Protestant Republicans managed to kill it two years later.[94] Yet for more than a century, government assistance to Catholic schools remained a vital issue; as recently as 1984, the Democratic Platform acknowledged the merits of tuition tax credits. Since then, the EDUCRATs completed their conquest of the party, and vouchers disappeared down the memory hole. Even as his colleagues in the cabinet were embracing empowerment, Education Secretary Richard Riley was notably reluctant to join them in support of anything even remotely voucherish—a clear indicator that the EDUCRATic mind-set still holds sway.

Earlier we suggested that public school teachers themselves might want to get out in front of the voucherization wave, cutting a deal that would guarantee them a leading role in the restructuring of education. That was the carrot. Now we can mention the stick: the times are a-changin'. Empowerment of parents and students will come more quickly if EDUCRAT cooperates, but it will come—even without that cooperation.

We have also considered the merits of voucherizing the Department of Veterans Affairs health system, enabling veterans to bypass the VA system in search of the best possible health care. Other aspects of the New Paradigm Big Offer, such as IRAs for Social Security and MSAs for health care, can be thought of as voucherlike in their empowering effect on retirement and health care.

So the time has come to voucherize EDUCRAT. The Upgrades have failed. If the status quo stands, if the dead hand of the past does not release us, then the cyberbell will toll for millions of undereducated Americans, doomed to low-value-added jobs. For their sake, the nation has no choice but to replace the Bureaucratic Operating System with the Market Operating System that will give them the skills they need to compete and win.

Vouchers are not yet an Alliance issue with the country as a whole. The rich look upon vouchers as gratuitous; they already have all the money they need to exercise all the choice they want. Indeed, vouchers might upset their cozy arrangements; as we have seen, rich communities can reap a huge tax subsidy through the deductibility of their local property taxes from their federal income taxes. Thus the rich can dedicate as much as $15,000 per pupil per year to their local public school, but their real after-tax cost might be less than $10,000, because other federal taxpayers make up the difference. Thus all Americans help pay for the "savage inequalities" of the current system.

As for the middle class, the arguments for vouchers are still coming into focus. People know that EDUCRAT no longer works, but they are reluctant to let go of what they know.[95] People like the idea of "neighborhood schools," even if they are no bargain, given their investment in them. Yet the public-school status quo is a paradigm: as with any paradigm, people won't let go of the system they know until they can visualize the replacement. So far, pro-voucher forces have failed to tangibilize the idea advantage of vouchers. In California, a voucher initiative was defeated more than 2:1 in 1993, adding to a string of anti-choice victories for EDUCRAT. The demagoguery of the Old Paradigm opponents of vouchers, led by the California Teachers Association, was a combination of lingering Synopticism and simple inertia, wrapped in the naked self-interest of CTA members anxious to preserve their monopoly. Yet vouchers are coming, for the reason that Cisneros and Reich both embraced them in their respective departments: nothing else works today.

One focus of the New Paradigm Big Offer should be specifically on the less advantaged. Earlier, we considered the transformational effect that full voucherization—for public, private, or religious schools—could have on African American parents: an education-improving wealth transfer vaster than even the Homestead Act. Since the current public school mandarinate traps the poor in its inward-folding web, the New Paradigm Big Offer could offer the one thing that decadent EDUCRAT can't give: escape from the tyranny of systematized failure.

If the middle class is content to stew in the Brezhnevian juices of the Old Paradigm, America should at least emancipate the poor from the yoke of bureaucracy. As a start, the New Paradigm leader would declare an education emergency and voucherize schools in afflicted areas, as measured perhaps by low test scores. If vouchers work for the poor, the idea would surely trickle up to the rest of society, although a voucher system could always be made "progressive" by phasing out and/or taxing vouchers for higher-income Americans.

In Wisconsin, a new pyramid of Alliance has already been built around the idea of vouchers. We have seen that in 1990, then-governor Bill Clinton wrote an admiring letter to a school-choice leader Polly Williams in which he lamented that visionaries are rarely embraced by the establishment.[96] Others have been inspired by Williams's example. In 1991, Indianapolis businessman Pat Rooney just up and did it: he started his own choice plan, out of his own pocket. Since then private groups in Milwaukee, San Antonio, and Atlanta have started similar programs, whereby some 6,000 children received $4.4 million in scholarships for the 1993–94 school year.[97] We can only speculate how much the world would change if institutions with deeper pockets, such as the Ford Foundation, decided to help children directly rather than subsidize EDUCRATic middlepeople.

In Jersey City, pro-voucher mayor Bret Schundler has pointed out the absurdity of spending $9,000 per pupil in the public schools when, for an average of $1,700, Jersey City's private schools do a better job of education. Imagine what would happen if that $7,300 differential were available to supplement poor children's education: for starters, every kid could have access to the Internet. Or consider what might happen if voucher-empowered students could break loose even $2,000 per year for tutoring: every kid could then hire himself or herself a Princeton student as a tutor; the voucherized student could be tutored for five hours a week, forty weeks a year, at $10 an hour. Such an arrangement would be a "win–win": the tutor would be paid more than he or she could make working at the library or for the dorm food service, and the child would get the benefit of an enthusiastic un-burned-out teacher; it would be the educational equivalent of barefoot doctors going to places where effective "professionals" are scarce.[98]

But is Schundler's plan, which includes parochial schools, constitutional? So far, Old Paradigm judges have said "no." But such opposition is an argument for new judicial thinking, not an argument against vouchers. If money from the GI Bill and the Pell program can go indiscriminately to religious universities ranging from Yeshiva to Brigham Young to Notre Dame, the same principle ought to apply to K–12 schools.

The fight for vouchers will not be easy; the hard work of empowerment never is. But Americans should not overlook opportunities to make incremental progress. Two strategies that could move the nation toward New Paradigm ideals include public school choice and the establishment of charter schools.

Public school choice, an amplification of the magnet school concept, enables students to choose from among the public schools in a particular system—a further move away from the old one-size-fits-all neighborhood school. Minnesota has had statewide public school choice for a decade, and fourteen other states have followed suit. Dozens of cities across the country have similar programs, the best known of which is in New York City's Community District Four. This East Harlem district, one of thirty-two such districts in the Gotham public school system, established its first three "alternative" schools in 1974. By 1982, a genuine choice system had emerged, ultimately blossoming into thirty-one different schools, devoted to everything from the performing arts to science and technology to maritime training. In the last two decades, East Harlem students went from dead last among the thirty-two districts to a middle rank today, scoring better than many more affluent districts.[99] The Manhattan Institute's Seymour Fliegel, himself a veteran of three decades in the city's schools, maintains that the positive results are "a miracle, but not a mystery." The answer, he says, is local autonomy: the right to experiment—to try, try, and try again—until the optimum approach for each individual student is found. So the essential concept behind public school choice is the same as with vouchers: school bureaucrats don't know best, so why let them have all the power?

Moreover, once that crucial point is conceded, it then becomes more difficult for the Old Paradigm Left to argue that poor children deserve less choice than rich children; it's harder to insist that poor children be limited to just the public schools. If the issue is choice, why should the choice be only among EDUCRATic schools? Jonathan Kozol warned his fellow progessives in the pages of *The Nation* that they risked an avalanche if they flirted with any form of choice: "Once we accept the ideology of competition as the engine of reform, we will be hard-pressed to say why only certain people ought to be allowed to be competitors."[100] Kozol is a sincere believer in old-style Synoptic paternal-ism; if we give parents an inch, he figures, they'll want a mile. And he's right: once people get in the habit of thinking for themselves, it's harder to order them around.

Charter schools, hybrid organizations that are publicly funded and privately managed, are another incremental step toward education reform. In California, Michigan, Massachusetts, and a dozen other states, organizations ranging from parent and/or teacher collectives to corporations to universities can seek a "charter" from the state to operate their own school. Groups obtaining charters have ranged from Brown University professor Ted Sizer's Coalition for Essential Schools to a group dedicated to the Reggio Emilia educational philosophy, which emphasizes the arts as the best learning tool,[101] to the San Diego chapter of the Urban League.[102] When these schools run well, they do so precisely because they are run autonomously. Even more than public school choice systems, charter schools can function like the best of private schools—nonbureaucratic, free to experiment, with an overrid-ing commitment to the education of children. Yet because they still operate at the sufferance of the state—as opposed to the behest of voucherized parents—the EDUCRATic establishment seeks to keep them on the tightest possible leash, litigating at every opportunity;[103] thus charter schools are still subject to all the crippling Bugs in the Bureaucratic Operating System.

Other strategies can also help nibble away at EDUCRAT's hegemony. Former Bush administration official Richard Darman has suggested offering vouchers for the incremental period of a lengthened school year. That is, if the school year is extended from 180 days to 200 days, students could use vouchers for special enrichment classes for the extra 20 days, whether at night, on weekends, or in summer vacation.

The reading tutorial firm Hooked on Phonics advertises: "We have a money-back guarantee. Don't you wish the schools did?"[104] Indeed, when we look at the hustle and innovation displayed by private "cram schools" that offer tutoring, such as Berlitz language courses, Sylvan Learning Centers, and Stanley Kaplan test preparations, we can begin to visualize what a part of the voucher world might look like. But only a part: with vouchers, more of the non-profit-minded would be able to participate in education. And parents would become the most important players of all. Today, parents who can afford it are already spending thousands of their own after-tax dollars on lessons and tutoring for their kids in everything from music to ballet to remedial reading; they spend even more today on CD-ROM encyclopedias and other learning software. Thus the cyberskew widens further. If the government were really on the side of helping parents help their kids, it would opt for a system flexible enough to include all these education programs as well.

Yet once we create diversity, we need information to help parents sort out their choices. For years, Americans have been seeking help from any number of guides and reference works, from *Money* magazine's listings of mutual funds to *Motor Trend*'s ratings of new cars. It may seem crass to compare education to investments or transportation, but it's a tragic mistake to pay for education without asking for accountability in return. In an information age, government ought to do all it can to empower people with the knowledge, as well as the wherewithal, to make the best possible decisions about their own welfare. In Britain, the government publishes "League Tables," rating how each school in the country is doing in terms of test scores. As Damian Green of the Policy Unit at 10 Downing Street notes, "The provision of information is a powerful weapon in the expansion of choice." Putting school-outcome data in plain sight helps British parents evaluate what they are getting for their money. If the U.S. government wanted to help, it could establish an easily accessible education-results database to benchmark different schools. And if such an information clearinghouse were to include international comparisons—which generally show that the U.S. is at the top among industrialized nations in education expenditure input and toward the bottom in education achievement output—that would further stir interest in profound educational reform. If parents saw their schools low on the list, they would comparison-shop for a better deal for their kids. Through such techniques, the power relationship between school bureaucracies and parents would start to shift, from a model that is driven by producers to one that is driven by consumers.

While the public schools continue to worry more about political correctness than personal computers,[105] people spending their own money in the free market are showing interest in the technological tools of empowerment. CompUSA, the Dallas-based computer superstore, offers teaching classes in seventy-five locations nationwide. Its cybercurriculum is at least as daunting as a high school math class, but it is made user-friendly thanks to 800 numbers, special support services, and easy-to-use training manuals. A single six-hour computer-training class costs $145; a year "membership," entitling one to attend any class during that time, costs $895. That seems like a lot of money—until we compare it to the $12,000 per pupil that the Newark schools spend every year. What's the argument against voucherizing education so that poor kids can learn computer skills in the same place that rich kids choose to?

The anti-choice forces aver that the public schools would be the dumping ground under a choice regime, as private schools "cream" the best students. Yet *every* student could be "creamed."[106] If there's shortage of "good" schools today, that's because there's a shortage of unencumbered money to pay for good schools. Experience has shown that where there's a demand, there comes a supply. Anyone who wants to buy such a vital educational tool as a computer has no trouble getting one—if he or she has the money to pay for it. And vouchers make that education money available to every student. Moreover, once all students have vouchers, good schools will spring into being almost as quickly as Blockbuster Video stores. Indeed, if we compare the potential size of the education market to the size of the video-rental market, we can imagine that the rush of new faces and voices into the education arena will come even more quickly than it did for home entertainment.[107]

The need for maximum flexibility clinches the argument for vouchers. So long as charter schools have a middleman-layer that looks to the government for funding, they will always be at risk of EDUCRATic takeover. Vouchers and tax credits are more straightforward than charters or contracting out, insofar as vouchers and tax credits break, once and for all, with the Old Paradigm of paternalism.

In 1994, four states—Connecticut, Pennsylvania, South Carolina, and Texas—elected strongly pro-school-choice governors. Politics has not yet caught up with the market, but it will. When Americans see the benefit of thinking for themselves and for their children—when the realization comes that letting EDUCRAT mismanage the job is not an option—they will rise up and demand vouchers.

Work

As we come to the last part of the New Paradigm Big Offer, we can reflect on what government can and cannot do to improve the commonweal. Honest economists have long known that government intervention, to protect or subsidize industry can make selected people rich; yet such playing-favorite policies cannot improve the overall well-being of society. And in the twentieth century, we have also learned that the grander dream of Synoptic government is an economic as well as social failure. After these hard and bitter lessons, we're left with a more modest economic mission for government that is nonetheless vital: the preparation of our work force to compete in the twenty-first century. As Robert Reich has put it, "The standard of living of a nation's people increasingly depends on what they contribute to the world economy— on the value of their skills and insights."[108]

President Clinton added another dimension to the discussion of work:

> I do not believe we can repair the basic fabric of society until people who are willing to work have work. Work organizes life. We cannot restore the family until we provide the structure, the values, the discipline, and the reward that work gives.[109]

But as we have seen, the onrushing cyber-economy has disorganized working life. According to Rae Nelson of the Center for Workforce Preparation, the average age at which an American youth assumes his or her first full-time job, with benefits, is twenty-eight. Since the typical high school student today graduates at nineteen, and since half of all young Americans will never even enter a four-year college—and half of those who enter a four-year college will not graduate—that means tens of millions of young Americans are milling around the "contingent" labor force, waiting for their first real job. Moreover, microeconomic trends—from defense downsizing to corporate restructuring to welfare reform—mean that more dislocated workers will be seeking new jobs, along with middle-aged homemakers, ex-offenders, and former welfare recipients.

This welter of complexity will overwhelm the mainframe mentality of AMERICRAT, collapsing the last distinctions between different categories of learning. Although the federal government funds more than 400 separate education and job training programs,[110] no bureaucratic system will be capable of the suppleness to assure that tens of millions of Americans receive the continuous training and retraining they need at different ages and stages to flourish in the cyber-economy. Skills delivery systems that run along Old Paradigm lines have proven incapable of providing the accountability that Americans should expect in return for the money. Technology, providing everything from interactive distance learning to special equipment for the handicapped, will be a vital part of any forward-looking worker empowerment strategy. The government could help accelerate innovations by empowering workers with vouchers, enabling them to make their own best arrangements. In this way, the rewards of work will be increased, and more Americans will enjoy what they do, confident that they are realizing their potential.

Welfare to Work

Both Left and Right have, in their different ways, been remarkably callous toward welfare recipients. The Democrats, the party of the New Deal and the Great Society, built the current system; they have an institutional interest in its preservation, but they have given little thought about what to do about the harm it is now causing. The Republicans want to defund, or at least diminish, the current system, but they have also given little thought about what to replace it with.

Virtually everyone with a voice in the ongoing debate over welfare reform maintains, at least in the abstract, that work is the answer. Indeed, for decades, the Left and Right have been talking past each other, with the former saying "guaranteed jobs" and the latter saying "workfare." Yet upon reflection, it's apparent that the two concepts are more similar than different.

When George Will observed that "statecraft is soulcraft," he was merely echoing what Franklin D. Roosevelt had said a half-century earlier, in his 1935 State of the Union address:

> The lessons of history, confirmed by the evidence immediately before me, show conclusively that continued dependence upon relief induces a spiritual and moral disintegration fundamentally destructive to the national fibre. To dole out relief in this way is to administer a narcotic, a subtle destroyer of the human spirit.[111]

Roosevelt is remembered as the father of the American welfare state, but he was very much against welfare. The "relief" programs of the New Deal were mostly work programs; the Works Progress Administration and the Civilian Conservation Corps were the essence of reciprocity—no handouts. FDR wanted America to work its way out of poverty.

Yet today, after decades in which AMERICRAT, in its later Upgrades, neglected FDR's wisdom, the welfare debate has assumed new urgency. In 1992 Clinton pledged to "end welfare as we know it" by "moving people from welfare to work."[112] The last significant welfare reform legislation, the 1988 Family Support Act, signed by Ronald Reagan, was ostensibly a plan for training people to get off welfare; yet instead of dependency declining, welfare roles went up by a third in the following five years, from 10.9 million recipients in 1989 to 14.3 million in 1994.[113] So one should approach the issue of welfare reform with intellectual humility; as James Q. Wilson says, we don't know what works. Yet humility should not be equated with hesitancy; America needs more experimentation, not procrastination. In the spirit of federalism, the federal government should de-Synopticize welfare, letting fifty flowers bloom in the fifty states.

Will the states use federalism as an excuse to abandon their responsibility to the poor? As we have seen, liberal Democrat Rivlin doesn't think so; she wants to turn back welfare and other federal programs to the states. This is a different country than it was thirty years ago, with different state governments. America can no longer barricade itself against the non-threat of Faulkner's Snopes family taking over Mississippi.

As Senator Nancy Landon Kassebaum (R-Kansas), chair of the Education and Labor Committee, says, "Let each state devise their own program that fits their state. I don't think we can fix it from Washington."[114] Virtually every state in the union is currently experimenting with some manner of welfare reform, from incentives for welfare mothers to stay in school to penalties for their having more children. Some states, such as Wisconsin, have reduced welfare roles, while others, such as New York, have seen them increase. Experts will debate cause and effect, but in the meantime, these fifty different laboratories of democracy are developing research data that all can study.

As we have seen, the New Paradigm Big Offer will help by block-granting the money the federal government currently spends on human services. The dollar amounts Uncle Sam spends on "welfare"—that is, means-tested entitlements, including AFDC, food stamps, SSI, and Medicaid—are dwarfed by Social Security and Medicare, but the total is nevertheless not small: approximately $200 billion a year. Combined with state and local expenditures, the total for antipoverty spending climbs to more than $300 billion a year, or about $8,000 for every poor person in the country. With that much money in the system, even the poorest states should be able to build on the pro-work consensus to find an end to welfare.

A New Civilian Conservation Corps

Yet even as it promotes federalism and decentralization, a New Paradigm federal government can make one signal contribution to the effort to turn America into what author Mickey Kaus has called "the work ethic state." It can bring back a New Deal program: the Civilian Conservation Corps.

Sometimes the best route to the New Paradigm future is through the memory palace of the Old Paradigm. In his first inaugural address, FDR said:

> Our greatest primary task is to put people to work . . . treating the task as we would treat the emergency of war, but at the same time, through this employment, accomplishing greatly needed projects to stimulate and reorganize the use of our national resources.

The Civilian Conservation Corps was created within weeks of FDR's taking office. Originally run jointly by the federal departments of Agriculture, Interior, and Labor, its operations were soon taken over by the uniformed military, with regimental commander George C. Marshall leading the effort in the Southeast. Yet its mission was domestic; as one chronicler put it:

> Critical as was the natural resource problem, the Nation had a more serious one in its youth population . . . Few of these youngsters had ever held a regular job. They were ready victims for the moral dry rot that accompanies enforced idleness and its resulting dejection. Insidiously, there was spreading abroad in the land the nucleus of those bands of young predators who infested the Russian countryside after the Revolution and who became known as "wild boys."[115]

Before it was phased out in 1942, the CCC planted 3 billion trees, developed 800 parks, and cleared 125,000 miles of trails. Lane Kirkland, a native South Carolinian, former president of the AFL-CIO, describes what the CCC did for his home region. Before the Corps arrived, he says, "The Southern U.S. was totally stripped of vegetation. Every river was thick with mud from erosion . . . Every farm had a gully. And every time it rained, the topsoil was just washed away." Then came the CCC: "You go down there and you see millions of pine trees that are the basis of the timber and pulp industry, planted by the CCC . . . the CCC paid for itself a thousand times over."

More importantly, the Corps offered honest, hard work to more than

3 million young men, saving a generation from despair. Its alumni went on to help defeat Hitler and power the postwar economic boom. By comparison, subsequent jobs programs have been tiny, even when the need was great. The Job Corps currently has about 60,000 recruits; the Clinton administration's AmeriCorps program promises "up to" 1,000 recruits for its own take on the CCC. Yet these jobs programs, along with others run by the government over the past few decades, such as the notorious Comprehensive Employment and Training Act of the seventies, have followed a flawed model. Instead of emphasizing the New Deal value of work, Great Society–type programs have dwelt on *preparation* for work—or worse, dwelt on nothing at all.[116] No wonder these newer programs have not been effective: social workers are less effective at the mobilization and motivation of young people, especially young men, than drill sergeants.

In times past, the nation could rely on the military to play its normal role as an employer of last resort for aimless, restless youth. Indeed, the armed services have been the federal government's best program for upward mobility, providing jobs, dignity, and discipline for the young and poor from all corners of the country. Anyone who doubts that the American Dream lives in the military should ask Colin Powell for his opinion. But today, in the post–Cold War era, the military's manpower needs are small and confined to those with clean records and good technical aptitudes.

America is not a left-wing country, nor is it a right-wing country: it is a *work* country. Work is one of the few values that Americans can agree on. That's why the current welfare system is so roundly despised: because it flouts the nation's deeply held bias against handouts. The national government could underline this belief in work with a New CCC, providing a "work standard" for welfare reform in the fifty states. The New CCC would accept young men and women without much regard to their circumstances prior to enlistment. Yet once young people volunteered for the New Corps, they would be required to live by its militaristic regimen. If situation determines consciousness, a more disciplined and gratification-delaying culture would emerge from this new tough-love environment.

The New Deal CCC succeeded because it was consonant with the American self-help ethos. The New CCC would not be forced labor;

it would offer meaningful jobs, although recruitment could be targeted to at-risk groups. It might begin with basic training, organized along military lines, to instill discipline and purpose into young men; it might be organized as a military unit without weapons—but with ranks, uniforms, honor, loyalty, and the inculcation of civic and patriotic virtues. By necessity, the Pentagon is decommissioning military bases and demobilizing its even more valuable cadre of drill sergeants. Yet such assets should not be frittered away; they are still needed for a new mission of national service. Thus would soldiers be reborn as Samurai bureaucrats.

The old CCC was tasked with outdoor environmental missions, such as planting trees and soil conservation. One New CCC mission could be reclaiming the Everglades for Mother Nature. In the past, the Army Corps of Engineers spent billions to pour concrete all through southern Florida; if a wetland environment is to survive, much of the concrete the Corps put in will have to be removed. Moreover, as Hugh Price, speaking at the National Urban League Convention, has suggested, the mission today could be extended to the cities as well:

> We taxpayers all know there's plenty of infrastructure work to do. Schools are crumbling. Subway and bus stations are strewn with graffiti and railroad rights-of-way are littered with trash. Public parks in cities and suburbs alike are poorly maintained.[117]

Both rural and urban environments could benefit from young people's meaningful work.

A New Paradigm leader might ask General Powell to run the New CCC. The argument to him would be simple: save a generation of young Americans. And if Powell were engaged in something even bigger, then his former subordinate, Norman Schwarzkopf, could be asked to assume command. More importantly, a CCC could be the common ground upon which Americans as diverse as Jesse Jackson and Bill Bennett could work together. Given that both Jackson and Bennett have been wrestling with the issues of self-discipline and virtue for some time, a New CCC could unite them in common cause.

People might argue that such a Corps would be expensive. Let's stipulate that it would be—$30,000 per recruit per year, maybe more.

So half a million recruits in a CCC would cost at least $15 billion a year. But those costs must be compared to costs the nation is incurring elsewhere. Jesse Jackson has a point: it *is* cheaper to send a kid to Harvard than to jail. Doubling the prison population in the last twelve years has not led to safer streets. We can't relocate San Quentin to Cambridge; what we can do is develop a better plan to deal with poverty and crime proactively. One problem with so many of today's social programs, like the Job Corps, is that the kids in them know that the programs are for "losers"; the stigmatization detracts from what they take away from the experience. Yet in serving their country honorably, doing productive work, young disadvantaged Americans could save themselves.

And if the nation ends up spending more money to promote the work ethic than it does now, so be it. So long as the CCC reflects American values—if it is run as a disciplined program, if its participants do real work—it will be popular as well as effective, no matter how much it costs. Since America was built on work, national policy ought to make sure that every American can find purposeful work.

The New Paradigm Big Offer will not solve all problems. The change that comes with choice, empowerment, and restructuring can also erode what T. S. Eliot called "the permanent things": our inherited values and traditions. The New Paradigm cannot guarantee that fathers will love mothers, that children will have happy homes; it can't completely answer the painful question: "why can't we just get along?"

A half-century ago the pessimistic economist Joseph Schumpeter wrote of the "creative destruction" of capitalism; it's plausible to spin out scary scenarios of cyber-alienation amidst affluence. Indeed, many of our deepest grievances are against modernity itself, which strips us of pastoral innocence and drops us on a sometimes darkling plain. Furthermore, we should recall that Sigmund Freud was writing about human nature itself—without regard to economic systems—when he titled his 1929 book *Civilization and Its Discontents*.

Yet in the era of the New Paradigm, perhaps the Synoptic Aspiration will be replaced by human-scaled Multiple Aspirations, a world in which people of all genders and colors are able to better themselves. This will be the new American community, although it remains to be seen exactly how new technology can be harnessed to create a high-tech *Gemeinschaft*.

No one can conserve the unconservable; once unleashed, Wienerian technology will never return to the tube—let alone the chip. It's possible that no matter what we do, a few generations more of tabloid TV will consign the entire canon of Western civilization to a few rarely downloaded CD-ROMs. But we can't go home again; history only spins forward.

Alfred North Whitehead once said that the test of civilization is the number of things it takes for granted. That's what Operating Systems are about—getting a system in place so that people don't have to think about it anymore, fully confident that it works. Yet as Whitehead also observed, "No period of history is ever great or ever can be great that does not act on some sort of high idealistic motives."

It's been said that ideas move nations. Ideas have certainly moved *this* nation. As we think about the time beyond our own lives, all we have is theory—and faith. And the New Paradigm prospect is that all Americans will be able to make the quantum leap into a better future.

Yet practicing politicians, more worried about reelection than immortality, have a right to ask: "What's in it for *me*?" The answer is: there are votes to be had. Whenever politics and reality are out of phase, a tremendous political opportunity exists for a leader or party to use the idea advantage to leapfrog over the opposition.

The Bureaucratic Operating System is not working. That's bad for incumbents. The Republicans were defeated in 1992, the Democrats in 1994. With power in Washington now divided, both parties have their fingerprints on the status quo. Yet that status quo is what's known in the military as "a target-rich environment." Any challenger, from any party, can make the point in 1996 that the system is still failing, that we're cascading ever closer to the chaos—so it's time once again to throw the bums out. Incumbents tied to the current system are going to be sitting penguins.

Yet if the two parties fail to meet the challenge, then the opportunity exists for a new leader or party to take the lead, to create a new Alliance to make the profound structural change America needs. The Bureaucratic Operating System is doomed, but its dissolution will be slow and uneven. If AMERICRAT is left in place to die with its Bismarckian boots on, the American Dream will have withered away long before.

Whoever makes the next Big Offer that unites the nation on behalf of constructive change will go down in history as a hero or heroine. After decades of hating politics, Americans hunger for leadership that will rekindle the best that they are capable of: a sense of the dignity and worth of the individual, a new commitment to colorblind upward mobility for all, a renewed confidence that the political system is effective as well as fair—in short, a new birth of freedom for the country.

This is the Big Offer the voters are waiting for. It will take several elections to set the New Paradigm in place, but let us begin. History will not wait for us; the Cyber Future looms. We are not past all hope, but the current course must be departed from—soon.

What comes next is up to the American people.

Notes

Introduction

1. Thomas Kuhn explains in *The Structure of Scientific Revolutions* (Chicago: University of Chicago Press, 1970) that scientists begin searching for new interpretations of data "when the profession can no longer evade anomalies that subvert the existing tradition" (pp. 6, 57). One reason for sticking to a failed paradigm is the perceived lack of an alternative: "Once it has achieved the status of a paradigm, a scientific theory is declared invalid only if an alternate candidate is available to take its place" (p. 77).

2. Kuhn, *Structure*, p. 67.

3. Ibid., p. 23.

4. Paul Manafort, quoted in Murray Kempton, "A Den of Sinners Looks to Its Master," *Newsday*, June 12, 1992, p. 70.

Chapter 1

1. Mario Cuomo, "A Case for the Democrats 1984: A Tale of Two Cities," keynote address, Democratic National Convention, San Francisco, California, July 16, 1984, p. 7.

2. William Gibson, *Neuromancer* (New York: Ace Books, 1984), p. 3.

3. The Trifecta of the Hugo, Nebula, and Philip K. Dick awards.

4. *Economic Report of the President, 1994* (Washington, D.C.: GPO, 1994), pp. 114–15.

5. Cuomo, "Case for the Democrats," pp. 7, 16.

6. Norbert Wiener, *Cybernetics: Or Control and Communication in the Animal and the Machine* (Cambridge: MIT Press, 1948). Wiener was a contrarian as well as cybernetician. Just a few years before, in 1943, the chairman of the board of IBM, Tom Watson, had said, "I think there is a world market

for about five computers." (Quoted in Ernst R. Berndt, *The Practice of Econometrics: Classic and Contemporary* [Reading, Mass.: Addison-Wesley, 1991], chap. 1.)

7. Lewis Beale, "No more starry-eyed visions of outer space," *New York Daily News*, July 17, 1994, City Lights section, p. 3.

8. Catherine S. Manegold, "Giuliani, on Stump, Hits Hard at Crime and How to Fight It," *New York Times*, October 13, 1993, p. A1.

9. Michael Novak, "Urgent Need for Virtuous Capitalism," *Los Angeles Times*, March 18, 1994, p. 2. See also Novak, *The Spirit of Democratic Capitalism* (Lanham, Md.: University Press of America, 1991).

10. Neal Stephenson, *Snow Crash* (New York: Bantam Books, 1992), p. 32.

11. Robert Reich, *The Work of Nations* (New York: Vintage, 1992), pp. 302–3 [first edition 1991].

12. Stephenson, *Snow Crash*, p. 2.

13. "Cyberpunk Era; William Gibson Interviews," *Whole Earth Review*, June 22, 1989, p. 78.

14. Tom Redburn, "Candidates See Distinct States, Each New York," *New York Times*, October 2, 1994, p. 1.

15. Sam Roberts, "Gap Between Rich and Poor in New York City Grows Wider," *New York Times*, December 25, 1994, p. 33. Data are for counties with more than 50,000 in population.

16. Mary Hellman, "William Gibson's Bold New World," *Washington Times*, October 17, 1993, p. D3.

Chapter 2

1. Ronald Reagan, "Remarks at a Reagan-Bush Rally" [September 19, 1984], *20 Weekly Compilation*, Presidential Document 1314.

2. Bruce Springsteen, in title track of *Born in the USA* (1984).

3. Aaron Bernstein, "Job One in America: Better Jobs," *Business Week*, June 13, 1994, p. 17. See also Richard B. Freeman, ed., *Working Under Different Rules* (New York: Russell Sage Foundation, 1994).

4. Ken Auletta, *Greed And Glory On Wall Street: The Fall of the House of Lehman* (New York: Random House, 1986), pp. 217–22. The Chairman of Lehman received $15 million, which seems paltry compared to the

"bulge bracket" totals the top six Wall Street firms are taking home when they clean out their desk for the last time. At such compensation scales, they can afford their own gold watches.

5. U.S. Department of Commerce, telephone communication.

6. Stephen Taub and David Carey, "The Wall Street 100," *Financial World*, July 5, 1994, p. 30. The *Washington Post* reports that Soros's total income, including personal investments, was $1.5 billion in 1993.

The hedge funds had a bad year in 1994, with the top fifteen losing an estimated $5 billion. But that still leaves them with around $30 billion, vastly more than even five years ago. (Laura Jereski, "The Wrong Stuff," *Wall Street Journal*, September 28, 1994, p. A1.)

7. Michael M. Thomas, *Black Money* (New York: Crown, 1994), p. 101.

8. Nick Gilbert, "Porous Soros," *Financial World*, November 8, 1994, p. 39. Soros is actually deferring his corporate income tax liability, not eliminating it altogether.

9. "War of the Worlds," *The Economist*, October 1, 1994, p. 3.

10. David Wessel, "What If the Dollar Doesn't Stay on Top?" *Wall Street Journal*, March 20, 1995, p. A1.

11. John A. Byrne, "Executive Pay: The Party Ain't Over Yet," *Business Week*, April 26, 1993, p. 56.

12. *Economic Report of the President, 1994* p. 25.

13. Katherine S. Newman, *Declining Fortunes: The Withering of the American Dream* (New York: Basic Books, 1993), pp. 43–44.

14. Patrice Hill, "Healthier Economy Fails to Lift Gloom," *Washington Times*, September 24, 1994, p. A1.

15. "Honey, They Shrunk My Raise!" *U.S. News & World Report*, September 12, 1994, p. 18.

16. "Trade Unions in America: Getting Their dues," *The Economist*, March 25, 1995, p. 100. There were 650,000 layoffs in 1993, despite a 5.6 percent increase in GNP. See Louis Uchitelle, "Job Losses Don't Let Up Even as Hard Times Ease," *New York Times*, March 22, 1994, p. A1.

17. John P. Kotter, *The New Rules: How to Succeed in Today's Post-Corporate World* (New York: Free Press, 1995), p. 13. Kotter, whose book includes data to 1992, estimates that by 1995, the percentage will have risen to 40 percent. (Judith H. Dobrzynski, "New Secret of Success: Getting Off the Ladder," *New York Times*, March 19, 1995, p. F14.)

18. Steven Pearlstein, "Large US Companies Continue Downsizing," *Washington Post*, September 27, 1994, p. C1.

19. "Soon to Hit the Unemployment Offices: Service Sector Workers," *Forbes*, April 11, 1994, p. 41.

20. Daniel Sutherland and David S. Hilzerath, *Washington Post*, May 2, 1995, p. A1.

21. Kotter, *New Rules*, p. 51.

22. Paul Krugman, "Europe Jobless, America Penniless," *Foreign Policy*, summer 1994, Krugman, p. 23.

23. Even law firms are now able to do much of their work with temporary lawyers. See Amy Stevens, "Big Companies Hire More Lawyer-Temps," *Wall Street Journal*, September 23, 1994, p. B1.

24. Lawrence Mishel and Jared Bernstein, *The State of Working America, 1994–95* (Washington: Economic Policy Institute, 1994), p. 4.

25. Douglas Coupland, *Generation X: Tales for an Accelerated Culture* (New York: St. Martin's Press, 1991), p. 11.

26. Brett D. Fromson, "The Golden Years: Wall Street's Prosperity Makes the Go-Go '80s Look Small Time," *Washington Post*, July 3, 1994, p. H1.

27. Lawrence Zuckerman "Shades of the Go-Go 80's: Takeovers in a Comeback," *New York Times*, November 3, 1993, p. A1. 1994 was the best year for hostile mergers and acquisitions since 1988, and the first quarter of 1995 showed a one-third increase from a year earlier. See Steven Lipin, "Mergers and Acquisitions in 1st Quarter Increased 35% From the Year Before," *Wall Street Journal*, April 4, 1995, p. A3.

28. "Call the Doctor: M&A Fever is Back," *Business Week*, October 18, 1993, p. 42. See also *Fortune*, October 18, 1993.

29. Christopher Farrell et al., "An Old-Fashioned Feeding Frenzy," *Business Week*, May 1, 1994, p. 34.

30. Dan Shaw, "Greedy for More? The 80's Sneak Back," *New York Times*, October 2, 1994, p. 43; Ellen Neuborne, "Luxury Items Back in Style," *USA Today*, November 17, 1994, p. 4B; Judd Tully, "At the Auctions," *Washington Post*, November 3, 1994, p. D2.

31. Leslie Eaton, "1980s Redux? Deals Making A Comeback," *New York Times*, July 17, 1994, p. F1.

32. Janet L. Fix, "Automation Makes Bank Branches a Liability," *USA Today*, November 28, 1994, p. B1. A teller transaction costs a bank $1.07, while an electronic transaction costs just seven cents.

33. Carolyn T. Geer, "For a New Job, Press #1," *Forbes*, August 15, 1994, p. 118.

34. William Bridges, "The End of the Job," *Fortune*, September 19, 1994, p. 62.

35. Joint Committee on Taxation, telephone communication.

36. Paul Gray, "Looking for Work? Try the World," *Time*, September 19, 1994, p. 44. The *National Review* cites data showing that 250,000 Americans may be emigrating each year ("Gekko," "Random Walk," *National Review*, December 31, 1994, p. 27). *Forbes* reports that the number of Americans renouncing their citizenship, apparently for tax purposes, has soared (Robert Lenzner and Phillipe Mao, "The New Refugees," *Forbes*, November 21, 1994, p. 131). The end of the Cold War suggests that it's safe for zillionaires to go where they may; call it yet another centrifugal result of the post–Cold War era.

37. Frank I. Luntz, *The American Dream: Renewing the Promise* (Arlington, Va.: Luntz Research, 1994), p. 30.

38. Ashley Dunn, "Skilled Asians Leaving US For High-Tech Jobs at Home," *New York Times*, February 21, 1995, p. A1.

39. Stephenson, *Snow Crash*, p. 2.

Chapter 3

1. Bureau of Justice Statistics, *Criminal Victimization in the United States, 1992* (Washington, D.C.: Department of Justice, 1992), p. 33.

2. *Meet the Press*, July 3, 1994. Nonetheless, some statistics suggest that crime is in fact still on the rise. The Justice Department's National Crime Victimization Survey, which interviewed 100,000 Americans over twelve years, showed that violent crime rose 5.6 percent in 1993, to a total of 10.9 *million*.

3. Tom Wolfe, *The Bonfire of the Vanities* (New York: Bantam, 1990), p. 56.

4. "Crime in America," *Washington Times*, December 21, 1993, p. A10.

5. Bret Schundler, "On The Waterfront: Police Unions Are Arresting the War Against Crime," *Policy Review* (summer 1994), p. 40.

6. CNN, *Inside Politics*, November 30, 1993.

7. See, for example, Arnold Hamilton "Rights Activists Brand Oklahoma Death Row Lockup a 'Concrete Tomb,'" *Washington Post*, October 9, 1994, p. A29.

8. Rick Bragg, "Chain Gangs to Return to Roads of Alabama," *New York Times*, March 26, 1995, p. 16.

9. Francis X. Clines, "A Futuristic Prison Awaits the Hard-Core 400," *New York Times*, October 17, 1994, p. A1.

10. H. Paul Jeffers, *Commissioner Roosevelt: The Story of Theodore Roosevelt and the New York City Police, 1895–1897* (New York: John Wiley, 1994), p. 100.

11. David Beard, "Puerto Rico Troops Fight Housing Project Crime," *Los Angeles Times*, January 2, 1994, p. A6.

12. *ABC World News Tonight*, November 3, 1994.

13. Mark Arax, "Fresno's War on Crime Heats Up," *Los Angeles Times*, December 22, 1995, p. B2.

14. Richard Cohen, ". . . And Common Sense," *Washington Post*, October 5, 1993, p. A19.

15. Richard Roth, *CBS Evening News*, December 22, 1993.

16. National Association of Federally Licensed Firearms Dealers, telephone communication.

17. U.S. Bureau of Justice Statistics; cited in Gary Blonston, "Crime Wave Across Nation Called a Mirage; Despite Fears, Figures Indicate Rate Isn't Rising," *Arizona Republic*, October 24, 1993.

18. Kelly Shannon, "If a home is a castle, this siding is armor," *Washington Times*, June 1, 1994, p. 1.

19. Jon Nordheimer, "In Atlantic City, Suspicion is a Way of Life," *New York Times*, March 22, 1994, p. B1.

20. Otis Port, "Pity Not These Ink-Stained Wretches," *Business Week*, July 25, 1994, p. 82.

21. Bruce Horovitz and Earle Eldridge, "Automakers Push Buyers' Security Button," *USA Today*, November 4, 1994, p. B1.

22. "Dispute in San Francisco Over Use of Special Security Patrols," *New York Times*, October 23, 1994, p. 23.

23. Ross Kerber, "Policing the Growing Security Business," *Washington Post*, September 6, 1993, Business section, p. 5.

24. William Sposato, "Reborn Times Square Ready to Usher in a Prosperous New Year," *Chicago Tribune*, p. 2.

25. Linda Wheeler, "In Georgetown, Private Guard Patrols Buy Peace of Mind," *Washington Post*, March 29, 1994, p. A1.

26. Clair Collins, "Hiring Private Security Guards to Cut Neighborhood Crime," *New York Times*, August 18, 1994, p. C6.

27. "East Side: $20 Million for Safe Streets," *New York Observer*, September 19, 1994, p. 4.

28. Ann Mariano, "Enclosed Communities: Havens, or Worse?" *Washington Post*, April 9, 1994, p. E1.

29. Iver Peterson, "Urban Dangers Send Children Indoors," *New York Times*, January 1, 1995, p. 29.

30. DeNeen L. Brown, "Afraid to Die, Afraid to Live," *Washington Post*, January 16, 1995, p. A1.

31. Joel Garreau, *Edge City: Life on the New Frontier* (New York: Anchor Books, 1992), p. 49.

32. James Trefil, "A Scientist in the City," *Washington Post*, January 24, 1994, p. B3.

33. The author is no relation to the Pinkerton Detective Agency or any other security company.

34. Stephenson, *Snow Crash*, p. 437.

35. William Gibson, *Virtual Light* (New York: Bantam, 1993), p. 97.

Chapter 4

1. Tony Kushner, *Angels in America, Part Two: Perestroika* (New York: Theater Communications Group, 1994), p. 14.

2. Karl R. Popper, *The Open Society And Its Enemies* (Princeton: Princeton University Press, 1950), p. 9. Plato gets good press as an intellectual in his search for Truth, Justice, Beauty, Wisdom, and so forth. That's the seduction of Plato: idealists of all kinds—anyone who can imagine a better world—are eventually seduced by Platonism. But, as Popper says, "Plato's political program, far from being morally superior to totalitarianism, is fundamentally identical with it" (p. 87).

3. The most familiar use of the term "synoptic" is in the phrase "synoptic Gospels," a reference to the fact that the first three Gospels of the New Testament (Matthew, Mark, and Luke) offer an account of events from the same point of view. But the word, which derives from the Greek, has other meanings. (Arthur W. Munk, *A Synoptic Approach to the Riddle of Existence A World View for a World Civilization* [St. Louis: Warren H. Green, 1977], p. 129).

The use of "synoptic" to describe a "mental act or faculty" dates back to 1852 and the work of James Martineau (1805–1900), whose *Essays on the Unity of Mind in Nature* (1891) refers to "taking a combined or comprehensive mental view of something." While maintaining its connotation of inclusiveness, the term has been used to describe different philosophical ideas, including the synoptic vision (or view) and the synoptic approach (or method). The first describes philosophy in the "grand manner," one that is not "simply the sum of self-intelligible atoms of inquiry" (C. F. Delaney, Michael J. Loux, Gary Gutting, and W. David Solomon, *The Synoptic Vision: Essays on the Philosophy of Wilfrid Sellars* [Notre Dame: University of Notre Dame Press, 1977], p. ix), whereas the second helps guide "the metaphysician in his attack on the tough, difficult, ultimate metaphysical PROBLEM from a vantage point that is universal, inclusive, and comprehensive" (Munk, p. 129).

Drawn from this intellectual pool, the "Synoptic Aspiration" is the quest for One Big Answer, a single, "one-vision," comprehensive solution. Such intellectual holism also has it roots in "Monism," a term first used by the German philosopher Christian Wolff (1679–1754) to describe "those systems which recognize only one basic metaphysical principle" (Munk p. 41). But this mind-set had it origins long before Wolff. As philosopher Arthur Munk writes, "Philosophic monism had its beginnings in that dim dawn of reflective thought when primitive philosophers began trying to reduce all their deities to modes or appearances of one deity." Since that time, philosophers have been propounding theories of inclusiveness. What undergirds all monists is the idea of unity, so when Plotinus viewed God as the "summit and Source of all being, as absolutely 'self-sufficient,'" and Hegel sought to "make his system into one Perfect Whole by attempting to show that it is able to overcome all difficulties and reconcile all differences," they were really talking about the same thing (Munk, pp. 42–43).

The lure of One Big Answer is indeed very strong, and many have been swayed by its siren song, not only because of its intellectual attraction but also its aesthetic. This may explain the rampant paternalism of modern politics, which has reared its head in the minds and policies of leaders from Bismarck on.

Why the acute desire to bundle everything up into one ball? Consider Munk's assertion that the monist thinks his "world view provides us with the only secure basis for a healthy optimism." One can make too much of this, but it is probably safe to say that the monist plays the vision game not just for the power but for the "abiding peace which comes to the troubled soul as it catches a vision of everything 'under the form of eternity'" (Munk, p. 49).

4. Now *this* is "Synopticism":

> At the *pinnacle* of the development of progressive thought Marxism arose at the junction of several sciences and ideological trends—philosophy, history, political economy, socialist and communist doctrines, and natural science. The founders of scientific communism synthesized the major achievements of German classical philosophy, ranging from Kant to Hegel (dialectical method) and Feuerbach (the materialistic interpretation of the central problem of philosophy), English classical political economy (Smith's and Ricardo's labour theory of value), the great Utopians—Saint-Simon, Fourier, Owen and other French, English and German Socialists and Communists (the idea of abolishing private property), French historians of the Restoration period (the theory of class struggle of Guizot, Thierry, Mignet, and Thiers), Lewis H. Morgan (a study of primitive society), and the 19th-century natural science (the three main discoveries which revealed the dialectics of nature: the cell theory of Schleiden and Schwann, the law of conservation and transformation of energy discovered and developed by Mayer, Joule, Colding, Grove, and Helmholtz, and Darwin's theory of evolution). The greater part of these achievements had already been assimilated by Marxism in its inception period, the others, mainly in the field of natural science, were used in the course of its development.
>
> The synthesis, the creative interpretation of these major achievements of human thought from the angle of the objective requirements of the class struggle of the proletariat and all further development of human society resulted in a series of outstanding discoveries by Marx and Engels, which led to the emergence of Marxism as a fundamentally new, integral system. In accordance with its three main theoretical sources, Marxism *arose as a unity* of its three component parts—philosophy, political economy and the theory of scientific communism. This, however, is not the mechanical sum total of three sciences, the result of the encyclopaedically diversified activities of their founders, but an organic synthesis of the three components of a single doctrine, each of which is internally linked with the whole. (B. N. Ponomarev, ed., *The International Working-Class Movement: Problems of History and Theory*, vol. 1: *The Origins of the Proletariat and its Evolution as a Revolutionary Class* [Moscow: Progress Publishers, 1980], p. 364).

Reading this, I thought of various theological texts and tracts that make the assertion that their true faith represents the highest stage of thinking.

5. Popper, *Open Society*, p. 227. The late author brands Hegel as "the father of modern . . . totalitarianism" (p. 218).

6. Arkady Plotnitsky argues that virtually all subsequent philosophy is a footnote of sorts to Hegel, including Marxism. "Hegel remains the thinker of the continuum," writes Plotnitsky, asserting that Einstein, for example, only comes "*after* Bohr, *after* Freud, *after* Nietzsche, *after* Darwin, *after* Marx" and of course, after Hegel. (Plotnitsky, *In the Shadow of Hegel: Complementarity, History, and the Unconscious* [Gainesville: University of Florida Press, 1993], p. 77.)

7. Ludwig von Mises, *Bureaucracy* (New Haven: Yale University Press, 1944), pp. 74–75.

8. Cited in Eugene Kamenka, *Bureaucracy* (London: Basic Blackwell, 1989). p. 120.

9. Robert Hughes, *The Shock of the New* (New York: Knopf, 1980), p. 11.

10. According to the German sociologist Max Weber (1864–1920), the leading student of bureaucracy, bureaucracy can be defined as:

> Fixed and official jurisdictional areas, which are generally ordered by rules, that is, by laws or administrative regulations. The regular activities required for the purposes of the bureaucratically governed structure are distributed in a fixed way as official duties. Methodical provision is made for the regular and continuous fulfillment of these duties and for the execution of the corresponding rights; only persons who have the generally regulated qualifications to serve are employed. (Weber, *Economy and Society*, ed. Guenther Roth and Claus Wittich [1922; reprint, Berkeley: University of California Press, 1978], p. 956)

11. Kamenka, *Bureaucracy*, pp. 94–95.

12. Weber, *Economy and Society*, p. 964.

13. Ibid., pp. 971–72.

14. Kamenka, *Bureaucracy*, p. 20.

15. Peter Green, *Alexander to Actium* (Berkeley, Calif.: University of California Press, 1990), pp. 3, 6.

16. Kamenka, *Bureaucracy*, p. 57.

17. Ibid., pp. 65–66.

18. Weber, *Economy and Society*, p. 973. Continuing, Weber offers a vision of idealized bureaucracy:

> The fully developed bureaucratic apparatus compares with other organizations exactly as does the machine with the non-mechanical modes of production. Precision, speed, unambiguity, knowledge of the files, continuity, discretion, unity, strict subordination, reduction of friction and of material and personal costs—these are raised to the optimum point in the strictly bureaucratic administration.

19. Thomas Bokenkotter, *A Concise History of the Catholic Church* (New York: Doubleday, 1990), p. 28.

20. Paul Johnson, *A History of Christianity* (New York: Atheneum, 1976), pp. 131–34.

21. Bokenkotter, *Concise History*, pp. 128–29.

22. As early as the time of Frederick the Great, Prussians brought discipline and professionalism not only to the army but to the overall society. The Prussians were the first Europeans to use exams for civil service (Kamenka, *Bureaucracy*, p. 104). Frederick "was the first model for the technocratic-based dictator of the twentieth century" (John Ralston Saul, *Voltaire's Bastards* (New York: Free Press, 1992) p. 190). Powered by the factorylike effectiveness of the *Kabinettsystem*, Prussia was the go-go country of *Mitteleuropa* in the eighteenth century, defeating the much larger Austrian Empire of the Hapsburgs in the Seven Years' War. As the Prussian poet Friedrich von Hardenberg Novalis put it in 1798, "No other state has ever been administered so much like a factory as Prussia since the death of Friedrich Wilhelm" (quoted in F.A. Hayek, *The Road to Serfdom* (Chicago: University of Chicago Press, 1994.) p. 9n.)

23. Merritt Ierley, *With Charity For All Welfare and Society, Ancient Times to the Present* (New York: Praeger, 1984), p. 127.

24. C. Northcote Parkinson, *Parkinson's Law: And Other Studies in Administration* (Boston: Houghton Mifflin, 1957), p. 33.

25. Ibid., p. 39.

26. Laurence J. Peter and Raymond Hull, *The Peter Principle* (New York: William Morrow, 1969), p. 25.

27. Ibid., p. 27.

28. Ibid., p. 151.

29. Milovan Djilas writes: "The greatest illusion [of Soviet communism]

was that industrialization and collectivization of the USSR, and destruction of capitalist ownership, would result in a classless society . . . The capitalist and other classes of ancient origin had in fact been destroyed, but a new class, previously unknown to history, had been formed" (Djilas, *The New Class: An Analysis of the Communist System* [New York: Praeger, 1957], pp. 37–38).

30. Irving Kristol, *Two Cheers for Capitalism* (New York: Basic Books, 1978), pp. 27–28.

31. Mancur Olson, *The Rise and Decline of Nations: Economic Growth, Stagflation, and Social Rigidities* (New Haven: Yale University Press, 1982), p. 77.

32. [C]ountries whose distributional coalitions have been emasculated or abolished by totalitarian government or foreign occupations should grow relatively quickly after a free and stable legal order is established. This can explain the postwar 'economic miracles' in the nations that were defeated in World War II, particularly those in Japan and West Germany. (Ibid., pp. 75–76).

Olson goes on to say that if the Japanese and Germans enjoy "continued stability," that will have "an adverse influence on their growth rates."

33. F. A. Hayek, *The Fatal Conceit: The Errors of Socialism* (Chicago: The University of Chicago Press, 1988), p. 85.

34. Wiener, *Cybernetics*, p. 162.

35. Kushner, *Angels*, p. 14.

Chapter 5

1. Sowell, *Ethnic America: A History* (New York: Basic Books, 1981), p. 33.

2. Ibid., p. xi.

3. Oliver E. Allen, *The Tiger: The Rise and Fall of Tammany Hall* (Reading, Mass.: Addison-Wesley, 1993), p. 81.

4. The stalwarts of Tammany worked to make themselves accessible to people still in the working class or slums. When Lincoln Steffens asked the boss of Boston, Martin Lomasney, about the role of the political machines, Lomasney replied: "I think there's got to be in every ward somebody that

any bloke can come to, no matter what he's done, and get help. Help, you understand; none of your law and your justice, but help." (Quoted in Wakin, p. 26). A page from George Washington Plunkitt's diary highlights his busy, multiethnic schedule:

2 A.M.: Awakened by a boy with message from bartender to bail him out of jail.

3 A.M.: Back to bed.

6 A.M.: Fire engines, up and off to the scene to see my election district captain tending to the burnt-out tenants. Got names for new homes.

8:30 A.M.: To police court. Six drunken constituents on hand. Got four released, by a timely word to the judge. Paid the others' fines.

9:00 A.M.: To municipal court. Told an election district captain to act as lawyer for a widow threatened with dispossession.

2–3 P.M.: Found jobs for 4 constituents. 3 P.M. an Italian funeral. Sat conspicuously up front.

4 P.M.: A Jewish funeral. Up front again, in the synagogue.

7 P.M.: Meeting of district captains and reviewed the lists of all voters, who's for us, who's agin.

8 P.M.: Church fair. Bought ice cream for the girls; took fathers for a little something around the corner.

9 P.M.: Back in clubhouse. Heard complaints of a dozen push-cart peddlers.

10:30 P.M.: A Jewish wedding. Had sent handsome present to bride.

Midnight: To bed.

(Cited in William L. Riordon, *Plunkitt of Tammany Hall* [1905; reprint, New York: Meridian, 1991], pp. 91–93).

A cursory glance reveals that the average machine politician was closely attuned to the basic needs of his constituents, much more so than those who make it their business to serve the poor today.

Yet BOSS, reviled by Republicans and reformers, managed to survive the onslaught of AMERICRAT until recently. One such place was Chicago, "the city that worked." Political scientist Harold F. Gosnell describes how Windy City politicos operated in the 1930s—and paints exactly this responsive, customer-driven picture. One precinct captain "passed out food, money for rent, coal, advice on getting hospital care, legal advice, adjusted taxes, and placed men in forest-preserve jobs." The good captain was "a master at adjusting himself to the particularities of the persons addressed." (Gosnell, *Machine Politics: Chicago Model* [Chicago: University of Chicago Press, 1937], pp. 58–61). So far from modern politics' goal of universal standard treatment, machine politicians put emphasis on the needs of the unique individual in a unique situation. BOSS may have been corrupt, but it contained much that worked. Gosnell's Chicago hacks prefigure business guru Tom Peters's emphasis on "MBWA"—"Management By Walking Around."

5. However, his Republican contemporaries were less admiring; Arthur was dropped from the ticket in 1884.

6. James Allen Smith The Idea Brokers: Think Tanks and the Rise of the New Policy Elite (New York: The Free Press, 1991), pp. 25–27.

7. U.S. Bureau of the Census Historical Statistics of the United States: Colonial Times to 1970 (Washington DC: GPO, 1975), pp. 105–106.

8. U.S. Bureau of the Census, *Statistical Abstract of the United States: 1994* (Washington, D.C.: Department of Commerce, 1994), p. 54.

9. Smith, *Idea Brokers*, pp. 34-36.

10. Quoted in Smith, *Idea Brokers*, p. 29.

11. Ibid. pp. 28-30. Milton and Rose Friedman take an even harsher view of German influence on the American intelligentsia:

> It may seem paradoxical that an essentially autocratic and aristocratic state such as pre–World War I Germany—in today's jargon, a right-wing dictatorship—should have led the way in introducing measures that are generally linked to socialism and the Left. But there is no paradox . . . Believers in aristocracy and socialism share a faith in centralized rule. (Friedman and Friedman, *Free to Choose* [New York: Harcourt Brace Jovanovich, 1980], p. 97).

"'We have a lot we can learn from the Germans,'" said Bill Clinton. "'The Germans are able to provide a very high-quality health care system at a much lower cost than we are, because they have much more discipline in the way it's organized and financed.'" Well, of course they do! "(Wilfred Prewo, "Germany Is Not a Model," *Wall Street Journal*, February 1, 1994, p. A14).

12. John Patrick Diggins, *The Rise and Fall of the American Left* (New York: W. W. Norton, 1992), pp. 72–76.

13. Samuel Haber, *Efficiency and Uplift: Scientific Management in the Progressive Era, 1890–1920* (Chicago: University of Chicago Press, 1964), p. ix.

14. Steven Fraser, *Labor Will Rule* (New York: Free Press, 1991), p. 132.

15. Frederick Winslow Taylor, *The Principles of Scientific Management* (1911; reprint, New York: Harper, 1947).

16. Judith A. Merkle, *Management Ideology: The Legacy of the International Scientific Management Movement* (Berkeley: University of California Press, 1980), p. 40.

17. U.S. Bureau of the Census, *Historical Statistics*, p. 224.

18. Merkle, *Management Ideology*, observes:

> The concerns of Scientific Management—centralized planning to promote the efficient use of resources, worker betterment through rationalization of working conditions, and the natural right of a guiding sector, or vanguard, to reform national conditions on this model—have more than a *coincidental relationship with Marxism-Leninism* [emphasis added]. One of the most curious episodes in the history of Taylorism is how this philosophy of private business came to be absorbed by its bitterest enemy, the first socialist state.

But there's a logic here: before "scientific management" was Marx's "scientific socialism." Merkle cites the semi-Synopticism of Taylor, referring to "the practical fusion of socialism, centralism, and bureaucratism that was effected under the aegis of Taylorism" (p. 103).

19. Robert H. Wiebe, *The Search for Order 1877–1902* (New York: Hill and Wang, 1967), pp. xiii–xiv.

20. Haber, *Efficiency*, p. 147.

21. John J. DiIulio, Jr., Gerald Garvey, and Donald F. Kettl, *Improving Government Performance: An Owner's Manual* (Washington, D.C.: Brookings Institution, 1993), p. 8.

22. Haber, *Efficiency*, p. 95.

23. Haber (ibid.) cites the following examples:

> On September 27, 1918, Wilson said that the Great War was "a people's war," which would bring "a full and unequivocal acceptance of the principle that the interest of the weakest is as sacred as the interest of the strongest"; "the final triumph of justice and fair dealing." In private, Wilson sounded like a socialist, saying that the world would change

after the war, with the government having to take over water power, coal mines, and oil fields. (p. 122).

On May 20, 1919, Wilson sent a message to Congress proposing "the genuine democratization of industry, based upon a full recognition of the right of those who work, in whatever rank, to participate in some organic way in every decision which directly affects their welfare or the part they play in industry." (p. 124).

24. Haber, ibid., p. 156.

25. Richard Norton Smith, *An Uncommon Man: The Triumph of Herbert Hoover* (New York: Simon and Schuster, 1984), p. 112.

26. Franklin D. Roosevelt, "Campaign Address on Progressive Government at the Commonwealth Club," *The Public Papers and Addresses of Franklin D. Roosevelt*, ed. Samuel I. Rosenman (New York: Random House, 1938), p. 753.

27. James Burnham, *The Managerial Revolution* (New York: John Day Press, 1941), p. 74.

28. William Strauss and Neil Howe, *Generations* (New York: Morrow, 1991), p. 265.

29. David Brinkley, *Washington Goes To War* (New York: Random House, 1988), pp. 62–63.

30. Eric Larrabee, *Commander in Chief: Franklin Delano Roosevelt, His Lieutenants, And Their War* (New York: Touchstone, 1987), p. 96.

31. Ibid., p. 117. Marshall had shown this ability to dance around the system before. In the 1920s, he was the assistant commandant and director of training at the Infantry School at Fort Benning, Georgia. Over the years, the process by which orders got transferred had become more and more ritualized, which "encouraged that tendency toward the elaborate and the time-consuming which lurks beneath the surface of every military organization" (pp. 109–12).

32. Michael Barone, *Our Country* (New York: Free Press, 1990), p. 76.

33. Weber, *Economy and Society*, p. 601.

34. Coupland, p. 25.

35. John Kenneth Galbraith, *The Affluent Society* (Cambridge: Riverside Press, 1958), p. 308.

36. Ibid., p. xix.

37. Jason Vest, "More Americans Use More Cocaine, Study Finds," *Washington Post*, June 14, 1994, p. A3.

38. Clinton and Gore, *Putting People First*, p. 3.

39. David Osborne and Ted Gaebler, *Reinventing Government: How the Entrepreneurial Spirit is Transforming the Public Sector* (Reading, Mass.: Addison-Wesley, 1992), pp. 166, 195.

40. Ibid., pp. 11–12.

41. Ibid., pp. 34–35.

42. Peter F. Drucker, "*Really* Reinventing Government," *Atlantic Monthly*, February 1995, p. 50.

43. Likewise, in an early eighties' high-hopes effort to control Medicare costs, the Reagan Administration gave birth to "Diagnostic Related Groups" (DRGs). These beasts would determine the correct reimbursement for each and every medical procedure. With careful monitoring, there could be no overcharging. DRGs sounded terrific—light at the end of the health-care cost tunnel. But within a month, Reagan-era Office of Management and Budget official Mike Horowitz recalls, software packages called DRG busters appeared, enabling doctors and hospitals to redefine one ailment as many— and bill the feds for all of them. Thus a relatively cheap tonsillectomy would be unbundled into the operation itself plus a zoo of tests and maladies to treat, from chest exams to sinus infections to throat cultures.

Realizing they were being rooked, the government came back with new rules to supersede the old. This made the health hustlers happy, because they could now sell another generation of system-torquing software. Horowitz describes the escalating spiral as "a legal-medical arms race." Medicare spending *quadrupled* in the last 12 years. It may be hard to do worse than that, but the Clintonians made the same mistake the Republicans made: trying to interpose the government into 250 million doctor–patient relationships.

44. Later in *Reinventing Governnment* (op. cit.), Osborne and Gaebler describe this deleterious phenomenon: "The real customers of the Department of Transportation have not been drivers and mass transit riders, but highway builders and public transit systems. The real customers of the Department of Housing and Urban Development have not been poor urban dwellers, but real estate developers" (p. 167).

45. Alan McConagha, "Inside Politics," *Washington Times*, January 13, 1995, p. A8.

46. Martin L. Gross makes similar calculations in his book *The Government Racket* (New York: Bantam, 1992), p. 9.

47. Paul C. Light, *Thickening Government: Federal Hierarchy and the Diffusion of Accountability*, chap. 4: "Where Does Thickening Start?" (Washington, D.C.: Brookings Institution, 1995), pp. 96–128.

48. GE and Frank Swoboda, "Up Against the Walls," *Washington Post*, February 27, 1994, p. H1.

49. John Judis, "Why Your Wages Keep Falling," *New Republic*, February 14, 1994, p. 28.

50. Janet Novack, "Antifreeze," *Forbes*, April 12, 1993, p. 46. On the other hand, author Mickey Kaus found that in 1990, for example, just 403 civil servants—out of 2.2. million—were fired for poor performance (Mickey Kaus, *The End of Equality*, New York: Basic, 1992, p. 98). That's one-fifty-fifth of 1 percent.

51. See Walter Pincus, "In Wake of Report, Woolsey Weighs What to Do Next," *Washington Post*, September 25, 1994, p. A1., and Pincus, "CIA's Woolsey Disciplines 11 in Ames Spy Scandal," *Washington Post*, September 29, 1994, p. A1.

52. John A. Byrne, *The Whiz Kids: The Founding Fathers of American Business and the Legacy They Left Us* (New York: Doubleday, 1993), pp. 7–8. Vietnam and the Great Society were the two failures that showed that AMERICRAT was no longer functional in the sixties, though the success of statism left AMERICRAT in a gleeful state of expansion. Nicholas Lemann describes the period at the dawn of the Great Society:

> The country was finally beginning to seem reliably liberal in its political mood for the first time since the Depression, and it looked like this liberal heyday would be better than the last one. In 1964, the economy was prosperous, eternally so, it seemed, because of the success of Walter Heller's Keynesian techniques—and the house of liberalism was in much better order than it had been in the 1930s because there weren't any destructive internal battles with communists this time around. (Lemann, *The Promised Land* [New York: Knopf, 1991], p. 148).

53. Deborah Shapley, *Promise and Power: The Life and Times of Robert McNamara* (Boston: Little, Brown 1993), p. 608.

54. John B. Judis, "Can Labor Come Back?" *New Republic*, May 23, 1994, p. 25.

55. Peter Brimelow and Leslie Spencer, "The National Extortion Association?" *Forbes*, June 7, 1993.

56. Sam Dillon, "Teacher Tenure: Rights vs. Discipline," *New York Times*, June 28, 1994, p. B1.

57. See, for example, "What's the CSEA [Civil Service Employees Association] Work Force Doing For New York?" *New York Times*, January 23, 1995, p. A15 [advertisement]. This particular ad touts the skilled services performed by CSEA members, from snow plowing to 911 operating to school-lunch preparing, leading one to wonder how one organization could have so much expertise in so many different fields.

58. Quoted in Fred Siegel, "Giuliani's budget victory: There's still a way to go." *New York Post*, June 24, 1994, p. 21.

59. Residents of big cities have begun to notice that their public servants are making twice as much as the average worker; this realization provoked a bitter labor dispute in Philadelphia between the city and its transit workers. See, for example, Michael Janofsky, "No Sign of an Ending to Philadelphia Strike," *New York Times*, April 7, 1995, p. A16.

60. Stephen Barr, "OPM Spells Out Un-Hatched Political Acts," *Washington Post*, September 22, 1994, p. A21.

One example of alleged politicization by federal employees was cited at the Department of Housing and Urban Development; in April 1995, Republicans accused HUD of staging rallies to oppose GOP budget cuts in New York, Detroit, and Atlanta. See Guy Gugliotta, "GOP Suspects Politics in HUD Urban Politics," *Washington Post*, April 6, 1995, p. A19.

61. Wendell Cox, "America's Protected Class: The Excess Value of Public Employment," *The State Factor*. June 1994.

62. Peter Peterson and Neil Howe, *On Borrowed Time* (New York: Touchstone/Simon and Schuster, 1989), p. 82.

63. Robert Marshall Wells, "Chapter 1 funding faces Senate rewrite in public school bill," cited in the *Washington Times*, July 18, 1994 p. A4.

64. James Bovard, "Draining the Agricultural Policy Swamp," in *An American Vision: Policies for the '90s* (Washington, D.C.: Cato Institute, 1989), p. 297.

65. Rich Lowry, "The Undeserving Rich," *National Review*, December 31, 1994, p. 21. The sugar program, actually a tariff on imports, is arguably the single most perverse program the federal government runs. The tariff raises the price of sugar—hardly a national-security commodity—by about $1.4 million to U.S. consumers, even as it denies potential export income

to struggling Latin American countries. Meanwhile, in the United States, the high price for domestic sugar encourages growers, like the aforementioned Fanjul family, to plow up the Everglades. This in turn upsets what's left of the South Florida ecosystem, forcing federal and state officials to spend more billions to try to restore some semblance of the natural wetlands habitat.

66. Meredith Bishop, "Fair Game: Government Welfare for the Well to Do," *Policy Review* (spring 1991), pp. 78–79.

67. Dean Baquet with Diana B. Henriques, "Abuses Plague Programs to Help Exports of Agriculture Products," *New York Times*, October 10, 1993, p. 1.

68. Ibid.

69. Ed Rubenstein, "Safety in (Small) Numbers," *National Review*, December 31, 1994, p. 15.

70. Jonathan Rauch, *Demosclerosis: The Silent Killer of American Government* (New York: Times Books, 1994), p. 117.

71. Kolb sees this as an example of "categorical" thinking—that is, worrying about where the money went, as opposed to the good it might have done. In 1981, he recalls, the Department of Education ran about 150 different spending programs. These "categoricals" were reduced in number to 120 in the next year, but by 1989, at the end of eight years of Reagan rule, categoricals had made a comeback—to over 200. Yet did education improve? The point is that categorical proliferation serves the interests of turf-building AMERICRATS, not America's students.

Chapter 6

1. U.S. Bureau of the Census, *Historical Statistics*, pp. 224, 1120. Data are from 1902, the first year for which federal, state, and local statistics are available.

2. Tax Foundation, *Facts and Figures on Government Finance, 1993 Edition* (Washington, D.C.: Tax Foundation, 1994), p. 5.

3. John Chamberlain, *American Stakes* (New York: Carrick and Evans, 1940), quoted in Smith, *Idea Brokers*, p. 81.

4. Theodore J. Lowi, *The End of Liberalism* (New York: W.W. Norton, 1969), p. x.

5. Ibid., p. 29.

6. Ibid., p. 298.

7. David S. Broder and Dana Priest, "As Momentum Slows, Clintons Said to Be Eager to Submit Health Care Bill," *Washington Post*, October 14, 1993 p. A4.

8. James Q. Wilson, "Mr. Clinton, Meet Mr. Gore," *Wall Street Journal*, October 28, 1993, p. A22.

9. William Greider, *Who Will Tell the People: The Betrayal of American Democracy* (New York: Touchstone, 1993), pp. 106–108.

10. James L. Payne, *The Culture of Spending: Why Congress Lives Beyond Our Means* (San Francisco: ICS Press, 1991), p. 13.

11. G. Pascal Zachary, "How Some Schools Get Fat with Federal Pork," *Wall Street Journal*, April 29, 1994, p. B1.

12. Jonathan Rauch, *Demosclerosis: The Silent Killer of American Government* (New York: Times Books, 1994), p. 69.

13. The new Bureaucratic Operating System encompasses both the remains of AMERICRAT and the new Orbitals. The Office of Economic Opportunity and its offshoots registered millions of new voters, making it possible for people to assert their rights through their own elected officials, just as Shriver and his colleagues intended. Nationwide, the number of black elected officials more than quintupled from 1970 to 1993 (U.S. Bureau of the Census, *Statistical Abstract*, p. 284.) Yet the most dramatic power gains for the poor have been in the cities. Those who have been elected as a result range from Marion Barry, the street activist-turned-mayor, to former Freedom Rider John Lewis to former Black Panther Bobby Rush. Lewis and Rush are now two of the forty-one African Americans in the 104th Congress, representing Atlanta and Chicago, respectively. Yet it must be noted that the rise of African American political power has been accompanied by a decline in the quality of life for many inner-city blacks.

14. Nicholas Lemann, *The Promised Land: The Great Black Migration and How it Changed America* (New York: Knopf, 1991), p. 247.

15. In which Moynihan argued that "the time may have come" for the Nixon Administration to slow down civil rights enforcement and the War on Poverty. 1970 was also the year that an ambitious hangover of the Great Society that carried over into the Nixon Administration, the Family Assistance Plan, calling for a guaranteed annual income, died in the Senate. Finally, 1970 was the peak year for OEO spending.

16. U.S. Bureau of the Census, *Historical Statistics*, p. 356. The current total of AFDC recipients is about 14.5 million people.

The cash value of the median AFDC peaked around 1970. The *Historical Statistics* (ibid.) show that per-family AFDC payments rose, adjusted for inflation, by 30 percent from 1962 to 1970 , while the *Green Book* shows that the real value of AFDC payments fell by 47 percent from 1970 to 1994 (U.S. House Committee on Ways and Means, *1994 Green Book: Overview of Entitlement Programs*, 103rd Cong., 2nd sess., WMCP: 103–24 [Washington, D.C.: GPO, 1994]).

17. U.S. House, *Green Book*, p. 1157.

18. Peter J. Ferrara, ed., *Issues '94* (Washington DC: Heritage Foundation, 1994), p. 122.

19. U.S. House, *Green Book*, p. 369.

20. Neil and Barbara Gilbert, *The Enabling State: Modern Welfare Capitalism in America* (New York: Oxford University Press, 1989), pp. 40–41.

21. Charles Reich, "The New Property," *Yale Law Review*, April 1964, p. 756.

22. Ibid., p. 786.

23. 397 U.S. 254 (1970).

24. Horowitz, personal communication.

25. Patrick J. Sloyan, "Harvard Lawyers' Public Interest," *Newsday*, February 18, 1994, p. 21

26. Lorraine Adams, "Complex Bureaucracy Makes It Hard to Get the Bloat Out," *Washington Post*, March 2, 1995, p. A1.

27. Paula Span, "Morristown's Man on the Street; He Sued the Town. It Paid Him a Bundle. So Why Is Richard Kreimer Still Homeless?" *Washington Post*, October 14, 1992, p. C1.

28. In February, 1995, a federal judge in New York ruled that Amtrak could no longer eject the homeless from Pennsylvania Station. The suit was brought by the Coalition for the Homeless. (Richard Perez-Pena, "Amtrak Told Not to Eject The Homeless," *New York Times*, February 22, 1995, p. B1).

29. Federal Bureau of Investigation.

30. "Merrill Wants Costs Tightened For Juvenile Programs," *Valley News*, January 27, 1995, p. A7.

31. James C. Wilson, "Inmates' Newly Expanded License to Sue," *Washington Times*, March 15, 1994, p. A19.

32. Ashley Dunn, "Flood of Prisoner Rights Suits Bring Effort to Limit Filings," *New York Times*, March 21, 1994, p. A1.

33. Wilson, op cit. On June 19, 1995, in the case of *Sandin v. Connor*, the Supreme Court restricted the ability of prisoners to file lawsuits. Chief Justice William H. Rehnquist opined for the majority that prisoner suits have "led to the involvement of Federal Courts in the day-to-day management of prisons, after squandering judicial resources with little offsetting benefit to anyone."

34. "Mugger Is Allowed To Keep Jury Award," *New York Times*, November 30, 1993, p. B8.

35. Walter K. Olson, "The New Chutzpah," *City Journal* (Winter 1994), p. 46.

36. *ABC News*, February 22, 1995.

37. Jacqueline Trescott, "Bush on Art vs. 'Filth,'" *Washington Post*, June 7, 1993, p. D4.

38. U.S. House, *Green Book*, pp. 208–209. Judges have not only expanded eligibility, but they have also mandated "outreach," to find more eligible children.

39. Ibid., p. 237; see also Spencer Rich, "GOP to Tighten Cash For Disabled Children," *Washington Post*, January 19, 1995, p. A23.

40. U.S. House, *Green Book*, pp. 251–52; Spencer Rich, "Ways and Means Panel Considering Republican Plan to Cut SSI Benefits," *Washington Post*, January 28, 1995, p. A7.

41. Joyce Purnick, "When Welfare Is Gone: A Cautionary Message," *New York Times*, February 20, 1995, p. B3.

42. As Senator Daniel Patrick Moynihan has observed, SSI as it functions is reminiscent of the guaranteed annual income that Richard Nixon proposed in 1969.

43. Heather MacDonald, "SSI Fosters Disabling Dependency," *Wall Street Journal*, January 20, 1995, p. A12.

44. Even with the Republicans in control of Congress, it is likely that much or most of money saved by "cuts" will be transferred to various treatment and rehabilitation programs.

45. U.S. Dept. of Commerce, *Historical Statistics*, pp. 126–27, 1100, 1102; U.S. Bureau of the Census, *Statistical Abstract, 1994*, pp. 319, 395.

46. "New York's Homeless: Of Cuts and Kindness," *Economist*, May 14, 1994, p. 28.

47. Jeffrey Goldberg, "The Decline and Fall of the Upper West Side," *New York Magazine*, April 24, 1994, p. 41.

48. Vernon Loeb, "A Promise Not Honored," *Washington Post*, January 22, 1995, p. B1.

49. Ian Fisher, "McCall Urges Moderation in Nonprofit Salaries," *New York Times*, February 9, 1994, p. B1.

50. Robin Kamen and Steve Malanga, "Non-Profits: NY's New Tammany Hall," *Crain's New York Business*, October 31–November 6, 1994, p. 1.

51. Alice Lipowicz, "Failing Centers Thwart NY Job Training Effort," *Crain's New York Business*, June 27–July 3, 1994, p. 1.

52. William Tucker, "Sweet Charity," *American Spectator*, February, 1995, p. 38.

53. Cited in Martin Morse Wooster, *Great Philanthropists and the Problem of "Donor Intent"* (Washington, D.C.: Capital Research Center, 1994), p. 18.

54. Leonard Silk and Mark Silk, *The American Establishment* (New York: Basic Books, 1980), pp. 138–39.

55. Reporter Evan Gahr reports that the same process continues, with the Ford and Rockefeller Foundations in particular funding "politically correct" curricula in higher education. See "Paymasters of the PC Brigades," *Wall Street Journal*, January 27, 1995, p. A8.

56. Independent Sector, Washington D.C., "Giving and Volunteering in the United States," October, 1994. In 1995, the *Los Angeles Times* found that in its first four years, the Points of Light Foundation took in $42 million; of that amount, $26.6 million was in federal funds. Yet it gave out only $4 million in grants; more than $22 million went for overhead, including travel and conferences (Glenn F. Bunting, "Bush-Inspired Charity Shadowed by Questions," *Los Angeles Times*, January 9, 1995, p. A1).

57. Lisa Myers of *NBC News* reported that Northeastern University garnered $142,000, none of which went for AmeriCorps volunteers but instead went to put together a plan to get more money the next year—this is the change we see in nonprofits (*NBC News*, February 16, 1995). However, it is also true, as AmeriCorps critic John P. Walters has uncovered, that many AmeriCorpians toil for the federal government itself, in departments ranging from the Department of Justice to the Legal Services Corporation to the National Endowment for the Arts.

58. Timothy Noah, "Losing Steam: So, What Do People At Energy Department Do All Day Long?" *Wall Street Journal*, December 15, 1994, p. A1. Greider, *Who Will Tell*, p. 115.

59. Tax Foundation, *Facts and Figures*, p. 5.

60. See, in particular, Peter Huber, *Liability: The Legal Revolution and Its Consequences* (New York: Basic Books, 1990); Walter Olson, *The Litigation Explosion: What Happened When America Unleashed the Lawsuit* (New York: Dutton, 1991); and Philip K. Howard, *The Death of Common Sense: How Law is Suffocating America* (New York: Random House, 1994).

61. George L. Priest, "The Invention of Enterprise Liability: A Critical History of the Intellectual Foundations of Modern Tort Law," *Journal of Legal Studies*, 14 (December 1985), p. 470.

62. Abram Chayes, remarks made at "Public Interest Law: The Second Decade," conference organized by the Council for Public Interest Law, January 3–4, 1980, Washington, D.C.

63. Peter Edelman, "The Next Century of Our Constitution: Rethinking Our Duty to the Poor," *Hastings Law Journal* 39 (1987), pp. 4, 28.

64. Huber, *Liability*, p. 9

65. Olson, *Litigation Explosion*, pp. 5–6.

66. Robert Pear, "Clinton May Seek Lid On Doctor Fees and Liability Suits," *New York Times*, March 9, 1993, p. A1.

67. Jeffrey O'Connell and Michael Horowitz, "The Lawyer Will See You Now: Health Reform's Tort Crisis," *Washington Post*, June 13, 1993, p. C3.

68. Dena Bunis, "Doctor Bills: Premiums for Malpractice Insurance in Area Up 14%," *Newsday*, July 27, 1993, p. 3.

69. Peter Passell, "Economic Scene," *New York Times*, October 14, 1993, p. D2.

70. After the schools had launched a $30 billion asbestos cleanup program, the Energy and Environmental Policy Center at Harvard released a study on the lifetime probability of premature death, per 100,000:

Being a pedestrian hit by a car	290
Tobacco smoke	200
Diagnostic X-ray	75
Bicycling	75
Miami/New Orleans drinking water	7
Lightning	3
Hurricanes	3
Asbestos in school buildings	1

(Peter Cary, "The Asbestos Panic Attack," *U.S. News & World Report*, February 20, 1995, p. 61).

71. Nancy E. Roman, "EEOC Lags Way Behind," *Washington Times*, February 9, 1995, p. A8.

72. Russell Mitchell with Jonathan Ringel, "The SWAT Team of Litigation," *Business Week*, January 23, 1995, p. 88.

73. Author Heather MacDonald calls it the "diversity industry." No one knows what its total cost is, although fees average $2,000 (some charge as much as $10,000) and perhaps half of the Fortune 500 companies are working on their diversity.

74. Huber, pp. 4, 12.

75. Philip Hermann, *The $96 Billion-Dollar Game*, cited in "The Price of a Suit," *Newsweek*, October 25, 1993, p. 6.

76. One Rand Corporation study on EPA's environmental cleanup superfund found that only 10 percent of funds go to cleanup (Michael Quint, "A Superfund Plan Divides the Insurance Industry," *New York Times*, June 10, 1994, p. D1). A good example of the new system at work is the superfund legislation. Since 1980, only 18 percent of superfund toxic waste sites have been cleaned up. Of the $6.7 billion spent in the past decade and a half, an estimated 85 percent has gone to lawyers. According to one estimate, only about 50 of 1,319 priority superfund sites have been completely cleaned up since the Superfund Fund law was enacted (M. R. Greenburg, "Superfund Reform, Still Contaminated," *Wall Street Journal*, July 14, 1994, p. A10).

77. See, for example, "Tort Bar Adjusts," an editorial in the *Wall Street Journal*, February 3, 1995, p. A12.

78. Neil Howe and Richard Jackson, *Entitlements and the Aging of America* (Washington D.C.: National Taxpayers Union Foundation, 1994), charts 3.2 and 3.4.

79. U.S. House, *Green Book*, p. 1250.

80. Capital Research Center, Washington D.C.

81. The Seniors Coalition, Washington D.C.

Chapter 7

1. Alexis de Tocqueville, *Democracy in America* (1835; reprint New York: Oxford University Press, 1947), chap. 18, p. 226.

2. Hedrick Smith, *The Power Game: How Washington Works* (New York: Ballantine, 1989), p. xvii.

3. Kuhn, *Structure*, pp. 10, 66.

4. Gary Wills, *Lincoln at Gettsburg: The Words That Remade America*, chap. 4, "Revolution in Thought" (New York: Simon and Schuster, 1992).

5. James M. McPherson's *Abraham Lincoln and the Second American Revolution* (Oxford: Oxford University Press, 1991), p. 40. McPherson argues that Lincoln initiated "the Second American Revolution" (p. 3). This led me to think of American history as a series of peaceful revolutions, or quantum leaps, or paradigm shifts.

6. Abraham Lincoln, in his Message to Congress in Special Session, July 4, 1861 (*Lincoln: Selected Speeches and Writings* [New York: Vintage, 1992]), p. 313.

7. McPherson, *Abraham Lincoln*, p. 35.

8. Norman Ornstein, Thomas E. Mann, and Michael J. Malbin, *Vital Statistics on Congress, 1933–1994* (Washington, D.C.: Congressional Quarterly, 1994), p. 40. In fact, Lincoln put a pro-Union Democrat, Andrew Johnson of Tennessee, on the ticket with him in 1864.

9. Benjamin P. Thomas, *Abraham Lincoln* (1952; reprint, New York: Random House, 1968), p. 493. Thomas quotes Lincoln associate Charles A. Dana: "Lincoln was a supreme politician. He understood politics because he understood human nature . . . There was no flabby philanthropy about Abraham Lincoln. He was all solid, hard, keen intelligence combined with goodness."

10. James David Barber in *The Presidential Character* (Englewood Cliffs, N.J.: Prentice-Hall, 1985), p. 65, refers to Hoover as an "active-negative" personality, and quotes William Allen White's description of Hoover as "constitutionally gloomy, a congenital pessimist who always saw the doleful side of any situation." A depressed character for a Depression—not the right leadership formula!

11. David Burner, *The Politics of Provincialism: The Democratic Party in Transition, 1918–1932* (Cambridge: Harvard University Press, 1986). See, in particular, Chap. 3, "The Divisive Themes."

12. Marcantonio, in the words of one biographer, "while not a Communist . . . presented positions on domestic issues from a working class perspective and approached foreign policy within a Leninist framework." The *New York Times* editorialized against his "faithful adherence to the Communist line" (Gerald Meyer, *Vito Marcantonio: Radical Politician 1902–1954* [Albany: State University of New York Press, 1989], pp. 1–2). The Communist Party in turn strongly supported him. Communist Party

chief Earl Browder recalled that Marcantonio "was actually our spokesman in Congress" (p. 65).

Ironically, thanks to the peculiarities of New York politics, Marcantonio was for many years elected to Congress as a Republican, where he was known as "the pink pachyderm" (Alan Schaffer, *Vito Marcantonio, Radical in Congress* Syracuse, N.Y.: Syracuse University Press, 1966, p. 32). Yet Marcantonio "frequently voted for important [Roosevelt] administration measures and at times found himself fighting for legislation that later became hallmarks of the New Deal" (p. 37). For his part, Roosevelt wrote to House Speaker Sam Rayburn in 1939, "I am inclined to think he will be with us more than against us" (p. 68).

As for Bilbo, his howling racism, anti-semitism and Klan sympathies (if not actual membership) are well remembered. For a small sample, see V. O. Key's *Southern Politics* (New York: Vintage, 1949), pp. 242–45. What is mostly forgotten is that, as Key put it, Bilbo "went down the line for the New Deal." As one biographer put it, from 1935 to 1940 "he had supported the Works Progress Administration, Social Security, the Agricultural Adjustment Administration, the Civilian Conservation Corps, the Tennessee Valley Authority, and the National Youth Administration" (A. Wigfall Green, *The Man Bilbo* [Baton Rouge: Louisiana State University Press, 1963], p. 95). Another historian asserts: "In Mississippi, New Deal liberalism found its most ardent disciple and its most effective missionary in Theodore Bilbo" (Chester M. Morgan, *Redneck Liberal: Theodore G. Bilbo and the New Deal* [Baton Rouge: Louisiana State University Press, 1985], p. 23).

That Roosevelt could hold the allegiance of a crypto-communist Republican and a racist New Deal Democrat is further proof of his political virtuosity.

13. William E. Leuchtenburg, *Franklin D. Roosevelt and the New Deal* (New York: Harper and Row, 1963), p. 11.

14. Ibid.

15. U.S. Bureau of the Census, *Historical Statistics*, p. 126.

16. Ibid., p. 177.

17. Jordan Schwartz, *The New Dealers: Power Politics in the Age of Roosevelt*, 1st ed. (New York: Vintage, 1993); see, in particular, chap. 3, "Jesse H. Jones: The Credit Revolution."

The Advisory Commission on Intergovernmental Relations published valuable data in *Regional Growth: Historical Perspective*, June 1980, p. 11. In 1930, incomes in the southeastern U.S. were less than half the national average, a low plateau they had been on since at least the turn of the century. By 1950, southeastern incomes had risen to nearly three-fourths of the national average. Incomes for the Southwest and West showed similar sharp gains.

The New Deal Big Offer worked politically: the South and West were the most Democratic areas of the country in the thirtiess and forties. In the five presidential elections of the New Deal–Fair Deal era (1932–1948), Roosevelt and Truman won 95 percent of the Sunbelt's electoral votes, compared to 76 percent of the Snowbelt's electoral votes.

18. Leuchtenberg, *Roosevelt*, p. 132.

19. Robert Penn Warren, *All the King's Men* (1946; reprint, New York: Harvest, 1984), p. 139.

20. Roosevelt, *Public Papers*, vol. 5, p. 235.

21. Merle Miller, *Plain Speaking: An Oral Biography of Harry S. Truman* (1974; reprint, New York: Berkley Books, 1986), p. 266.

22. Cited in *The American Reader: Words That Moved A Nation*, ed. Diane Ravitch (New York: HarperCollins, 1990), p. 298.

23. Assuming that all Wallace voters would have voted for Truman otherwise, his candidacy cost Truman the electoral votes of Maryland, Michigan, and New York. However, only in New York was Wallace's influence substantial—he won more than 8 percent of the vote in the Empire State.

24. The exact quote from Prime Minister David Lloyd George, "a fit country for heroes to live in," dates from 1919, but it still captured the spirit of the times three decades later.

25. Robert J. Donovan, *Conflict and Crisis: The Presidency of Harry S Truman* (New York: Norton, 1977), p. 125.

26. Ibid., p. 303. In June of 1947, Truman vetoed the Taft-Hartley bill, which outlawed the closed shop. Truman rejected all attempts at compromise, and was overridden in the Senate and House by 3:1 and 4:1 margins, respectively. Principle aside, Truman understood the long-term politics of the issue. The postwar backlash against unions would subside, he reasoned, while the muscle of the labor movement would be fully flexed on his behalf in the 1948 election.

27. Ibid., p. 653.

Chapter 8

1. Lawrence B. Lindsey, *The Growth Experiment. How the New Tax Policy Is Transforming the U.S. Economy* (New York: Basic Books, 1990), p. 41.

2. David Stockman, *The Triumph of Politics: How the Reagan Revolution Failed* (New York: Harper and Row, 1986), p. 229.

3. Lindsey, *Growth Experiment*, p. 83.

4. Robert Lenzner and Phillipe Mao, "The New Refugees," *Forbes*, November 21, 1994, p. 131.

5. *Economic Report of the President, 1995*, pp. 321, 345.

6. Lindsey, *Growth Experiment*, pp. 46-47.

7. In fairness to Reagan, the complete sentence is as follows: *In this present crisis,* government is not the solution, government is the problem" [emphasis added]. In the same inaugural, Reagan later said: "Now, so there will be no misunderstanding, it's not my intention to do away with government. It is rather to make it work—work with us, not over us; to stand by our side, not ride on our back. Government can and must provide opportunity, not smother it; foster productivity, not stifle it." One can see the door being opened to dramatic qualitative reform, and there were a number of imaginative empowerment-oriented conservatives in the early Reagan years. However, most had left the administration by the end of his first term.

8. Lindsey, *Growth Experiment*, p. 83. Congressman Dick Armey of Texas cites IRS data showing that the bottom nine deciles of taxpayers all paid a declining share of the income tax burden through 1989. Meanwhile, the share of taxes paid by the top 10 percent of taxpayers jumped substantially, while the taxes paid by the top 1 percent of taxpayers grew by nearly half, from 17.6 percent in 1981 to 25.2 percent. Interestingly, these trends reversed after 1990.

9. Thomas Ferguson and Joel Rogers, *Right Turn: The Decline of the Democrats and the Future of American Politics* (New York: Hill and Wang, 1986), p. 124.

10. Stockman, *Triumph*, p. 8.

11. U.S. Bureau of the Census, *Statistical Abstract of the United States: 1993* (Washington, D.C.: Department of Commerce, 1993), p. 368. Other data on the same page in the *Abstract* reveal that state and local social welfare expenditures more than doubled, from $190 billion to $392 billion. For purposes of comparison, the consumer price index rose 50.5 percent from

1980–89, while federal social spending rose 86 percent, and state and local social spending rose 106 percent.

12. Tax Foundation, *Facts and Figures*, p. 41.

13. David Frum, *Dead Right* (New York: New Republic Books, 1994); see especially chap. 3, "The Failure of the Reagan Gambit."

14. The idea that an urban underclass existed received some attention in the seventies, but it was *New Yorker* writer Ken Auletta's book *The Underclass*, published in 1982, that first got people thinking that something was happening in their urban midst.

David Stoesz, of the School of Social Work at San Diego State University, observes that the furor over Daniel Patrick Moynihan's report, *The Negro Family: A Case for National Action*, published in 1965, silenced a generation of social scientists. Comments Stoesz: "The reluctance of liberal social scientists to chronicle the deterioration of life in inner city ghettos coincided nicely with an incoming Reagan administration which held as a primary tenet that social problems were artificial constructs by academics; city life was not as bad as had been portrayed."

15. Martin C. Anderson, "Welfare Reform," in Peter Duignan and Alvin Rabushka, eds. *The United States in the 1980s* (Stanford: Hoover Institution, 1980), p. 145.

16. Charles Murray, *Losing Ground: American Social Policy, 1950–1980* (New York: Basic Books, 1984); Daniel Patrick Moynihan, *Family and Nation* (San Diego: Harcourt Brace Jovanovich, 1986).

17. Paul Klebnikov, "Showing Big Daddy the Door," *Forbes*, November 9, 1992, p. 149.

18. *Budget of the United States Government, Fiscal Year 1996, Historical Tables* (Washington: GPO, 1995), pp. 76–77.

19. As of 1994, at least sixteen former Reagan officials had been convicted of HUD-related crimes.

20. *Economic Report of the President, 1995*, p. 366. On the other hand, Reagan did succeed in cutting, for example, the number of pages printed annually in the *Federal Register*—a handy indicator of federal activity—from its all-time high of 87,012 pages in 1980 to 53,376 pages in 1988; a 40 percent reduction (Ornstein et al., *Vital Statistics*, p. 158).

21. Tax Foundation, *Facts and Figures*, pp. 19, 20.

22. John H. Makin and Norman J. Ornstein, *Debt and Taxes* (New York: Times Books, 1994), p. 9.

23. Richard C. Cornuelle, "New Work for Invisible Hands," *Times Literary Supplement*, April 5, 1991.

Chapter 9

1. Strauss and Howe, *Generations*, p. 263.

2. Ornstein et al., *Vital Statistics*, p. 40, and U.S. Bureau of the Census, *Historical Statistics*, p. 1083. For the trivia pursuers, the other two such presidents were Zachary Taylor and Richard Nixon.

3. Adam Clymer, "The Gridlock Congress: The 102d Will Be Remembered as Much For Its Embarrassments as Its Legislation," *New York Times*, October 11, 1992, p. A1.

4. Major Garrett, "It's 'Operation Domestic storm,'" *Washington Times*, March 8, 1991, p. A1.

5. Tom Raum, "Bush's Homefront Agenda: Call It 'Operation Desert Storm,'" Associated Press, March 13, 1991.

6. *Economic Report of the President, 1994*, pp. 359, 362.

7. Milton Friedman, "The Real Free Lunch: Markets and Private Property," *Cato Policy Report*, July/August, 1993, p. 13.

8. Doyle McManus and James Gerstenzang, "Candidates Conjure up Heroes Past, *Los Angeles Times*, September 21, 1992, p. 1A.

9. Steve Holland, "Truman Caught in Fight between Bush, Clinton," Reuters, September 7, 1992.

10. A year after the election, Bush admitted that he was "far less articulate and convincing on the domestic stuff," adding that he was nonetheless "satisfied" that history would judge him kindly ("Bush 'Satisfied,'" *Washington Times*, October 3, 1993, p. A2). Bush had some reason for optimism, for reasons outside the scope of this book. As Charles Krauthammer wrote after the election, "Bush's was not a failed presidency, but a completed one. History called upon him to do two things: to close out the Cold War and thwart the ambitions of a reckless tyrant in the Persian Gulf" ("Bush: Two Great Challenges Met," *Washington Post*, November 23, 1992, p. A21).

Chapter 10

1. Sam Fulwood III, "Clinton Modifies Plan for 100-Day Legislative Agenda," *Los Angeles Times*, June 24, 1992, p. A12.

2. Stanley B. Greenberg, *Middle Class Dreams* (New York: Times Books, 1995), p. 42.

3. Stanley Greenberg, "Reconstructing a Democratic Vision," *The American Prospect* (Spring 1990), p. 82.

4. Bob Woodward, *The Agenda* (New York: Simon and Schuster, 1994), p. 25.

5. Ibid., p. 60.

6. Quoted in Marilyn Milloy, "For some, No Change: Health Reforms Won't Affect All," *Newsday*, May 7, 1993.

7. Washington author Elizabeth Drew asserts that Hillary Rodham Clinton probably supported the single-payer plan all along, but restrained her enthusiasm as a matter of political expediency (Elizabeth Drew, *On The Edge: The Clinton Presidency* [New York: Simon and Schuster, 1994], p. 193.)

Tom Hamburger, Ted Marmor, and Jon Meacham assert that the Clintonians' dissembling on health care began before he was elected. In November 1991, Clinton said that he agreed with the arguments of the single-payer, Canadian-style plans but would publicly advocate a more modest "play-or-pay" program during the upcoming campaign. One suspects that this duplicity did not go unnoticed on the Left, nor unsuspected on the Right, leaving Clinton's health care plan fatally betwixt and between ("What the Death of Health Reform Teaches Us about the Press," *Washington Monthly*, November 1994, p. 35).

8. The *Washington Post* reported that Hillary is "replacing Madonna as our leading cult figure." *People* wrote that she is "a political pragmatist driven by a deep sense of spiritual mission." *Time* described her as "the icon of American womanhood." *Family Circle*, equally eager to please but mindful of its less hip readership, called Hillary a "brilliant woman," but, also highlighted her oft-overlooked "traditional side."

9. Robert Pear, "Economic Advisers Caution President On Medical Costs," *New York Times*, May 22, 1993, p. 1A.

10. P. J. O'Rourke, *Parliament of Whores* (New York: Atlantic Monthly Press, 1991), p. xx.

11. Quoted in Hillary Stout and Jeanne Saddler, "Health Plan Will Limit Aid For Small Firms," *Wall Street Journal*, September 17, 1993, p. A3.

12. "Incalculably Inaccurate," *Economist*, August 20, 1994, p. 22. See also Tax Foundation, *Facts and Figures*, p. 92.

13. Dana Priest, "A Second Opinion As Debate Begins: First Lady Doubts Mitchell Bill," *Washington Post*, August 10, 1994, p. A1.

14. Scholar-turned-New York-lieutenant governor Elizabeth McCaughey actually read the Clinton health care bill. In a long article in *The New Republic*, she zeroed in on thirty-one specific items. Alarmed that someone was actually reading what they had written, the Clinton White House took the nearly unprecedented step of writing a nine-page critique of her critique, which of course fueled the conflagration. A second McCaughey article put another below-the-waterline torpedo into the Clinton bill and vaulted her from think-tank obscurity to a bright political career ("No Exit: What the Clinton Plan Will Do For You," *New Republic*, February 7, 1994, p. 6; see also "She's Baaack! Clinton's Health Care Plan on the Ropes," *New Republic*, February 20, 1994, p. 6).

15. Donald Lambro, "Questions Slow Momentum of Clinton Health Care Plan," *Washington Times*, October 12, 1993, p. A5.

16. Dana Priest, "A Second Opinion As Debate Begins: First Lady Doubts Mitchell Bill," *Washington Post*, August 10, 1994, p. A1.

17. "The Week," *National Review*, October 18, 1993, p. 12.

18. Donald Lambro, "Shalala Seeks Plan to be Polished Later," *Washington Times*, September 30, 1993, p. A1.

19. *CNN/USA Today* poll, August 10, 1994.

20. Ann Devroy and Dana Priest, "Clinton Plan Is Officially Laid to Rest," *Washington Post*, July 23, 1994, p. A1.

21. J. Jennings Moss, "Health-plan Changes Repackage Old Ideas," *Washington Times*, July 23, 1994, p. A1.

22. William Kristol, "Health Care: Why Congress is Now More Dangerous than Clinton," *Project for the Republican Future*, July 26, 1994.

23. Adam Clymer, "National Health Program, President's Greatest Goal, Declared Dead In Congress," *New York Times*, September 27, 1994, p. A1.

24. Apologies to Eric Alterman.

25. Editorial, "Total Quality Madness," *New Republic*, October 3, 1994, p. 7. Writing in the same magazine two weeks later, Fred Barnes wrote

that the Democrats were "breathtakingly wrong in reading the public mood. They bought the line of historian Arthur Schlesinger Jr. that Clinton's election marked 'the arrival of a new liberal phase'" ("Earthquake," *New Republic*, October 17, 1994, p. 16).

26. Robert J. Samuelson, "Health Care: The 'Con' That Failed," *Newsweek*, October 10, 1994, p. 35.

27. Gloria Borger, "The Land of Lost Opportunity," *U.S. News & World Report*, August 22, 1994, p. 43.

28. Dan Goodgame et al., "Tales from the Crypt," *Time*, September 19, 1994, p. 42.

29. Paul A. Gigot, "Stan Recants! Or Why Health Care Is a Dud," *Wall Street Journal*, August 12, 1994, p. A10.

30. Jonathan Gruber and Alan B. Krueger, "The Incidence Of Mandated Employer-Provided Insurance: Lessons From Workers' Compensation Insurance," in David Bradford, *Tax Policy and The Economy* (Cambridge, Mass.: National Bureau of Economic Research, 1987), pp. 134 and 139.

31. Richard L. Berke, "Advice for Democrats in Fall: Don't Be Too Close to Clinton," *New York Times*, August 4, 1994, p. A1.

32. David S. Broder, "Health Care: Virtually Invisible As a Midterm Campaign Topic," *Washington Post*, October 27, 1994, p. A25.

33. Howard Kurtz, "In 1994 Political Ads, Crime Is the Weapon of Choice," *Washington Post*, September 9, 1994, p. A1.

34. Susan M. Eckerly, "The Triple Threat to Government Red Tape," *Commonsense* (Fall 1994), p. 66.

35. Linda Grant, "Shutting Down the Regulatory Machine," *U.S. News & World Report*, February 13, 1995, p. 70.

36. Al Kamen and Ann Devroy, "Clinton Warns of Horrors if GOP Wins," *Washington Post*, November 3, 1994, p. A27.

37. CNN, October 20, 1994.

38. William Kristol, "Memorandum To Republican Leaders," Project for the Republican Future, November 4, 1994.

39. Katharine Q. Seelye, "Voters Disgusted with Politicians As Election Nears," *New York Times*, November 3, 1994, p. A1.

40. *ABC News World News Tonight*, October 17, 1994.

41. CNN, "Inside Politics," November 10, 1994.

42. Woodward, *Agenda*, pp. 64-71. On p. 135 Woodward describes Greenspan as "in some ways the ghostwriter of the Clinton plan."

43. Greenspan compared the Clinton presidency to that of Gerald Ford, while Robert Reich compared it to that of Calvin Coolidge (Ibid., pp. 71, 133).

44. Ibid., p. 165.

45. Senate Library, *Presidential Vetoes, 1789–1988* and *Presidential Vetoes, 1989–1991* (Washington DC: GPO, 1992). President Garfield also vetoed no bills in his six months as president before he died September 19, 1881.

46. Bill Clinton in Georgetown, Delaware, quoted by *White House Bulletin*, September 3, 1993.

47. See Crane Brinton, *The Anatomy of Revolution* (New York: Vintage, 1957).

48. See, for example, James B. Shuman and David Rosenau, *The Kondratieff Wave* (New York: Dell Publishing, 1972).

Chapter 11

1. Jefferson was the leader of the Republican Party; the term "Democrat-Republican" is a convention of historians, enabling them to distinguish Jefferson's party from the still-to-come Republicans.

2. Ironically, Roosevelt put his weight behind a major Jefferson renaissance: the Jefferson nickel was first minted in 1938, the same year as the groundbreaking for the Jefferson Memorial.

3. Alan Ehrenhalt, *United States of Ambition*, p. 217.

4. The total number of political action committees rose from 608 in 1974—at the dawn of reform—to 4,195 in 1992. In 1992, Democratic incumbents in the House of Representatives raised more than $79 million from PACs, while Republican challengers that year raised just $4 million (Ornstein et al., *Vital Statistics*, pp. 95, 99).

5. The personal staffs of Members of Congress and Senators—most of whom can be reasonably construed to spend most of their time furthering their boss's career—jumped from 1150 in 1930, to 5,804 in 1967, to 11,572 in 1191 (Ibid., p. 128).

6. According to Congressman Bill Thomas (R-California), chairman of the House Oversight Committee, in 1992, an election year, Congress spent $54 million on franked mail. In 1993, that figure dropped to $25 million, but rose again to $42 million in 1995—an average of $80,000 a lawmaker.

7. It should also be noted that Ehrenhaltianism—politics as the best, and sometimes only, job—continues even after Ehrenhaltians leave office. The

National Taxpayers Union reports, for example, that Tom Foley is actuarially likely to receive $3.3 million in pension benefits over the remainder of his life. In 1995 alone, he will receive an annual pension of $123,804, which compares quite favorably to the average Social Security beneficiary, who receives $8,088 per annum. Even former congressman-turned-governor Tom Ridge of Pennsylvania, born in 1945, is entitled to $1.4 million in lifetime benefits.

Finally, Ehrehnaltianism continues even into prison. Former congressman Nicholas Mavroules, who served fifteen months for taking a bribe, collects $37,000 per annum in pension benefits. Kentucky's Carroll Hubbard, sentenced to three years for illegally diverting campaign funds to personal use, collects $45,000 a year for his eighteen years' service. An estimated $10 million has gone to jailbird lawmakers since 1970 (*ABC News*, April 3, 1995).

8. See, for example, Dionne, *Why Americans Hate Politics* (New York: Simon and Schuster, 1991), chap. 1: "Freedom Now: The New Left and the Assault on Liberalism."

9. Randall Rothenberg, *The Neoliberals: Creating the New American Politics* (New York: Simon and Schuster, 1984), pp. 121, 20, 27.

10. Ibid., pp. 125–26. During the same period, Gephardt also cosponsored a market-oriented health care bill with his Republican congressional colleague David Stockman; he was also active in tort reform.

11. Charles Peters, "A New Politics" *Public Welfare* 18 (1983), pp. 34–36.

12. Another name for this group was "Atari Democrats," after the bankrupt videogame maker.

13. Rothenberg, *Neoliberals*, p. 151.

14. Paul E. Tsongas, *The Road From Here* (New York: Knopf, 1981), p. 254.

15. Ibid., pp. 11–18; Rothenberg, *Neoliberals*, pp. 42–44.

16. Paul E. Tsongas, *A Call To Economic Arms: Forging A New American Mandate* (Boston: Tsongas Committee, 1991), pp. 15, 5.

17. Ibid., p. 11.

18. Ibid., p. 12.

19. Coelho had wheeled his way up the greasy pole to the no. 3 job in the House Democratic hierarchy in just ten years in Congress. In the early eighties, as neoliberals spun fine ideas about what they might do if they retook the White House, Coelho focused on what the congressional Democrats should do with the power they did have: committee chairmanships. Noticing that business political action committees were giving much of

their money to Republican candidates, Coelho went to the PACmen and made them an offer they couldn't refuse, in essence: stop giving money to Republicans; start giving money to us. In his scathing look at the campaign financing of the House, *Honest Graft*, journalist Brooks Jackson writes that Coelho's tactics "resembled a legal version of the old protection racket" (Jackson, *Honest Graft: Big Money and the American Political Process* [New York: Knopf, 1988], p. 78.)

Once Coelho and the business community reached their new *modus vivendi*, Coelho went to work to cement the new Democrat–Fatcat entente. Jackson details the missionary work that Coelho did on behalf of real estate, wine, and oil interests, to name just a few richies that Coelho enriched further (ibid., pp. 114–20). Few businesspeople are so free-market pristine that they can resist ponying up a few thousand dollars in return for tax breaks or subsidies worth millions. In 1989, Coelho had to resign under the proverbial ethical cloud.

20. Robert B. Reich and John D. Donahue, *New Deals: The Chrysler Revival and the American System* (New York: Times Books, 1985). The authors write hopefully that "The Chrysler bailout marked a turning point in American capitalism." The To-the-Finland-Station sense of destinarianism quickly seeps in: the authors aver that the bailout "was a dramatic culmination of trends that had been long under way in the relationship among business, labor, finance, and government" (pp. 4, 6).

One big lesson of the bailout, the authors assert, is the synergistic effect of government intervention, which leveraged additional private investment into Chrysler and provided more valuable information for private parties. Hence, the "final lesson concerns the *power* of public intervention" (pp. 283–87).

21. Ira C. Magaziner and Robert B. Reich, *Minding America's Business: The Decline and Rise of the American Economy*, 1st ed. (New York: Vintage, 1982), p. 259.

22. What the anti-Hegelian philosopher Arthur Schopenhauer said of the German intelligentsia's relationship to the *Reich* in the last century applies to Reich as well in this century: "Governments make of philosophy a means of serving their state interests, and scholars make of it a trade." Quoted in Popper, *Open Society*, p. 229.

23. Hobart Rowen, "Big Business Should Be a Friend of Bill," *Washington Post*, October 23, 1994, p. H2.

24. "Social justice" is a popular Democratic argument for intervention and industrial policy in some form or fashion. But the Okunian wealth-transfer bucket has become ludicrously leaky; the Democrats defend the current

system at their political peril. Just how mendacious "social justice" can become inside the Beltway was revealed in early 1995, when the Federal Communications Commission's "tax certificate" program, which enabled corporations to win enormous tax breaks in return for selling broadcasting and cable companies to minority-owned firms, came to national attention. Viacom, the billion-dollar communications (Paramount, Blockbuster, MTV) conglomerate, was in line to receive a special tax abatement of some $600 million in return for selling a $2.3 billion cable system to one Frank Washington, an African American who just happened to have Tele-Communications, Inc., the nation's largest cable operator, as his "partner." Washington personally stood to gain perhaps $2 million in return for front-manning a deal between two white-owned corporations. The deal was ultimately killed by the Congress, but it symbolizes the decadence of the AMERICRATic system in the nineties: a single black man, a millionaire to begin with, stands to reap millions from a government program, and a company that couldn't remotely be called disadvantaged nets 300 times as much. Such economics demonstrate the conundrum of AMERICRAT 4.0 observed earlier: how it is possible to spend trillions in the name of the poor and yet find out that the middle class—or even the rich—have sucked up most of that compassion-money, leaving little to actually trickle down to the needy (Jackie Calmes, "Senate Committee Votes for Repealing Tax Break Crucial to Viacom Cable Sale," *Wall Street Journal*, March 16, 1995, p. A2; Geraldine Fabrikant "Other Options Appear Open to Viacom in Cable Sale," *New York Times*, March 17, 1995, p. D5; and Jeffrey H. Birnbaum, "Turning Back the Clock," *Time*, March 20, 1995, p. 36).

Revealingly, even after the Viacom deal was preempted, at least one other similar arrangement was allowed to continue. Proving that the Old Paradigm is bipartisan, Senator Carol Mosely-Braun, Democrat of Illinois, and Senator Bob Packwood, Republican of Oregon, worked to secure a $30 million break for Rupert Murdoch's News Corporation and a $13 million break for the Tribune Company, all to facilitate the sale of Atlanta and New Orleans TV stations to a company headed by the black musician Quincy Jones (Edmund L. Andrews, "Little-Noted Tiptoe Through a Closing Loophole," *New York Times*, April 7, 1995, p. A1).

25. U.S. Bureau of the Census, *Statistical Abstract, 1994*, p. 157.

26. National Commission on Excellence in Education, *A Nation at Risk* (GPO, Washington D.C., 1983), p. 1.

27. Federal spending on education per public elementary and secondary school pupil rose from $2,955 (4,291 1993 dollars) in 1982–83 to an

estimated $5,721 in 1992–93, an increase of 33.3 percent in real terms and 93.6 percent in unadjusted terms: U.S. Department of Education.

28. See, in particular, Charles Peters and Phillip Keisling, *A New Road For America: The Neoliberal Movement* (Lanham, Md.: Madison Books, 1985), pp. 19-33. In one stinging passage, the authors trash "the National Education Association official who accused Reagan of trying to 'destroy public education' with his proposal to give $500 tuition tax credits to parents of private school students. He, too, sends his son to a private school."

29. Roy Ulrich, "Progressives Drop the Ball on Vouchers," *Los Angeles Times*, October 18, 1993, p. A11.

30. Letter on State of Arkansas stationery dated October 18, 1990, courtesy of Polly Williams.

31. Charles Peters, "What We've Won and What We've Lost: A *Monthly* Scorecard," *Washington Monthly* (December 1994), p. 28. Out of step with his party as always, Peters noted in this piece that he had always been a strong supporter of public education. Yet he recalled that "Public education had fallen on hard times by the seventies, mostly because teachers' unions and self-protecting administrators resisted reform." Peters conceded that the cause of de-bureaucratizing education would have to rely on bureaucracy-busting ideas, such as alternative certification of teachers and charter schools (p. 30).

32. E. J. Dionne Jr., "Credit Check," *Washington Post*, September 6, 1994, p. A17.

33. As Congressman Barney Frank of Massachusetts put it, "Voters are angry with politicians like me. And they're angry with you in the media. Well, let me tell you something: The voters are no bargains either!" (quoted in Richard Harwood, "The Voters' IQ," *Washington Post*, October 24, 1994, p. A19). Frank can afford such an attitude: he was unopposed in 1994. Not many other Democrats had it so easy.

34. "GOP tide rolls by dock on the Bay," *Washington Times*, November 12, 1994, p. A4.

35. Quoted on *ABC News*, March 12, 1995.

36. Gordon S. Black and Benjamin D. Black, *The Politics of American Discontent: How a New Party Can Make Democracy Work Again* (New York: Wiley, 1994), p. 16.

37. Quoted in Robert D. Novak, "Winning Democrat," *Washington Post*, April 6, 1995, p. A21.

Chapter 12

1. David Blankenhorn, *Fatherless America: Confronting Our Most Urgent Social Problem* (New York: Basic Books, 1995), p. 223. In 1962, 58 percent of Americans met the definition of the traditional nuclear family—husband, wife, and kids. By the year 2000 that share will be down to 25 percent.

Other estimates show that if present trends continue, half of all babies born in the U.S. in the year 2004 will be born out of wedlock. However, it is worth noting that illegitimacy rates are rising around the world.

That's the bad news. The good news is that people keep trying; divorce is up, but so is remarriage. One in seven American children live in blended families (Barbara Vobejda, "Study Alters Image of 'Typical Family,' " *Washington Post*, August 30, 1994, p. A3). Grandparents, spryer in their golden years than they once were, are stepping in when parents fail. Popular culture reflects this hunger for successful role models, as endless reruns of the TV sitcom *The Brady Bunch* flit across the small screen.

2. Richard Weaver, *Ideas Have Consequences* (1948; reprint, Chicago: University of Chicago, 1984), p. 130.

3. NBC, "*Meet the Press*," November 13, 1994.

A major work of conservative synthesis is James Q. Wilson's *The Moral Sense*. Wilson seeks an essentially secular social reinforcement for people's innate feelings of right and wrong:

> To say that people have a moral sense, is not the same thing as saying that they are innately good. A moral sense must compete with other senses that are natural to humans—the desire to survive, acquire possessions, indulge in sex, or accumulate power—in short, with self-interest narrowly defined . . . But saying that a moral sense exists *is* the same thing as saying that humans, by their nature, are potentially good. (Wilson, *The Moral Sense* [New York: Free Press, 1993], p. 12).

The moral sense helps explain why even crooks fail lie detector tests.

Thus a modest but realistic goal: nurture the good that is in people's nature. However, Wilson's own pragmatic sense tells him that 250 million Americans will never buy into One Big Moral Answer; his patient argument owes more to sociobiology than to grace, more to knowledge than to faith.

4. Daniel R. Feenburg and Harvey S. Rosen, *Recent Developments in the Marriage Tax—Working Paper No. 4705* (Cambridge, Mass.: National Bureau of Economic Research, 1994), p. 20.

5. CNN, "Both Sides With Jesse Jackson," November 12, 1994.

6. If the debate between Culturalists and Economists rages at the abstract national level, it has been settled where the solon meets the citizen. At the grassroots, preaching means little, and problem solving means much; the dilemmas of schools, streets, and sewers can be solved only by the Economists.

Republicans who want to win at the local level have taken the Democrats head-on, challenging the Old Paradigm presumption that urban quality of life depends on more bureaucrats. Stephen Goldsmith, the Republican mayor of Indianapolis, says we need a "small government response to big city problems" (speech to the National Taxpayers Union, Washington D.C., November 18, 1994). One Goldsmithian solution: eliminating all existing urban grant programs, and replacing them with a 15 percent tax deduction to urban residents. With a commonsense approach to cutting costs while getting the job done, Goldsmith has balanced the budget of the twelfth-largest city in the country without a tax increase by reducing spending in real terms. Other Republican mayors—Rudy Giuliani of New York, Dick Riordan of Los Angeles, and Bret Schundler in Jersey City—all demonstrate an ability to use microeconomic tools to reengineer their cities' governments.

In the statehouses, Republicans, in the majority for the first time since 1970, also govern to the Economic side of the Economist–Culturalist debate. Michigan's John Engler, Wisconsin's Tommy Thompson, and Massachusetts' Bill Weld are divided on the issue of abortion, but they have all gambled their popularity on AMERICRAT-reforming policies, from spending cuts to privatization to charter schools to school choice. All three were reelected in 1994, with percentages of 61, 67, and 71, respectively. Thompson has shown that we can end at least some welfare as we know it. His ideas—tying continued relief to continuing education, linking social work to actual work—have proved that dependency can be humanely reduced. Since 1987, when he took over in Madison, nationwide welfare recipiency has increased by 30 percent (U.S. House, *Green Book*, p. 395). Yet in the Badger State, the caseload has fallen from 99,000 cases down to 74,000—a 25 percent cut. For purposes of comparison, the runner-up to Wisconsin is Iowa, which has seen about a 3 percent reduction. How did Thompson do it? Through a combination of carrots and sticks: On the one hand, the governor energetically involved himself in the welfare issue, pressing the full utilization of job-training resources. On other hand, Thompson was tough. Jason Turner, Director of the Welfare Replacement

Program of the State of Wisconsin, is blunt: "Thompson reintroduced the stigma of welfare dependency." Thompson, Republicans should note, proves another point about New Paradigm politics—he is the longest-serving governor in Wisconsin history.

7. Forty years ago, Buckley formulated the mission of his new conservative magazine, *National Review*: "It stands athwart history, yelling Stop, at a time when no one is inclined to do so, or to have much patience with those who urge it" (William F. Buckley, Jr. "Publisher's Statement," *National Review*, November 19, 1955, p. 5). Gingrichian conservatism offers a completely different image: the irresistible force crashing through the barricades of liberalism.

8. Cyber Future evidence abounds. For example, during the 1994 Christmas holidays, a San Francisco church announced a food giveaway; the line before the church even opened its doors was seven blocks long. By the end of the day, 12,500 people had waited for help (*NBC News*, December 22, 1994). Yet, as noted in Mario Cuomo's keynote speech in the same city a decade before, the question is causation.

9. Black and Black, *Politics*, p. 16.

10. The 1992 Republican Platform advocated a Human Life Amendment to the Constitution but conspicuously omitted the familiar "rape, incest, and life of the mother" exceptions: "the unborn child has a fundamental individual right to life which cannot be infringed" (Republican National Committee, *The Vision Shared: Uniting Our Family, Our Country, Our World*, Houston: Republican National Committee, 1992, p. 39).

On p. 145 of their book, authors Gordon and Benjamin Black (op. cit.) adduce data showing that only 9 percent of the American people supported the 1992 Republican platform language. In their book *The Second American Revolution*, (New York: William Morrow, 1994), authors James Patterson and Peter Kim conclude that 11.7 percent of Americans support that position (p. 256).

A *New York Times* poll in 1994 found that just 28 percent of Republicans were firmly pro-life, compared to 34 percent who were pro-choice; 37 percent were in between (editorial, "The GOP's Pro-Choice Majority," *New York Times*, February 19, 1995, p. E11).

The Republican Party's own National Policy Forum found that 43 percent of rank-and-file Republicans are pro-choice.

11. Dan Quayle, *Standing Firm* (New York: HarperCollins, 1994), p. 348.

12. Armstrong Williams, "Abortion and the GOP Whigs," *Washington Times*, March 29, 1995, p. A25.

13. Lloyd Grove, "Drawling Power," *Washington Post*, August 11, 1994, p. B1.

14. George Weigel and William Kristol, "Life and the Party," *National Review*, August 15, 1994, p. 53.

15. Speech to the Conservative Political Action Conference, Washington D.C., February 4, 1995.

16. Two academics from the City University of New York, Barry A. Kosmin and Seymour P. Lachman, surveyed the spiritual beliefs of 113,000 Americans in 1990 for their book *One Nation Under God: Religion in Contemporary American Society* (New York: Harmony Books, 1993), pp. 192, 199, 204.

17. Chris Bull, "The Tolerant Bully," *The Advocate*, June 28, 1994, p. 24.

18. Ibid.

19. Rich Tafel, "Inside Politics," *Washington Times*, October 12, 1993, p. A6.

20. Marjorie Connelly, "Portrait of the Electorate: Who Voted for Whom in the House," *New York Times*, November 13, 1994, p. 24.

21. Chris Bull, "Outward Bound," *The Advocate*, October 4, 1994, p. 40. Headline referred to in the text was on the cover of that issue. The two self-professed gay Congressmen are Barney Frank and Gerry Studds, both of Massachusetts. Gunderson declared himself to be overtly gay in the March 10, 1995, issue of *The Washington Blade*, p. 27.

22. Chandler Burr, "Congressman (R), Wisconsin. Fiscal Conservative. Social Moderate. Gay." *New York Times Magazine*, October 16, 1994, p. 43.

23. Patrick J. Buchanan, "Global Trade's Toll," *Washington Times*, October 5, 1994, p. A19.

24. Buckley never writes an easy-to-parse sentence if he can help it, but here is what he wrote in the *National Review* in 1991: "I find it impossible to defend Pat Buchanan against the charge that what he did and said during the period under examination [the time of the Gulf War against Iraq] amounted to anti-Semitism, whatever it was that drove him to say and do it: most probably, an iconoclastic temperament" (quoted from *In Search of Anti-Semitism* [New York: Continuum, 1992], p. 189).

25. Patrick J. Buchanan, "The Isolationist Myth," *New York Post*, December 3, 1994, p. 11.

26. Patrick Buchanan, "Back Door Bailout after the Rout?" *Washington Times*, February 1, 1995, p. A17.

27. *CBS News*, February 22, 1995.

28. Senator Pete Domenici (R-NM) the chairman of the Budget Committee, did propose a seven-year pay freeze for Congress. More than half of the new Republicans elected in 1994 had never before held elective office. These tyros qualify as "citizen legislators," but we can expect some of them to have some rough edges—and thus be vulnerable to a more polished Ehrenhaltian Democrat down the road.

However, many of the freshmen Republicans will find that they like politics and so they Ehrenaltianize themselves in office. One good prospect: Michael P. Flanagan, the thirty-one-year-old Republican who giant-killed Democrat Dan Rostenkowski in Chicago, lived at home and earned $7,000 the year he was elected. His promotion to the U.S. Congress means nearly a twentyfold increase in his annual income to the congressional salary of $133,600. Fear of falling, careerwise, guarantees that he'll be a tenacious incumbent.

Another indicator that the new Republican majority might find ways to entrench itself, Coelho-style was a piece in the *New York Times*, the headline of which tells it all: "Republicans Rule Lobbyists' World With Strong Arm: Past Slights Recalled: New Congressional Majority Seeks to Collect Donations and Change Allegiances" (Richard L. Berke, March 20, 1995, p. 1).

29. See, for example, Richard L. Berke, "Poll Finds Public Doubts Key Parts of GOP's Agenda," *New York Times*, February 28, 1995, p. A1; Michael K. Frisby, "Americans, Polled on GOP and 'Contract,' Like Big Picture but Have Trouble with Small Print," *Wall Street Journal*, March 9, 1995, p. A20; and Richard Morin, "Public Growing Wary of GOP Cuts," *Washington Post*, March 21, 1995, p. A1.

30. Pete DuPont, "Selections for a Contract Encore," *Washington Times*, March 29, 1995, p. A22.

31. NBC, *Meet the Press* November 13, 1994.

32. For an example of admiration from the Right, see George F. Will, "Presidential Minimalism," *Newsweek*, March 20, 1995, p. 72. From the Left, see Richard Cohen, "Lugar's Principled Stand," *Washington Post*, March 3, 1995, p. A25.

Just what a legal scandal farm subsidies had become was further revealed by the Washington-based Environmental Working Group, which found that $1.3 billion in federal agriculture payments have gone to "city slickers"—Americans who are not only not poor, but also not farmers. Recipients live in some of the poshest ZIP codes in New York, Washington, D.C., and Southern California.

33. An interesting discussion of baselines is found in Michael Wines, "Are 'Cuts' Really Cuts? That Depends," *New York Times*, March 25, 1995, p. 13.

34. The Balanced Budget Amendment (BBA) was defeated in March 1995, but it will be back. If it ever does pass, all the duplicitous politicization squeezed out of the system on baselines and tax expenditures will come back in the guise of enforcing the amendment. Put simply, everyone will cheat on everything: revenues, expenditures, unfunded mandates, what spending goes on- and off-budget, and on and on, for as long as Washington is Washington. And when the whole legal contrivance comes crashing down, as they said in the film *Ghostbusters*, who're you gonna call? A judge? Republicans in particular should have learned by now not to give the judiciary more jurisdiction.

Finally, what's to stop some future government from trying to balance the budget, not by reducing spending but by raising taxes? If the Republicans really wanted to level with the American people, they would argue, as Milton Friedman does, that the deficit isn't the issue; the real issue is the government's overall burden on the economy, whether expressed in taxes or borrowing. It would be far better to scrap the BBA altogether and strive for an amendment to limit the real growth of government spending, or capping the federal government's percentage of GNP is more promising than a BBA. Of course, no fiscal machine will work unless the people operating it are committed to making it work.

35. C-SPAN, March 24, 1995.

36. Cornuelle, *Reclaiming the American Dream* (New Brunswick, N.J.: Transaction Publishers, 1965), p. 8.

37. Reagan's lost battle against the Legal Services Corporation (LSC) illustrates the uphill slog the Right faces when it foresakes the idea advantage. The LSC is a $400 million-a-year government organization that, as we have seen, subsidizes much Reichian litigation nationwide. It is perhaps surprising that the government finances lawsuits against itself—especially when those lawsuits so often serve to expand the size and scope of government, injuring innocent bystanders, the taxpayers. And yet the nominal mission—but the bulk of its caseload—of the LSC, to provide legal help to the indigent, is a noble mission. However, in the early eighties, Reaganaut Ed Meese, looking upon the LSC as a single monolithic entity, tried to kill the whole agency. The Reagan administration failed to separate out in

its own mind—let alone the public's—the difference between the PC politics of the LSC and its ongoing mission of protecting the poor against force and fraud. In going after both with a blunderbuss, the Republicans bagged neither. A more effective idea would have been a plan to fund poor people's legal defense but defund the activists' legal offense. Coupling the abolition of the LSC with the extension of legal access for the poor through some other mechanism, such as tax deductions or tax credits for pro bono representation, might have gathered a critical mass of votes from those who applauded the LSC's Gideon's Trumpet justice-for-the-poor goal, even as they were appalled by its Kunstlerian techniques.

38. On days when he is not explaining what he meant to say, Gingrich has shown that he understands the moral and political opportunity spread out before the Republicans. Here is what Gingrich said in early 1995, during one of the District of Columbia's fiscal crises, after Mayor Marion Barry appealed to the federal government for help. Speaking to the members of Congress charged with D.C. oversight, he said they should "focus on the people of the District, not the government." Continuing, Gingrich said,

> We want to focus on the children, we want to focus on neighborhoods, we want to focus on public safety; let's worry about making D.C. a capital we can be proud of and then let's come back to the secondary question, which is how can we work with the city government. But let's not get ourselves mired down in a political argument where everybody gets to blame each other while children get killed . . . We cannot tolerate the level of violence and the level of brutality and the level of degradation that is happening to our children. And everyone of us ought to look at them as our children. They're Americans, they're part of our extended family. . .We want to cooperate in finding a solution that is good for the children and the people of D.C. (C-SPAN, February 1, 1995)

Democrats and other anti-Gingrichians may dismiss anything the Georgian says, but they should ask themselves if they disbelieve the message or whether they merely distrust the messenger. If the message is right, then they ought to think about finding their own reformist voice.

Chapter 13

1. For example, in the last 150 years, the Whigs/Republicans and Democrats have, at various times, switched places on issues including, but

not limited to, the following: big government/industrial policy, the gold standard, isolationism/interventionism, abortion, free trade, aid to private and parochial schools, and immigration.

2. Beth Donovan and Ilyse J. Vernon, "Freshmen Got to Washington with Help of PAC Funds," *Congressional Quarterly Weekly Report*, March 27, 1993, p. 724.

3. Editorial, "The Freshman Flop," *Roll Call*, October 13, 1994, p. 4.

4. Milton Friedman, "The Real Free Lunch: Markets and Private Property," *Cato Policy Report* (July/August 1993), p. 13.

5. Black and Black, *Politics*, pp. 25, 155.

6. Ibid., p. 17.

7. CNN, *Evans & Novak*, October 8, 1994.

8. Perhaps America needs more issue-oriented third-party presidential candidates who run not to win, but to sway. Norman Thomas, the socialist, ran in every presidential election from 1928 to 1944; he was never a contender, but his honest advocacy of collective economic action influenced the New Deal.

9. However, even those riding wave of history need a helmsperson. U.S. history reminds us that fate's fickle finger, applied to individuals, can make a huge difference. For example, what would have happened if Robert E. Lee had accepted Lincoln's offer to command the Union troops in 1861? Or, four years later, what would have been the consequence if John Wilkes Booth had missed? In 1933 one Joseph Zangara shot and killed Chicago's Mayor Cermak, but he was aiming at Franklin D. Roosevelt, riding in the same car. And what would America be like today if Lee Harvey Oswald— or whoever—had missed John Kennedy in Dallas in 1963?

10. When we last heard from Paul Tsongas, he had helped redefine Democratic thinking in the eighties; then he lost to Bill Clinton in the 1992 Democratic primaries. In late 1994 he said America needs "the kind of moral authority the administration clearly does not have and that the 'Contract with America' cannot provide, since it is also poll-driven." Tsongas listed his "precepts"—tolerance, a balanced budget, entitlement reform, the abolition of capital gains held for five years or more—and called for "a coalition party" that would "unite well-meaning Americans under a common banner." It's "a coalition that already exists," but "is unaware of its existence," he said. "It is the coalition of social liberalism and fiscal conservatism," aiming to "ride the wave of history rather than seeking shelter in the failed policies of the past." (See David M. Shribman, "Tsongas

Suggests 3d Party—Sees Powell as a Candidate," *Boston Globe*, December 12, 1994, p. 1.)

11. We should also note the danger of negative alliances: When, as Will Marshall of the Progressive Policy Institute puts it, "the two parties are both losing market share," it's not surprising that entrepreneurs such as Perot rush in to make the big score. Yet Perot could give throw-the-bums-out political vigilantism a bad name. Perotistas without principles or paradigms could do anything—although the one thing we know they want to do, put up protectionist barriers that would wreck the international trading system, is bad enough.

Pat Buchanan seems most eager to pull together the single issue that Perot chose to most associate himself after 1992: opposition to trade liberalization. Buchanan seeks to pull together a protectionist alliance that transcends the Republicans, or even the Right. Improbable? Can't happen here? Consider: if Buchanan, Ross Perot, Richard Gephardt, Jesse Jackson, and Ralph Nader all have the same view of free trade, what else might they ally on? Indeed, in a warning to the GOP on the eve of the 1994 GATT vote, Buchanan's group, the Coalition for the American Cause, bought full-page ads shouting "Wake Up, Republicans! You Are Courting A Third Party!" (Advertisement, *Washington Times*, November 29, 1994, p. A9).

12. Notoriously, Gingrich also said, "I think people want to change, and the only way you get change is vote Republican." Quoted in *The Hotline*, November 7, 1994.

13. William Booth, "Abortion Clinic Slayer Is Given Death Penalty," *Washington Post*, December 7, 1994, p. A1.

14. PBS, *To the Contrary*, May 8, 1993.

15. "Judge Draws Protests After Cutting Sentence of Gay Man's Killer," *New York Times*, August 17, 1994, p. A15.

16. Mellman and Lazarus/MassMutual American Family Values Program, "1991 American Family Values Study: A Return to Family Values," Washington D.C., 1991, p. 13.

17. "Remarks of Hillary D. Rodham, President of the Wellesley College Government Association and member of the Class of 1969, on the occasion of Wellesley's 91st Commencement, May 31, 1969," p. 2.

18. Charles Reich, *The Greening of America* (New York: Random House, 1970), p. 3.

19. Paul Krugman, *Peddling Prosperity, Economic Sense and Nonsense in the Age of Diminished Expectations* (W.W. Norton New York, 1994), p. 155.

20. And pay they have. In Mario Cuomo's cyberized Empire State, the top state income tax rate of 7.875 percent kicked in for a family earning just $26,000. *New York* magazine's Jacob Weisberg puts his finger on this debauching of fairness, pointing out the injustice of poor people paying taxes at rich people's rates: "Wall Street billionaires and their bootblacks, therefore, pay state taxes at the same rate." Maybe that's one reason Cuomo lost. See Jacob Weisberg, "Why We've Fallen Out Of Love With Mario," *New York*, August 8, 1994, p. 22.

21. Once the experts warned us that too much leisure would be a major social problem; now we see that the task is time management. Harvard's Juliet Schor, author of *The Overworked American: The Unexpected Decline of Leisure*, cites studies showing that over two decades, time on the job for the average employed American increased by 163 hours a year, or an extra month (Schor, *The Overworked American: The Unexpected Decline of Leisure* [New York: Basic Books, 1992].) Not only are individual earners working harder, so are entire families. As Columbia's Katherine Newman puts it, "The only reason that the American middle class has managed not to fall through the floorboards is that a record number of families are bankrolled by two wage earners" (Newman, *Declining Fortunes*, p. 42.)

22. William R. Mattox, Jr., "The Parent Trap," *Policy Review* (Winter 1991), p. 6. Mattox cites a University of Maryland study showing that in 1965, parents spent thirty hours a week with their children. By 1985, such interaction had fallen 40 percent—to seventeen hours a week.

23. In an interview, Clinton went so far as to say: "I think Murray did the country a great service. . . . I think his analysis is essentially right." But then he demurred on the Murray solution, to abolish welfare altogether: "Now, whether his prescription is right, I question." The president conceded that Murray's end-welfare solution "would work" to reduce illegitimacy, but he wondered whether it would be "morally right."

24. CNN, September 9, 1994.

25. Quoted in "Lunch," *Lear's* (April 1993), p. 22.

26. Robert A. Nisbet, *The Quest for Community* (New York: Oxford University Press, 1953), p. 231. Nicholas Lemann offers an interesting perspective on this ironic unity in "Paradigm Lost: The Shortcomings of the Small-Town Solution," *Washington Monthly* (April 1991), p. 46.

27. Amitai Etzioni, *The Spirit of Community* (New York: Crown, 1993), p. 122.

28. Jon Meacham, "What the Religious Right Can Teach the New Democrats," *Washington Monthly* (April 1993), p. 42.

29. CNN/*USA Today* poll, May 11–14, 1995.

30. Juan Williams, "Blacked Out In the Newt Congress," *Washington Post*, November 20, 1994, p. C1.

31. Maudlyne Ihejirika, "Jackson: Coalition Must Be Reawakened," *Chicago Sun-Times*, November 26, 1994, p. 6.

32. Gary Wisby, "Jackson: Don't Turn Back the Clock," *Chicago Sun-Times*, November 24, 1994, p. 16.

33. Janet Cheatham Bell, *Famous Black Quotations* (New York: Warner Books, 1995), p. 62.

34. Khalid Abdullah Tariq Al-Mansour, *Betrayal by Any Other Name* (San Francisco: First African American Press, 1993), p. 703. Afrocentric spirituality is not the only approach to the inculcation of productive values. Some recent literature asserts that Black Christian churches are playing an increasingly valuable role as well, as they reach out to black men. The Reverend Johnny Ray Youngblood, pastor of St. Paul Community Baptist Church in a poor Brooklyn neighborhood, says, "Good isn't weak. Good isn't milquetoast. Good isn't namby-pamby." A sympathetic chronicle of Youngblood's work points out that the African American minister practices "a policy of theological affirmative action," emphasizing the role of black men in the church. See Samuel G. Freedman *Upon This Rock: The Miracles of a Black Church* (New York: HarperCollins, 1993), p. 58. A broader survey of this phenomenon is found in Tucker Carlson, "That Old-Time Religion," *Policy Review*, Summer 1992, p. 13.

35. Eugene H. Methvin, "A Scandalous Law That's Costing Taxpayers Billions," *Reader's Digest* (December 1994), p. 123.

36. Congressional Budget Office, *Reducing the Deficit: Spending and Revenue Options* (Washington, D.C.: GPO, 1994), p. 194.

37. David Breskin, "Spike Lee: The Rolling Stone Interview," *Rolling Stone*, July 11–25, 1991, p. 63. In the shadows and interstices of federal regulation, a substantial underground economy has emerged in many poor areas, as people eke out a living doing repairs, running errands, or driving jitneys. Hernando De Soto, in his landmark study of the spontaneous "informal" economy of Peru, made the point that Third World peoples, who had never heard of John Locke or Adam Smith, were nevertheless developing

market institutions, in spite of the best efforts of their socialist/mercantilist/crony capitalist governments to squelch them (Soto, *The Other Path: The Invisible Revolution in the Third World* [New York: Harper and Row, 1989]). See, for example, Neal Templin, "Off the Books: For Inner-City Detroit, The Hidden Economy Is Crucial Part of Life," *Wall Street Journal*, April 4, 1995, p. A1. The Washington-based Institute for Justice, a libertarian legal activist group, has taken up the cause of many striving capitalists of color.

38. George Fraser's *Success Runs In Our Race: The Complete Guide to Effective Networking in the African-American Community* (New York, William Morrow, 1994), pp. 34, 40, 42. Another book by an African American of a similar nature is Les Brown's *Live Your Dreams* (New York: Avon, 1992).

39. Walter E. Williams, *The State Against Blacks* (New York: New Press, 1982).

40. *Meet the Press*, July 25, 1993.

41. Eleanor Clift, "The Black Power Outage," *Newsweek*, November 28, 1994, p. 32.

42. The same *Advocate* survey found that 59 percent of its gay readers would marry another man if they could, with 26 percent saying they might. One in ten of those polled were fathers; another quarter said they would like to father a child. See Janet Lever, "Sex and Sexuality," *Advocate*, August 23, 1994, p. 15.

43. There is one significant Constitutional obstacle to gay marriage: Article IV, Section 1, the "full faith and credit" clause. It holds that states shall recognize "the public Acts, Records, and judicial Proceedings of every other State." Thus it could be argued that if New York, for example, were to sanctify gay marriage, then Utah would be required to accept such a union if a New York couple were to move to the Beehive State. This is not a small concern; yet one can hope that creative problem-solvers, respectful of both sides of this issue, could work out some sort of evolutionary compromise.

44. David Nimmons, "Playboy Interview," *Playboy*, September 1993, p. 66.

45. Diane Werts, "Epidemic Epic," *Newsday*, September 5, 1993, Fanfare section, p. 10.

46. Janet Lever, "Sex and Sexuality," *Advocate*, August 23, 1994, p. 15.

47. Gabriel Rotello, "The Insistent Dead Drove The Living to Washington," *Newsday*, April 29, 1993, p. 112.

48. Hastings Wyman Jr., "Election leaves Gays in a precarious position," *Washington Blade*, November 18, 1994, p. 41.

49. Nimmons, "Playboy Interview," p. 66.

50. "Domestic Partnership Bill Vetoed in California," *New York Times*, September 13, 1994, p. A14. Nonetheless, many corporations, such as Apple, Microsoft, Capital Cities/ABC, and Time-Warner, have offered fringe benefits to the domestic partners of employees.

51. W. H. Auden, *Collected Poems* (New York: Vintage), pp. 141–42.

52. In Song X, Auden says to his lover, "O marry me, Johnny, I'll love and obey" (Ibid.). The late John Boswell of Yale wrote that "many— probably most—earlier Western societies institutionalized some form of romantic same-sex union" (John Boswell, *Same-Sex Unions in Premodern Europe* [New York: Villard Press, 1994], p. 282).

53. Bruce Bawer, *A Place at the Table: The Gay Individual in American Society* (New York: Poseidon, 1993), pp. 19-20.

54. National Center for Education Statistics, *Digest of Education Statistics* (Washington, D.C.: GPO, 1993), p. 24.

55. Ibid., p. 164.

56. Ibid., p. 74.

57. Ibid., p. 85. In constant dollars, teachers in public and elementary schools earned $29,319 in 1979–80, which rose to $35,235 in 1989–90. Two school years later, that figure had dropped slightly, to $35,163.

58. Patterson and Kim, *Second American Revolution*, p. 107

59. John Larrabee, "Teachers fight running public schools for profit," *USA Today*, August 3, 1994, p. 5D.

60. Mark Perry, "The Educational Octopus," *Choice Comments*, Harrisburg, Penn., March 15, 1995. Perry has assembled some other data to prove that Parkinsonianism is rampant in EDUCRAT. For example, New York City's public schools have 4 times as many students as the parochial school system, but 250 times the number of administrators. Also, the Chicago Board of Education's 3,300 employees exceed the entire Japanese Ministry of Education.

61. National Center for Education Statistics, p. 90.

62. Bruce S. Cooper, Robert Sarrel, and Toby Tetenbaum, "Choice, Funding, and Pupil Achievement," unpublished doctoral dissertation, cited in *Issues '94* (Washington, D.C.: Heritage Foundation, 1994), p. 176.

Chapter 14

1. Kushner, *Angels*, p. 13.

2. For a longer discussion, see Robert J. Shapiro, *Cut and Invest: A Budget Strategy for the New Economy* (Washington: Progressive Policy Institute, 1995), Chap. 2: "The United States in the Global Economy: The Crisis of Slow Growth." Shapiro and his colleague M. Jeff Hammond have assembled some compelling data comparing international growth rates from 1975 to 1992. Average real growth for the U.S. during this period was 2.4 percent, putting us ahead of Germany, France, the United Kingdom, and most other Western European countries. Yet the average for all advanced economies was 2.6 percent, with Japan's growth rate of 4.0 percent leading the group. Interestingly, the average for all nonadvanced economies around the globe was 4.7 percent, with Asian economies growing at 6.6 percent per year—nearly three times the U.S.'s rate of growth.

In the case of Europe, the next decade will be instructive: will the great advantage of freer trade with the European Union be overcome by the proliferation of rule-writing, red-taping Brusselscrats?

3. Tax Foundation, *Facts and Figures*, p. 118.

4. Economist James L. Payne argues that the true total cost of collecting $1 through the federal income tax is 65 cents, which he breaks down as follows: 24 cents for compliance, 35 cents for forgone production, 2 cents for enforcement, 3 cents for avoidance and evasion, and 1 cent for IRS overhead (Payne, "Inside the Federal Hurting Machine," *Freeman*, March 1994, p. 124).

5. Senator Connie Mack (R-Florida) says that those 6 billion person-hours are equal to the total needed to produce all the cars, trucks, and airplanes made in the U.S. each year.

6. Indeed, Bob Dole used the exact same words—"a blank piece of paper"—on April 2, 1995, when he announced a tax reform commission, to be led by Jack Kemp.

7. David Hage, David Fischer, and Robert F. Black, "America's Other Welfare State," *U.S. News & World Report*, April 10, 1995, p. 34.

8. Quoted in Kenneth Eskey, "Flat income tax reborn in conservative minds," *Washington Times*, September 22, 1994, p. A9.

9. Washington economist Bruce Bartlett estimates an absolute flat rate, with no deductions or exemptions or anything, could be reduced to just 9.2 percent, but that *would* be a regressive tax.

10. Harvard economist Dale Jorgenson estimates that a flat tax would boost the national wealth by $1 trillion (Daniel J. Mitchell, "A Brief Guide to the Flat Tax" [Washington, D.C.: Heritage Foundation, 1995], p. 2).

11. The best discussion of the flat tax is in Robert E. Hall and Alvin Rabushka, *The Flat Tax* (Stanford, Calif.: Hoover Institution Press, 1995). Other variations on the flat-tax theme calling for a "two-tier" flat tax, with rates of perhaps 11 and 21 percent, might resolve this question; it's no longer a pure flat tax, but the goals of simplicity and lowering marginal rates are still achieved.

12. Republican pollster Frank Luntz argues that people support the flat tax because they currently think that the rich pay less than they do, or nothing.

13. Senators Sam Nunn and Pete Domenici, cochairmen, *The CSIS Strengthening of America Commission First Report* (Washington, D.C.: Center for Strategic and International Studies, 1992), pp. 96–102.

14. Indeed, antipathy toward any kind of direct tax on individuals—on either income or consumption—has led some on the libertarian right to advocate abolishing the IRS altogether, and installing instead a national sales tax. While some, such as Indiana senator Richard Lugar, argue that such a tax could be made progressive through rebate schemes, it would still leave state and city income taxes in place and so the intrusive burden of income tax collectors would still be felt.

15. Rauch, *Demosclerosis*, p. 135.

16. Peter Drucker, *The Effective Executive* (1966; reprint, New York: Harper Colophon, 1985), p. 104.

17. The pretax rate of return on corporate capital has moved in a range of 8–12 percent since 1955. It is the pretax return that matters because what is at issue is the value to society of additional investment. Government's share of the total return must therefore be added to what private individuals get for their money. Three excellent research works on this subject include Feldstein, Dicks-Mireau, and Poterba's "The Effective Tax Rate and the Pretax Rate of Return," *Journal of Public Economics* 21 (1983): 129–58; Ando and Auerbach's "Cost of Capital in the United States and Japan, A Comparison," *Journal of the Japanese and International Economies* 2 (1988): 134–58; and Kopke's "Profits and Stock Prices: The Importance of Being Earnest" in the *New England Economic Review* (March-April 1992), pp. 26–44.

18. Aaron Bernstein and Paul Magnusson, "How Much Good Will Training Do?" *Business Week*, February 22, 1993, p. 77.

19. Children's Defense Fund, "We Are the Children's Defense Fund: We Are Making a Difference in Children's Lives; You Can Make A Difference Too," pamphlet, 1993. Even if we assume that the $7 return is accurate, we may not, to use the economistic reductionist terms that the CDF itself utilizes, be getting a very good deal. That early childhood investment probably "pays off" to society during the individual's early work- and child-bearing years. Let's assume for argument's sake that the $7 is saved between the ages of eighteen and thirty-eight and that 10 percent is the rate of return that society gets on investment. Then $1 spent at birth on a CDF program has a value of only 59 cents. Alternatively, we might think of society borrowing at 10 percent in order to get a 7.5 percent rate of return. Such thinking may be too roundheaded for some, but those who seek, for whatever reason, to define social spending not as "compassion" but rather as hard-headed dollars-and-cents calculation, must be prepared to defend their data on the intellectual turf of economists.

20. National Opinion Research Center and Lewin-VHI, submitted to the Department of Alcohol and Drug Programs, *Evaluating Recovery Services: the California Drug and Alcohol Treatment Assessment* (Caldata), July 1994, p. 1. Estimates of a three- to sevenfold "return" on drug treatment dollars are common; see, for example, the testimony of Columbia University's Dr. Herbert Kleber before the Senate Finance Committee, March 27, 1995.

21. Sheryl Stolberg, "Drug Treatment Yields Big Savings," *Los Angeles Times*, August 29, 1994, p. A1.

22. We might not have to wait until then. Bob Herbert of the *New York Times* details the case of Leslie Fay, the Pennsylvania apparel company, which decided to dispose of the low-skilled jobs that remained in the United States after years of successful production. Herbert writes, correctly, that "big business is about making money, not stroking the tender feelings of sentimental long-time employees." The problem is that making money, like making sausages, can be a messy business:

> The logic behind the company's move is irrefutable. Leslie Fay's American production workers, mostly middle-aged women, earn about $7.80 an hour. Who would pay such an excessive wage when, in this wonderful new world of global competition, you can get your dresses made by young girls in Guatemala or Honduras for 40 or 50 cents an hour? ("Leslie Fay's Logic," *New York Times*, June 19, 1994, p. E17).

In the rugged cyber-economy, Herbert's question answers itself; low-value-added labor has become just another commodity. Herbert may be a sentimentalist, but he understands that such huge wage differentials can have but a short half-life in the cyber-economy.

Fifteen years after Sally Field won an Oscar for *Norma Rae*, one wonders whether those heroic textile workers won a union only to lose their jobs. The International Ladies' Garment Workers Union complains that Leslie Fay already does 75 percent of its production overseas. But it may be too late for collective bargaining, strikes, or even media campaigns—Leslie Fay declared bankruptcy in 1993.

Returning to the case of Leslie Fay, we find that Honduran workers can do the same routine production work as Americans for one-fifteenth the wage. Yet there's an even bigger differential between what Pennsylvania spends per pupil, per year in the public schools ($5,073, according to the Pennsylvania Department of Education) and what Honduras spends ($205, according to the Honduran Embassy and the United Nations). In terms of hard-nosed competitive cost–benefit analysis, we should hope that for twenty-five times greater investment, Keystone State educators could give future workers more than a 15:1 earnings ratio. But as we have seen, the expensively educated but poorly skilled Pennsylvanians cannot preserve even the 15:1 wage advantage over little Honduras. The bottom line is that we have to do better with the money we have: we need to increase the return on public investment, not the public investment itself.

23. Bookshelves sag under the mass of tomes denouncing wasteful government spending. Three of the better books, Martin L. Gross's *The Government Racket: Washington Waste from A to Z* (New York: Bantam, 1992), Brian Kelly's *Adventures in Porkland: How Washington Wastes Your Money and Why They Won't Stop* (New York: Villard Books, 1992), and Peter G. Peterson's, *Facing Up: How to Rescue the Economy from Crushing Debt & Restore the American Dream* (New York: Simon and Schuster, 1993) are quite specific in itemizing costly and wasteful spending-cut candidates.

24. Congressional Budget Office, *Reducing the Deficit: Spending and Revenue Options* (Washington, D.C.: GPO, 1994), pp. 54, 186, and 272.

25. Furthermore, many science projects that may be quite meritorious—on grape virology, screw worms, and cranberry breeding—are hurt by their arcane subject and silly-sounding names. Of the hundreds of projects the government funds, many are pure pork; yet the one sure way not to improve the system is to judge such spending by their titles.

26. Similarly, the easiest groups to impose tax burdens on are generations yet unborn; hence, the deficit.

27. Citizens United to Terminate Subsidies, "The Green Scissors Report," Washington, D.C., January 1995. In the words of the report:

> The General Mining Law of 1872 permits anyone to enter open public lands to explore for hardrock minerals including gold, silver, lead, copper, zinc and many others. Anyone can file a claim to extract minerals found. There are hundreds of thousands of claims on federal lands operating under the 1872 Mining Law.
>
> There are three factors that prevent a fair return to the taxpayer. First, mining companies pay no royalties to the federal treasury on the mining each year of approximately $3 billion worth of minerals from public lands.
>
> The second factor involves "patents." Mining companies can "patent"—or buy—20-acre tracts of land for $5 an acre or less . . .
>
> The third factor is the massive abandoned mine cleanup costs left for taxpayers. The Mineral Policy Center places the cost of such cleanups at $32 billion to $72 billion.

28. Department of Defense, *Base Closure and Realignment Report* (Washington, D.C., March, 1993), p. 2.

29. Connie Mack, U.S. Senate, *Congressional Record*, March 24, 1994, p. S3587.

30. See, for example, Joe Cobb, *Establish a Spending Reduction Commission* (Washington, D.C.: Heritage Foundation, 1995).

31. Peterson, *Facing Up*, p. 106. However, as with any Old Paradigm one-size-fits-all institution, Social Security isn't equally good to everyone. George Mason University's Walter Williams makes the point that Social Security is stacked against black males, who have an average life expectancy of 64.2, whereas white males live on average to be 73. Yet people don't qualify for full Social Security benefits until they are 65. Williams puckishly suggests that the retirement age for black men be reduced to 56 (Walter Williams, "A stretch of racial ratios," *Washington Times*, November 17, 1994, p. A18).

32. CNN, *Crossfire*, February 24, 1995.

33. The current FICA tax consists of the 7.65 percent "contribution" from both the employer and the employee, for a total of 15.3 percent; the division of the tax burden is nothing more than a ploy to make the tax more palatable.

34. Alan J. Auerbach and Laurence J. Kotlikoff, *Saving the American Dream*

(New York: Merrill Lynch, 1994). The Senate Budget Committee, citing Clinton administration data, found that a baby born in 1995 would face a lifetime net tax rate of 84 percent.

35. The Clinton administration disputes the Kerrey–Danforth Commission's findings: Medicare won't go bust in 2001, the Clintonians say, it will be in 2002. See Spencer Rich, "Trustees Warn of Medicare Collapse," *Washington Post*, April 4, 1995, p. A4.

36. Senators Robert Kerrey and John Danforth, *Letter to President Clinton and Congressional Leadership* (Washington, D.C.: Bipartisan Commission on Entitlement and Tax Reform), dated December 14, 1994.

37. However, in the 1960 case *Flemming* v. *Nestor*, the Supreme Court ruled that workers do not have any property rights in Social Security. In other words, benefits are a function of politics, not contracts.

38. David Frum, "Republicans: What Now?" *Wall Street Journal*, November 10, 1994, p. A16.

39. Life expectancy from 1871 through 1880 was 37 years; life expectancy from 1891 through 1900 was 42.3 years. So 40 years is a compromise between the two. Klaus J. Bade, *Population, Labour and Migration in 19th and 20th Century Germany* (New York: St. Martin's Press, 1991), p. 21; originally from P. Marschalck, Bevölkerungsgeschichte Deutschlands im 19. und 20. Jahrhundert (Frankfurt, 1984), pp. 164–488.

40. Shapiro, *Mandate for Change*, p. 36.

41. Office of Management and Budget.

42. Peterson, *Facing Up*, p. 104.

43. Charles Peters assembled a useful list of spending and deficit reductions in "Beyond Paper Cuts: Eight smart ways to make real in-roads to deficit reduction," *Washington Monthly* (October 1993), p. 30. Peters cites data analyzed by Phillip Longman and Neil Howe for the *Atlantic* in 1992, which show that "20 percent of Social Security's outlays—or $55 billion—go to households making more than $50,000. Take the COLA away from them and you save roughly $8.25 billion by 1998, assuming 3 percent inflation."

44. John C. Goodman and Gerald L. Musgrave, *Patient Power* (Washington: Cato Institute, 1994), p. 31.

45. An excellent summary of an IRA-type Social Security reform comes from Peter J. Ferrara, of the National Center for Policy Analysis, Dallas, Texas, in a 1994 paper, entitled *The President Proposes a Private Option for Social Security*.

46. Madison added: "The powers delegated by the proposed Constitution to the federal government are few and defined. Those which are to remain in the State governments are numerous and indefinite."

47. The efficacy of modern bureaucratic politics was one thing that the Right and Left wings of modern politics agreed on. Leftist muckraker Lincoln Steffens traveled to the Soviet Union and came back saying, "I have been over into the future, and it works" (William Safire, *Safire's Political Dictionary* [New York: Ballantine, 1978], p. 782). And the now-trite expression "the wave of the future" is actually the title of a 1940 book by Anne Morrow Lindbergh, an apologist for fascism. She saw fascism as the solution for what she called the "type of decay, weakness, and blindness into which all the 'Democracies' have fallen." (Lindbergh, *The Wave of the Future: A Confession of Faith* [New York: Harcourt, Brace, 1940], pp. 33–34). It's interesting to note that these two figures from the Right and the Left were describing supposedly irreconcilable regimes in suspiciously similar terms.

48. Alice M. Rivlin, *Reviving the American Dream* (Washington, D.C.: The Brookings Institution, 1992), p. 9.

49. Ibid., p. 98. Ways of reckoning the federal government vary. Syndicated columnist Donald Lambro, a veteran waste-watcher, cites the Government Accounting Office finding that the Department of Commerce, for example, "shares its mission with at least 71 federal departments, agencies and offices." Lambro cites another GAO report: "12 federal agencies spending about $1 billion annually spend. $1 billion annually to administer about 35 laws governing food safety and quality. Fundamental differences in agencies' missions, responsibilities, and authorities have led to inconsistent oversight, inefficient use of resources, and poor interagency coordination." Lambro piles it on, finding 75 different antipoverty programs spending $210 billion a year and 125 job training programs spending another $16 billion. Lambro mocks the Clinton administration proposal to cut 1,000 Agriculture Department offices, pointing to the 10,000 that would remain. (See Lambro, "Shrinkage potential beyond the obvious," *Washington Times*, December 26, 1994, p. A16.)

50. Ibid., p. 17.

51. At least not deliberately. The celebrated "Rivlin Memo," dated October 3, 1994, delineating various presidential options for cutting spending, including entitlements, and raising taxes, leaked later that month, to the delight of Republicans.

52. *John McLaughlin's One on One*, January 29, 1995.

53. Editorial, "Taking on Big Byrd," *Wall Street Journal*, September 27, 1994, p. 12.

54. Robert W. Poole Jr., "Privatizing Essential Services," pp. 215–18, in *Market Liberalism: A Paradigm for the 21st Century*, ed. David Boaz and Edward H. Crane (Washington: Cato Institute, 1994), pp. 209–10.

55. An excellent study of the DVA is Robert E. Bauman's *70 Years of Federal Government Health Care: A Timely Look at the U.S. Department of Veterans Affairs* (Washington, D.C.: Cato Institute, 1994). Bauman makes this important point: "for most of this century the U.S. government has owned and operated the largest health care system in the nation . . . with 171 hospitals, 362 outpatient clinics, 128 nursing homes, a $16 billion 1994 budget, and 266,000 employees, the VHA is socialized medicine writ large." While Americans can draw their own conclusions about the quality of VA health care, Bauman notes that costs have risen 900 percent since 1970, and more than 250 percent since 1980. The VA spends half a billion dollars a year on hospital construction, a building boom driven by pork politics, not need. In Florida, for example, the DVA has built two new hospitals, even though the five existing VA hospitals are one-third empty. The General Accounting Office found that the VA pays twice as much as others for nursing care, and still finds the money to pay for nineteen golf courses (Jack Smith, *ABC News*, April 9, 1995).

56. Edmund L. Andres, "Winners of Wireless Auction to Pay $7 Billion," *New York Times*, March 14, 1995, p. D1.

57. Peter Saunders and Colin Harris, *Privatization and Popular Capitalism* (Buckingham, England: Open University Press, 1994), pp. 5–6, 26.

As one British Tory leader put it, "Our aim is to build upon our property-owning democracy and to establish a people's capital market, to bring capitalism to the place of work, to the high street, and even to the home. As we dispose of state-owned assets, so more and more people have the opportunity to become owners . . . These policies also increase personal independence and freedom, and by establishing a new breed of owner, have an important effect on attitudes."

58. Ibid., p. 143.

59. Ernst and Young, *Privatization: Investing in State-Owned Enterprises Around the World* (New York: Wiley, 1994), p. 3.

60. Lynn Scarlett, *Privatization Report* (Santa Monica, Calif.: Reason Foundation, 1994), p. 1. The privatization boom is expected to continue, with another $40 billion in privatizations for Western Europe alone anticipated

in 1995. See Digby Larner, "OECD Warns Privatization Might Push Stock Markets Lower," *International Herald Tribune*, March 25–26, 1995, p. 19.

61. E. S. Savas, ed., *Privatization for New York: Competing for a Better Future: A Report of the New York State Senate Advisory Commission on Privatization*, January 1992, p. ix.

62. Andrew Young, "Thinking About Cities in the 1990s" in *Thinking About America: The United States in the 1990s*, ed. Annelise Anderson and Dennis L. Bark (Stanford: Hoover Institution Press, 1988), pp. 421–22.

63. Peter Behr, "Solving the Privatization Puzzle," *Washington Post*, February 13, 1995, Washington Business section, p. 1. Yet the public is best served not by rote privatization, but rather by competition. In many cities, notably Indianapolis and Phoenix, reorganized and reenergized public employees have underbid private firms seeking city business; even New York City's employees are getting into the spirit. See for example, Steven Lee Myers, "Union Outbids Private Competitors for Street-Sign Work," *New York Times*, March 26, 1995, p. 40.

64. Poole, "Privatizing," pp. 215–18.

65. "FDA to leave firms to devices," *Washington Times*, April 7, 1995, p. A6.

66. "Across the USA: News From Every State," *USA Today*, April 12, 1993, p. 8A.

67. The Postal Service has at least 40,000 facilities in the U.S.; nobody knows how much they're worth, but the total must be in the billions, or even hundreds of billions. However, the market-unfriendly nature of the Postal Service has assured that no credible valuation has ever been made for those assets; that's why markets are needed, to ascertain something close to reality in subjective judgments.

68. The Cato Institute's Paul Craig Roberts cites a case in Los Angeles, in which LA county sheriff's deputies, reinforced with DEA agents and even the National Guard, broke into the home of one Donald Scott and shot him dead. The suspicion is that the feds thought that if he were a drug user they could confiscate his $5 million home and keep the money (Roberts, "A police state or a nation of laws?" *Washington Times*, August 31, 1993, p. F1).

69. Weber, *Economy*, p. 965.

70. See also, David Heilbroner, "The Law Goes on a Treasure Hunt," *New York Times Magazine*, December 11, 1994, p. 70.

71. In 1994 the General Accounting Office surveyed students on thirteen

college campuses to gauge their attitudes toward government service; the GAO found that college students view government as the "employer of last resort." As one student put it, "Why be part of the problem?" (*Federal Employment: How Government Jobs Are Viewed on Some College Campuses*, September 1994 [GAO/GGD-94-81], pp. 13–14.)

72. Howard, *Death of Common Sense*, pp. 182–83.

73. Ibid., p. 177.

74. James Fallows pointed out in the *New York Review of Books*, January 12, 1995, p. 3., that the Contract with America contains nary a word on health care cost control.

75. Irene Wielawski, "Congress' Failure May Reinvigorate Health Care," *Newsday*, October 4, 1994, p. 36.

76. Erik Eckholm, "While Congress Remains Silent, Health Care Transforms Itself," *New York Times*, December 18, 1994, p. A1.

77. U.S. Bureau of the Census, *Statistical Abstract*, 1994, pp. 854–55. Clearly, personal behavior accounts for many of America's health care problems; the costs and tragedies of sex, drugs, and violence defy therapeutic solutions. In 1995, for example, the Centers for Disease Control reported a nearly sevenfold increase in the percentage of babies born with fetal alcohol syndrome from 1979 to 1993.

78. Milt Freudenheim, "Health Costs Paid by Employers Drop for First Time in a Decade," *New York Times*, February 14, 1995, p. A1.

79. Gerald F. Seib, "Washington Wire," *Wall Street Journal*, December 16, 1994, p. A1. The runner-up issue was "unreliable retirement benefits," while unemployment was a distant third.

80. Goodman and Musgrave, *Patient Power*, p. 75.

81. "Cost of Health Care in the United States is Continuing to Grow," *New York Times*, November 27, 1994, p. 35.

82. Tax Foundation, *Facts and Figures*, pp. 32, 44.

83. Goodman and Musgrave, *Patient Power*, p. 112.

84. Ibid., p. 28. Goodman and Musgrave's work informs this coming section.

85. Peter J. Ferrara, unpublished paper, "Medical Savings Accounts at Work" (Washington: National Center for Policy Analysis, 1994), pp. 21–24.

86. The Cato Institute's Michael Tanner points out that in a given year, just an eighth of employees have health insurance claims exceeding $2,000.

If that is the case before employees can earn money by staying healthy, we could look forward to even positive feedback once an MSA plan is in place. (See Michael Tanner, "Returning Medicine to the Marketplace," in *Market Liberalism: A Paradigm for the 21st Century*, Washington, D.C.: Cato Institute, pp. 185–86.)

87. Judy Licht, "States Review Hospitals' Performance," *Washington Post*, February 28, 1995, Health section, p. 9.

88. Christopher Connell, "Accrediting group finishes first-ever HMO report card," *Washington Times*, February 24, 1995, p. B9. See also Ron Winslow, "New 'Report Card' on Health Care Uses Standardized Criteria, Audited Data," *Wall Street Journal*, February 28, 1995, p. B6.

89. The percentage of Americans over the age of sixty-five will nearly double from 1990 to 2050, to nearly a quarter of the population.

90. Goodman and Musgrave, *Patient Power*, p. 41.

91. David Wessel and John J. Fialka, "White House Proposes Giving Vouchers, Choices to Residents of Public Housing," *Wall Street Journal*, December 20, 1994, p. A16. Cisneros himself unveiled plans in January 1995, to cut more than a third of HUD employees by the year 2000. See Guy Gugliotta, "Cisneros Plans to Cut 4,400 Workers at HUD," *Washington Post*, January 7, 1995, p. A1.

92. Robert B. Reich, "The Choice Ahead," remarks to the National Press Club, January 5, 1995, p. 6.

93. CNN, December 15, 1994. See also Paul Magnusson, "Here A Cut, There A Cut . . . ," *Business Week*, January 9, 1995, p. 38.

94. Oliver E. Allen, *The Tiger: The Rise and Fall of Tammany Hall* (Reading, Mass.: Addison-Wesley, 1993), p. 110.

95. Yet those that should know the public schools best—public school teachers—are far less likely than the general population. As the writer Mark Perry has noted, "Public school teachers send their own children to private schools at more than twice the national average—22 percent of public educators' children are in private schools compared to the national average of 10 percent." In big cities, Perry adds, the percentage is much higher: 50 percent in Chicago, 46 percent in Milwaukee, 44 percent in New Orleans, etc. (Perry, *Choice Comments*, March 15, 1995).

96. That letter to Rep. Williams, who represents inner-city Milwaukee. Williams, the mother of four, gave up on the public schools in the eighties. She first turned to her fellow Democrats for new thinking, but Badger State Democrats were terminally EDUCRATed. So Williams joined with

Republican Governor Tommy Thompson to start a voucher pilot program so that black students trapped in miserable inner-city schools—schools that spend much more than the national average—could have the chance to go to the school that would help them learn the most. Williams and Thompson managed to get a 1,000-pupil pilot program, covering just 1 percent of the public school population, in 1990. The vouchers were worth only $2,500, less than half of what the Milwaukee public schools were spending per child. It was a small breach in the wall, but much national attention poured through. Friend and foe alike understood the significance of the Williams–Thompson achievement: a proto-Alliance between black and white, poor and prosperous, Democrat and Republican, based on the New Paradigm.

Williams put her finger on the difference between vouchers and top-—down systems:

> If the focus in the public school was on the child—on educating children—then all the other problems . . . would just go away. But the focus of the public schools is maintaining that system. It is not about educating children. The only ones who care about educating children are the parents. (*This Week with David Brinkley*, ABC, August 29, 1993).

To forestall a church-and-state constitutional challenge, the pro-choice forces in Wisconsin deliberately excluded religious schools from the voucher program, but that didn't stop the anti-choice forces from suing. Having lost the battle in a Democratic vote, Wisconsin EDUCRATs challenged the voucher plan in court.

A look at the list of plaintiffs and defendants tells us everything we need to know about the moral and intellectual bankruptcy of the Old Paradigm bureaucracy. On one side were Lonzetta Davis and her daughter Sabrina, Velma Frier and her daughter Shavonne, Thais Jackson and her daughter Tamika, the Urban Day School, and the Harambee Community School. On the other side were the Wisconsin Association of School District Administrators, the Wisconsin Federation of Teachers, and the Milwaukee Teachers Education Association. The Wisconsin Supreme Court ruled in favor of the voucher program; Justice Louis Ceci wrote that the choice program "attempted to throw a life preserver to those Milwaukee children caught in the cruel riptide of a school system floundering upon the shoals of poverty, status-quo thinking, and despair."

97. Allyson M. Tucker and William F. Lauber, *School Choice Programs:*

What's Happening in the States (Washington, D.C.: Heritage Foundation, 1994), pp. 1–2.

98. Just such an infusion would enable an idealistic program such as Princeton alumna Wendy Kopp's Teach for America program to dramatically expand its good work. Teach is a wonderful program, but since it is run as a volunteer program, it is still within the province of charity. In the future, if it is to survive, it will need, to use the Weberian term, to have its charisma rationalized. It could apply directly to the government for funding, in which case it would suffer a Veal fate, or it could participate in some postvoucher education market.

99. Seymour Fliegel with James Maguire, *Miracle in East Harlem: The Fight for Choice in Public Education* (New York: Times Books, 1993), p. 226.

100. Jonathan Kozol, "Whittle and the Privateers: Corporate Raid on Education," *Nation*, September 21, 1992, p. 272.

101. William Celis III, "Private Groups to Run 15 Schools in Experiment by Massachusetts," *New York Times*, March 19, 1994, p. 1.

102. K. L. Billingsley, "Urban League Obtains Charter to Run Schools," *Washington Times*, December 26, 1994, p. A1.

103. In Michigan, for example, the state ACLU chapter teamed up with the teachers to block state funding of charter schools. A state judge granted them an injunction. Even the threat of such costly litigation is an impediment to full experimentation. (See Rene Sanchez, "Michigan Develops Bold Lesson Plan for Educational Overhaul," *Washington Post*, December 27, 1994, p. A1.)

104. Editorial, "Teaching for Hire," *Wall Street Journal*, March 27, 1995, p. A26.

105. See, for example, an April 1995 General Accounting Office report that found that schools are lagging behind on the use of technology: GAO: "School Facilities: America's Schools Not Designed or Equipped for 21st Century" (Washington: GAO, April, 1995).

106. Educational expert Daniel McGroarty has found that the public schools in dozens of cities, including New York, Washington D.C., and Milwaukee, already send special-education and at-risk students to private schools. Such students are surely not "cream," but there is a market for serving them as well.

107. The Hudson Institute's Lewis J. Perelman offers a visionary look at the future of all education. "A new generation of technology," he writes, "has blown the social role of learning inside out." We are on the verge of

"hyperlearning," which he defines as "an unprecedented degree of connectedness of knowledge, experience, media, and brains—both human and nonhuman" (Perelman, *School's Out: Hyperlearning, the New Technology, and the End of Education* [New York: William Morrow, 1992], pp. 22–23). Yet it may turn out that technology is only a supplement, not a substitute, for individual instruction. Maybe the oldest model of all—a teacher working one-on-one with a student—will make a comeback. But even here, vouchers can help. The truth is that almost every American is an expert in something worth knowing. In a New Paradigm marketplace, those that know something will be completely free to teach those that want to learn.

108. Reich, *The Work of Nations*, p. 154.

109. Editorial, "Mr. Clinton's Promising Speech," *New York Times*, November 17, 1993, p. A26.

110. Rene Sanchez, "Goodling Vows a Fresh Look at Education," *Washington Post*, January 10, 1995, p. A15.

111. Franklin D. Roosevelt, "Annual Message to the Congress, January 4, 1935," *Public Papers and Addresses of Franklin D. Roosevelt* (New York: Random House, 1938), p. 19.

112. One who has put forth a plan is author Mickey Kaus, who calls for a return to the "work ethic state"; he dismisses incrementalist 'welfare reform' and argues instead for a full-fledged Rooseveltian work-not-welfare program. "Instead of attempting to somehow teach mainstream culture to people who spend most of their day immersed in ghetto culture," he asserts, "we could make ghetto culture economically unsustainable" (Mickey Kaus, "The End of Equality," Youth Policy 14, nos. 7 and 8 [December 1992], p. 17). Kaus's concept is simple and straightforward:

> If you could work and needed money, the government wouldn't give you a check and then try to cajole you into working . . . It would give you the location of several government job sites. If you showed up and worked, you would be paid for your work. If you don't show up, you don't get paid. (Ibid.)

Kaus estimates that his program would cost between $43 and $59 billion a year (Ibid., p. 135). That's a small amount compared to the $5 trillion in current dollars that the federal government has spent in the last three decades on the War on Povery; yet wary Americans have a right to be skeptical of any bright idea emanating from Washington, given that the poverty rate bottomed out in 1973 and has been drifting upward since (Heritage Foundation, *Issues '94*, pp. 122–23).

113. House Ways and Means Committee, *Green Book*, p. 395.

114. *The Hotline*, November 28, 1994.

115. J.J. McEntee, *Final Report of the Director at the Civilian Conservation Corps* (Washington, D.C., Federal Security Agency, June 30, 1942, pp. 3–4).

116. Abuses of the CETA program were well publicized in the seventies, and led to a substantial backlash. See, for example, Robert P. Hunter, "The Department of Labor," in Charles Heatherly, ed., *Mandate for Leadership* (Washington, D.C.: Heritage Foundation, 1981), pp. 476–80.

One more recent don't-know-whether-to-laugh-or-cry tale of CETA in action two decades ago was provided by Laurie Abraham in "Jerky Boys," *New Republic*, February 20, 1995, p. 20. The author recalls her experience as a CETA supervisor in Cleveland, during which time the CETA "workers" imbibed, skylarked—and masturbated—while "on the job."

As for today's Job Corps, Senator Nancy Kassebaum has found that nearly half of all Jobs Corps students drop out after just six months. The biggest single factor is "a pattern of uncontrolled violence"; some twenty-three Job Corps students have been convicted of murder in the past three years. The Job Corps looks less like the military and more like the 'hood many young people desperately sought to leave behind.

117. Hugh Price, Keynote Address, National Urban League Convention, Indianapolis, Indiana, July 24, 1994, p. 14.

Index